Howard Zinn's Southern Diary

Howard Zinn's Southern Diary

Sit-ins, Civil Rights, and Black Women's Student Activism

ROBERT COHEN

Foreword by **ALICE WALKER**

The University of Georgia Press
Athens

This publication received generous support from the
Stephen M. Silberstein Foundation.

Designed by Melissa Bugbee Buchanan
Set in Minion Pro and Myriad Pro
Printed and bound by Thomson-Shore, Inc.
The paper in this book meets the guidelines for
permanence and durability of the Committee on
Production Guidelines for Book Longevity of the
Council on Library Resources.

Most University of Georgia Press titles are
available from popular e-book vendors.

Printed in the United States of America
22 21 20 19 18 P 5 4 3 2 1

Library of Congress Cataloging-in-Publication Data

Names: Zinn, Howard, 1922–2010, author. | Cohen, Robert, 1955 May 21–
editor, writer of added commentary. | Walker, Alice, 1944– writer of
foreword.
Title: Howard Zinn's Southern diary : sit-ins, civil rights, and black women's
student activism / Robert Cohen ; foreword by Alice Walker.
Description: Athens : The University of Georgia Press, [2018] | Includes
bibliographical references and index.
Identifiers: LCCN 2017059453| ISBN 9780820353227 (hardcover : alk. paper)
| ISBN 9780820353289 (pbk. : alk. paper) | ISBN 9780820353234 (ebook)
Subjects: LCSH: Zinn, Howard, 1922–2010—Diaries. | Spelman College—
History. | Southern States—Race relations—History—20th century.
Classification: LCC PS3576.I538 Z46 2018 | DDC 818/.5403 [B] —dc23
LC record available at https://lccn.loc.gov/2017059453

In memory of Marilyn Young (1937–2017), whose brilliant historical scholarship challenges us to confront America's addiction to war.

And to Spelman College activists, past and present, in their courageous struggle for a more just and democratic world.

CONTENTS

What Nurtured My Outrage, Really?   **Alice Walker**

When Spelman College's president, Albert Manley, fired Howard Zinn, my favorite teacher, it never occurred to me not to react. I was completing my sophomore year and had studied one semester with Zinn, yet it was obvious to me that he was a great teacher and an extraordinary person. He was fired at the beginning of summer, as his family prepared to transition to New England for the season. This was rude and awkward timing that caused unnecessary suffering after such an unexpected blow. I thought this manner of ejecting a controversial teacher extremely cowardly and could not bear to seem to condone or accept it.

I wrote a letter of protest that was published in our student newspaper, a letter that led inevitably to my own exit from a school that I struggled with, but deeply loved.

But what nurtured my outrage, really? I have been contemplating this question since Robert Cohen, the author of this book, asked me to write a foreword for it. And I must say, I have uncovered many beautiful reasons why I knew instinctively that I must stand up for Howard Zinn, "my slim teacher," as I sometimes thought of him. But these beautiful reasons Zinn never knew about, because the world we live in is so fragmented that our family histories are rarely depicted in ways that show how they influence each other, connect, or intertwine.

I stood up for Howard Zinn, a Jewish teacher of History, a husband and father in his forties, because I in fact come from a community that venerates teachers.

Reaching this understanding only recently brought tears, as I allowed my deep appreciation for my southern black, farming, and sharecropping community to blossom once again in memory. In fact, "memory" encompasses years before I was born, when my father, riding a mule, went off in search of teachers for the school the vibrant but struggling community built, against nearly impossible odds, for its young.

One of the people he found became my first grade teacher, Miss Reynolds,[*] a black descendant of white Reynolds Plantation folks. Never to have children of her own, she gifted my mother with my very first clothing. She married one of our cousins, also a descendant of a local white landowner. (This explains how he kept his land when other black farmers, after Reconstruction, were dispossessed.) This cousin provided the land for the school, and Miss Reynolds offered the love and guidance that kept it going. An earlier school, whose ruins remained visible for years in our church's cemetery, had been burned to the ground by local whites. I mention the mixed ancestry of this couple to place them squarely at the heart of this "poor" community. There was a sister of the landowner cousin who behaved as though she were white, but we noticed, as she taught us grudgingly and with "high yellow" condescension, that she consumed a lot of prunes.

It is sometimes thought that in small isolated communities such as ours it is the preacher who is most cherished. It is true that on his monthly or bimonthly visits his was the honored seat at our pine board table. His was the plate with the most butter beans, greens, Irish potatoes, yams. Certainly the biggest and most crisp piece of fried chicken. His word was virtually law, as he hemmed and hawed his way through biblical stories he entertained us with in church. Sometimes he made very little sense because we knew none of the folks he talked about, all white, and very hairy, from a land that existed not only geographically and mythically far, but also may not have existed at all. It was a puzzle that was never solved, just who these people were, or how they ended up in our church. Besides, and lucky for us, we had our own animal folktales about animals we actually knew and saw sometimes (in the case of rabbits) several times a day. Church was always saved by song. Passion. Compassion. The genius of soul expressed in melodies whose high notes could curl your toes. There was laying on of hands and washing of feet. Folks fainting. Women in white from head to toe fanning anybody who looked queasy.

But it was the teacher who was truly cherished. Though I sense, from the distance of many decades, that the folks had to be careful to hide how much adoration they gave to those who taught their children, and sometimes themselves, how to read and write.

Without our teachers we were destined to sharecrop, to be maids and butlers, forever. Grownups got that, though many children did not. I was lucky that books held a revered place in our rustic shack, which my mother managed to make appealing through a genius for creating beauty that left her family in awe. And we were storytellers. If stories were hidden in books, as we discovered

---

[*] Miss Reynolds's married name was Mrs. Birda Simmons, but no one in our family ever called her that.

they were, it was our job to bring them out. We could only manage that by reading them.

Magic.

And so, with this history of my parents feeding teachers, my grandparents providing housing for them in the form of a spare room in their small house, my mother's sending of cakes and pies, on a monthly basis, to whomever was teaching her children, my father and grandfather cutting cords of wood to keep whatever teacher they'd enticed to our community warm for a winter, I understood that teachers are never to be treated shabbily.

That wherever a teacher is treated badly is no place for a person from my family or from my community.

I did not know what I would do after writing my anguished letter about the cruel treatment of Howard Zinn (and his family); I didn't even consider this. Nor did I have any clue how I, a scholarship student, could continue my education if Spelman threw me out. All I knew was that where I came from people stood with their teacher, if that teacher was respected and loved.

Howard Zinn was *so* respected and loved at Spelman College. His diary shows his constant concern for his students, as we, with his often quite cheerful help, dismantled segregation in Atlanta and attempted to leave the Victorian age behind us at Spelman. Anyone who reads his great work *A People's History of the United States* will have a glimpse of what he was about. Liberation, not only for the students at Spelman, whom he clearly loved, but for all of us.

PREFACE

As a writer and historian, the late Howard Zinn's fame is most closely associated with his book *A People's History of the United States*, an introduction to American history from the perspective of those that textbooks typically slighted, including workers, women, Native Americans, other people of color, immigrants, and the poor. Since its publication in 1980, the book has sold more than two million copies. It is one of the most popular and widely read history books ever written. Zinn was a great storyteller whose narrative skills, along with his eye for telling historical details, his focus on abuses of power, and his emphasis on the dissenters and rebels who fought for social justice, make his historical writing extraordinarily dramatic.

Zinn displayed these same skills in his unpublished diary, which documented events in African American history, including black women students' struggles against paternalistic restrictions on their campus life that he witnessed and participated in during the heyday of the southern civil rights movement in 1963. The diary has only recently become available with the opening of Zinn's papers at the Tamiment Library at New York University (NYU), in the part of the collection covering his years (1956–63) as a young professor, activist, and mentor to black student sit-in organizers at Spelman College, the oldest and most well-known historically black college for women. The diary had been placed by Zinn in an unbound file, whose simple handwritten cover, "Journal 1963," gave no hint of its importance. Zinn briefly quoted this diary in his memoir, *You Can't Be Neutral on a Moving Train* (1994), but said nothing that would indicate how powerful a document his diary would turn out to be. This accounts for how surprised I was upon first reading the diary and observing how effective Zinn was in encapsulating and almost effortlessly bringing to life on the written page the history he was witnessing and making.

Covering his last semester at Spelman, which culminated in his politically charged firing, the diary offers a window onto the Atlanta sit-in movement, the Student Nonviolent Coordinating Committee (SNCC), the Spelman campus and its student rebellions, the larger political atmosphere at Atlanta's black colleges, and race and gender as lived both on campus and off. Coming in at ninety pages—some handwritten, but most typed single-spaced, in a small typeface, by Zinn—the diary provides rich insights and intricate detail on the Atlanta racial scene and on the status of black women students. The diary leaves you feeling that you are there with Zinn and his students in this time of protest, repression, solidarity, and liberation. And because it was written by Zinn, the diary has an edge to it, reflecting a keen political intelligence, democratic historical sensibility, and striking awareness that the history he was observing and making was of great importance in the struggle for freedom and equality. Even before I finished reading the diary, it seemed obvious that this document ought to be published so it could reach a larger readership, and in the pages that follow you will have the opportunity to read Zinn's diary.

Zinn was a pioneer in oral history who made extensive use of in-depth interviews—including with his current and former students—in his most influential book on the civil rights movement, *SNCC: The New Abolitionists*. So it seems evident that had he published his southern diary he would have first done oral histories with his students and colleagues to provide historical background and cross-generational perspectives on the events covered in the diary. This is precisely what I have done, since I suspected that Zinn's diary could be best understood if its events were contextualized in an introductory essay that tapped into the memories of those who knew Zinn best in his Spelman years and that drew on relevant archival records as well as the private papers of Zinn's closest friends. And just as the diary itself proved absorbing, so did the oral histories of Zinn's circle of students and colleagues, offering arresting insights from a wide array of former and current Spelman community members. These included poet and novelist Alice Walker; civil rights attorney Betty Stevens Walker; antiwar leader, historian, and labor lawyer Staughton Lynd; Martin Luther King adviser, Mennonite leader, and historian of black protest Vincent Harding; actress Marie Thomas; women's studies pioneer Beverly Guy-Sheftall; sit-in leader Roslyn Pope; and many others. Their interviews explore the complexities of politics, power, freedom, repression, race, and gender at Spelman and in Atlanta (and the South) in the 1950s and early 1960s, and so does my introductory essay. I came to recognize that the task of understanding Spelman and Zinn in 1963 was dialogical, best accomplished if there was a dialogue between history and memory. This meant putting Zinn's diary and the archival record from 1963 in conversation with those who in our own century retained vivid memories of their days and Zinn's at Spelman.

At times the interviews and the diary align closely, even poetically, as when both capture the camaraderie and love between Zinn and his Spelman students. But some of the oral histories offer views of the political controversies at Spelman that conflict with Zinn's perspective and with each other. Such conflicts at times give the introductory essay a *Rashomon*-style quality, especially with regard to Spelman president Albert E. Manley, the campus official who, just as the diary ends in summer 1963, fired Zinn. Manley emerges in some of the Spelman alumnae oral histories as a strict but caring paternalist, while other alumnae and faculty oral histories, and Zinn's diary, cast Spelman's president in a harsher light—as an autocrat suppressing and punishing student and faculty dissidents. Among the oral histories of Zinn's former colleagues there is agreement that Manley's firing of Zinn was unjust, but disagreement over whether Zinn was courageous or reckless in his defiance of Spelman's first African American president. There is also disagreement over whether race played a role in Manley's firing of Zinn, the college's most outspoken white radical faculty member.

Rather than perceiving these disagreements as a troublesome problem that needed to be resolved in my introductory essay, I came to value them as useful entry points into key controversies narrated in Zinn's diary. They are thought provoking and add other voices that supplement and at times challenge Zinn's— on how he made sense of the Spelman scene and his role in it. Instead of acting as an omniscient narrator and historical umpire, as historians often do in their monographs, my role is more that of a provocateur raising questions for readers to consider as they make their way through Zinn's diary. This does not mean that I am or pretend to be neutral on such disputes. I do indicate my perspective, but not—I hope—in a way that forecloses debate when both sides have valuable arguments and evidence to offer. Thus the introduction aims not to impose my historical judgments with respect to all such contradictions but rather to equip readers to make their own judgments, reflecting on how the oral history interviews and archival evidence in the introductory essay compare with the assertions Zinn made and the assumptions he held in his southern diary.

These disputes are especially interesting because they involve evidentiary questions that morph into historical methodology and even philosophy of history problems concerning the relationship between time and historical judgment. As time passes and passions cool, do our historical judgments about events in the distant past become more mature, objective, and accurate? If so, that would mean privileging the retrospective oral history interviews over the views recorded by Zinn in his diary in 1963. Or does the passage of time tend to distort rather than clarify, clouding historical judgments because of nostalgia or fading memories? In that case it is the diary itself, Zinn's perspective in 1963 as a young historian, and the archival paper trail from that time, that ought to carry the most weight. These are questions worth considering as you read the introductory essay and move on to Zinn's diary to assess this dialogue between the present and the past.

No matter what verdict you reach on these controversies, the oral histories, correspondence, and Zinn's diary itself afford you an opportunity to interact with one of the most influential historians and social critics of our time, his colleagues, and students—who included some of the most critically minded, egalitarian, courageous, and politically effective young activists ever to set foot on an American college campus. We are especially fortunate that, though Zinn's is a man's diary, it narrates an important yet neglected chapter in women's history. The students closest to Zinn, and most prominent in his diary, were young African American women whose struggles for racial equality and against sexist paternalism have not been accorded the historical attention they deserve. Reading Zinn's diary, contextualized and queried by the historical essay that precedes it, should enable you to virtually relive and reflect upon the cauldron of social change that black Atlanta and its college campuses had become as the freedom struggle surged in 1963.

Zinn's connection with Spelman did not, however, end in 1963. Fired from Spelman College back then, Zinn some four decades later would be awarded an honorary degree and featured as the college's commencement speaker. How could the same college fire Zinn and later honor him? The answer to this question is, of course, that Spelman in the twenty-first century is not the same college it had been in 1963; it has been transformed into a more progressive institution led by its first African American women presidents. Zinn and his students were precursors, and some of his former students also active contributors, to this transformation, a story that is told in the epilogue. It is a story that attests that Spelman, no less than Zinn himself, has an extraordinary history that unfortunately has attracted precious little attention from the historical profession. My hope is that this volume will encourage readers to explore, and historians to further document, these neglected chapters in African American women's history.

ACKNOWLEDGMENTS

This book would not have been possible without NYU's Tamiment Library, which houses Howard Zinn's papers and his Spelman College diary. The papers were acquired when the late Michael Nash was Tamiment's archivist, and I am much in his debt. Michael's successors Tim Naftali and Tim Johnson were very helpful, particularly in making accessible and digitizing important Zinn audiotapes from his Spelman years.

Myla Kabat-Zinn's support was essential to this project. She made her father's papers available to the Tamiment Library and generously granted permission to publish his southern diary. Myla was equally generous in sharing her insights about her father and his Spelman years and was a consistent source of helpful advice in making sense of this complicated history. I am also grateful to her for sharing photos from her family collection, some of which appear in the pages that follow.

Holly A. Smith, Spelman College's archivist, was tremendously helpful in making my research trip to Spelman so productive—not only enabling my effort to search all the relevant collections there but also connecting me with Spelman alumnae for oral history interviews that deepened my understanding of Spelman's history. Her help with my photo research proved invaluable.

My thanks to Kathy Shoemaker of Emory University's Manuscript, Archives, and Rare Book Library for assisting me in locating important oral histories with Zinn and his Spelman students. Vakil Smallen, archivist at the George Washington University Libraries, and Jordan Kurland of the American Association of University Professors (AAUP) were of great assistance in giving me access to the AAUP files on Zinn's firing at Spelman. I am indebted to the Wisconsin Historical Society, the University of Wisconsin Library, and the NYU Elmer Holmes Bobst Library's interlibrary loan department for enabling me to access on microfilm Howard Zinn's civil rights papers that are housed in Madison, Wisconsin. Columbia University's Rare Book & Manuscript Library made accessible important oral histories with Albert E. Manley and other presidents of historically black colleges and universities (HBCUs).

The oral history work that did so much to bring Spelman's history alive for me was made possible by the generosity of Spelman alumnae and friends and former colleagues of Zinn's who devoted considerable time to our interviews, including Roslyn Pope, Betty Stevens Walker, Marie Thomas, Beverly Guy-Sheftall, Alice Walker, the late Vincent Harding, Staughton Lynd, and Henry West. I am grateful to former Spelman president Beverly Daniel Tatum for both her insightful interview on her role in the awarding of an honorary Spelman degree to Howard Zinn and the documents she provided me on that important moment in Zinn's life. The current president of Spelman, Mary Schmidt Campbell, was very welcoming, and the fact that I had the opportunity to meet with her and also interview former president Tatum—speaking with two Spelman presidents in one research trip—I hope conveys what a warm and special place Spelman is. I am grateful to the late Samuel DuBois Cook and Sylvia Cook for sharing their memories of Howard Zinn in his Spelman years, and to Karen Cook for facilitating our correspondence.

I am much indebted to Beverly Guy-Sheftall, the founder and director of the Spelman College Women's Research and Resource Center, for sharing with me her unrivaled knowledge of Spelman's history, her advice on some important conceptual questions regarding African American women's history, and her critical reading of my introductory essay and epilogue.

Betty Stevens Walker provided documents and photographs from her personal papers on her Spelman years that were very helpful, and I benefited as well from her unique perspective as one who was close friends with both Zinn and Albert Manley. Sarah Thompson, who in 2003 was the eloquent Spelman student activist that helped introduce Zinn when he made his first speech at Spelman since his firing forty years earlier, shared her memories of that occasion and the tape of Zinn's speech that day—and for both I am deeply grateful.

I was fortunate to receive helpful criticism of my analysis of and writings on Zinn and Spelman from Wesley Hogan of Duke University; John Inscoe of the University of Georgia; Bettina Aptheker of the University of California, Santa Cruz; and two anonymous readers from the University of Georgia Press. Wesley also offered some very useful suggestions on the editing of Zinn's diary. Gregg Parrish provided crucial technical assistance with the initial scanning of the diary that was a great help at an early stage of this project.

I learned much about Spelman and the student movement there in the early 1960s from Alice Walker, and I am grateful to her for writing her beautiful and moving foreword to the book.

I also offer my thanks to Mick Gusinde-Duffy of the University of Georgia Press for his support, advice, and faith in this project. I am grateful to Kay Kodner for her careful copyediting work.

I join with the publisher in gratefully acknowledging the generous contribution to this book by Stephen M. Silberstein.

Harry G. Lefever's pioneering study of Spelman College and the civil rights movement and Martin Duberman's biography of Howard Zinn provided essential background for my study, and I am grateful to both of them for their valuable scholarship. I also want to express my gratitude to Gwendolyn Zoharah Simmons and Marian Wright Edelman for the memoirs they wrote of their Spelman years, which were of such great use in this study, and to the City of Atlanta Student Movement Commission for its excellent work in completing and making accessible oral histories with Atlanta sit-in leaders and activists. Martha Prescod Norman Noonan helped spark my interest in African American women's student activism, and I am grateful to her for that as well as her friendship, and to Martha and her fellow editors of the landmark anthology *Hands on the Freedom Plow: Personal Accounts by Women in SNCC*, which helped inspire my work on this book. My thanks to Charlayne Hunter-Gault and Calvin Trillin for teaching me so much about the struggle for racial equality in 1960s Georgia.

My interest in African American history and 1960s student activism has roots that stretch back to my inspiring teachers, Jesse Lemisch, Leon Litwack, and Philip Altbach, an interest reinforced by my friendship and collaborative work with the late Tom Hayden and the insights Bob Moses shared with me in a memorable oral history interview and in a collaboration with Bob's Algebra Project. Had I not been the lucky recipient of all this learning and inspiration, this book would not have been possible.

Among the greatest challenges in this book was the historical detective work required for the diary annotations, since it involved tracking down many of those in Zinn's circle of African American colleagues and friends who were underrepresented in online reference sources. This task of uncovering neglected but fascinating historical figures was made easier—as were the other challenges of editing the Zinn diary—by the experience I gained in documentary editing as consulting editor for the Emma Goldman Papers project, and for that experience and her friendship I owe a huge debt to Goldman project director and biographer Candace Falk.

Books often take longer to complete than one plans. And in this case that was both true and painful, because this book's completion came too late to share with my dear friend and colleague Marilyn Young. Marilyn, like Howard Zinn, was a brilliant radical intellectual with Brooklyn working-class roots; they'd been close friends since their days studying Asian history at Harvard in the early 1960s. She shared with Zinn a passionate opposition to the American war machine and a desire to teach Americans the lessons of the Vietnam War, lessons all too few have heeded. Marilyn shared with me both her insights about Zinn and her private correspondence with him during his final Spelman years. It was Marilyn who first urged me to explore the Zinn papers at NYU. Marilyn also played a pivotal role in bringing the Zinn papers to NYU. If not for Marilyn, this book would not exist. Co-teaching with Marilyn our NYU course on the politics and culture of 1960s America has been one of the great pleasures of my life, as was our friendship. The book is dedicated to her memory.

The book's other dedication is to Spelman's student and faculty activists, past and present, and their struggle for a more democratic world—free of racism, sexism, homophobia, and war. It's been an honor and a pleasure to meet, interview, and learn from the generations of Spelman students and professors who have worked so courageously to make freedom and equality more than just words.

Words can't quite convey how much my work and life owe to Rebecca Hyman and Daniel Hyman Cohen, my wife and son, who inspire me every day. I hope they will view this book as I do, as much theirs as mine.

Howard Zinn's Southern Diary

MENTOR TO THE MOVEMENT

Howard Zinn, SNCC, and the Spelman College Freedom Struggle

Writing and Making History in the Black Freedom and Student Rights Struggles

If there was a capital city of the civil rights movement in the early 1960s, Atlanta would have a good claim upon that title. Atlanta was the hometown of Martin Luther King Jr. and the church he preached in, Ebenezer Baptist, and the place where the civil rights organization King headed, the Southern Christian Leadership Conference (SCLC), had its headquarters. The Student Nonviolent Coordinating Committee (SNCC), the most dynamic, egalitarian, and action-oriented organization in the black freedom movement, also had its headquarters in Atlanta. And in fact, Atlanta emerged as a hub of black student activism even before SNCC's founding in April 1960. The month before SNCC was born, students from Atlanta's distinguished consortium of six historically black colleges, the Atlanta University Center—especially from Morehouse College (male) and Spelman College (female)—launched and led the largest and arguably the best-organized sit-in movement against Jim Crow lunch counters in the wake of the Greensboro sit-ins in February 1960. Martin Luther King Jr. was among those arrested in the second wave of these student-led sit-ins in Atlanta in October 1960 (an arrest that led to John F. Kennedy's historic phone call to Coretta Scott King and the release of King from a Georgia prison at the height of JFK's presidential campaign, which won Kennedy black votes that helped carry him to the White House). The Atlanta University Center would contribute to the civil rights movement some of its most accomplished organizers, including sit-in leaders Lonnie King (Morehouse) and Herschelle Sullivan (Spelman); SNCC leaders Julian Bond (Morehouse) and Ruby Doris Smith (Spelman); the primary author of the Atlanta student movement's Appeal for Human Rights Roslyn Pope (Spelman); the Mississippi freedom movement's dynamic lawyer Marian Wright (Spelman); the Mississippi Freedom Schools' leader Staughton Lynd (Spelman faculty); the civil rights movement's eminent novelist and poet Alice Walker (Spelman); M. L. King adviser and speechwriter Vincent Harding (Spelman faculty); and the movement's chronicler and oral historian, who also served as a SNCC executive committee member and was a teacher and mentor to some of the Atlanta movement's most talented student activists: Howard Zinn (Spelman faculty).[1]

Zinn was the first to shine a national spotlight on the prominent role that female students from Spelman College were playing in the Atlanta sit-in movement. In August 1960 he published, in the *Nation*, "Finishing School for Pickets," an article whose title and content dramatized the conflict between the new student activism and the conservative traditions and confining gender norms of the South's most famous historically black women's college.[2] Spelman, as Zinn noted, was founded in the late nineteenth century by "staid New England women missionaries" and, even in 1960, promoted a social ethos that was "pious, sedate, encrusted with traditions of gentility and moderation." If the college's strict curfews, compulsory chapel, and restrictions on student visits off-campus made it seem an unlikely launching pad for student protests in downtown Atlanta, so did the Spelman ideal of young womanhood, which, as Zinn put it, stressed being "well mannered and lady-like, don't speak loudly, and don't get into trouble. . . . The 'Spelman girl' walked gracefully, talked properly, went to church every Sunday, poured tea elegantly and, in general, had all the attributes of a fine finishing school." But these conservative traditions were powerless to prevent a determined core of Spelman students from helping to initiate and lead Atlanta's sit-ins against Jim Crow in March 1960. "Several carloads of Spelman students" rode to downtown Atlanta the first morning of the sit-ins, "without the knowledge of" the Spelman administration, and participated in protests at "ten different eating places." Fourteen of the seventy-seven students arrested in the first Atlanta sit-ins were Spelman students.[3]

Nor were these sit-ins the start of Spelman student activism, which, as Zinn described in "Finishing School for Pickets," was already stirring in the late 1950s. Back then Spelman students protested against segregation in the Georgia legislature's Jim Crow gallery and participated in a successful campaign to desegregate Atlanta's public library.[4] Spelman students in the late 1950s also defied the city's Jim Crow bus-seating restrictions and worked to end segregation at the Atlanta airport restaurant.[5]

In explaining how such activism could arise at Spelman despite its conservative traditions, Zinn argued that there was "something fundamental at work which is setting free . . . the anger pent up in generations of quiet, well bred Negro college women." That something was the beginning of a transformation of Spelman (as of other historically black colleges), which was "losing its provincial air" thanks in part to exchange programs that brought students from the newly independent African nations to campus and the international scholarships that had sent Spelman students abroad, making them a part of a "global revolution in expectations" as old hierarchies of race and empire were challenged and toppled. The increased presence of liberal white faculty at Spelman and the growing contacts with white college students via interracial exchanges, forums, and other academic programs were also, in Zinn's words, "helping to break down the mixture of awe-suspicion-hostility with which deep-South Negroes generally regard whites. And for Spelman, unexpressed but obvious pressure to adopt the manners and courtesies of white middle class society breaks down, as Spelman girls get a close look at how whites really behave."[6] Thus "the tame-sounding phrase 'cultural exchange'" could have, in Zinn's estimation, "revolutionary political implications."[7]

What Zinn failed to mention in this *Nation* article—but would discuss decades later in his memoir, *You Can't Be Neutral on a Moving Train* (1994)—was that far from being merely an observer of the process of change and rising student activism at Spelman, he had been a key facilitator of the Spelman student movement. It had been his students in 1957 and 1958—along with a few of their Morehouse counterparts—who challenged Jim Crow seating in the gallery of the Georgia state legislature. It was the Spelman Social Science Club, the student group Zinn mentored as faculty adviser, that took him up on his suggestion that they "undertake some real project involving social change" by launching a campaign to desegregate the Atlanta public library—a campaign whose success was expedited by Zinn's outreach to black faculty at both Spelman and Atlanta University, whose threats of a legal suit against the library forced it to integrate and serve black patrons.[8] Zinn also had gone to bat repeatedly for students who challenged and criticized the campus's paternalistic social restrictions, even when this led him into conflicts with the Spelman administration. So by the time of the Atlanta sit-ins in 1960, Zinn was such a trusted and beloved figure among Spelman student activists that they held meetings in his apartment on campus; gave him advance notice of the first sit-ins; borrowed his car to travel to the sit-in sites; and had him serve as their initial press contact, so that a few minutes after the start of those sit-ins, he would notify reporters and encourage them to cover the protests. Even the founding statement of the Atlanta student movement, "An Appeal for Human Rights," which would be published in the *Atlanta Constitution* and attract national attention to the movement, had a Zinn connection; it was drafted by his student Roslyn Pope and typed at his home by Julian Bond on Zinn's typewriter.[9]

Zinn's involvement with the Atlanta student movement and his closeness to Spelman's leading student and faculty activists gave him an insider's view of that movement and of the political and intellectual world of Spelman, Atlanta University Center, and SNCC.[10] Thus it was no surprise that Zinn would write the first nationally circulated accounts of the Spelman movement in the *Nation* and then in his book *The Southern Mystique* (1964); the most detailed contemporary report on the black freedom struggle and its segregationist foes in Albany, Georgia (for the Southern Regional Council), *Albany: A Study in National Re-*

sponsibility (1962); and the first book-length history of SNCC, *SNCC: The New Abolitionists* (1964).[11] Zinn would always view his years at Spelman (1956–63), which connected him to the civil rights movement and a remarkable generation of Spelman students, as among the most significant in his life, which is why he devoted the first three chapters in his memoirs to that time.[12]

It is only now, however, well after Zinn's death in 2010, and the opening of his papers at New York University's Tamiment Library, that we can see that some of his most memorable writing on his Spelman days are from a daily journal he kept in his last semester there, during the winter-spring of 1963, which he never published. Not even his close friends, students, and colleagues at Spelman in that era were aware at the time that Zinn was keeping a diary. It was only with the publication of Zinn's memoir in 1994 that the existence of the journal was even mentioned publicly—when he quoted from it as he narrated the story of his escalating conflict with the Spelman administration that led to his firing in June 1963. Similarly, historian Martin Duberman, drew on the diary to go over this same story in his biography, *Howard Zinn: A Life on the Left* (2012). Most recently, historian Staughton Lynd, a close friend and colleague of Zinn in his last three years at Spelman, used excerpts from the diary in an insightful essay on Zinn in his book *Doing History from the Bottom Up* (2014), in which he shows that Zinn thought strategically and deeply about the ways that legal change and interracial contact could overcome old patterns of racial discrimination.[13]

Mere excerpts from the diary cannot, however, do justice to its historical significance. Read from start to finish, the diary, which has more than fifty entries on the student and faculty conflicts with the Spelman administration, is one of the most extensive records of the political climate in a historically black college in 1960s America—a time when students at those colleges were on the cutting edge of that decade's new student activism. Insightful as Zinn's memoir and Duberman's biography of Zinn are on his battles at Spelman, the unabridged diary offers a more in-depth view than either of the book chapters—recording in real time the free speech, academic freedom, and student rights battles that rocked Spelman in 1963 and led to Zinn's firing and the abrupt ending of his Spelman years. The diary, in other words, merits publication because it illuminates far more than Zinn's own story. It captures a pivotal time in the history of student protest in the 1960s, foregrounding the activism of African American young women and capturing the way race was lived in Atlanta—the relationships between that city's black and white academics and activists and their generational and ideological tensions when the most idealistic among them were engaged in historic desegregation struggles. Zinn in Atlanta during the early 1960s was, as his wife Roslyn wrote their friends Ernie and Marilyn Young, "in the right place and at the right time."[14] Zinn had been at Spelman since 1956. But beyond this, he was a gifted writer and searing social critic who would go on later in the 1960s to write widely circulated books opposing the Vietnam War and defending civil disobedience, and in the 1980s he published the best-selling radical history of his time, *A People's History of the United States*.[15] So by 1963 even his immediate responses in his diary to the events he observed and was a part of in Atlanta, both on and off campus, were written with great clarity, and carried with them the insights of a veteran movement activist who had longstanding friendships in black Atlanta and had lived and taught in that community for years. For Zinn, living and teaching on a historically black college campus had opened a window onto black America to which few whites had access. Even when the Zinn diary's accounts of events are incomplete or less than entirely persuasive, they often raise important questions about social and political life at a historically black women's college and how this conservative institution navigated a time when its students became central actors in a revolution in southern race relations.[16]

Zinn's journal offers a vivid view of Spelman student activism during one of its most significant yet least well-known phases. Most of the historical writing on and commemorations of the Atlanta student movement and Spelman student protest have been devoted to the sit-in movement, especially in 1960, the historic first year when demonstrations in downtown Atlanta brought about the initial cracks in the Jim Crow line in Atlanta stores and eateries.[17] By the time Zinn was recording his diary during the winter-spring semester of 1963, Spelman students and other activists from the Atlanta University Center, joined by a core of white progressives from Emory University, were engaged in a series of sit-ins and demonstrations to follow up on those of prior years, since the majority of restaurants and hotels in Atlanta—despite the desegregation agreement brokered by the city's Chamber of Commerce president in 1961—were still racially segregated.[18] While for Spelman students this ongoing struggle for racial justice remained central, they became increasingly engaged with a second kind of freedom struggle—one that occurred not downtown but on their own campus and that was about personal freedom, gender liberation, and free speech. They were seeking to end the paternalistic policing of their social lives by an overbearing administration, which treated them as though they were immature girls who needed constant chaperoning and rigid curfews and sought to suppress their free speech rights whenever they dared to protest these and other restrictions.[19]

Here, as Zinn's diary shows so clearly, you had Spelman students who had played very adult roles, committing civil disobedience downtown, getting arrested, and even risking their lives in sit-ins against Jim Crow, but on their own campus these young women were still regimented like children. This contradiction seemed increasingly glaring and intolerable to the college's student activists. As Spelman civil rights activist Brenda Cole recalled, after the second wave of sit-ins during the fall of 1960–61 secured the rights of African Americans to be served on a nondiscriminatory basis at some of Atlanta's largest commercial establishments, such as Rich's department store, she and her classmates "started looking around and saying 'what has it profited us to go to Rich's when [because of Spelman's restriction on students traveling downtown] we've got to get five or six girls to go with us? We can't even leave campus after a certain time or . . . ride in cars. . . . Then we started looking at the . . . rules on campus . . . a lot closer and said . . . 'we're still not free.'"[20] Activists at Spelman became convinced, as student movement veteran Lana Taylor (Sims) explained, that their college was "just too paternalistic. That you have women who . . . couldn't go around the corner by themselves. . . . The institution was just working against the thing that they were supposed to be fostering—growing up and maturity."[21] And so the struggle against racial discrimination downtown, and its liberatory ethos, fostered a critique and revolt against gendered restrictions of their campus lives at Spelman.

It would not be an overstatement to term this a proto-feminist revolt for a freer campus, which erupted before the term "second-wave feminism" had even been coined, and to see this as a significant free speech movement, riling the Spelman campus more than a year before Berkeley's Free Speech Movement of 1964 rocked the University of California. A key reason this Spelman on-campus rebellion for student rights is not better known is because it failed. That failure attests to the difficulty of waging a two-front freedom struggle—for an end to segregation off campus and to secure student rights on campus. The failure of the student rights campaign was also made inevitable by the unwillingness of students to deploy on their black campus the civil disobedience tactics they had used so effectively against segregationists downtown.[22] At Spelman it would be the college president, appropriately named "Manley," who prevailed, beating back this women students' rights campaign, clamping down on free speech so effectively that he managed to get away with firing the professor most active in defending this struggle for student rights: Howard Zinn.

Another reason why the antipaternalist revolt that led to Zinn's firing at Spelman has not gotten its due from historians, from the African American community, or even from Spelman itself is that race trumps gender in historical memory, making it difficult for many to see racialized and intersectional sexism.[23] The battle against Jim Crow was of such epochal significance, and the Atlanta University Center's male and female colleges' alliance in that struggle was so dramatically played out, first in downtown Atlanta and then in SNCC, that this crusade on race has taken center stage. Indeed, there is today a street bordering Spelman and Clark-Atlanta University named for the Atlanta student movement, and there is also a historical marker that pays tribute to the antiracist student crusade.[24] But one would never know from such historical commemorations that, unlike their male counterparts from Morehouse and the city's other historically black colleges, the Spelman women in the 1960s not only battled racism off campus but also fought infantilizing restrictions on their social and political lives on campus. As Spelman student activist Ann Ashmore Hudson recalled, "As Black women, we not only had to fight for our freedom as a people but we had to fight on campus at the same time [for] basic fundamental freedoms. It was absurd. . . . The guys [at Morehouse] were not as restricted as the [Spelman] women. We were much more restricted than they were. And so we had to fight for freedoms they didn't."[25] So while Spelman students were contending with gender as well as racial discrimination, their gender-based, antipaternalist struggle has been little studied or remembered, let alone commemorated. Here it is helpful to bear in mind the insightful scholarship of Johnnetta Cole and Beverly Guy-Sheftall, who have written critically of the tradition of "race only" discourse in the black community—the idea that feminism is a white phenomenon. This tradition too plays a role in a kind of collective amnesia about Spelman's campus revolt, since it leads us to associate the Atlanta student movement with its sit-ins on race downtown and not to follow the Spelman students back to their campus to see how gender was lived and how gendered restrictions were challenged.[26]

All this is further complicated by the fact that the Spelman revolt came before second-wave feminism had invented such new terms as "sexism" with which to describe and critique gender discrimination. So the revolt's feminist character was implicit rather than explicit. Spelman students resented the limits on their access to the Morehouse library, but they lacked the feminist vocabulary and fully formed late-1960s-style feminist consciousness to demand that male and female students be treated equally, and instead they bemoaned being treated like children and insisted they were adults.[27] The aspiration toward intellectual rigor (and social responsibility) that Spelman's student rebels articulated was at odds with Spelman's devotion to teaching female students the social graces, which is why one heard them insisting that "when a woman leaves home to go to college she is interested in becoming elevated academically. If she has a desire to elevate her social graces she should enter charm school not a college."[28] So there was an emerging ideal of a new Spelman woman as so intellectually serious that she would look down on the ideal of women as merely socially decorous.

Similarly, though Zinn did not use the word "feminist" in connection with the revolt on Spelman's campus, as early as 1958 he realized that the rights consciousness of the civil rights movement had made Spelman's activist students politically independent and assertive, as uncomfortable with violations of their social and political freedom on campus as with Jim Crow itself, or as Zinn put it: "The movements for desegregation have created a new spirit among Negro young women of college age."[29] And one needs to be careful not to dismiss these concerns about campus freedom as secondary matters for Spelman students, for however important it was to end Jim Crowism downtown, it was also true, as Beverly Guy-Sheftall (Spelman class of 1966) recalls, that students who lived in Spelman's dorms spent much more time on campus than downtown, and so their daily lives as students were impacted more by the sexist social restrictions of the campus than the racist practices of white merchants downtown.[30]

Still, keeping in mind that this campus revolt was only a feminist-*tinged* rebellion, and one that came too early to be celebrated as part of the new feminist movement, it is little wonder that it has been largely forgotten while the antiracist actions of these very same activists have been honored as milestones in the black freedom movement. One of the great values of Zinn's diary is that it reminds us that *both* the female rights rebellion on campus and the sit-ins against Jim Crow downtown were important and inspiring freedom struggles.

Zinn never explained why, after more than six years at Spelman, he decided to keep a diary in what would turn out to be his final semester at the college. Staughton Lynd, one of Zinn's closest friends and colleagues in the college's history and social science department, which Zinn chaired, thinks Zinn kept the diary because he knew the student rights struggle at Spelman and the escalating conflicts between students, their faculty supporters, and the Spelman administration were reaching a boiling point, yielding new levels of campus polarization.[31] There is no question that Zinn knew his energetic support of the students' struggle against the paternalism of the Spelman administration had antagonized Spelman president Albert E. Manley. In fact just over a month after Zinn began keeping the diary, he confided to friends that he doubted his Guggenheim fellowship application would get anywhere since he lacked the required presidential endorsement, "which I don't have because we've been fighting a cold war over student freedom."[32] Perhaps Zinn wanted a record of the semester's conflicts in order to be more effective in his role as the leading faculty supporter of the student rights campaign. Or it may be that Zinn was thinking as a historian here, keeping a diary because he recognized the importance of the student rights revolt and wanted a record of it in order to write about it in one or both of the two books he was working on about the black freedom struggle, *The Southern Mystique* and *SNCC: The New Abolitionists*. Zinn was an early practitioner of oral history and had taped many interviews with SNCC organizers for *The New Abolitionists* in this same period. He carted his reel-to-reel machine to Spelman's most tumultuous student rights protest meeting of the semester and recorded its whole two hours. That tape to this day is stored with his papers, suggesting again that Zinn saw the revolt as a historically significant event that he was eager to document.[33]

The Spelman student rights struggle and its hardening of the divisions between pro–student rights faculty and the paternalistic administration often occupies center stage in Zinn's diary. The evolution of this struggle gives the journal its book-like quality, as it is a plot line that simply won't stop. On the one side was Zinn, the youthful, forty-year-old department chair, a New York Jewish radical, who viewed the student rights struggle on campus as a natural extension of the civil rights protests in downtown Atlanta, a sign that Spelman students who had acted as courageous adults in the sit-ins downtown were no longer willing to be treated like little girls by their paternalistic college administration. And on the other side was Spelman's first African American president, Albert E. Manley, who saw the college's students as "young ladies" whose success in their Christian college and beyond would be impossible unless they obeyed all the campus rules and adhered to Spelman's socially conservative Christian traditions that protected them and ensured the smooth functioning of the college.[34] The diary shows that under the pressure of their profound disagreement about the student rights struggle, the Zinn-Manley relationship steadily deteriorated, much like a doomed marriage, whose intensely personal conflicts kept erupting and escalating, growing so heated that a final and very messy divorce seemed inevitable. Things grew so bad that Zinn came up with a mocking term, "Spelmania," which he used repeatedly in his diary to describe the administration's enforcement of nineteenth-century-style social restrictions and heavy-handed attempts to suppress student dissent against those restrictions.[35]

Though central to the Zinn diary, the history of the Spelman student rights struggle was not the only historically significant story Zinn recorded in its pages. While Spelman was the most important part of Zinn's academic, political, and personal life, there were five other higher educational institutions affiliated with the Atlanta University (AU) Center with which Zinn interacted. Zinn had close colleagues, friends, and students from the other AU-affiliated campuses, especially Morehouse and Atlanta University itself. Indeed, if one gets the impression from Zinn's diary that Spelman was behind the times in its strict social regulations and extreme paternalism, the AU Center itself comes across as ahead of its time politically, intellectually, and racially. Zinn was acutely aware that this was one of the very few places in Atlanta, in Georgia, or even in all of the South where interracial intellectual events occurred on a regular basis and where genuine dialogue was possible across racial lines—and this was because the faculty was multiracial, predominantly African American but with a cadre of vocal white progressives. Both groups participated actively in a number of forums and speaker series, as did blacks and whites from outside the university.[36]

It was through such events and interaction that Zinn came into regular contact and developed friendships with African American colleagues beyond Spelman. In fact, as the diary shows, when his friend Samuel DuBois Cook of the Atlanta University political science department, a prominent black academic, went on leave, Zinn—at Cook's request—served in his place as organizer of the Town Hall political and intellectual forum and speaker series sponsored by Clark College. Zinn also presided over a Spelman-sponsored non-Western-speaker series.[37] The multiracial interactions and friendships that came out of such regular shared experiences had a major impact on Zinn's thinking about race, helping to convince him that racial prejudice and exclusiveness could be overcome by consistent and close interracial contact, a view that he would advocate forcefully (if a bit too optimistically) in his forthcoming book, *The Southern Mystique*.[38]

In addition to participating in and organizing these interracial faculty events, Zinn was an astute observer of them—eagerly analyzing their significance and practiced at digging below the surface of race relations in the university community and beyond. Zinn's sharp eye and narrative skill in recounting such interracial events were evident in his correspondence even before he started keeping his southern diary. For example, in May 1962 Zinn's letter to his friends and fellow historians Ernie and Marilyn Young offered a brilliant account of a panel and audience discussion of Communist China that he had organized, and which in a surprising way turned into a tense discussion of racism in the Jim Crow South. According to Zinn's account, the remarks of panelist Richard Walker, a white professor from the University of South Carolina, ignited a firestorm of dissent from black faculty. After Walker spoke with unremitting hostility of Communist China's "absolutist tyranny," Horace Mann Bond, the dean of Atlanta University's education school, rose up and "his very first question—or rather comment—threw the whole place into a state of excitement that never let up." Bond, as Zinn put it, spoke "in the kind of resonant and cultivated tone that [W. E. B.] Du Bois has," and remarked, "This is not hospitable but I will say it anyway. Professor Walker's statements on the tyranny of Communist China come with little grace from a man who teaches at a University in a [Jim Crow] state which is as tyrannical, as brutal, as barbarous as any place on this earth."[39]

Zinn likened the reaction of the crowd to the "general excitement and agitation" provoked "as Khrushchev was reciting Stalin's crimes at the 20th Congress." In reply, Zinn noted, "Walker walked slowly to the microphone—it seemed like a mile—and said 'Sir, in the time that I have been at the University of South Carolina, I do not recall a single execution!' This, in turn, sparked an angry retort by panelist William Worthy, a prominent radical African American journalist, who said curtly 'If Negroes tomorrow asserted their full rights as American citizens, there would be executions.'" As the focus shifted from China to the Jim Crow South, another white panelist spoke and, in Zinn's view, "said just about the worst thing anyone can say to a Negro . . . in the South today: 'I know full well we have severe problems in race discrimination. But it will take time.'" Zinn then inventoried the politically and racially diverse audience's reactions to these heated exchanges: "Leaving the meeting, Negroes were sharply split: faculty and administration people for the most part strongly critical of Bond and Worthy ('I was embarrassed'), students for the most part gung-ho for them, white radicals for them, white Birchers venomous, white liberals shook up by the depth of feeling in the Negro community which they had not expected."[40]

After describing the uproar, Zinn stepped back and analyzed it, arguing that Walker "infuriated Bond and other Negroes in the audience because . . . his wheedling voice, his too holy attitude about the United States, his confident black-and-white assertions about China . . . [were] irritating." Zinn viewed Walker as "the epitome of the white colonialist trying to con the natives with soft-hard talk." And Zinn saw in this explosive meeting a larger significance: "For years Negroes have separated their traditional pro-American [foreign] policy attitudes from their race resentment. But beneath the surface the tie exists, a potential for linking race to other American issues. Under certain conditions this tie jumps above the surface. . . . Out of Negro militancy can . . . come foreign policy neutralism, criticism of civil liberties deprivations, etc. . . . just beginning to assert itself."[41] Of course Zinn's conclusions here were influenced by his Left perspective on the southern scene, as was his diary. And though one may disagree with his form of optimistic radicalism, he also displayed a keen awareness of the generational divisions within the black community, an ability to question both Cold War liberalism and the right, and an insistence on probing below the surface of interracial discourse, often giving his analysis a striking seriousness and depth.

What comes across in Zinn's observations about race in Atlanta and the South more generally during the early 1960s is how good a listener he could be when it came to racial politics. It wasn't just that he was living in the black community and had been for years, but that he had a keen awareness of its critical voices, really heard them, and melded them with his own Left perspective. For example, Zinn's tough-minded assessment of the harsh reality beneath the cheerful headlines and optimism of Atlanta's moderates, in commenting on the city's limited school desegregation in 1961, reflected both his own critical sensibility and that of a local National Association for the Advancement of Colored People (NAACP) leader. That fall Zinn wrote:

Atlanta's schools are integrated, successfully, quietly, picayunely. Nine Negro kids in 11th and 12th grades in four different high schools. I drove Myla to her new school, Brown High, in a lower middle class quiet tree-lined section of Atlanta. Squad car in front of the school. Plain clothesman in front of the school. Motorcycle cop in front of the school. Policeman walking a policedog in front of the school. Policeman and paddywagon on corner. A hundred newspapermen and photographers across the street. Two Negro kids entering the school. As I drove away after dropping Myla I heard two high school girls talking animatedly on their way to school, about getting on the cheering squad. Atlanta has been in an orgy of self-congratulation ever since. Columnists, politicians, League of Women Voter-nicks and everyone weeping with hysterical joy that Atlanta has done such a marvelous thing. A bit of truth and justification, but enough to make one nauseous. Only dissonant voice was our friend Sam Williams (philosophy teacher at Morehouse, minister of a nearby Baptist church, head of Atlanta NAACP) who sermonized that Sunday "Why is Atlanta So Proud[?]" and pointed to nine kids swallowed up in thousands of others after a hundred years beyond slavery. Meanwhile the Negro kids in some of the schools, including Myla's, are having a hard time—no friends,—sitting alone in the cafeteria, cursed and shoved in the hallways.[42]

Observations such as these on school desegregation, and many others like them, remind us that Zinn in 1963 was not only writing with great perception but doing so at a crucial moment in the history of Atlanta, Georgia, and the South. It was a time when the color line was being challenged, an era of hopefulness for the freedom movement in Georgia. Desegregation had taken place not only in the public schools of Atlanta but also at the University of Georgia in Athens, the Peach State's legislature and its galleries, and some of Atlanta's biggest stores. In addition, black voter registration was surging in Atlanta.[43] One can see in the writings in Zinn's diary how the pace of protest and expectations of change intensified in May 1963.[44] Both black and white students in Atlanta were inspired toward greater activism by the Birmingham freedom struggle—whose televised encounters between nonviolent protesters and Bull Connor's vicious police dogs and high-powered fire hoses shocked the nation and unleashed a wave of civil rights protests across and beyond the South. Yet at the same time, even in Atlanta, the Georgia city that prided itself on being a center of commerce "too busy to hate," resistance to integration persisted at the city's leading hotels, in the housing market, and in many restaurants.[45] Zinn's diary documents both this ongoing resistance to integration and the determination of Zinn and his fellow civil rights activists to overcome it. An emblem of that resistance, and a reactionary "folk hero," was the arch-segregationist Lester Maddox, who would ride the wave of publicity from his violent threats against integrationists at his Atlanta restaurant till it carried him all the way to the governorship of Georgia in 1966. Maddox makes an appearance in Zinn's diary, which tells of the physical ejection of Morehouse civil rights protesters from his Pickrick restaurant.[46] So Zinn was writing at a moment of transition, when the black freedom movement in Atlanta and Georgia had considerable momentum, but where victory was far from complete or even assured. This too makes Zinn's diary especially valuable as a window onto a time of change.

By the time Zinn started keeping his southern diary, his own education on race in Georgia was extensive and went well beyond Atlanta. The year before his final Spelman semester he had completed an in-depth report for the Southern Regional Council on the freedom struggle in the South Georgia city of Albany, whose segregationist leaders were considerably more extreme than their counterparts in Atlanta. Zinn's eye for revealing details and critical sensibility, combined with an ironic sense of humor, can be seen even in the short summary he sent to two friends in describing "Things I didn't get into my report":

(1) The Faulknerian atmosphere of this little Georgia city—the smell of slavery still in the air in spite of Sears Roebuck.

(2) My verbal duel with chief deputy sheriff Lamar Stewart who wouldn't let me into the county jail to see Lenora Taitt, my former student and one of the Freedom Riders— . . . and then my shouting out at her through the jailhouse window and her shouting back hoarsely—her voice gave (she slept for five nights in a narrow bunk with two other students).

(3) My very brief interview with Police Chief Pritchett, a red-faced chunk of former football player who had one line before ending the interview "There'll be no change in the nigger situation in Albany."

(4) Interview with nervous-to-the-point-of-hysteria white official at the Chamber of Commerce, who, when I took out a notebook and pencil said "If you quote me, I'll kill you!"

(5) The story of one of the Freedom Riders who took into jail with him copies of *Tropic of Cancer* and *Strange Fruit* and the sheriff passing over the *Tropic* . . . reading the first pages of *Strange Fruit* and shouting "This is pure *obscenity*" (Big word for a sheriff).[47]

Though Zinn's Albany report (1962) focused on the struggle against white supremacy in that southwest Georgia city, it had larger implications that serve as an important introduction to his diary and its politics.[48] The subtitle Zinn chose for his Albany report was *A Study in National Responsibility*, and what Zinn was driving at both in his report and in its subtitle was that those with power nationally, namely, the Kennedy administration and the Federal Bureau of Investigation (FBI), had behaved *irresponsibly*, sitting on the sidelines or worse while Albany's black freedom movement waged an uphill struggle to secure civil rights for its African American citizens. "My report," as Zinn later explained, "focused on the failure of the federal government to enforce constitutional rights in Albany."[49] Zinn had been especially scathing with regard to the FBI, noting that its agents aligned themselves with the Albany police force that was deployed to deprive blacks of their rights and that the FBI did nothing to stop racist violence against civil rights workers.

Such criticisms in Zinn's Albany report made considerable waves nationally. They were picked up in a front-page story in the *New York Times* and also elicited a statement by Martin Luther King Jr. seconding Zinn's criticisms of the FBI—a statement that would infuriate FBI director J. Edgar Hoover and help fuel Hoover's ugly, deep, and lasting vendetta against King.[50] In his December 1962 *Nation* article, "Kennedy: The Reluctant Emancipator," Zinn would underscore his Albany report's critical take not only on the FBI but also on the Kennedy "administration, whose collaboration with the racist South—by inaction—was to," as he put it, "become a persistent issue throughout the struggles of the movement for equal rights."[51] Thus in his 1963 diary, even though it was written when John F. Kennedy resided in the White House, President Kennedy and his brother Robert, the attorney general, rarely appear except to be criticized or even mocked.[52] For Zinn, much as for Martin Luther King Jr.'s biographer Taylor Branch, writing decades later, 1963 was part of the King era—or Zinn might term it the "SNCC-King era"—and its profound struggle for interracial democracy, not Kennedy's ephemeral New Frontier, since for Zinn it was the black freedom movement that was shaping and defining the central moral struggle of this time.[53]

Zinn's discussion with friends about his writing of the Albany report reflected another strong part of his Left outlook that appears in his southern diary as well: a refusal to go along with Communist bans and red-baiting popularized by McCarthyism and sustained into the early 1960s by ongoing Cold War tensions. Thus Zinn would not hesitate to quote Communists when he thought they illuminated social problems he was discussing. This came up in relation to W. E. B. Du Bois in Zinn's writing of the Albany report. As Zinn explained, he had "an argument with the staff of the Southern Regional Council [SRC] going over my report—one of them said—is it *necessary* to quote Du Bois (he had just joined the Communist Party)—and I said, it's not *necessary*, but is Du Bois now an Orwellian non-person? And the director of the SRC, a soft-spoken Virginia guy said quietly 'Leave it in.'"[54] So in his diary we repeatedly encounter not only Zinn's insistence on opposing red-baiting, whether directed against others or himself, but the great pleasure he took in making the case for the abolition of the House Committee on Un-American Activities, in a debate on that issue—a debate that was for him one of the high points of his final semester in Atlanta.[55]

A strong awareness of social class is also evident in Zinn's Spelman writings, which reflects his personal experience growing up working class, along with his Left background and a Marxist influence.[56] And this helped to shape the way he viewed Spelman, leaving him intensely aware and critical of its leadership's bourgeois orientation and aspirations and concerned about the ways Spelman often distanced itself from the larger working-class and poor black community, including the one that bordered the campus. Thus in one letter from his later Spelman years, Zinn noted, "It's now 12:30 PM [*sic*]—everyone's asleep.

I'm looking out of my five-windowed study at the blackness outside (no more lights across the street, they've razed the little framed houses Negroes lived in—to build a Fine Arts bldg. for the college!—this is civilization, the middle class sitting on the poor)."[57]

Zinn's radicalism comes across strongly in many ways in his southern diary, and it enabled him to connect with like-minded activists—so that his diary gives us glimpses of their stories as well as his own. The diary makes evident, for example, that Zinn was not alone among the faculty in his willingness to risk arrest and controversy to challenge Jim Crow and to join with students in such risky acts of defiance. Zinn had a small group of faculty allies in his struggle to support the Spelman student rights campaign. He did not see such activism as being in conflict with his role as a teacher, as he regarded activism itself as an invaluable form of education. For Zinn, the boundary between the classroom and outside political work was at the very least porous, and he often brought issues from that outside work into the classroom for debate and discussion. Zinn used his authority as a teacher to try to expand the horizons of his students outside the classroom as he worked to bring them to white campuses, crossing the color line to promote interracial student contact. And this was, as Zinn later recalled, not an easy thing to do in that segregated time, when "hav[ing] a visiting delegation of Black students from Spelman go over to Agnes Scott [College]" was such a departure from the norm that "it was all carefully planned—all worked out in advance as if you were planning D-day."[58] With Zinn's diary showing us that in his academic work as well as in his outside political organizing he was challenging the color line, we see the white universities and colleges of the Atlanta area surprisingly present in the life of Zinn and his students.

Whether it was crossing the color line with his students at white campuses, challenging racism at the Yale Club, sitting in at a Jewish delicatessen in Atlanta, or confronting Spelman's president over his attempts to stifle student dissent, we see Zinn in his diary constantly pushing for change. In an almost complete and quite profound way, Zinn, in matters of race and educational democracy, lived his politics—no mean feat considering the fact that he regarded himself as a radical, perhaps even as a revolutionary (though one committed to nonviolence).[59] Indeed, for Zinn the challenge was recognizing the need at times to hold back and not be too pushy or unrealistic in his political expectations.[60] Living on the Spelman campus, Zinn had become so immersed in the black community that for him going to any event with a mostly white crowd seemed strange.

Given his record of challenging Jim Crow long before the sit-ins, and the prominence of Atlanta sit-in veterans—including his students—in founding SNCC, it was natural that Zinn had close ties to these dynamic young activists. And so SNCC was a major presence in his diary. The diary shows us Zinn attending and speaking at SNCC meetings, being asked and agreeing to help document the civil rights abuses SNCC encountered, working on writing SNCC's history, and being very aware of the historic role that these young militants were playing in the black freedom struggle.[61] Zinn never had any doubts that this activist role was compatible with his work as a historian, and in fact at several points in the diary we see his discomfort with academics who viewed their work in purely a careerist way, disconnected from the struggle for social justice.[62] Indeed, it is clear from his earlier correspondence that Zinn did not have a high opinion of the historical profession based on the racism he had encountered within it. Thus in December 1961, Zinn wrote with disgust of the resistance he had encountered in "my battle in Chattanooga . . . at the business meeting of the Southern Historical Association" while attempting "to get them to stop meeting in hotels where Negro delegates can't sleep—historians are a pitiful lot as human beings."[63]

Though as both a teacher and an organizer Zinn's egalitarianism on race was a constant, reflecting his deep commitment to equality, his radical vision extended beyond race. He never thought his students' questioning spirit should be confined only to matters of race simply because they were black. In this sense he was the exact opposite of critics of Martin Luther King Jr.'s stand against the Vietnam War, who chided him for meddling with foreign policy, as if an African American leader's area of expertise ought to be confined to domestic race relations and civil rights issues. Zinn often tried to bring his students' attention to international issues, and he was deeply committed to opposing the Cold War and battling its domestic manifestations—intolerance of dissent and radicals. Zinn's cosmopolitanism, marked by his strong internationalist sensibility, was a carryover from his radical youth when his class consciousness and antifascism drew him close enough to the Young Communist League to be mistaken for a member.[64] He remained willing to support Communist-led campaigns and organizations during the late 1940s when their stances on labor, civil liberties, and other issues comported with his own, despite the pariah status of the Communist Party in these tense Cold War years.[65] Zinn, disillusioned with his role as a World War II bombardier, gradually evolved into a kind of anarchist with pacifist tendencies, who had broken with the Communist movement, but he retained strong opposition to colonialism, U.S. militarism, and Cold War American exceptionalism and sustained an ongoing and passionate commitment to the peace movement.[66]

Zinn's internationalism found strong expression in the role he took on at Spelman, founding and heading the non-Western studies program. He developed and taught courses first in Russian history and later in Asian history after a sabbatical at Harvard, where he did extensive coursework on Chinese history. Zinn was an avid promoter of international student exchange programs; he grew close to the visiting African students at Spelman and also to philanthropist

Charles Merrill, whom he encouraged to fund more scholarships for Spelman students' study abroad.[67] In short, though he did not say so in his 1960 *Nation* article on Spelman student activism, the internationalist challenge to the college's old provincialism, which he saw as a crucial building block for that activism, was something he had been promoting for years—and in that sense the *Nation* article was implicitly autobiographical.

The diary also shows how engaged Zinn was with his teaching. Zinn was a well-trained historian, a Columbia University PhD who had written a prize-winning dissertation on Fiorello La Guardia, and he was a very talented lecturer and discussion leader. There are more than forty teaching-related entries in the diary, many of which document how innovative he was, holding debates and using simulations, music, novels, and visiting experts to enliven class discussions. His diary attests that he cared deeply about how well the classes went and took great pleasure when his students became intellectually engaged, when debates were intense, or when students came to him after class and asked, for example, to borrow a record of Woody Guthrie's labor union songs he had played in class.

One can, of course, connect Zinn's passion for his teaching and engagement with black students in his classes to his politics. Decades later, in his memoir, Zinn noted that his working-class background and life experience before becoming a teacher—such as blue-collar work in the Brooklyn Navy Yard, where black workers were discriminated against, and serving in the air force and seeing how blacks were segregated in the armed forces "in a war presumed to be against Hitler's racism"—were all good preparation for teaching at a historically black college since they had raised his awareness of the pervasiveness of racism and the need to battle it.[68] But his work with students at Spelman became much more than some kind of political obligation. Spelman was a small college, with enrollment of well under a thousand students during Zinn's years there, and that mattered as well in contributing to the close relationship he had to his students. Zinn and his family lived on campus and it was quite common for students to drop by and for him to interact with them extensively beyond the classroom— serving as teacher, mentor, and political adviser.[69] It is almost impossible to imagine a professor today writing a diary in which students loomed so large as friends and as subjects of concern.[70] We see Zinn in his diary constantly working to get his students into graduate school, pushing them for fellowships, motivated mostly by his great respect for their work and their abilities but also by his determination to ensure that race or any form of discrimination did not prevent them from realizing their potential.

Since Howard Zinn wrote this diary, and it reflects his political acumen, historical sensibility, and personal biases, it is, of course, his diary in terms of authorship. But in terms of historical agency, the diary belongs as much to Spelman College's student activists as it does to Zinn. It was their courageous organizing for freedom on campus that generated the protests and conflicts with the Spelman administration that likely prodded Zinn to keep this diary in the first place. And their attempt to break with archaic traditions of infantilizing restrictions on student life and political expression on campus so inspired Zinn that it led him to do battle with President Manley on their behalf, yielding a series of tense arguments whose consequences monopolize the final part of the diary and document the sad ending of his Spelman years. One could say that his admiration, even love, of the students and their rebellion fired him up and then ended with his firing.

Depressing as that ending may be, the rebellion itself, and Zinn's narration of it in his diary, are very much in keeping with the reputation he later earned with his best-selling *A People's History of the United States*, which viewed history from the perspective of those outside the national elite—workers, African Americans, Native Americans, and women. On these diary pages Zinn, the people's historian, is reminding us that the freedom struggles waged by these young African American women were a part of the 1960s worth remembering even if the students did not initially prevail in their demands for democratic change at Spelman. This is why Zinn ended his memoir's final chapter on Spelman with the focus not on his firing but on the Spelman students whose activism so moved him. "It was," Zinn explained, "those students and so many others who made the Spelman years, with all that turmoil—even with being fired—such a loving, wonderful time. Watching them change in those few years, seeing their spirit of defiance to established authority, off and on the campus, suggested the extraordinary possibilities in all human beings, of any race, in any time."[71]

Spelman and Zinn from a Colleague's Perspective: Henry West

Even a diary as illuminating as Zinn's has its limitations. In Zinn's case the most obvious limitation is temporal since his journal covers only one semester, winter-spring 1963, plus a few weeks prior to the start of the semester and two months following its end. The other limitation is, of course, that the diary centers on Zinn's perceptions and so tells us far more about how Zinn saw his colleagues, students, and friends in Atlanta than how they saw him. To offset these limitations, and to provide the historical, political, and personal context and background that can make a reading of the diary as meaningful as possible, I offer a summary here of oral histories commenting on the Spelman political scene before, during, and after the period covered in Zinn's southern diary. These enable us to see how the events documented so evocatively by Zinn in his diary in 1963 fit into the larger picture of Zinn's whole Spelman period that dated back to his hiring as professor and chair of the history and social science department in 1956. Interviews with Zinn's students, friends, and colleagues also enable us to dig deeply into the events he covered in the diary by probing how others on the scene saw those events and Zinn's role in them. There are also memoirs by Zinn (plus his post-firing narrative of the Spelman administration's abuses), his students, and colleagues as well as correspondence from the Zinn papers, the Spelman College archives, and the personal collections of those close to him at Spelman that need to be considered as we seek to contextualize the world Zinn describes in his diary. Readers need to be aware, however, that since some of the events discussed in the diary were controversial and complex, there are areas of disagreement both between Zinn and his contemporaries and among those contemporaries. By bringing out such disagreements (some of which cannot be settled definitively by the archival records), the oral histories expedite a deeper reading of the Zinn diary since they enable readers, as they review the diary, to consider some of the most important and difficult historical questions it raises, especially regarding Zinn's tactical sense and the motivations of those in author-ity—most notably Spelman president Albert E. Manley—who ended up using their power against Zinn.

To get at the historical context for the 1963 semester covered by Zinn's diary, we have to begin at the start of Zinn's Spelman years in the 1950s when he was a young historian in his mid-thirties. In those early years Zinn already had a core of close friends on the Spelman and AU Center faculty, black and white, radical and liberal, with whom he socialized extensively. Since this was more than a half-century ago, most of that circle of friends is gone now. Fortunately there is one exception: Henry West, one of Zinn's younger friends from those years, with whom Zinn was close. West was Zinn's neighbor who lived in the same building on the Spelman campus, and he was also Zinn's colleague in the history and social science department. He remained so close to Zinn after his Spelman years that West and his wife Pat shared a vacation home on Cape Cod with Zinn and his wife Roslyn. While Zinn had come to Spelman in 1956, West joined its faculty two years later as a philosopher who taught sociology there. West had a remarkable political history. Though he was a white southerner, born and raised in the segregationist environment of Athens, Georgia, his religious convictions led him to break radically with the Jim Crow regime and to become an avid in-tegrationist and advocate of racial equality. Upon completing his graduate work at Union Theological Seminary in New York, West was determined to return to the South and contribute to the civil rights movement, which was why he decided to only seek jobs at historically black colleges and eventually joined the Spelman faculty.[72]

Henry and Pat West participated in one of the early civil rights protests initi-ated by Zinn and his students. This was a reprise of a 1957 protest that Zinn, his students, and some from Morehouse had mounted in the gallery of the Georgia state legislature, defying its segregated seating practices. In 1958 Howard and Roslyn Zinn, the Wests, and the students in the Spelman Social Science Club, which Zinn served as faculty adviser, returned to the legislature's gallery. This racially integrated delegation, as West recalls,

> sat in the white section and five to ten minutes went by, and someone called attention to the master of arms, the presiding officer, that there were "colored" students in the white section. He banged the gavel, interrupted the proceedings and said, "Sergeant at Arms, get those colored students out of the white section! We have segregation in the state of Georgia!" So then the Sergeant at Arms came and told everybody in our delegation to move into the colored section. Well, we all moved [there]. Howard Zinn and his wife, me and my wife. So we sat there four or five minutes. Someone went to the chairman and pointed to the balcony [where the interracial delegation was now sitting in the "colored" section], and he said, "Sergeant at Arms get those white people out of the colored section! We have segregation in the state of Georgia!" So the Sergeant at Arms came and told me and my wife, Howard and Roz and one of the [African American] students who looked white, for the five of us to move to the white section. Well we'd made our point so we left.[73]

This protest against Jim Crow at the state capitol attracted press attention. According to West, their protest "actually made the front page of the *Atlanta Constitution*." Rather than please Spelman's African American president, this publicity upset him. "Manley didn't like the fact that we were making news," West explained. "He wanted Spelman to be a nice quiet finishing school for young ladies. . . . Manley disapproved of Zinn's activism." According to West, tensions with the Spelman administration over Zinn's activism grew as the Atlanta student movement surged in 1960, West's last year at Spelman. The big sit-in at Rich's, Atlanta's most prestigious department store, involved not only students but a handful of activist faculty, including West and Zinn. "Manley disapproved of that" faculty activism, West said.[74]

Compounding these tensions were the Spelman administration's strong disapproval of any student attempt to challenge the social restrictions on their lives on campus and Manley's resentment of faculty support for such student dissent. The campus seemed to breed such dissent because the rules were so strict. As West recalled,

> Students were not allowed to wear socks. They had to wear stockings and skirts. No shorts, except for athletics. . . . They were supposed to be in their dormitory rooms by 7:00 on [at night], unless they checked out to go somewhere on campus [and then] they would have to be back in their rooms by 9:00. They could not leave the campus after dark, not even to go across the

street to the library that was shared with Morehouse.... They had to have their window shades at half-mast during the daytime and pulled down as soon as they turned on a light at night.[75]

West saw such rules as part of "an effort to take these first-generation college students," who included the "daughters of janitors and maids, and instill in them what were [assumed to be] the values of . . . middle-class genteel . . . young ladies, [as in a] . . . finishing school."[76] Such overbearing regulation and surveillance of student behavior seemed at odds with the atmosphere of a free college, and so, as West put it, "Howard a radical, and I a radical, thought a lot of this was absurd . . . just crazy."[77] So when students objected to such restrictions both West and Zinn were supportive of them.

West, along with Zinn, was involved in an early conflict with Manley over the right of students to criticize these social regulations. In January 1958 Herschelle Sullivan, a student of Zinn's, was chastised by Manley for publishing an allegorical story in the student newspaper, the *Spelman Spotlight*, that parodied life at Spelman, mocking his autocratic governing style. It began: "Once upon a time in the country of Atlintio-Georgio, there was a small kingdom of Spielmon which was isolated from the rest of the world . . . smothered by a tradition curtain. This little anachronistic kingdom was not as advanced technologically as the surrounding kingdoms because at Spielmon it was customary to do things as they had been done in the past. Their ideally democratic government was in reality an oligarchy. The ruler was a benevolent despot."[78]

Upon learning that Sullivan had been rebuked by President Manley for this parody, Zinn rose to her defense because, as Zinn explained in his memoir, "I felt . . . I should not remain silent if one of my students, perhaps influenced by my classes, spoke her mind freely about what troubled her on campus." Zinn fired off a letter of protest to Manley asserting that in his history classes he "had been stressing the need for independent thought, for courage in the face of repression, and that any administrative effort to discourage freedom of expression was a blow at all the values crucial to liberal arts education."[79] In this dissent, Zinn was joined by five colleagues who also wrote Manley, protesting not only the president's response to Sullivan's parody but to the way "the intellectual and social growth of students at Spelman was limited by needless restrictions. . . . Students should be encouraged to develop self discipline rather than have discipline thrust upon them."[80] Clearly irked by this criticism, Manley responded to none of these faculty letters of protest.

Manley was not silent, however, with regard to all of the faculty supporters of the Sullivan parody. West was the faculty adviser to the Spelman student newspaper when the controversial Sullivan story was published. Soon after its publication, Manley summoned West to his office. According to West, Spelman's president "asked me if I'd read that [Sullivan parody]. And I said 'Yes, I read the copy to see that there were no grammatical mistakes and so forth.' And he said, 'And you allowed that to be published?' And I said, 'Yes, I thought it was very clever.' And he said: 'Well, I think that was bad judgment on your part.' And so I was removed as adviser to the newspaper. That's the kind of benevolent despot that he was."[81]

Incidents like this left West convinced that "Albert Manley ran the place like a high school . . . a finishing school," with little respect for the free speech rights of students or for their dissenting opinions or the academic freedom of the faculty. And this situation, so evident back in the 1950s, in West's view, paved the way for the escalating student rights movement in 1963 and the heightening of the Zinn-Manley tensions that would lead to Zinn's firing. West stressed that the authoritarian administrative style embodied by Manley was by no means confined to him and that it pervaded the whole Spelman administration. As an example of this West cited a new regulation issued by the dean of students, declaring that "the students could not visit the apartments of male faculty members." When West questioned this new policy at a faculty meeting, asking why such a policy had been adopted, the dean replied, "I don't need to give a reason." West found it troubling that she was "implying there was misbehavior on the part of the male faculty without specifying that." She "just arbitrarily . . . with the president's approval" banned Spelman students from visiting the apartments of their male teachers.[82]

West saw the conflict between Zinn and the Spelman administration as not just political but a cultural clash. Citing E. Franklin Frazier's classic critique of the African American middle class and historically black colleges in his *Black Bourgeoisie*, West noted that colleges such as Spelman, founded by missionaries, "New England Puritans," had a strong tradition of social conservatism, adhered to especially by the senior administrators and older faculty who were "Black puritans." But at the same time these colleges drew faculty from the Left, whose racial egalitarianism led them to teach on black campuses. And, as West pointed out, these progressives, who were often, like Zinn, "New York radicals," tended to be secular and did not share the administration's puritanical fear that if Spelman's "young ladies" were not policed carefully they "would get a bad reputation" and be "endangered by going across the street and getting pregnant with Morehouse" students. Even the library at Spelman was affected by this puritanism, as West explains:

> I taught this [sociology] course on marriage and the family. And one of the books that I selected was . . . *Ideal Marriage* [which included discussion] about how to have good sex. Well I put this book on reserve in the library for students. . . . And the students came to me and said, "It's not there." So I went to the library

and I said, "I put this book on reserve. And the students are saying 'it's not there.'"
And the librarian . . . a black librarian, woman . . . said, "I don't want to have a
book like that in my library." And I said, "I'm teaching a course and I want my students to have access to it." And she said, "Well, I'm not going to have it in my library." Now her "library" was just a reading room, just one room at Spelman. The
big library was across the street shared by Morehouse. So I went to Manley and
I told him that the librarian was not allowing my students to read a book that
I had placed on reserve and recommended to them. So he called the librarian
and said to make the book available to them. . . . Students came and said, "It's
still not available." And so I went to the librarian and said, "The students say this
book is still not available, although president Manley said that he was going to
tell you to make it available." She said, "I have it locked in my desk. I don't want
it on the shelves for just anyone to read it." So there was this puritanical streak
of the [older] black faculty and of the administration. They wanted to keep the
young ladies under control. And to keep them from harm, especially sexual
harm. That was the reason for all the parietal rules.[83]

Though West left Spelman before the period covered by Zinn's diary, he
stayed in close touch with him. When Zinn went on leave in 1960–61 to study
East Asian history at Harvard, West was doing graduate work there and they
saw a good deal of each other. Zinn kept him posted on the Spelman scene after
that. West recalled Zinn discussing what he saw as one of the worst of Manley's abuses, the punitive action against Spelman student Lana Taylor.[84] She had
been among the students who in the spring of 1962 were inspired to petition for
student rights when Marian Wright, a Spelman alumna and Yale law student,
gave a speech at Spelman urging students to become a force for social change.
(Wright, a former Zinn student, had been in 1960 a key organizer of the Atlanta
sit-ins and student movement, and she had gone to jail in this battle against
Jim Crow. It was, in fact, the notice Wright had posted on a Spelman bulletin
board, recruiting students for the sit-in by asking for "young ladies who can
picket," that had inspired Zinn to so name one of the Spelman chapters of his
memoir.)[85] The petition asked for change at Spelman, charging that the college
was "not preparing today's women to assume the responsibilities of today's rap-
idly changing world. . . . Intellectual inquiry requires social freedom as the pur-
suit of excellence is enhanced by a feeling of self-direction. We are asking . . .
for the responsibility of personal freedom as college women. We feel a college
should not assume the responsibility of a mother along with the role of an educator."[86] The petition urged that students should be allowed to go into the city
more freely, that they should be allowed individual dating, and that Spelman
generally should liberalize student life and improve the academic reputation of
the college.[87]

Taylor had chaired the meeting at which this student rights petition had been first circulated on campus. For that role she would be denied a scholarship after Manley claimed she had displayed "poor citizenship," even though she was an honors student who had been elected president of the senior class. Manley had also pressured the student newspaper editor not to publish the petition. The fallout from the Taylor case was considerable since, as Zinn told West, Manley proved to be curt, uncooperative, and angry when Zinn sought to revisit the decision to punish Taylor. Zinn told West that when he

discovered that her scholarship had been withdrawn [and] so [though] . . . she had been elected president [of the senior class she] could not serve because she was not enrolled . . . he began to raise the question of why was her scholarship withdrawn. And, as he told the story to me, when the faculty meeting would assemble—Manley presided at faculty meetings, by the way—Howard would say that he wanted to raise a point of order, that he wanted to know why the student's scholarship had been withdrawn. And Manley would say, "That is out of order." And when Howard continued to raise the question, Manley would simply adjourn the faculty meeting. And this went on through the year.[88]

When West heard that Manley fired Zinn, he was surprised that Manley had gone that far since Zinn was a full professor and department chair. He thought Manley had gone out on a limb because such a firing was so improper. But politically the purging of the campus's leading dissenting faculty member seemed to West completely in character for Manley both as West had known him in the 1950s and as Zinn had described him in the early 1960s. According to West, Manley's response to Zinn was much "like a high school principal with a teacher who was insubordinate, and felt that he had the power to get rid of him. . . . Manley . . . wanted to be in control. And when he was not in control because a student [Lana Taylor] was advocating student power he got rid of that student. And when Zinn was protesting his getting rid of that student he got rid of Zinn."[89]

West's perspective on Manley's role in Zinn's firing, though based in part on his conversations with Zinn (along with West's own interactions with Manley), actually differs from the way Zinn ended up depicting the firing in his memoir, *You Can't Be Neutral on a Moving Train*. Zinn implied that the Spelman board of trustees had played a central role in his firing. In fact, Zinn titled the chapter in his memoir on his firing, "A President Is Like a Gardener," which was a quote from a speech given at a testimonial dinner for Manley by New Jersey banker Lawrence J. MacGregor, chair of Spelman's board of trustees, a few months before Zinn's firing. The full quotation (which Zinn initially recorded in his diary) has MacGregor noting that, like a gardener, a college president "must make sure things grow in their place—and if anything grows where it's not supposed to grow he must get rid of it."[90] Zinn in his memoir indicated that he "felt a certain sympathy for President Manley" who was "under pressure from all sides," including "the Board of Trustees."[91] West, to the contrary, thinks the decision to fire Zinn "could easily be explained just by Manley" and his long-simmering feud with Zinn over student rights (and student activism both on campus and off) "with the support of the Board but without the initiative of the Board."[92]

The archival paper trail at Spelman on Zinn's firing is not large because Manley apparently purged his extensive papers of his files on Zinn. Even so, the few revealing documents on the decision to dismiss Zinn that are in the Spelman and American Association of University Professors archives and in Zinn's own papers do not suggest that the Spelman board of trustees initiated Zinn's firing. In fact, some board members did not even know of the firing until they received letters from Zinn's colleagues protesting his firing. One board member, Judge Elbert Tuttle, indicated that there had been no discussion of the Zinn case at any board meeting before his firing. There is evidence that Manley had briefed the board's executive committee on the firing, and board chair MacGregor told his fellow trustees that Manley had kept him "fully informed at all times" on Zinn's dismissal, but there is no evidence at all that anyone other than Manley initiated the firing. In fact, at the crucial meeting in November 1963 when Spelman's board of trustees discussed Zinn's firing—almost a half-year after the firing—MacGregor's introduction to that discussion made it clear that this was the board's first "opportunity to state their views and discuss the matter fully," and that the firing was Manley's decision, and a good one, so "the matter should be left entirely in President Manley's hands."[93]

Why then did Zinn foreground the MacGregor quote in his memoir, implicating the board of trustees in his firing? It may be that this was, at least subconsciously, an implication that attracted Zinn because it accorded with his radical politics. From a Left perspective it was obviously preferable to blame an elite group of mostly conservative, rich white trustees for the firing rather than view it as solely the work of Spelman's first African American president using his power to terminate an insubordinate white faculty member. In any case, the archival record tends to support West's view of the firing as Manley's handiwork over Zinn's version blaming the trustees as well as Manley.[94]

One ought not be too quick, however, to dismiss Zinn's suggestion that the trustees had a hand in his firing. Even if the trustees did not initiate the firing and Manley did because he was fed up with the student rebellion and Zinn's championship of it, one must ask why Manley felt so threatened by that rebellion and Zinn. He may well have felt that such student and faculty challenges to his leadership had the potential to undermine his authority, and that this could prove embarrassing and undercut the board's respect for him. In other words, since Manley defined his job as president in terms of maintaining good order and old traditions on campus and saw those as prerequisites for maintaining good relations with the college's mostly conservative white trustees, then that board can be said to have played a role, if an indirect one, in Zinn's firing.

Zinn, moreover, was more correct than he even realized in depicting board chair MacGregor as a toxic force with regard to dissent at Spelman. Zinn, as we have seen, quoted MacGregor's purge-friendly public statement about the president needing to rid the campus of things that don't belong, as a gardener does. But Zinn did not know that MacGregor had privately suggested to the board at its November 1963 meeting that Zinn ought to have been dismissed earlier, "that Mr. Manley had been most lenient toward Dr. Zinn in that he had been retained as long as he had."[95] A few weeks after that meeting MacGregor sent a private letter to Manley, in the wake of the assassination of President John F. Kennedy, which chillingly compared Spelman's dissidents—unnamed but apparently referring to students and faculty protesting Zinn's dismissal (all of whom were nonviolent of course)—to JFK's assassin (or to the killer of the assassin). "The events in Dallas during the past few days," MacGregor wrote, "provide a terrible illustration of the ultimate outcome when people refuse to abide by established procedures and take matters in their own hands. It may be that you will have an opportunity to point this out to anyone at Spelman who is concerned about the loss of 'freedom.'"[96] Having a board chair with such conservative inclinations could not help but reinforce Manley's authoritarian tendencies.

West admired Zinn not only as a fellow activist in the struggle against Jim Crow and an ardent defender of student rights but also as an effective teacher "beloved by his students, maybe the most beloved member of the faculty. It was clear that he was interested in the students, he respected them. He thought highly of them." West points out that the academic weaknesses as well as the strengths of Spelman students need to be understood in order to grasp why Zinn was so popular with the students. "Most of the students had gone to segregated high schools in Georgia and really didn't have the skills to do really good college work." But while "poorly prepared for college . . . when you gave them a writing assignment they [initially] thought a paper was one page," Spelman students "were intelligent" and able to "discuss issues in class as well as any [students at such leading research universities as] MIT and the University of Chicago." Owing to these problems with their students' academic preparation, "some of the older faculty put them down, said 'you've got to learn to read better . . . to write better.'" Such faculty, as West put it, "were not encouraging the way that Howard was encouraging to the students to make the best of their abilities. So he was not only friendly to the students, but was encouraging to the students and they recognized that."[97]

Zinn's popularity with Spelman's students was also linked to a shared disdain for the Jim Crow system. Even though Zinn tended to be closest to the small core of students who were most active in the civil rights movement, his prominent role in working with and writing about the movement appealed to the larger student body, which, as West notes, was strongly supportive of that movement. As West points out, even though it was a small percentage of Spelman students who dared to risk arrest in the sit-ins, this militant minority was "not unrepresentative" with regard to their enthusiasm for a revolution in race relations. "In my classes," West recalls, "every member of classes was concerned about racial justice and the fact that they were discriminated against, and that they didn't like their position in society and they wanted society to change."[98]

Zinn as Mentor: Marian Wright (Edelman)

The best sources on Zinn's relationship to his students are the students themselves, and both their oral histories and memoirs offer extensive discussion of what Zinn meant to them and to the Spelman student body. Marian Wright Edelman, in her *Lanterns: A Memoir of Mentors*, devotes a chapter to "Spelman—A Safe Haven," and while discussing the important mentors from that period in her life named only one Spelman faculty member, Howard Zinn. She was among the students Zinn "welcomed to gather, explore ideas, share hopes, and just chew the fat" at his home "in the back of the Spelman College infirmary," along with his wife and his children Myla and Jeff. Wright Edelman credited Zinn as an intellectual and well as a political mentor, whose work in the classroom was valued as much as his work on the picket line, teaching her

> to question and ponder what I read and heard and to examine and apply the lessons of history in the context of daily political, social, and moral challenges like racial discrimination and income inequality. He combined book learning and experiential opportunities to engage in interracial discussions; partnered with community groups challenging legal segregation; and engaged students as participants, observers, data collectors, and witnesses in pending [civil rights] legal cases. . . . He listened and answered questions as we debated strategy for conducting sit-in demonstrations to challenge segregated public dining facilities. . . . In short, he was there for us through thick and thin, focused not just on our learning in the classroom but on our learning to stand up and feel empowered to act and change our own lives and the community and region in which we lived . . . [to be] active and proud claimants of our American birthright.[99]

Zinn played a similar mentoring role for her fellow activists in SNCC, being supportive and offering advice without coming across as their leader or their better. As Wright Edelman explained,

> He conveyed to me and to other students that he believed in us. He conveyed to members of the Student Nonviolent Coordinating Committee whose voter registration and organizing efforts he chronicled in his book *SNCC: The New Abolitionists* that he believed in, respected, and supported our struggle. He was there when two hundred students conducted sit-ins and seventy-seven of us got arrested. He provided us a safe haven in his home to plan civil right activities by listening and not dictating. . . . He was passionate about justice and his belief in the ability of individuals to make a difference in the world. Not a word-mincer, he said what he believed and encouraged us as students to do the same.[100]

Wright Edelman was with Zinn and other students when they sat-in at the white section of the Georgia legislature's gallery. Having grown up in the racially segregated world of South Carolina, her school experience prior to Spelman had been confined to fellow African American students, which is why she felt "indebted" to Zinn for including her in one of his efforts to cross the academic color line, providing her "first interracial [student] experience with a discussion group at the YMCA on international relations." For many students at Spelman, educated at segregated schools, Zinn was their first white teacher. And for Wright Edelman, who came from a religious background, Zinn was her first non-Christian teacher. Zinn "stretched her religious tolerance beyond childhood limits." She initially felt "shock and confusion when he announced in class that he did not believe in Jesus Christ. There were few Jewish citizens in my South Carolina hometown. Through him I began to discern that goodness comes in many faiths and forms which must be respected and honored."[101] Zinn further broadened her intellectual horizons by helping her to secure a Merrill Scholarship to study in Europe, just one of many ways Wright Edelman felt that he "helped prepare me to discover my leadership potential."[102]

Though aware that the "Black Spelman establishment did not like Howard Zinn," Wright Edelman thought of this as a plus. In her view, Zinn made "Spelman's president Albert Manley . . . [and] some teachers and administrators uncomfortable by challenging the comfortable status quo." In fact, part of the reason she found Zinn such an appealing teacher was that he represented so dramatic a break with Spelman's staid academic style both in the classroom and out: "We called him Howie and felt him to be a confidant and friend as well as a teacher, contrary to the more formal and hierarchical traditions of many Black colleges. He stressed analysis and not memorization: questioning, discussions, and essays rather than multiple choice questions and pet answers." This too carried over into the political realm as Zinn, in the early stages of the sit-in movement, according to Wright Edelman, "reassured us of the rightness of our cause when uncertainty and fear crept in and some of our college presidents [at Spelman and other AU-affiliated campuses] sought to dampen our spirits and discourage our activities."[103]

With regard to President Manley and his administration at Spelman, then, Wright Edelman's memoir aligns closely with Henry West's oral history in that both show him uncomfortable with the new student activism even as it targeted Jim Crow. Also in much of her memoir, she, like West, attests to a generational divide between the politically daring student civil rights activists and their at least tactically conservative elders—the latter characterized most of the college presidents at historically black campuses affiliated with the AU Center. Indeed, in the excerpts from her college diary from 1960, she noted that in the initial planning stages of the sit-in movement in early March "the college presidents have been a big hindrance" to the movement."[104] Manley comes off especially poorly in connection with a planned student march on the capitol in May 1960, on the anniversary of the *Brown* decision, which the movement planned to hold despite KKK threats. Wright Edelman recalled making a speech in the Spelman chapel urging "my Spelman sisters to join me and students from other colleges in front of Atlanta University's Trevor Arnett Library at the appointed hour to begin our march to the Capitol." But rather than show solidarity with her and the freedom movement, to Wright Edelman's "shock and dismay, Dr. Manley . . . stood up after I sat down and urged Spelman students not to participate. He stressed all the dangers but none of the values at stake. . . . [And] we learned that nearly all of the college presidents had done as Dr. Manley did and discouraged students from joining our march. Clark College's president Dr. James P. Brawley had gone so far as to lock the dormitories to try to make it impossible for students to leave the campus."[105]

This is not to say, however, that the generational divide was impermeable or that the college presidents were uniformly unpopular with the student protesters. Indeed, in contrast to her memoir's critical portrait of Manley, Wright Edelman offers a flattering portrait of Morehouse College president Benjamin Mays, mentor to Martin Luther King Jr. and a longtime civil rights advocate, whom she named and described as one of her three important mentors during her Spelman years. It is also true that even the more conservative presidents in Atlanta could and did at times shift with the political winds. Though too timid to embrace the sit-in movement early or consistently, they did not always oppose it. In fact, that same march on the capitol that Manley and other presidents had opposed drew a very different reaction from them once it turned into a big success that drew more than a thousand students and support from adult civil rights leaders. This can be seen in Wright Edelman's description of the church reception that followed the march: "The tumultuous welcome from the packed crowd at Wheat Street church, the grinning welcoming committee of college presidents lined up across the stage and the surprise entrance of Dr. King who'd flown up from Montgomery to encourage our youthful efforts taught me some lifelong lessons: hang on when life gets rough for pain and progress are Siamese twins."[106] Most of these presidents sympathized with the civil rights movement but were uncomfortable with civil disobedience, especially if it involved putting their students at risk.

Defying Spelman's Administration to Join the Freedom Movement: Gwendolyn Robinson (Zoharah Simmons)

Though Wright Edelman's account took Manley and the Spelman administration to task for at times standing in the way of the student wing of Atlanta's civil rights movement, it is by no means the most critical account of Manley's administration written by a Spelman alumna who was a civil rights activist in Zinn's Spelman years. That distinction belongs to SNCC Mississippi field organizer Gwendolyn (Robinson) Zoharah Simmons, whose essay "From Little Memphis Girl to Mississippi Amazon" was recently published in *Hands on the Freedom Plow: Personal Accounts of Women in SNCC* (2010). Zoharah Simmons, who was known as Gwendolyn Robinson in her student days at Spelman, portrays the Manley administration as placing barrier after barrier in the way of students who wanted to be active in SNCC, the Atlanta sit-ins, and the Mississippi Freedom Summer.[107]

Zoharah Simmons arrived at Spelman in 1962, so she was there when Staughton Lynd had been hired. Lynd was a radical historian who would become one of Zinn's closest friends and political allies at Spelman. Zoharah Simmons writes of the influence that Lynd and Esta Seaton (another close friend of Zinn's who was a poet teaching in Spelman's English department) had on her through a course they co-taught on American history and literature, which "acquainted her for the first time with the history and protest writing of my people." Another Zinn friend, Vincent Harding, and his wife, Rosemary Freeny Harding, at that time codirectors of the Mennonite House and prominent civil rights activists, had a hand in fanning "the flame" of Zoharah Simmons's "black pride and identity." She also cited Zinn as fostering that pride in his "illuminating lectures on the African American contribution to the expansion of democracy in the United States," which was also fostered through her membership in Ralph David Abernathy's church in Atlanta and hearing Martin Luther King Jr.'s sermons there. All of this drew Zoharah Simmons to the civil rights movement, as did her visits to the SNCC office, which was near campus, jumping with activity, and led by such dynamic organizers as James Forman and Ruby Doris Smith.[108]

But Zoharah Simmons's move toward SNCC and civil rights activism was slowed by her status as a low-income student who needed to keep her scholarship if she was to stay in school and fulfill her dream (shared by her working-class parents) of obtaining a college degree. And it quickly became apparent that civil rights activism would jeopardize her scholarship. "Spelman administrators warned us Spelman women," recalled Zoharah Simmons, "to stay clear of any involvement with the Movement. We were there, we were told, to get an education, not to get involved in demonstrations and protests. They made it clear that any young ladies who got involved would be summarily dismissed, especially those of us who were on scholarships." So initially Zoharah Simmons tried to stay clear of involvement with SNCC. But she found the freedom struggle too compelling and so tried to move toward low-key activism, doing office work for SNCC but staying "out of the limelight and definitely away from any news cameras or paddy wagons."[109]

This approach worked during her freshman year when Zoharah Simmons kept her involvement in the movement secret from her family and Spelman officials. But during her sophomore year, in part because of the inspiration of the March on Washington, she became more involved: she was elected to SNCC's board, the coordinating committee for the student movement for the Atlanta University Complex, and was arrested in a desegregation protest at Lester Maddox's restaurant. Press coverage alerted the Spelman administration of her arrest and led to her being summoned to the dean's office, where she was chastised for having "left the campus without permission, lied on the dorm sign up sheet, and disobeyed the school's regulations regarding participating in civil rights demonstrations." The dean warned her that she was putting her scholarship in jeopardy, and he called her grandmother, who was very upset with Zoharah Simmons. She was placed on probation for "lying" and "bringing dishonor" on the college.[110]

After her second arrest in a desegregation protest at Krystal's restaurant, and "because of the rallies" she had "organized on campus related to more campus freedoms," Zoharah Simmons was summoned to a meeting with both the dean and Manley. Spelman's president astonished her, as Zoharah Simmons recalls, when he "asked me if I were a Communist and had been sent to foment dissent and chaos on the campus. A Communist? I hardly knew what that was. A *paid* instigator? Boy, I was poor as Job's turkey, with hardly a penny to my name." The dean then informed her that her scholarship had been revoked and that she should pack her bags and leave the college.[111] It took a SNCC-organized strike threat and a rally outside the president's home, in which he was burned in effigy, to get Manley to back down and reduce her punishment to strict probation.

The administration got back at Zoharah Simmons again when the dean learned of her plan to travel to Mississippi in 1964 to join with Lynd, Zinn, and others from Spelman who had volunteered to participate in the SNCC-led voter registration and freedom school crusade, Freedom Summer. Without notifying Zoharah Simmons, the dean had contacted her mother, who came to Spelman to whisk her home so that she could not be a part of that dangerous freedom struggle. Her mother was so opposed to her going to Mississippi that, as Zoharah Simmons put it, "I was literally kept a prisoner when we got home." Only after repeated attempts and with her friends' assistance, and funding from Lynd, was she finally able to get away from her mother and travel to Mississippi.[112]

Tough Love? Rethinking the Manley Administration: Betty Stevens (Walker)

Clearly, then, one of the key tasks readers will need to confront in reading Zinn's diary is determining the motivations, character, and politics of Manley, who by 1963 had become Zinn's nemesis. Although this may seem a simple matter in light of the cogent black-and-white accounts of Manley and his administration in the West interview and the Wright Edelman and Zoharah Simmons memoirs, making sense of Manley's behavior and that of his administration is actually complex, and his record in dealing with the Atlanta student movement was more inconsistent, contradictory, and debatable than these damning accounts suggest. The most revealing source on these complexities is Betty Stevens Walker, the Spelman student activist mentioned in Zinn's diary more than any other student.[113]

Stevens Walker was a student of Zinn's who had been equally active in the civil rights sit-ins in downtown Atlanta and the struggle for student rights at Spelman. In February 1961 she had spent thirteen days in jail after being arrested in one sit-in as part of SNCC's "jail no bail" campaign to flood the jails with civil rights protesters. On campus she was a leading voice of criticism of the Manley administration for its strictness in enforcing rules governing student life, its punishing of students who flouted those rules, and its attempt to silence those who dared to raise their voices against this harsh regime. She was involved in organizing the largest protest meeting of the spring 1963 semester demanding change on campus—the meeting, held in March and described in Zinn's diary, was titled "On Liberty at Spelman"—and it was so offensive to Manley that Zinn's attempt to get the president to heed the grievances raised there played a role in his firing after that semester ended.[114]

Stevens Walker also figured prominently in Zinn's diary because Zinn was concerned that Manley would use his power against her as payback for her dissident leadership. He, as well as other progressive faculty, became convinced that this leadership by Stevens Walker was the reason she did not win a Merrill Scholarship to study abroad. So Zinn helped convince philanthropist Charles Merrill to provide her with a summer scholarship to study at Harvard—a move Manley (in one of the diary's most fascinating entries) came close to stopping but then backed down, telling Merrill that she had demonstrated "poor citizenship," yet with some apparent reluctance conceding that she should get the summer scholarship anyway. The diary reveals that her classmates admired her campus citizenship, electing her president of the student body despite administration attempts to find a candidate to defeat her. And when Zinn was fired she was among the students most upset, writing a letter of support to Zinn and a public letter of protest to the administration. If any Spelman alumna was qualified to assess Manley, Zinn, and their conflict in 1963 it was Stevens Walker, who was on the scene and involved in the key events that escalated that conflict.[115]

Stevens Walker acknowledges that she had intense disputes with President Manley on student rights and his administration's tendency to go overboard in regulating student life. But her retrospective view of Manley is considerably more positive than the biting assessments offered by West, Wright Edelman, and Zoharah Simmons. Stevens Walker contends that Manley was supportive of the civil rights movement, and that given the constraints of his job he did as much as may have been possible to support students' participation in that movement. She stresses that Manley had the almost impossible job of representing the movement-oriented students, their cautious parents, and conservative trustees, while safeguarding the financial state and survival of this historically black college. Parents had sent their daughters to Spelman to be educated and earn a college degree, not to get arrested or injured putting their bodies on the line in civil rights protests. Stevens Walker notes that when she was in jail for almost two weeks following her arrest in a sit-in, Spelman's president and dean visited her repeatedly to look after her needs and show the police that the college was concerned about her welfare.[116]

One document Stevens Walker cites in defense of this more positive view of the Manley administration is a letter her mother received in February 1961 from Mercile L. Johnson, Spelman's dean of women, during the time that Stevens Walker was in jail for sitting-in. The letter reassured her mother that "Betty is getting along well and her morale is unusually high. She is being treated kindly and with much concern on the part of jail personnel. The food is adequate and all have beds contrary to news reports. The young ladies are housed in one large room which enables them to assist each other to such an extent that they have become a close knit and determined group."[117]

The dean explained that she and President Manley visited the imprisoned students "several times a week," and implied that they were a part of discussions aimed at securing their release. She indicated that she and Manley would continue to bring to the jail "whatever they needed and encourage them by our visits although we do not agree with their decision [to refuse bail since the prolonged jail time was interfering with their school work]." The dean urged Stevens Walker's mother to "write encouraging and reassuring letters" to Betty in jail whether or not she approved of her getting herself arrested in a civil rights protest. And her letter concluded with a line that made clear that whatever she and Manley thought of the sit-in and "jail no bail" strategy, they saw the protest's goal as laudable, writing that "the struggle has been long and tiring, but we hopefully look forward to the time when all men are treated with dignity and respect."[118] Such documents, in Stevens Walker's view, take us beyond the youthful impatience that she and her fellow activists felt toward the administration back in the early 1960s, when they hoped for but did not get Manley's unqualified support for the sit-in movement.[119] The dean's letter suggests that even though not on the ramparts of the civil rights revolution she and Spelman's president were—at least at times and in their own way—helpful to the sit-in movement.

Similarly, at the beginning of the school year in which the dean sent that letter to Stevens Walker's mother, President Manley had himself reached out to the parents of Spelman students. Manley's letter informed parents of the likelihood that the student protests, "sit-ins, stand-ins, kneel-ins and related demonstrations" against Jim Crow would continue in the 1960–61 academic year "with the possible participation of your daughter who is enrolled in Spelman College." He pointed out that "these activities could lead to arrest, and jail terms if bail is refused." The administration's position, Manley claimed, was to respect the students' right to engage in such protests and even civil disobedience: "Although we shall continue to consult with and offer advice to the students, the decision whether or not to participate in demonstrations is one to be made by each individual student." Whether or not Manley actually believed in such adult-like autonomy for Spelman students, in asserting it here he was freeing his administration from any liability for the demonstrations. In other words, since it was the students' decision not the college's to defy the Jim Crow laws, Spelman, as Manley wrote, "cannot accept responsibility for any of these demonstrations and the possible consequences." This can, of course, be seen as an opportunistic posture since it placed all the risks and costs of the desegregation struggle on the students, but it was not hostile to the sit-in movement. Indeed, as with the dean's letter, Manley's was supportive of the movement's quest for racial equality, as he wrote: "Spelman College sympathizes with the students in their goal to achieve full human rights."[120]

There are other examples, too, of the Spelman administration displaying sympathy toward the sit-in movement. The administration allowed Martin Luther King Jr. to give a speech at the campus chapel in April 1960,[121] warmly endorsing the sit-ins and praising the rise of black student activism. That same semester President Manley and his wife served as sponsors and attended a fundraiser at Clark College for the Committee on Appeal for Human Rights, the organizing body for the Atlanta sit-ins. Manley even went so far as to praise the sit-ins in his speech at the Spelman graduation ceremony in 1960, paying tribute to the student activists for "participating in these demonstrations," showing "the characteristic of discipline and your willingness to sacrifice and suffer . . . demonstrating that college students are not apathetic but can become involved in great causes when the moment arrives."[122]

It was the historically black state colleges and universities, dependent on segregationist white legislatures and governors for their funding, not their private counterparts like Spelman, that tended to have presidents who were most intolerant of student-led sit-ins and other protests against Jim Crow. Thus when students at Albany State were arrested attempting to desegregate the bus terminal in Albany, Georgia, that college's president, William Dennis Jr., expelled them and would end up dismissing forty of his school's civil rights activists. Manley allowed some of them to transfer to Spelman, attesting that he was more tolerant of students protesting Jim Crow off campus than he was of students demanding student rights on campus, which he saw as a direct challenge to his authority.[123] Zinn's diary reveals, however, that some of these transfer students chafed under the social restrictions enforced by the Manley administration, and quickly realized that Spelman too placed limits on their freedom.[124] Nonetheless, Stevens Walker's memories of Manley offer a useful reminder that on the spectrum of intolerance of student civil rights activism Spelman was by no means the worst historically black college in the South or even in Georgia.

Though Stevens Walker's assessment of Manley was considerably more positive than Zinn's, Zinn did acknowledge that Manley proved capable at times of voicing surprising support for the student desegregation struggle. Indeed, in his initial *Nation* account of Spelman student activism in 1960, Zinn even highlighted the way Spelman's president broke with his conservative past by praising the sit-in movement in his commencement speech. Zinn interpreted this as a reflection not of Manley's politics or character but rather of the impact of the Spelman student movement itself, offering an optimistic reading of that movement's power to pressure and shame its more conservative elders into expressions of solidarity. In Zinn's words,

> The new Spelman girl is having an effect on faculty and administrators. Many who were distressed and critical when they first learned their sweet young things were sitting behind bars later joined in the applause of the Negro community. . . . Spelman's President Albert Manley, who inherited the traditions of conservatism and moderation when he took the helm seven years ago, has responded with cautious but increasing encouragement to the boldness of his young women. At the college commencement exercises this year, Manley

startled the audience by departing from the printed program and the parade of parting platitudes with a vigorous statement of congratulations for breaking with the "docile generation" label with its sit-ins, demonstrations and picketing.[125]

But Zinn soon came to realize that his *Nation* article had been overly optimistic about Manley's ability to embrace change and warm up to the new student activism. In fact, as Zinn noted in the Spelman narrative he wrote in July 1963, the month after his firing, Manley "resented the *Nation* article. What was important to him was not that I was hailing Spelman's future" as a center of student activism "but that I was demeaning its past" as a "semi-monastic" college that treated young women as if they were immature adolescents. Zinn came to see that even if willing on occasion to take a public posture sympathetic to student civil rights activism, consistent support of such activism was not forthcoming, and that when it came to student activism on behalf of greater freedom on campus Manley did not even go in for liberal posturing but instead responded "in a tyrannical manner."[126]

Zinn would later make several attempts to explain Manley's response to the sit-in movement. Unlike the *Nation* article, where he suggested that the movement was demonstrating the power to change the Spelman administration and awaken it from its conservatism, Zinn in an oral history interview in the 1990s argued that the movement had earned so much support from the black community that Manley and other presidents of historically black colleges felt pressure to seem publicly supportive, when in fact they remained privately troubled by the movement's radical antiauthoritarianism and civil disobedience tactics. "Black administrators found that the students were," in Zinn's words, "always going farther than they wanted them to go, and yet, because of the Black community they could not really oppose that."[127] This was the way he came to see Manley's 1960 commencement remarks that paid tribute to the sit-in movement: "Manley [was] trying to ingratiate himself with the students. 'I'm not an ogre. I'm not reactionary.' So he might commend them publicly and then privately try to slow things down."[128]

At his angriest, Zinn, in the wake of his firing, may even have compared Manley to the classic image of the two-faced historically black college president, the fictional Dr. Bledsoe, in Ralph Ellison's *Invisible Man*—which was itself drawn from Ellison's own experience at Tuskegee—in the *Herald Tribune Book Week* interview Zinn did with Dick Schapp (which accompanied Ellison's review of Zinn's *Southern Mystique*) in November 1964. After telling Schapp of Manley's growing discomfort "as the students pushed harder for freedom on campus and off," and Manley's use of censorship and punishment of student rights advocates, Zinn spoke of how he "became more and more disillusioned with President Manley," and the Bledsoe analogy came up. According to Schapp's article, "Dr. Zinn calls President Manley a 1960s version of Dr. Bledsoe, the Negro College President in Ralph Ellison's *Invisible Man*. It is not a flattering comparison. Dr. Bledsoe was an Uncle Tom to his white patrons, while feeding his Negro students all the . . . attitudes . . . needed to keep them . . . in their places. Dr. Bledsoe was a traitor to his students."[129]

Zinn did, however, write *Book Week*, objecting to the way Schapp quoted him on Ellison's book. While acknowledging that in the interview with Schapp he said "yes I *had* made the connection after reading Ralph Ellison's *Invisible Man*, between the college he described and the one where I was teaching. But I never compared my college president to Dr. Bledsoe. Both men and situations are far more complex than is implied by the quick, harsh judgment stated in the interview."[130] Schapp in turn wrote a letter to Zinn expressing his puzzlement over Zinn's letter backing away from "the Manley-Bledsoe comparison." Schapp wrote that the reason he had interviewed Zinn on that topic was that he had heard

> that you indicated to the people at Knopf . . . that you likened President Manley to Dr. Bledsoe. . . . You said, according to my notes, that it struck you "immediately" that Ellison's description "was so much like the situation we were in." Now, Ellison's description depended, beyond any doubt, upon the character of Dr. Bledsoe. Is it in any way possible to connect the Spelman campus with the Ellison campus without connecting Manley and Bledsoe? I don't see how. But you did indicate to me that there were differences, that the atmosphere created by the student revolt was the main difference, and so I said "a 1960s version of Dr. Bledsoe." . . . Your letter sounds to me like you are unhappy not with my account, but with seeing in print your own feelings towards President Manley. Obviously, you don't like hurting someone else. Your compassion is admirable, but unless I completely misinterpreted your words and your emotions, I doubt that you will mourn when President Manley leaves the Spelman campus.[131]

Whatever Zinn did say to Schapp about Manley, the *Invisible Man* analogy was not the harshest comparison he made about his Spelman nemesis. That came in the Spelman student rights narrative that Zinn wrote the month after his firing. Here he went so far as to compare Manley and his administration to the Jim Crow regime. Zinn wrote of the

> startling analogy between the arguments of those who would keep Spelman old-fashioned and rigid and authoritarian, and the arguments of the Southern segregationists who have been trying so desperately to maintain the status quo. . . . Both speak of "tradition," of "our way of life," having drawn their breaths

for so long in stagnant air, the first breezes of change appear as a hurricane threatening to overturn society. . . . Both say: look how much progress we have made under the old system. (Even under segregation some great Negroes came out of the South; even under paternalism some brilliant students came out of Spelman.) . . . Both say, again and again: "These people are really content with the way things are; agitators are stirring them up." The myth of the happy, singing slave dies hard. . . . Both point to the "backgrounds" of those striving for greater freedom, whisper about their sins, and say "they're not ready for their freedom." When Dr. Manley tried to draw my attention to stealing in the dormitory I couldn't help thinking how the traditionalist South tries to keep attention focused on Negro crime and illegitimacy. In both situations what needs to be constantly reiterated is that there are certain basic rights which human beings should have—rights which may be independent of their faults as individuals, faults which may very well be a response to the denial of those rights. . . . Both pooh-pooh signs of discontent as just ordinary "griping" and refuse to recognize their meaning until the "griping" explodes in a full-scale rebellion.[132]

It is on this analogy with segregationists that Stevens Walker's view of Manley and his administration differs the most from Zinn's. Stevens Walker stresses that although both the protest movements involving Spelman students were for greater freedom—liberation from Jim Crow discrimination off campus and freedom from overbearing paternalistic regulation and restrictions on campus—the origins, nature, and dynamics of the conflicts differed dramatically. For Stevens Walker the key difference was that in the battle for greater freedom on the Spelman campus you were "fighting" the "authority" of black elders, who "you knew deep down inside of you have some caring for you, . . . some concern for you, . . . even on some level some love for you." This was profoundly different from the white segregationists the students were battling in downtown Atlanta, where the antagonist you were "fighting [constituted] an authority that you know despises you, an authority that you know hates you or that marginalizes you so much that you virtually don't exist." This difference in turn led to, as Stevens Walker points out, a major difference in the kinds of risks protesters hazarded in the two movements. In the protests against the Manley administration's paternalism "you may lose your scholarship. And that's not good." But there was nothing like the "same level of risk" students faced against the Jim Crow authorities and racists downtown where "you could lose your life. You're not pleased with the other. But you do know the consequences are greater and can be deadly, certainly more devastating than the other."[133]

There was for Stevens Walker a familial quality to the battle with the Manley administration that also set it apart from the off-campus crusade against Jim Crow. "I had," she recalled, "an understanding even before I came to Spelman—I was from Raleigh, North Carolina— . . . a sense of place and the overwhelming desire of black authority to protect the young." And so even while disagreeing with and opposing the overbearing way Manley wielded that authority, she knew that in their own misguided way Spelman's paternalistic officials were trying to protect students and their black college from the "danger that our young people faced since these black colleges were sitting in hostile territory" in the Jim Crow South. She "didn't like" the harsh rules Manley enforced, and she avidly championed "the need for us to be trusted with more freedom" on campus. But there was "never a lack of understanding of the need [our elders felt] to be protective of us," though "we felt we didn't need to be protected. So that the rules and regulations were stifling." Yet she was aware that in Georgia "we lived under state sponsored terror . . . that you have these [black campus enclaves so] older people were very cautious of the dangers. . . . I think I always had that understanding. . . . That's why I could have these battles [with Manley over student rights], but they were not personal in the sense that hostile feelings grew in me. I had an understanding . . . [as with] kids, they get upset with their parents but they understand on one level. . . . They don't like it. But they understand that 'you're trying to protect me.' I think I was always clear about that. I don't think I ever demonized anyone."[134]

For Stevens Walker the familial nature of her relationship was not merely metaphorical but was present literally. She had a warm personal relationship with President Manley's wife Dorothy. So President Manley and Stevens Walker would have, as she put it, "very heated battles" over student rights and "he would walk into his home in the evening and I would be at his dinner table because his wife was very fond of me. And I don't think he was very happy to see me there at his dinner table." Such close ties would have, of course, been impossible with segregationists, as would Stevens Walker's subsequent role after graduating from Spelman and Harvard Law School as attorney and friend of Albert Manley.[135]

Obviously Stevens Walker was unusual in having so warm a relationship with Mrs. Manley. But her larger point about the familial nature of the relationship between some students and administrators, and the bonds of racial solidarity that linked students to their campus officials on historically black colleges— which seem to have eluded Zinn—is of great importance for understanding the dynamics of the Spelman student movement. Because they recognized that these black elders were heading a black educational institution in the hostile territory of the Jim Crow South, Spelman students in the early 1960s never considered using their most powerful weapon, sit-ins/nonviolent civil disobedience, against them. That weapon was in this era reserved for those whom they regarded as their political enemies—white segregationists downtown. Spelman students did, of course, protest and petition for their rights on campus, but they would not escalate their tactics against their own elders on campus and risk damaging their school or bringing hostile white police onto their black campus. On some historically black campuses these bonds of racial and familial solidarity would eventually come to fray and break when black power militancy inflamed generational conflict, leading to building takeovers on black campuses in the late 1960s.[136] But in the early 1960s those bonds still held, and as we have seen, had the power to lead black college administrators to visit their jailed student civil rights activists (something that was unimaginable for their white counterparts on majority white campuses, such as the University of California, Berkeley) and to lead students to keep *on-campus protests* relatively tame tactically. This is why students from historically black colleges, though the first students to sit-in off campus, lagged behind white New Left student activists in engaging in civil disobedience *on campus*. Thus it was at Berkeley in 1964 rather than at a historically black college that students first used the mass sit-in tactic on campus—in their Free Speech Movement. It is also why the Spelman free speech protests failed while Berkeley's succeeded. Civil disobedience was the great equalizer that empowered the student movement and weakened repressive campus administrations, and being unable to imagine deploying this weapon on campus meant that Spelman's student rights advocates had no effective political response when Manley stonewalled and suppressed their movement.

Stevens Walker believes that, despite all the conflicts, both sides on the Spelman political scene wanted "the same thing for all our people: justice, equality, and freedom." But given the political and economic realities of the financially frail black colleges and the dangers from racists outside the college gates, there were restraints on all members of the college community. So in this sense the fundamental dynamic politically back then was, in her view, "that neither president nor professor nor student was free."[137]

This is not to say, however, that Stevens Walker viewed the Spelman student rights struggle as any less significant than did Zinn. She too saw it as an extension of the student civil rights freedom struggle downtown. She stressed that after having spent thirteen days in jail for sitting in against segregation it was almost impossible to accept the old college rules that treated students like children: "You cannot do that and then go back to campus and not fight against the curfew. I think that stuff is all part of the same process" of seeking more freedom. "It puts you in conflict" with campus authority.[138]

For all Stevens Walker's differences with them in her view of Manley, her perspective on Zinn himself and his role at Spelman aligns closely with that of West, Wright Edelman, and Zoharah Simmons. Stevens Walker admired Zinn as a teacher and loved him as a caring person and mentor who transcended racial barriers and radiated respect for the young African American women he taught at Spelman. According to Stevens Walker,

Howard Zinn saw us in a very unequal environment as equals. And we knew that. . . . It was not something that was on a subconscious level. On a very conscious level and with a real sense of knowing, K-N-O-W-I-N-G. I like it better than cognition. I like it better than acknowledgment. I like it better than awareness, that sense of knowing. We knew that he respected us. And we knew that he saw value in us. He honored who we were in the world in a way that we had not experienced by non-black people. And that's why he was *huge* in presence and in spirit on the campus, not just for people like me, people who were actively involved in the movement, and not just his students, but all of the students. He was a presence on the campus that was so embracing of all the students. . . . He saw us beyond what other people saw. And he saw possibilities. He saw probabilities. He saw worth. He saw intellectualism. He saw things that many other people would not associate with us. . . . He also interpreted us to people [such as the Yale Law School dean, described in the diary, who Zinn tried to convince of Stevens Walker's impressive intellect] who didn't see those things.[139]

As a teacher and mentor Zinn did more than teach his students history. He inspired them to have confidence in themselves and in their abilities to change the world for the better through both the knowledge they gained at college and the activist ethos they imbibed there. This is what Stevens Walker was referring to when she observed that "Howard Zinn was a transformative figure on Spelman's campus. And when I say transformative I mean he made us not just better students, but better people, better human beings. . . . Helping people to see possibilities that they had never seen before." For Stevens Walker that was why, with Zinn's firing, "the loss was enormous. And it was a loss. And it was a grief. And the enormity of the loss was that this was someone who was so important. And then keep in mind this was the tumultuous '60s. And for the person to no longer be there, a sense that you knew you were going to experience this sense of absence when you felt that you really needed the person to be there. I'm speaking now from the perspective of a Movement person, somebody who was more than just his student. Someone who was in the Movement. For me it was up close and personal."[140]

Courageous? Reckless? Staughton Lynd's Take on Zinn's Battle with Manley

One limitation of oral history done so long after Zinn's firing is that those who are still alive and available for interviews were young in the early 1960s. The Spelman students of Zinn and his younger colleagues all were and remain fond of Zinn. The generation of administrators, Manley and his deans, were decades older and so these critics of Zinn are not around to share their less lofty views

of him. And Manley's memoir is mute on his conflicts with the student protesters and Zinn. Fortunately, however, one of Zinn's surviving colleagues from
the early 1960s, Staughton Lynd, though also one who loved Zinn dearly, is a
historian and student of social movements as well as a veteran organizer. In our
interview he was able to bring a critical eye to Zinn's role as the most outspoken dissident on the Spelman campus. Unlike West, who cast all the blame on
Manley for Zinn's firing, Lynd raised questions about Zinn's tactics with respect
to Manley and discussed evidence that Zinn's own mistakes helped to pave the
way for his firing—an event that Lynd viewed as tragic for Spelman—which led
Lynd himself to leave Spelman a year after Zinn's departure.[141]

Lynd agreed with both West and Zinn about Manley's flaws as an educational
leader, his autocratic manner, and his intolerance of dissent from both students and faculty. But Lynd also pointed out that some of Zinn's faculty friends
thought and told Zinn that his approach to Manley was too confrontational,
that "Howard was unnecessarily combative." Criticisms along these lines were
in fact mentioned in Zinn's diary. Lynd believes there was a racial dimension
to the Zinn-Manley conflict, "that," as Lynd put it, "it really wasn't feasible for
a white person" on the Spelman faculty "to be so aggressive in confronting a
black administrator" on a campus whose faculty and administration were overwhelmingly black. This, in Lynd's view, was connected as well with the school's
traditional mission in the black community and Zinn's and his own status as
white outsiders deemed a threat to that mission. As Lynd explains, "the whole
idea of Spelman was to be a kind of finishing school to prepare women to marry
black professionals. And there were strong concerns, not just political and racial
but sexual, that these [Spelman] girls needed protection. And that the last thing
they needed, in the view of black faculty members [and administrators], was
itinerant white radicals Lynd and Zinn to stir them up."[142]

The small size of the college, in Lynd's view, made matters worse because, unlike in a big university, the president had direct contact with the faculty, and so
the disputes between Zinn and Manley were at close range, and they occurred
repeatedly since there was not a layer of bureaucracy separating the two. And
because of this intimacy the president, as the diary shows, regularly encountered Zinn at faculty meetings, where the two tangled with each other. Given
all this, readers of the diary will need to consider whether such conflicts show
Zinn at his most admirable, standing up for the students he admired and even
loved—and their right to free expression and dignity—or at his most stubborn
and tactless. Was Zinn courageous or reckless in confronting Manley? Or both?

Even if Zinn is accorded some responsibility for the conflicts with Manley
that led to his firing, Lynd insists that Manley's duplicity ought not be overlooked, for without it the firing would likely never have happened. "Unfortunately," explains Lynd, "Manley rather than dealing with Howard directly and

saying 'Look, this has to stop or A, B, and C are my next steps,'" instead "was surreptitious, waiting till the students had left and then axed Howard."[143]

As for his own view, Lynd "wasn't sure then" in 1963 whether Zinn had been too combative with Manley, and Lynd "hasn't been sure since how I feel about it." The reason for his indecision on this is because, at Spelman, though Lynd opted to avoid the confrontational approach Zinn used with Manley, Lynd's own strategy did not prove effective either. Lynd had thought it wise not to antagonize Manley, and to instead focus on helping the students directly through informal study groups and personal assistance—as when he helped Alice Walker, for example, to attain admission and funding to attend another college after Zinn's firing had disillusioned her with Spelman. Yet Lynd found that his low-key approach bought little goodwill from the administration. "Manley had a very low opinion of my role as well," recalled Lynd. "I remember vividly one conversation the next winter after Howard had gone, where he [Manley] kind of accused me of being duplicitous. You know among my many characteristics that tends not to be one. So no one [critical of his administration] was very successful" at relating to Manley.[144] This comparison with Lynd implies that even had Zinn been more tactful it may simply have been impossible for a white radical dissenting faculty member to have gotten along well with Spelman's president.

Did Race Matter? Reflections on the Zinn-Manley Conflict by Lynd, Vincent Harding, Willis Laurence James, and Gloria Bishop

Zinn himself differed from Lynd in one important respect in interpreting his conflict with Manley, and that is on the role of race in that conflict. Where Lynd seems certain that race loomed large in this dispute, Zinn insisted that race was not a factor in his conflicts with Manley or in his firing. In fact, in the Spelman narrative Zinn wrote the month after his firing, he made a special point of denying that race influenced these events. "At this point," wrote Zinn,

> I want to mention the unmentionable, mainly in order to set it firmly aside. The unmentionable is race. It needs to be said, because we live in such an intensely race-conscious society that the fact of dismissal of a "white" college professor by a "Negro" college president (I put them in quotes because civilized people of the future will surely see the absurdity of such designations) is outside of what we call "the race question." In the controversy between liberals and conservatives at Spelman, people of both races were on both sides. That there seemed to be more white teachers on the liberal side occasionally brought comment among faculty and students, but I believe most of them soon realized that the factors were not racial but cultural; more of the white teachers came from northern colleges where they were more accustomed to liberal

atmospheres. When I received my notice of dismissal it was a dark-skinned student from Africa who put her head in her hands and wept. And it is the negro students of Spelman who have been the chief victims of, and the sharpest protesters against, administrative malpractice. Because there is so much racial tyranny in this country, we easily forget that tyranny can be non-racial or bi-racial. Ralph Ellison showed this brilliantly in his portrait of the Negro college in *The Invisible Man*.[145]

Lynd did not find Zinn's argument here at all convincing. In fact, when I read him the quote above Lynd told me he "thought 'Howard, what planet were you living on?'"[146] Yes, there were, as Zinn claimed, whites and blacks on both sides of the debates about student rights at Spelman, but that doesn't mean that the dispute lacked a racial dimension, especially since the most vocal and passionate faculty advocate of the student rights cause was white (Zinn) and the key administration official opposing the student rights rebellion (and viewing it as an intolerable threat to his own power) was Spelman's first black president (Manley). Nor was it the case that the line of division was simply between liberals and conservatives since Zinn was a radical, not a liberal. One can understand why Zinn would make this argument on race, since viewing his firing as a response to his championing a biracial struggle for freedom on campus was a more idealistic explanation than seeing himself as a white professor who lost his job because he had disrespected black authority. And in fact both those arguments are true. He lost his job both because he championed that campus freedom struggle and because he had defied black authority far more brazenly than any other faculty member at Spelman.

There is evidence suggesting that some of Manley's more loyal supporters among Spelman's African American faculty saw the Zinn-Manley conflict at least in part in racial terms. Willis Laurence James, an African American professor of music and friend of Manley's, who had been at Spelman for decades, organized nine like-minded faculty to write a joint letter to Spelman's president, in the wake of Zinn's firing, expressing "complete support and confidence in regard to your judgment in handling the administrative affairs of Spelman College."[147] In a private letter to Manley, James was even more forceful in backing Manley against Zinn. James's message, without explicitly mentioning race, seemed to carry a racial subtext—that Zinn's challenge to Manley was "insulting" and that Manley had to stop Zinn to preserve his "self-respect"— phrasing that suggests that Spelman's first black president had no choice but to act against an insubordinate white professor. James wrote Manley that "I have never in all my years of teaching seen a college president put through ~~the long insulting~~ an ordeal comparable to that which you were subjected during the past school year by Dr. Zinn and certain of his satellites. Your patience was unique and I can see no other course you could have taken in the interest of self-respect, Spelman College, and its future than to relieve Dr. Zinn of further unhappiness and agitation at Spelman College and to relieve the college and the majority of the faculty of him and the liability his presence and announced policies were fabricating."[148]

This all begs the question of what would have become of Zinn had he been a black rather than a white radical professor who had been critical of the administration. Would he still have been fired by Manley? Of course we cannot answer that question definitively since Zinn was white. But Vincent Harding, Zinn's successor as chair of the history and social science department at Spelman, who was a good friend of Zinn's during and after his Spelman years—and had sought unsuccessfully to convince Manley to reconsider the firing, and even asked his friend Martin Luther King Jr. to help appeal the firing—was also a radical, who would emerge as one of the most prominent African American historians of his generation. When asked in 1964 to take over as chair of the history and social science department, the year after Zinn's firing, Harding hesitated at the idea of replacing Zinn under such circumstances. But when he spoke with Zinn about this decision, Zinn "insisted that the young activist scholar take the appointment," stressing that "the Black students needed him" and that as department chair Harding would have the power to promote change at Spelman.[149]

In his own way Harding would prove at least as effective as Zinn in promoting political and intellectual change at Spelman. Where Zinn had been close to SNCC and Atlanta's black freedom movement as an activist and had initiated curricular change through his leadership of Spelman's non-Western program, Harding, an adviser to Martin Luther King Jr., was among Atlanta's most prominent civil rights and antiwar activists and had championed curricular change as a pioneer in African American studies and founder of the Institute for the Black World. Both Harding and Zinn served as mentors to Atlanta's black student activists. In fact during our interview, Harding agreed that the tribute Lerone Bennett Jr. had paid to him as a source of inspiration to the student movement in Atlanta applied as well to Zinn: "It was in his classrooms at Spelman College that some of the . . . merry mischief of the Atlanta revolution was developed. It was in his classrooms that student minds and spirits first touched the fire."[150] It seemed essential, then, to get Harding's perspective on the way race worked with respect to Manley's decision to fire Zinn and to see how Harding and Manley got along in comparison to the way Zinn and Manley related to each other.

Harding's perspective was similar to Lynd's, not Zinn's, on this question of whether there was a racial dimension to Zinn's firing. Harding acknowledged that such events can be complicated, "but one thing is clear. You cannot at that point in history, especially in a place like Atlanta, figure out any of these things without factoring race into them."[151] Harding thought that his own experience with Manley offered a useful point of comparison with Zinn's. According to Harding, during his years on the Spelman faculty,

> I on some occasions felt the need to challenge Manley on decisions, on one kind of issue or another. But I was a black man and Howard was not. And I think that some place at deep, deep levels it is simply impossible for there not to be a difference in response. Now what one does with that difference, what are the results of the difference, all of those are controlled by very conscious kinds of mechanisms. But at the level below consciousness, I am quite certain that part of it was the fact that I had known Manley before I came there [as a professor]. I had been on the campus, spoken with him and spoken with the students. Students from the campus had come over to the Mennonite House [which Harding headed]. All of that was a part of the story. I think some place even further back and deeper was the fact that my parents were originally from the Caribbean, from the West Indies [as were Manley's], so I think Manley felt a kind of special relationship, connection. And so I could do things, I could raise questions, I could speak up and not have them ring all the bells that Howard's speaking up and challenging might call forth. And, of course, we were very different people. I tended to be more diplomatic than Howard.[152]

Manley's decision to hire Harding to replace Zinn is itself a testament to the political complexity of Spelman's president. Were Manley simply a conservative it would be hard to imagine him replacing one radical professor with another. Harding views it as "part of the ambiguity of the man" that he was not opposed to the civil rights movement or faculty activism per se, and so was willing to take a chance on Harding, perhaps hoping that, though a radical, Harding as an African American would understand—in a way Zinn did not—the need to be respectful of Manley's authority as the head of a black educational institution. Harding, however, saw Manley in terms quite similar to the way Zinn had. In Harding's view Manley was

> a part of the tradition of black college presidents who were always watching their backs in terms of their boards and in terms of their contributors. It was very clear to me that he was not a very powerful supporter of [the black freedom] movement externally but he knew that the movement was a necessary development. But he was always going to be very careful about how many of his [Spelman's] young women would be arrested and what people would say about that. He was a *very* political person. . . . He was always conscious of, aware of the people he was dealing with, what their connections were, how those *connections* might benefit and not benefit him.[153]

With this in mind, Harding, in responding to his job offer, made it clear to Manley that "'while he was no wild man from outer space" and would respect the Spelman administration's authority, he would not compromise his activism— that he was "going to be working outside the institution, inside the institution, and around the institution . . . in a way that would sometimes challenge the institution."[154]

Harding not only proved true to his word about remaining an activist while on the Spelman faculty, and at times challenging Spelman to change, but kept Zinn apprised of this work. In a letter he wrote to Zinn in January 1967, Harding described some heated faculty meetings where "the feces really hit the fan, as far as President Manley is concerned," when Harding made "some extended comments on the purpose of Spelman College," stressing the need for the college to "capitalize on its uniqueness" by doing far more to stress the teaching of African American history and culture and developing courses that would prepare Spelman students to address the needs of the black community. That Spelman should attempt "to create a stronger sense of Negroness, of what the Negro experience has really meant, and what it portends for the future." What Harding "had in mind was a program of Negro American Studies encompassing not only history, but Negro American art, music, religion, sociology, the freedom movement, education and politics—giving a more unified, integrated vision of the Negro in America and the America which he sees. It would be aimed, in part, at an activist problem-solving end." Harding confided to Zinn that resistance to these ideas was considerable among the older faculty: "fossils who had been slumbering in the somnolent ooze of Negro higher education were roused to roar, and Spelman hasn't had a faculty meeting like that one since you were here, I'm sure."[155]

In this same letter to Zinn, Harding recounted the attempt of the Spelman administration to bar SNNC's controversial black power advocate, Stokely Carmichael, from speaking on campus. Harding would publish an article, "When Stokely Met the Presidents: Black Power and Negro Education," on the clashes between Carmichael and the presidents of what Harding labeled "two of Atlanta's most self-consciously elitist Negro colleges."[156] In that article Harding documented the dubious rationale behind the attempt to bar Carmichael: "The president of the school vetoed the invitation" the students had made to the SNCC leader to speak on campus, "saying that the meeting had not been planned well enough to prevent the students from being 'brainwashed' by the articulate and persuasive black speaker."[157] Though not allowed to speak in a lecture hall, Carmichael did, at the students' insistence, get to speak, but from the top of a Volkswagen bus in a campus parking lot. Carmichael's speech not only questioned the educational mission but the rich, white funders of the college. According to Harding, Carmichael, standing before students whose education had depended for so long on such patrons of the black [colleges,] he almost spat out the [Rockefeller] family name most revered by some of the Atlanta administrators. Then Carmichael said, "Your presidents call these people philanthropists. I'll tell you what they really are: They're the thieves. If you don't believe me look at how they make their money. Look at how they're getting it now. Look at their South African investments, especially through the Chase National Bank." The stir of excitement which passed through the crowd as they heard these words was almost visible.[158]

Obviously Manley would not have been pleased with Harding's article given its critical view of black college leaders and their white financial angels (Rockefeller funding had been so central to Spelman College that the college itself had been named for Laura Spelman Rockefeller and her parents). It is possible that Harding's political sensitivity in not indicating in his article the names of the two black colleges involved in the disputes with Carmichael helped prevent an explosion with President Manley. But it is nonetheless striking that, despite the article and Harding's other activism and moves to change Spelman, he was never fired and that he and Spelman's president, in Harding's words, "always had basically an amicable relationship."[159]

The contrast between Harding's and Zinn's relationship with Manley would suggest that race, as Harding indicated, made a crucial difference and contributed to Zinn's firing. However, Zinn does have a point in pushing against a monocausal racial explanation of his dismissal from Spelman. The case of Gloria Wade Bishop offers an instructive comparison in this regard. Bishop in 1964 was a young African American instructor in English and education at Spelman who was active in the sit-in movement. She had been arrested picketing Leb's, the same segregated delicatessen in Atlanta that Zinn, as he noted in his diary, sought to desegregate in 1963. Bishop's activism led to conflicts with the Spelman administration. A Kenyan student had grown close to Bishop—a friendship that college officials sought to disrupt. According to Bishop, this "student was *told* by the dorm mother that I was bad company and should be avoided. The accusation is that I have taken a foreign student to demonstrations . . . [and that this student] wants to leave [the college] only because I have planted negative feelings toward Spelman in her little foreign mind." The Kenyan student was called into a meeting with college officials, including President Manley, whose purpose "was to convince her to break off her relationship with Bishop." She told Bishop that during that meeting, whenever Bishop's "name was mentioned, Dr. Manley shook his head and frowned."[160]

Bishop's fate was similar to Zinn's. Where Zinn was fired without warning after classes had ended in 1963, Bishop too was dismissed without warning in

1964. As she explained in a letter to Zinn, "Yep, Manley fired me in a really devious manner." Manley claimed that Bishop had indicated that she wanted to stay on only if she could keep teaching in the English and education departments, and that since there was no opening in English "he couldn't hire me next year." He also claimed that Spelman needed a more experienced instructor in education. Bishop placed her own firing into the context of the larger crisis at Spelman in the year since Zinn's dismissal, and concluded that "I consider myself among the chosen, for everybody of any importance is leaving this year. Nine instructors are leaving, four of them PhDs and all white with the exception of little black me. . . . In the English department only three Negro Spelman graduates are left. Poor Albert [Manley]. He has a job on his hands. I wonder does he realize just what is happening at Spelman."[161]

Perhaps it was gender, or Bishop's youth, but it is clear that race alone was not enough to deter Manley from wielding the ax. The Bishop comparison suggests that it may have been Harding's status as an established religious leader (he had headed the Mennonite House), his ties to Martin Luther King Jr., and the Caribbean background he shared with Manley as a black man that helped to shield him from the fate that Bishop and Zinn met on account of their dissidence.

Evening Theater Party Verboten: Spelman Memories of Marie Thomas

Since Zinn and the students he was closest to were so involved in the Atlanta civil rights movement and SNCC, and since Zinn himself cared so deeply about war, peace, civil liberties, and class inequality, much of our discussion here has focused on politics—dissent, freedom, and power both on campus and off. But as the diary makes evident, Zinn was also deeply concerned about the state of student social and cultural life at Spelman and how it was warped by regimentation. He, along with the student movement, wanted this changed so students would be treated with respect and in an adult manner rather than like children by campus officials. Spelman alumna Marie Thomas's oral history reminds us that these sociocultural issues mattered and impacted far more than a small core of student activists at Spelman.

Though Thomas had participated in civil rights protests downtown, her main focus at Spelman was her work in theater. An aspiring actress, she was a theater major who had acted in numerous drama productions at college. After graduation Thomas would act on the Broadway stage and go on to roles in television and movie productions as well. Her conflicts with the Spelman administration would come not from political actions but from the way Spelman's stern social restrictions clashed with her theater work, turning a happy event—her lead role in the Tennessee Williams play, *Summer and Smoke*—into a tense battle with Spelman officialdom.[162]

Raised in Atlanta, the daughter and niece of Spelman graduates, Thomas was familiar with and eager to avoid subjecting herself to the college's strict restrictions on student social life. She chose to live at home and commute to Spelman her first three years, delaying the one year of required campus residency until her senior year. So she was a senior when she was first affected by and chafed under those restrictions. Having rehearsed for three hours every night for the Williams play, she and the other actresses wanted to hold their cast party, as was customary, after the play on Saturday night. But, as Thomas recalls,

> Dr. Manley decided—for some reason, he had it in for the theater department—that our cast parties were, I guess, too flamboyant. He moved the cast party to Sunday afternoon. Well anybody that's in show business knows that after you've finished something that's exciting like that you like to have a celebration, no matter how brief. And I just thought that [decision to forbid an evening cast party] was so punitive and so unnecessary. The young ladies, the four other [Spelman] girls [that had been in the play,] went back to the dormitory. . . . I didn't sign in and I didn't lie. I just left with friends and I went to a friend's home [to celebrate]. And the girls showed up because they knew where I was going. And . . . they snuck out and they had already signed in. I don't know if they signed me in or what the circumstances were but that alerted the house mother everybody was not there anymore. . . . [When Thomas's mother found out about this] she felt the best thing to do was to get us back to campus as quickly as possible before there was a major situation about it. [But it was too late,] and the next thing you know we are called up on charges.[163]

The disciplinary proceedings were so rushed and with no semblance of due process that, as his diary reflects, they outraged Zinn, as did the punishment, which was initially ruled to be suspension for a semester.[164] Since later the period of suspension was reduced, for Thomas the worst part of the punishment was losing her scholarship. She really needed the scholarship since her father, a postman, and mother, a teacher, were not affluent. The loss of the scholarship was a real hardship. Thomas found the restrictions "inane" and the punishment deeply offensive, especially because her "four years at Spelman were spent with people picketing, people going to jail [in civil rights sit-ins], my junior year some of the girls went to jail for two or three weeks. And this [curfew violation] was so minor and so ridiculous. I still consider it that." She found it remarkable that with "all this civil rights stuff going on and here they are treating us like we were a bunch of twelve-year-olds."[165]

Even more emotional was Thomas's encounter with the dean after the hearing. One of the other suspended students needed a place to stay before going back home for the semester to St. Louis. So Thomas asked the dean if this student could stay with her until her flight left, and she said yes. But, in Thomas's words,

> The next thing I knew the dean reneged on it. I didn't know what was going on. It all seemed so deceitful in many ways to me. And being the emotional actress person I was, I stormed into the dean's office. I think I scared her because she moved behind the desk. I said, "I don't know what you're trying to do here. What is this all [about]? It doesn't make any sense." And I think I alluded to the fact people had been picketing, that this was stupid. Long story short, they changed the sentence to two weeks.[166]

From that point on Thomas decided to be "Miss Goody Two-shoes" to avoid violating any campus rules and just focus on graduating and getting out of Spelman since this was her senior year.[167] She even opted to attend a theater rehearsal rather than risk participating in the semester's major campus protest meeting, "On Liberty at Spelman," documenting Spelman's oppressive social regulations. But Thomas did send a letter that Zinn read at the meeting, which received "tremendous applause" from her fellow students. The letter contrasted her three years of freedom living off campus with the unfree final semesters she endured living on campus; and it eloquently discussed why the paternalistic regime on campus was deemed so oppressive by students—that the issue was not merely the petty regulations and punishments themselves, but the way this overly regulated environment corrupted values and disrupted personal growth, maturity, individual thought, and freedom. In her letter, Thomas explained her experience living off campus:

> For three years I enjoyed what one might call a "normal" kind of college life. . . . Not only was I learning in the classroom but I was learning in other aspects of life also. I had no chains, no stifling bonds drawing me in each time I sought to have an interesting conversation over a cup of coffee with an individual, a fellow or a girl, about a new book, current event, an interesting piece of literature, a bit of philosophy. . . . I felt no piercing, waiting, hoping, suspecting eye preparing for my "one false move." . . . I felt free. . . . hopeful about my future life, anxious to express myself, desirous to be Marie, to think, to feel, and to know the world I lived in. Now my hopes are all blurred. . . . I no longer know if thinking for myself, being an individual is the thing to do. I am told where to go, when to return, how to get there, and what to do when there. . . . I am no longer Marie, but a Spelman girl.
>
> When I was going through my period of repentance for my "crime" [of violating curfew] . . . if I ever learned anything worthwhile . . . it is that people with power fear themselves, and . . . try with persuasive and petty powers to make their followers fear themselves also. The old but true saying of "smile . . .

but watch out from behind" is prevalent at this school. Its entire atmosphere thrusts one's mind into a state of fright, frustration. One can no longer do anything except ask . . . "Whom do you trust?" The answer: no one. One learns to lie, cheat, sneak. . . . If she's lucky, she's an uncaught criminal.

I say let us become aware of ourselves. Check back our traditional, antiquated, medieval, and aged standards, rules, and regulations. What do they mean to a modern girl growing normally and learning in our modern world today? Times have indeed changed. God give us the strength, knowledge, and understanding to change with them.[168]

But Spelman would not change as Thomas hoped in her years there. The old campus restrictions remained, and their leading faculty critic, Zinn, would lose his job for his role in championing the grievances aired in Thomas's letter. As for Thomas, she headed for New York and her acting career and tried not to think of that "whole missionary slave thing" that, in her view, yielded such authoritarian traditions at Spelman. And reflecting back, she notes that "it took me a long time to even think in terms of Spelman again, maybe a good ten years before . . . [I could] look on it with a different heart." But she still thinks the paternalistic campus ethos was "absurd. . . . We didn't need [the dean and president as] parents. We had parents."[169]

For Thomas the final irony involved Manley. A decade after graduating from Spelman (and after all that turmoil with the administration), she was acting in a play on Broadway. Thomas was stunned to see President Manley "sitting in the first row and smiling up at me like we'd been old friends. . . . He also included me in his memoir [in the section listing the achievements of distinguished Spelman alumnae]." She and most of her classmates "didn't care for him very much because he seemed very stern and not approachable," so it struck her as ironic that in the wake of all the conflict and distance he would see her as one of his students and take pride in her achievements—perhaps seeing her as one of the beneficiaries of his tough love.[170]

In Prose and Poetry: Alice Walker on Zinn and Spelman

The most famous writing on Spelman in the 1960s came not from Zinn, or any published history or memoir, but from the imagination of Zinn's most famous student from his Spelman years, Alice Walker, the Pulitzer Prize–winning novelist and poet. Walker would publish a classic civil rights novel, *Meridian* (1976), and include in it a less than flattering section on a fictionalized version of Spelman, which she dubbed "Saxon College." Walker also appears several times in Zinn's diary, once when he noted her remarkable talent as a writer; again as he noted her reflections on a class debate; and yet again when he wrote happily that she had composed a poem to him, and that he in turn had written a poem for her, which read in part:

Alice, Alice
in the palace of your mind
pure thoughts do reign . . .
clear and fiery
like champagne.[171]

Zinn thought so highly of Walker's ability as a writer that he used her words in the conclusion of his narrative on his firing and the crisis at Spelman, as part of his appeal to the trustees to reverse his termination and end oppressive social regulations and free speech violations on campus. Noting the lack of democratic governance and student rights at Spelman, Zinn asked, "Are we teaching our students that democracy is something to be talked about, but not practiced? That freedom is good as an abstraction, but not as a concrete reality? . . . Will the trustees of the college affirm to our students that democracy can work?"[172] Zinn then quoted the conclusion of "Spelman junior Alice Walker's paper 'On Djilas and Kolakowski,'" that she had written the previous semester for his class on the Soviet Union, in which she concluded: "Every country should have a Kolakowski, someone who questions the unanswerable, but who nevertheless prods the people into thinking before they act. 'Will it be possible to formulate a general principle of regulating the mutual relationship between our knowledge of historical necessities and our moral conviction? Between the world of being and the world of values?' These are the questions which were voiced by Polish skepticism after the Stalinist era. Do not they apply to all countries and all societies for all time?"[173] And Zinn added, "A student who thinks and writes like this deserves nothing but the best,"[174] meaning that she deserved a college free and democratic enough to be worthy of the name. Ultimately, Walker would leave Spelman before graduating, feeling that with Zinn's firing Spelman was no longer a place for her. With assistance from Staughton Lynd and his mother who taught there, Walker transferred and completed her college education at Sarah Lawrence.[175]

Before leaving Spelman, Walker, writing, as she later put it, "through tears of anger and frustration," published in the Spelman student newspaper an open letter to her classmates protesting Zinn's firing. She suggested that his firing testified "to what was said at many a stormy session last spring on 'liberty at Spelman,' that freedom of expression and to dissent does not, indeed exist at Spelman. . . . The action against him was not only premeditated but also a direct result of his militant effort to aid the student body in obtaining the same personal rights for which men have died."[176] Walker praised his role in diversifying the curriculum through his leadership and courses in the non-Western studies program, his advising students in the sit-ins, and his work to desegregate the Atlanta public libraries and statehouse. She termed his writings the best on the "Negro movement in general and the Negro student movement in particular." Walker expressed admiration for Zinn as a teacher, whose "classes all really serious and inquiring students aspired to attend." While critical of the unfair and "abrupt" way Zinn was terminated—in the summer when the students were not present to protest—and "without warning," Walker suggested that the biggest loser in this firing was not Zinn but Spelman, which had lost its way politically, morally, and intellectually:

> I am not sorry for Dr. Zinn in the usual sense of the word, the world takes care of its own and history favors great men—the more injustices overcome and profited from, the greater the personality. I am sorry though for us, as a group of presumably mature and civilized individuals, if we can settle down to "business as usual" with only a second thought to what we have lost and to what we have become in the process of forgetting our loss too quickly. How many of us I wonder are still familiar with the poem which begins—"I have to live with myself, and so, I want to be fit for myself to know."
>
> Let us never exchange complacency for personal values and beliefs and comfort for conscience. Self-gain comes to nothing if in the process of gaining the world one loses his soul. Let us not desert the battle because a leader has moved to another part of the field; it was for us, the student body, Spelman College itself, that Dr. Zinn fought.[177]

She urged that Spelman pay its overdue debt to Zinn by standing "together in some positive action to have him reinstated." Walker concluded by stressing that her letter was "written not in anger, but from regret," and that her words were directed toward her fellow students "to rumple the complacency of my Spelman sisters so that if they do not share my regret they can at least properly appreciate our loss."[178]

Despite her youth, Walker as an undergraduate was, as her letter protesting Zinn's firing indicates, already an extraordinarily skilled writer. And Zinn was not the only Spelman faculty member to recognize this. Staughton Lynd, another of her history professors, wrote Zinn that Walker's letter to the *Spotlight* was "long and typically beautiful."[179] Walker had used her writing skills to craft a letter that was forceful and eloquent in protesting Zinn's firing, yet also restrained compared to her personal feelings of outrage over the loss of Zinn. She was aiming in the letter to convince as many Spelman students as possible that this was a terrible loss for their college, so she avoided sounding irate or hotheaded. Indeed, as we have seen, Walker said in the letter that it had been written "not in anger, but from regret" that Spelman was losing such an inspiring teacher, mentor, movement historian, and activist. Privately, however, in sending a draft of her *Spotlight* letter to Zinn, Walker confided that "in some ways" that letter "is not what I'd really like to express at all—what I'd really like to do is show such anger & wrath that Sisters Chapel would dissolve into a shuddering heap of rusty old bricks & pious old ladies!"[180]

In reflecting back on Spelman in the early 1960s one might expect that Walker would simply be negative. After all, she'd left the college because of its lack of freedom a half-year after the Zinn firing that had so angered her, and later wrote very critically of the bourgeois self-absorption of the Spelman-like fictional Saxon College in *Meridian*. Walker's Spelman experience, as she later explained, enabled her in *Meridian* to "explore the misuse of gender-based power from the perspective of having experienced it."[181] But Walker urges that we keep in mind the role that Spelman played in serving the black community; that at least in the arts it excelled; and that one ought not overlook the attractions of Spelman, especially for its students from blue-collar and poor backgrounds, including her. "Don't underestimate how beautiful it was in spite of all the problems," said Walker in our interview on her Spelman experience.

> You could write it, you could go to the position that "Oh it was a kind of prison." And in a way it was. But at the same time when you think about where many of the students came from it was like being in a garden. A garden that did have a fence around it, but by golly it was a garden and you were used to a cornfield. So don't underestimate what medicine any of us received from at last being in a space with towering trees and open space, and beauty all around us, and the culture that was there and came through there.
>
> We were so well versed in . . . poetry, literature, and music. It had its values and they are not to be ignored. It's just that we also wanted to be free. We wanted to be seen as people with personal agency and insight.[182]

Walker also points out that unpleasant as the conflicts with the Spelman administration were, they could not negate what was so inspiring about the Atlanta student movement of the time—its sense of purpose, community, and solidarity as well as its intelligence about strategy in the struggle against Jim Crow. In this respect Walker and Zinn echoed one another, for, as we have seen, he viewed his Spelman years and his work with the Atlanta movement and SNCC as among the best in his life despite his firing. In fact, when asked whether she felt nostalgic for that time in Atlanta, despite eventually feeling the need to leave Spelman, Walker replied:

> Well how could you not? I mean, I remember the first time I sang "We Shall Overcome." I did it at the AU Center under cherry trees arm-in-arm with Julian Bond. And he was really cute [laughs]. It was like that. It was like wow! A recent thing that happened made me think of us. This young [African Ameri-

can] woman who climbed the [flag] pole [to take down the Confederate flag by the South Carolina state capitol in Charleston]. She reminded me of us. That kind of centering with your circles and choosing how you were going to proceed. That was very, very much how we were—[deliberating carefully on] who was going to sit-in where, how you're going to dress because that was really important. And whether you're going to be arrested, how many books you're going to take with you. It was a moment of awakening to our activism. So precious, so priceless. And it just so happened that we were coming out of this school that had some restrictive policies that cramped our spirits.[183]

Perhaps most surprising of all is Walker's take on Manley. One might expect that since his firing of Zinn figured so prominently in her decision to leave Spelman she would be bitterly critical of Spelman's president. But this is not the case. While, of course, Walker strongly opposed the firing, she retained a certain sympathy for Manley, and in that respect her view of the Spelman administration was closer to that of Stevens Walker than to West, Wright Edelman, Zoharah Simmons, or Thomas. Walker traces her views on Manley to her own social background. She came to Spelman from Eatonton, "a little place" she "was born in right in the middle of the state" of Georgia, from a poor sharecropping family, and arrived at college only seventeen years old. "I was very impressed with Manley because I had never seen a college president. And I'd certainly never seen a black one."[184] She had a respect for his effort to promote black education.

It's not that Walker was uncritical of Manley. But she attributed his failures to his limited power as compared to the rich and powerful whites he needed to report back to on the college's board of trustees. She not only saw him as an intermediary for whites but linked this to "class colorism" within the African American community. Manley, she points out "was very light-skinned and that factored into nearly everything." Though Manley was born in Honduras, Manley's parents were Jamaicans and he resembled

> those pink Jamaicans Zora Hurston described in some of her early work . . . they were the offspring of masters and enslaved women who then became known as . . . interim managers and rulers of the island. . . . I was used to seeing this class colorism when the person [of color] with lighter skin is placed in the position between the black people and white people . . . and get to be the kind of overseer of whatever plantation they're on, including the college campus. So there I was at seventeen seeing this and seeing his very light-skinned wife, because that is also part of the package.[185]

So if Manley could seem two-faced—at times supporting and at times repressing student civil rights activism—Walker saw this not as some character flaw, but as a reflection of his lack of power and need to placate white trustees and donors: "In his position, he has to be two-faced." And here she paraphrased the poet Paul Laurence Dunbar's "We Wear the Mask," on "'the face that laughs and the face that cries,' and which one you show when and where. And it's a very delicate dance, and there's a built-in insecurity among that class."[186]

Her view of Manley as a fair-skinned middle manager doing the best he could while subject to white power left her in the awkward position of being both angry over the dismissal of Zinn yet empathetic to the administrator who had let that happen. As Walker explains,

> I politically had to stand on the side of what was right. That it was wrong to fire Howie and in the way Manley did. At the same time there was a connection between me and Manley, even though I was only seventeen and eighteen. You know I left Spelman when I was I guess eighteen or nineteen. And it [this connection to Manley] was so real that when I left—and I don't think I ever said this to Howie even. But the day I left I went to his [Manley's] house and knocked on the door, and I kissed him on the cheek. And it wasn't so much about sweetness either. It was about even at that age understanding the position that such a person is placed in by birth, by race, by political chicanery, and violence. . . . And so I never bought the idea that at Spelman he was just a mess politically. I think he was probably really astute politically.[187]

Walker was convinced that for all their limitations and paternalism Manley and his administration did care about the students. They often expressed it in ways that were objectionable since they policed student life excessively, at times even ridiculously, as when she was rebuked for reading French poetry in the middle of the night. But "we never felt unloved," according to Walker. "In their own way they cared. They were daily proving that. It's just in the area of protest they were *afraid*. And we understood they were afraid [because] our parents were afraid."[188] And the administration's determination to monitor and restrict student travel off campus and to keep the young women of Spelman as much as possible behind the campus's high wall, which Zinn at one point compared to a "chastity belt,"[189] did have a logic to it given the way race and sex worked in the South. As Walker put it: "If you lived in the South you would understand the reasoning. There was so much rape" of African American women by white men. That's "the reason there are so many different colors of black people . . . [it's] because of the white rapists. Although they [whites] never look at that. They'd rather pretend that black people were raping them. It's insane."[190]

Regarding Manley, Walker knew from direct personal experience of his concern for her welfare. Walker had been offered Spelman's most prestigious fellowship, a Merrill Scholarship, to study in Europe. But because she wanted to "keep working in the South"—apparently in the black freedom movement and on her poetry—she turned the Merrill down, and was the first student ever to do so. Manley noticed, and in Walker's words, "probably thought I was throwing away a great opportunity. . . . I think he totally understood my rebellion. He may not have liked it because he was in power to keep us at a certain level."[191] Manley intervened. He "somehow maneuvered to get [philanthropist] Charles Merrill to walk across the campus together" with Walker to see if Merrill could convince her to take the travel scholarship rather than remaining in the South to focus on her poetry. The plan backfired because Merrill, in an uncharacteristic bout of snobbishness, managed to insult Walker. It was raining as the aspiring poet and the wealthy philanthropist walked across the Spelman campus, and evoking the scene vividly, Walker recalled:

> I was so conscious of the fact that I had this little pair of shoes that didn't keep the rain out (my feet were soaked), and that he, Merrill, had these excellent shoes, excellent raincoat . . . excellent hat . . . excellent umbrella. He was rich and he had all this stuff. And I had none of it. I had this parka that someone had given my mother and was wearing that to keep warm and dry, which couldn't really work. . . . So there we were walking along and he was basically trying to tell me that I was being foolish. . . . But anyway he actually said, "I don't think a sharecropper's daughter growing up in a shack with no books"—or a few books, I don't remember which it was—"would make much of a poet."[192]

Disastrous as it was, the fact that Manley had sought to help her by getting Merrill to meet with her showed Walker that he did care.

Walker was aware, however, that it was possible for a black college president to stand up to white authority and back the black freedom movement more vigorously than Manley did. As with Wright Edelman, Walker saw another AU-affiliated college president, Benjamin Mays of Morehouse College, as the epitome of a strong black college president. Mays was not only an outspoken civil rights activist and mentor to Martin Luther King Jr. but also a tall, dignified, dark-skinned African American leader who looked very much like the commanding leader that he was. Of her first encounter with Mays, Walker recalled, "The first time I saw Benjamin Mays I was still believing in God . . . as a person in a way. And that's who I thought God would look like. . . . God, he was so incredibly impressive. And Manley had none of that. He [Manley] was what he was created to be in a way, that buffer, that overseer. . . . Mays you felt really represented some rootedness that was really unshakeable."[193]

As for the social atmosphere fostered by the old conservative Spelman traditions that Manley was too timid to change, Walker obviously found it oppressive since she left before graduating. But she also acknowledges that it had an upside: "The thing about Spelman women and Morehouse men was that they were incredibly dignified. . . . There was an expression 'A Morehouse man, a

Spelman woman, you can tell by looking at them.' It had to do with how they carried themselves, what they thought and spoke about, and all that." But being groomed by Spelman's regimented social codes was for her ultimately too stultifying and "frustrating . . . the need to be so careful with everything you say, everything you think, and everything you do, everything you wear. . . . It makes for a stilted quality. It's really anti-life in a way."[194]

For Walker staying too long in an excessively overregulated environment such as Spelman's was too much a "limitation on . . . [the] imagination. It is deadly. . . . That's how it felt to me. Like I could think as far as the window, but I didn't dare think about opening the window and going out there [or] thinking more on the other side of the window." A prime example of this was when she got in trouble at her dormitory for reading French poetry in the middle of the night. "I don't know why they taught you French if they didn't want you to read French poetry in the middle of the night. I mean *really* [laughs] what sense does that make?"[195]

The basic problem with the whole fossilized social system maintained by the Spelman regime was, in Walker's view (and in Zinn's), that it derived from a repressive and even anti-intellectual social world from a dead white past. As Walker put it, at Spelman the conservative administration was

> copying the finishing schools of the white upper class. And those people suffered too. Learning how to pour tea properly, and the whiteness of the glove, the guilt, the general reticence. You see this sometimes in the old movies and the recently made things like *The Forsyte Saga*. These things from the Edwardian period in England, where you had a specific way of being depending on your sex. And you just weren't permitted to think [if you were female] or to act (you could maybe think if you could fake how you looked while you were thinking). But you could not act beyond a certain [very narrow] range of behavior.[196]

It was, of course, Zinn's firing that made what had been oppressive at Spelman just intolerable to Walker, which is why she wrote Zinn, "there is really nothing here for me. It's almost like being buried alive."[197] She recalls that soon after writing her open letter protesting Zinn's firing she was packing her bags to transfer to Sarah Lawrence College even though she had—prior to Staughton Lynd's helping her transfer there—"never heard of Sarah Lawrence." She "just knew that I had very little attachment to a place that could be so shortsighted in terms of the liberation of our people and the real education of our students."[198]

With regard to Walker's own writing, as mentioned earlier, her classic civil rights novel *Meridian* had some of its roots in her Spelman experience. Walker agrees that "Spelman is definitely there" in *Meridian* since it was at Spelman that she "got to understand a lot of that culture" of historically black women's colleges. And the book is dedicated to Staughton Lynd. But she warns us that it is a work of fiction so we ought not confuse the events in the novel with those that actually occurred, since Saxon College came from her imagination. Walker does, however, see a connection thematically between the Saxon College segment of *Meridian* and what happened at Spelman with the purging of Howard Zinn. In *Meridian*,

> One of my points was to focus on how people destroy what nurtures them. The symbol of that [at Saxon College] is the Sojourner tree, which had been the protector. It amuses me because people do go to Spelman and they try to find the stump. But it's totally from the imagination. Every culture, no matter what the culture is, has a tendency to destroy the very thing that is most precious because they reach the point of such rage against whatever calamity they are facing and they have nowhere to vent this rage. And it's so crazy. That's part of what I was showing: how a university or school that is so, should be so, honored as a place that nurtures can be just destroyed because you feel like you have no choice but to cut at your own foundation. And firing Howie was to cut at your own foundation because what was being built there with his great alliance with us was something really nurturing, sheltering, blossoming and beautiful.[199]

Walker would remain a close friend of Zinn's for the rest of his life. The two corresponded frequently over the years. He spoke at the opening of her papers at Emory University, and she sent him and Roslyn her new poems over the years. She would publish a poem on Zinn, "My Teacher," which paid tribute to his populist historical scholarship, compassionate activism, and inspiring teaching and mentorship:

> When the students
> where we were rose
> against
> the local bosses, the reactionary cowards
> of that age
> my teacher rose with us
> When the country
> rose
> against racism
> and war
> there at the front
> of everyone was my

slim teacher. . . .
My teacher has written books
that empower
the spirit . . .
the first true history
of the United States. It is
called a People's History, because
we are all there!
My teacher
has taught
laughter
and subversion
and how to stay
reasonably sane
in a world
gone insane.[200]

At his death in 2010 Walker moved from poetry to prose, publishing a column remembering Zinn being "magical as a teacher." In the classroom he "was witty, irreverent, and wise," loved "what he was teaching and clearly wanted his students to love it also." His visibility as a civil rights activist—"Howie . . . was constantly in our midst, and usually somewhere in front"—in the protests to desegregate Atlanta helped embolden her in her own activism. "Because I was at Spelman on a scholarship, a scholarship that would be revoked if I were jailed, my participation caused me a good deal of anxiety. Still, knowing that Howard and others of our professors . . . supported the students in our struggle, made it possible to carry on." Walker saw Zinn as playing "a role in one of the many births of my feminism. A feminism/womanism that never seemed odd to Howard Zinn, who encouraged his Spelman students, all of them women, to name and challenge oppression of every sort."[201] And for Walker, not only Zinn's friendship but also his influence lasted a lifetime:

I was Howard Zinn's student for only a semester but in fact I have learned from him all my life. His way with resistance: steady, persistent, impersonal, often with humor is a teaching I cherish. Whenever I've been arrested, I've thought of him. I see policemen as victims of the very system they're hired to defend, as I know he did. I see soldiers in the same way. In some ways Howie was an extension of my father . . . [who] was also an activist . . . and was one of the first black men . . . to vote in our backwoods county; he had to pass three white men holding shot guns in order to do this . . . . [Both] saw injustice as something to be acknowledged, confronted, and changed. And . . . looked for signs of humanity in . . . opponents.[202]

Unlike Zinn, Manley never was close to Walker, but Manley nonetheless sought to maintain contact with her after her Spelman years, much as he had with Marie Thomas. In fact, when I told Walker of how Manley showed up for Thomas's Broadway debut, Walker responded: "That was me. He used to show up everywhere. I couldn't be up on the East Coast near Washington without seeing this elderly gentleman in the audience, beaming, clapping. It was *so* interesting."[203] And as with Thomas, Manley would include Walker in the section of his memoir on distinguished Spelman alumnae. But here too he never alluded to the political turmoil at Spelman caused by his paternalistic regime. Nor did he mention that his firing of Zinn helped precipitate Walker's departure from Spelman. It seems that for all its harshness, his paternalism did reflect his genuine and enduring affection for and pride in Spelman students, even the dissidents.

Herschelle Sullivan (Challenor), 1963: On Zinn and Spelman's Past and Future

Oral history and memoir can offer a larger perspective, informed as they are by hindsight. As time passed, Spelman alumnae, in middle age and beyond, could reflect back on Spelman and Manley long after their anger faded. It may be, for example, that the generous reading of Manley's intentions and limitations offered by alumnae who came to admire and even love Manley, such as Betty Stevens Walker, and the empathy that Alice Walker expressed for Manley are balanced and insightful ways to view the Spelman administration. But one could as easily argue that this long view distorts as well as illuminates. In seeking to be understanding of Manley, we may risk losing touch with why students were so angry in the first place—why Alice Walker, for example, chose to leave Spelman and turned down a prestigious scholarship in search of a freer campus. This is why documents from 1963, such as Zinn's diary, are so useful in reminding us of what it was like for students to endure paternalistic restrictions and how and why such limitations on their freedom generated anger and protest. With this in mind, it seems fitting to turn away for the moment from oral history and memoir to a dissident Spelman voice from 1963, a time when that revolt and Zinn's firing were immediate concerns rather than a distant memory. Zinn's former student, Spelman class of 1961, Merrill scholar, and leader in the Atlanta sit-in movement Herschelle Sullivan (Challenor), as a Columbia doctoral student, wrote to Manley in October 1963 protesting his firing of Zinn, leaving us with one of the most memorable and authentic voices of Spelman's dissident student culture from Zinn's Spelman years.[204]

Sullivan had been, as we have seen, involved in one of the earlier conflicts with Manley, which took place over an editorial she published in Spelman's student newspaper in 1958 mocking his authoritarian administrative style—a dispute in which Zinn, West, and several other faculty had sided with her right to dissent. She opened her October 1963 letter to Manley by recounting the infantilizing restrictions on her freedom that she had experienced first as a new undergraduate and then as an advanced student at Spelman. As a freshman, she explained,

> I recall wanting to attend a Town Meeting at Atlanta University [which is a short walk from Spelman]. I was told that this would be impossible if I could not find an upperclassman to go with me. Later that year I remember receiving a letter from the Dean of Women reprimanding me because I had ventured over to Morehouse Chapel to hear a Cantata. In my sophomore year I am reminded of the threatened expulsion by you because of an editorial written in the college newspaper. You called me into your office in the spring of my junior year to inform me that I had been "tentatively" selected by the faculty committee to study abroad, but that there were some reservations because of the "bad marks" on my record. You asked me at that time if I would "embarrass Spelman overseas."
>
> Now Spelman had thoroughly embarrassed me [by firing Zinn].[205]

For Sullivan, however, this was not about some personal conflict with Manley, but a larger concern that the firing of Zinn ran counter to what should have been "Spelman's *raison d'être* . . . to prepare educated women to cope with the pressures and problems of the twentieth century." Though implicitly rather than explicitly feminist, this sexually egalitarian mission required of Spelman intellectual and academic excellence as well as political engagement—an aspiration toward cosmopolitanism and leadership in the struggle for a more just society. And this was a mission that, in Sullivan's words, had been well served by

> Dr. Zinn's accomplishments in his seven years at Spelman. We are both familiar with his initiation of the exchange program [across the academic color line to and from predominantly white campuses], his concern for student political awareness that prompted him to personally take students to weekly world affairs discussions sponsored by the American Foundation for Political Education, his work with the Town Meeting, the realization of his non-Western studies program financed by the Ford Foundation. . . . His initiation and finally realization of the desegregation of the public libraries and the state legislature. A stimulating professor who expected more of his students than the mastery of a text, he found time to write many articles, complete one book and start two others.[206]

Like Zinn himself, Sullivan saw Spelman's administration as paternalistic and provincial, falling behind the times and in need of serious reflection on "what its role for the future would be" and how it, like other "Private Negro institutions," would adapt to the "critical period in the socially and politically evolving decade of the sixties." Her fear was that the lack of freedom on campus was leaving Spelman mired in mediocrity, causing many students "to leave after their freshman year." "Something is wrong when the faculty turnover is as high as Spelman's and the Dean of Women changes five times in seven years." As faculty such as Zinn from leading universities were driven away, the result Sullivan saw was a "high rate of inbreeding of [instructors who were] Spelman graduates without advanced degrees or with those having advanced degrees from Atlanta University. Diversity, not homogeneity, is needed at institutions of higher learning."[207]

The heart of the matter for Sullivan in the firing of Zinn was whether Spelman and other historically black colleges could jettison the old parochialism and be free enough to "stop preparing Negroes for a segregated society." She saw Manley's paternalistic regime as a relic of the Jim Crow era, reflecting its undemocratic ethos: "the unquestioned authority of the Negro College president over faculty as well as students reflects the absolute authority pattern of white officials over the Negro community." But a new day was dawning, and Spelman students could only be prepared for it with the freedom required to become educated participants who would not only be a part of this new world but also help to shape it. "Realities of the contemporary world require that Negro students be given the opportunities on their respective campuses to articulate their concern, assume greater responsibilities, be treated as adults, socially and intellectually. Otherwise we will not have the cadres to effectuate the changes that we as Negroes are demanding in American society."[208]

Zinn's firing was for Sullivan out of sync with the freer and more cosmopolitan ethos of Spelman women who had undergone their political baptism in the sit-in movement against Jim Crow. And it was, she thought, futile for Manley to try to turn the clock back because students who had played adult roles in the black freedom movement were not going to stand for being treated like children when they returned to campus. "Can we," asked Sullivan "demand that Negro college youth stand up for their civil rights, protest against unjust city ordinances and state laws, make decisions about going to jail that may jeopardize their parents' jobs, successfully negotiate with city officials, study and travel in Europe without surveillance, and yet not permit them to make constructive criticisms in their college newspapers, distrust them in their social relationships, thwart decision-making in student government councils?"[209]

Despite the irate tone of the letter, Sullivan avoided bitterness, telling Manley that she had written him "personally to air my feelings about this to you. I have always felt that I could discuss things with you." She expressed the hope that her words would "serve as a stimulus . . . to alter what appears to many of us to be an undesirable climate on Spelman's campus."[210] Sullivan was not demonizing Manley, but rather calling upon him to reinstate Zinn, restore academic freedom, and recognize that Zinn, like the student movement he was fired for supporting, represented the kind of intellectual and political qualities Spelman ought to be aspiring toward.

Insubordination or Intolerance? The First Explanations of Zinn's Firing

The last part of Zinn's 1960s Spelman story began just as his southern diary was ending in the summer of 1963 when he started working with the American Association of University Professors (AAUP) to appeal his firing. The AAUP agreed to consider taking Zinn's case because of the academic freedom and due process issues it raised. Zinn, after all, was a longstanding critic of Manley's authoritarian administrative style, and he was also a full professor and department chair, who in those roles and during his seventh year at Spelman assumed he had tenure. He had been dismissed abruptly, without notice, after playing a prominent role in supporting the administration's increasingly vocal student critics. President Manley's initial response to the AAUP's inquiries was largely procedural, centering around the question of whether Zinn did in fact have tenure. Manley claimed that Zinn had not been in the tenure-track ranks long enough to have permanent tenure, arguing that since he was promoted to full professor early he fell short of Spelman's seven-year tenure requirement. And Manley held that the year of leave taken for a Harvard fellowship in 1960–61 should not count toward Spelman's tenure track, even though Spelman had given permission for that leave and paid Zinn half his salary that year. Manley maintained that as such Zinn was not entitled to tenure, an explanation of his firing, or due process since he had simply been a contingent faculty member whose contract the college chose not to renew. So Manley's initial correspondence with the AAUP and his letter of termination to Zinn offered no explanation for his dismissal.[211]

The most direct evidence as to why Manley chose to fire Zinn came from Professor Samuel DuBois Cook, of Atlanta University's political science department, a friend of Zinn's who was close to Morehouse president Benjamin Mays. Manley as a friend and fellow AU-affiliated college president confided to Mays about Zinn's firing. Mays, in "a long talk with" Cook in July 1963, repeated Manley's explanation for the firing, an explanation that will surprise no one who reads Zinn's southern diary or Zinn's subsequent accounts of his firing. Cook recounted in a letter to Zinn that President Mays "said that Manley told him of a long-standing feud between the two of you and that the Social Science meeting (with the tape recording of student gripes) was the straw that broke the camel's back."[212] In other words, Zinn's continuing criticism had irritated Manley, who saw the "On Liberty at Spelman" meeting, in which students demanded major changes in his administration, as Zinn's handiwork and as an insubordinate act—"the straw that broke the camel's back"—that necessitated his firing.

In defense of academic freedom, tenure rights, and Zinn's many contributions to the campus and community, Cook and sixteen other Spelman, Morehouse, Atlanta, and Clark college faculty wrote a letter of protest to Spelman's board of trustees urging reconsideration of Zinn's dismissal. While acknowledging that "many would not have chosen Dr. Zinn's direct methods of dissent" against the Spelman administration, they maintained that if the college valued freedom such dissent ought to be honored rather than punished: "No impartial judge can seriously maintain that Dr. Zinn posed a menace to the administration. He merely refused to accept an authoritarian discipline—for himself, for the students, or for his colleagues. Our educators speak for the need for free inquiry, the need for non-conformity, even for rebels. Why then this arbitrary ejection of an instructor who, in his teaching, in his scholarship, in his publications, by his general influence in the community and by his personal qualities, was an outstanding member of the Spelman faculty?"[213]

Such faculty correspondence and Manley's initial private statements offer two contrary views of Zinn's firing—that of Manley, which blames the firing on Zinn's insubordination; and that of Zinn and his faculty supporters, which blames the firing on Manley's political intolerance and authoritarianism. There is, however, a third interpretation of the firing, which R. B. Pearsall, chair of Spelman's English department, offered in a letter to the AAUP. Pearsall's view is distinctive because in offering it he expressed admiration for both Zinn and Manley, whom he termed "the two best men on the campus, and the most profitable to the college."[214] According to Pearsall:

> The gradual estrangement of Dr. Zinn and President Manley, the dismissing officer, had three prime causes. One is a general situation of strain evident not only here but in many southern colleges and most Negro ones. The second is a general obsolescence of principles which affects communication and control in those groups of colleges. The third and saddest is lethargy, cynicism, and perhaps fear among Mr. Zinn's colleagues on the Spelman faculty. . . . The estrangement and culminating dismissal followed naturally from these three causes. Dr. Zinn became the spokesman for courageous and modern principles in areas affecting students, faculty, and administration. In a conventional situation this responsibility would have been shared by many. At Spelman he [Zinn] found himself almost alone. The president was alone. Inevitably differences of principle and tactics shifted to mutual distrust and dislike, and to the emotion-filled finale.[215]

Neither Zinn nor Manley was "to blame" for the firing, claimed Pearsall. Instead, he blamed himself and other senior faculty, whose voices were needed to sway

Spelman's reluctant president to embrace meaningful administrative reform, but who had not risen to the occasion: "In any singling out of guilty individuals," Pearsall concluded, "priority would need to be given to the half-dozen senior members of the faculty who could have manipulated a different outcome, and failed to do so. I am one of these."[216]

Each of these three interpretations contribute to our understanding of Zinn's firing. Manley's authoritarian tendencies and intolerance of student and faculty challenges to his authority led to the years of conflict between Spelman's president and Zinn. Zinn himself admitted in his memoir that his open criticism and defiance of President Manley, which even some of Zinn's friends and colleagues had advised him to tone down, did constitute insubordination.[217] Pearsall seems to be on solid ground in arguing that too much of the burden of reforming the Spelman administration fell on Zinn's shoulders since few other senior faculty were so vocal—though, of course, there is no way of knowing whether the voices of additional senior faculty would have made a difference in winning such reforms or avoiding Zinn's firing given how hostile Manley was to criticism and to challenges to his authority.

Sex, Lies, and Racist Cops: The Escalating Battle over Zinn's Firing and Manley's Autocracy

The final, and by far the most explosive, explanation of Zinn's firing came belatedly and privately from Manley; Spelman's president first mentioned it to the AAUP more than a half-year after the firing. In private letters to Zinn and the AAUP in 1964, Manley, attempting to stave off a formal AAUP investigation of his firing of Zinn, offered a new rationale for the firing, a morals charge—implying that Zinn had an affair with a Spelman student and had lied to the college about it. In his initial letter to Zinn raising this charge, in January 1964, Manley warned that if the AAUP investigation proceeded, "documented facts . . . concerning your personal and private relationships with a student" would come out, raising questions about "your fitness to serve as a faculty member in this or any other institution." To avoid "unnecessary embarrassment . . . to yourself and others," Manley urged Zinn to "agree that the most graceful way to dispose of the pending matter before the A.A.U.P. would be for you to communicate with the A.A.U.P. and inform them that you and the college have worked out a settlement of your differences."[218]

Manley's correspondence with the AAUP indicates that this allegation against Zinn referred to an incident back in January 1960 when Zinn and his student, Roslyn Pope—a Merrill scholar, who would become a key leader of Atlanta's sit-in movement in March 1960—had been sitting in a parked car at night when police arrested them for disturbing the peace.[219] Zinn had never tried to hide this incident, which he promptly sought to report back to Manley. Zinn also wrote about the arrest in his soon-to-be-published book on race in the South, *The Southern Mystique* (1964), as an example of the "mystique of race consciousness . . . that expresses itself in the rage which inflames some white southerners who see a white and a Negro together as friends." The rage Zinn was referring to here was that of the Atlanta police officers who arrested him and Roslyn Pope. "If you're arresting us," Zinn asked, "what is the charge?" To which the "older patrolman replied: 'You sittin' in the car with a nigger gal an' wantin to know what is the charge?'"[220] Defended by Donald Hollowell, the attorney for Martin Luther King Jr., Zinn quickly got the charge—of disturbing the peace—dismissed. Zinn in March 1964 wrote an irate letter to Manley expressing outrage that sexual impropriety was now being read into this incident, especially since the arrest had occurred almost four years earlier and had never been mentioned or sexualized by the Spelman administration until Zinn had filed an appeal contesting his firing.[221]

Manley in his AAUP correspondence on this 1960 incident wrote that he had evidence of dishonesty and sexual impropriety by Zinn, claiming that in 1963 new information on the arrest had come to the college from "unimpeachable sources." Manley wrote that "the College has eyewitness reports from two Atlanta policemen" indicating that Zinn had lied about the circumstances leading to the arrest. Manley seemed aware of how odd it looked for him to have gathered this information and for a black college president to be taking the word of two white arresting officers over that of a Spelman professor and student (in an incident that brought an arrest ending with the dismissal of all charges). So Manley, in his AAUP correspondence, even went so far as to defend the integrity of Atlanta's white police officers, asserting that "contrary to what may be a popular belief elsewhere, the Atlanta police force is not composed of rabid racists," and that the arresting officers "had no interest adverse to Dr. Zinn and the young lady involved."[222]

Manley's motive for making such a charge seems transparently political. He needed leverage to get Zinn to abandon the AAUP appeal and stop a potential AAUP investigation of the firing since he likely realized how difficult it would be for Spelman to win such an appeal (because at most colleges full professors and department chairs, such as Zinn, would be assumed to have tenure). Beyond this, Manley was furious that even after firing Zinn he had not been able to rid himself of Zinn's scorching criticism of his administration. In fact, the firing had only intensified such criticism and offered damning new evidence of political intolerance at Spelman that Zinn had long bemoaned. Manley at times seemed more upset when he discussed this ongoing criticism than when he discussed Zinn's alleged sexual impropriety. Manley complained to the AAUP that since his dismissal Zinn had embarked upon a holy crusade to reform Spelman College, despite the fact that the trustees and the majority of faculty members and alumnae do not agree with his views on how the College should be administered. Dr. Zinn over the past several months has been trying to achieve his objective by broad-scale charges from afar about a lack of student freedom which he has caused to be given widespread circulation on the Spelman campus. . . . Dr. Zinn now appears to be trying to enlist the AAUP in this cause by asking for "all the facts about Spelman College to be brought out into the open by an investigation." It remains to be seen whether the AAUP will let itself be used for such a purpose. I do not think any useful purpose would be served by commenting further upon Dr. Zinn's half-truths and wild charges about the College's atmosphere and his theories about how the College ought to be administered.[223]

Although it incensed Manley, Zinn's decision to go public with his criticism of the Spelman administration after his firing was in its own way among the most impressive acts he made in connection with the college. Though it might be tempting to dismiss such criticism as merely revenge for his dismissal, there was actually a selfless quality to Zinn's "holy crusade" to end autocratic rule at Spelman in the wake of his firing. The AAUP had advised Zinn to avoid public criticism of Manley so as to make possible a settlement of his case that might include his reinstatement or financial compensation. Zinn did hold off such criticisms temporarily so as not "to foul up the mechanism by which the A.A.U.P. handles matters like this."[224] But from his first conversations with the AAUP, Zinn made it clear that his own job status and finances were secondary to the battle for freedom at Spelman, "that I want reinstatement at Spelman, but not at the expense of hushing up the situation at the college. A basic factor in maintaining the atrocious conditions there has been the ignorance of the trustees about what goes on: if nothing else is accomplished by this controversy the trustees should finally get a picture of how the college is run." Zinn told the AAUP that he was "willing to risk" losing his reinstatement battle via public criticism of Spelman if that would work "for the good of college reform," and expressed the hope that the AAUP would join him in being as "concerned with democracy in college government and academic freedom as with tenure and employment rights of professors."[225] By the end of the summer of 1963 Zinn went public with his criticism of Spelman's autocratic governance and his own dismissal.

And what criticism it was! Zinn used his considerable narrative power as a historian to construct a detailed, thirty-five-page, single-spaced history of political repression and administrative abuses at Spelman dating back to his early days at the college in the mid-1950s and covering all the major attacks on both student and faculty rights. Written when he was still angry over his firing, the narrative at times became polemical, as when he likened the Spelman administration to segregationist officials in their narrow-mindedness and intolerance. But overall the narrative is compelling and impressively documented, offering a devastating indictment of Spelman's administration and a ringing call for reform. It may well be the most extensive and powerful report ever written on the lack of democratic decision making and campus freedom at a historically black college—and Zinn circulated this report to Spelman's trustees, students, faculty, alumni, and the public.[226]

Faced with such criticism, Manley had no intention of backing down. And ultimately, he wore Zinn down. Zinn and the AAUP realized that even if eventually disproven the charge of sexual impropriety would itself be damaging and a legal challenge would be lengthy and costly. After a bout with pneumonia and having obtained a new job as a professor of government at Boston University, Zinn finally in late 1964 ended his appeal.[227]

Most of the documents relating to Manley's morals charge against Zinn seem to have been purged before he donated his huge collection of presidential papers (covering his more than two decades as president) to the Spelman College Archives. There is no file dedicated to Zinn or his firing and none of the evidence Manley claimed to have gathered documenting lies Zinn told about the 1960 arrest or any misconduct at all. And though there are multiple copies of the board of trustees minutes from the November 1963 meeting where Zinn's firing was discussed, they are all missing the same pages in which the trustees aired their views on the Zinn case. Nor is there a copy of the confidential statement Manley sent out to the trustees in preparation for this November 1963 board discussion of the Zinn case.[228] The few documents that have been preserved in the Manley papers do not support his charge of sexual impropriety. In fact, Manley, in his private letter to the trustees in September 1963 attempting to rebut the open letter sent to Spelman's trustees by Zinn's supporters protesting the firing, did not even mention the existence of a morals charge. Instead Manley pointed out in the letter that the total number of faculty supporting Zinn was small: only seventeen Atlanta University Center faculty from its six affiliated colleges, which combined had some three hundred faculty, had signed and only three of Spelman's forty-three faculty had signed.[229]

Even when Manley finally did raise the morals issue before Spelman's board of trustees in November 1963, his tone was muted when compared to what he told the AAUP. In Manley's correspondence with the AAUP raising the issue of sexual impropriety, he had lambasted Zinn, claiming that he lacked the "moral fitness to serve as a faculty member at a Christian college for young ladies."[230] And he had threatened that if these charges and the evidence became public, "embarrassment and disgrace" would result for Zinn.[231] This contrasts quite markedly with what he told the board. Indeed, in Manley's summary to the board of the confidential statement that he had sent the trustees on the Zinn case, the top two reasons for his firing were that he was "deficient" in that "1. He neglected his academic responsibilities; 2. He would not work within the rules of the college community." The morals issue came last, and it was expressed in a far more tentative way than his scorching attack on Zinn to the AAUP. Here, with the Spelman board, what Manley said of the final reason for his firing was simply that "3. He was of questionable moral character."[232]

Manley never commented publicly on his firing of Zinn. And in 1963 when Zinn's friends, Leslie Dunbar and Vincent Harding, met with Manley on the firing, Manley refused to comment, saying this was an internal college matter.[233] Nor did Manley even mention the Zinn case in his memoir of his Spelman presidency, published in 1995.[234] But while working on those memoirs, Manley did confide to Beverly Guy-Sheftall, director of the Spelman Women's Research and Resource center (who frequently dined with and discussed his memoir with Manley), that "one of his regrets" from his presidency was firing Zinn, a remark that would be difficult to explain if the morals charge he had raised against Zinn in 1964 had been true.[235]

Staughton Lynd, Zinn's close friend at Spelman, looks back on Manley's handling of the Zinn case as disgraceful. Lynd is dismissive of the morals charge, viewing it as the worst example of the "dirty pool" being played by Manley against Zinn. Lynd finds it "inconceivable" that Zinn would have had an affair with a student "because if there was anyone sensitive to the misuse of faculty power it was Howard Zinn, and any [sexual] relationship with a student is from my point of view just prima facie off the table because there isn't genuine equality. I am still of the opinion that it was a scandalous attack."[236]

The final word with regard to Manley's accusations concerning Zinn's arrest and his allegedly improper relationship with Roslyn Pope ought to belong to Pope herself. Manley never told Pope about his morals charge against Zinn or any concerns the president of Spelman had about her arrest with Zinn. In fact, because this charge was made privately by Manley to Zinn and the AAUP, and never became public, Pope never knew (until I interviewed her for this book more than a half-century after Zinn's firing) of this charge or its use by Manley in his correspondence with the AAUP regarding Zinn's firing. Pope was shocked and appalled by this accusation. She told me that Zinn's narrative of their arrest in his memoir was truthful. The police had behaved in a racist manner that night; they were nasty; they used a racial slur against her, just as Zinn had indicated in his published accounts of the arrest; and the police had only arrested them because of her race. She was never involved in a sexual relationship with Zinn, and found Manley's accusation not merely false, but "shameful." She regarded Zinn as an inspiring teacher, activist, and friend, but had not the slightest romantic interest in him. Nor he in her. Pope expressed regret that she was never told about these accusations and so had no opportunity to refute them when they were used so unethically to discourage Zinn from having the AAUP investigate his firing.[237]

Both the gender and racial dynamics of this episode are painful to reflect upon. Taking Manley at his word, and assuming he did gather affidavits from the two arresting officers in 1963, three years after the arrest, it is striking that he never went back to Roslyn Pope to get her perspective on the arrest or the morals charge. It's not merely that Manley took the word of two white policemen while ignoring the perspective of a stellar Spelman student—who had distinguished herself as a Merrill scholar, president of the Spelman student body, and prime author of the Atlanta student movement's Appeal for Human Rights—but that he made the morals charge against Zinn without extending to Pope the courtesy of informing her of it so she could respond. It was as if her view did not matter even though the arrest and morals charge involved her. Manley apparently did not want to afford her the opportunity to attest that the morals charge was groundless and that the police were indeed racist. Learning of all this so many years later, Pope was literally stunned by what she termed "the treachery, betrayal, and dishonesty displayed by President Manley," which she concluded "show him to be an unmitigated villain, a wolf in sheep's clothing. Such an example of perfidy is unforgivable." Pope thought it was "sad" that Zinn "had to go through that," being falsely accused of a morals charge by Manley, which she termed "a radical betrayal" and something that Manley "pulled out of his hat to justify the firing of Howard."[238]

What Manley seemed never to have reflected upon was what it was like for Pope as a young African American woman to have been arrested at night with her white professor by two hostile white policemen. For Pope the experience was horrible. The police arrested her and Zinn, as Pope put it, "for no reason at all . . . it was harassment. . . . Had I still been in Paris, [where as a Merrill fellow she had spent the prior year free of the Jim Crow South's racism] no attention would have been paid to my riding in a car with a white male. The fact that we were stopped at all is a testament to the racist attitudes of the two policemen." The police officer who referred to her as a "nigger gal" she could sense "was a very hate-infested person. . . . I remember just being stricken with fear." Fearing for her own safety, Pope felt almost relieved after the arrest that "at least we're in jail, we're alive."[239] For Pope the way Manley overlooked the racist nature of this encounter with the police was as outrageous as the false morals charge that he contrived against Zinn and sought to connect with their arrest: "Apparently Manley just seized on that as if we were the culprits when it was really the Atlanta police department."[240]

Although not so egregious as Manley's, Zinn's handling of this controversy was also problematic. Pope was mystified as to why Zinn never told her of Manley's charges. "It's somewhat distressing that it's all transpired behind my back,"

Pope reflected.[241] Whatever motive Zinn had for keeping Manley's charges secret, it was wrong of him to leave Pope in the dark about a morals charge that
involved her. Zinn also exhibited a kind of tone deafness to the impact that
the arrest had on Pope, which suggests that for all his insight and experience
as an observer with regard to race he did not understand the emotional aftermath such an encounter with racism could leave on a young African American
woman. He seemed unaware that for Pope, as she later reflected, "in my seventy-
seven years on earth, that incident was the most humiliating and degrading experience of my life. It was totally devastating, especially as I remembered Paris."
While neglecting to discuss with Pope the impact of their arrest and failing to
help her work through her distressed feelings about the arrest, Zinn went ahead
and discussed the arrest in his books. Pope found it "offensive" that "Howard
discussed it in print. . . . Apparently he didn't realize that I was severely affected."[242] In a sense, then, both Manley and Zinn used Pope and the arrest for
their own purposes, Manley to make scurrilous charges against Zinn, and Zinn
as dramatic material for his publications on southern race relations.

While Manley's sexual accusations regarding Zinn and Pope were false,
Manley was not the only one who thought Zinn may at some point have had
an inappropriate sexual relationship with a student at Spelman. According to
Lynd there were rumors that sometime later in his Spelman years, well after the
1960 arrest, that Zinn "did become involved with a student" other than Pope.
The rumor of this other alleged affair "circulated among the black faculty."[243] It
also circulated among some Spelman students, and Alice Walker recalls hearing
"gossip" about this after leaving Spelman.[244]

Unlike Lynd, Alice Walker is not dismissive of these rumors of an affair. She
thinks such an affair was "completely possible," though she has "no idea" if the
rumors were true. The reason she thinks an affair could have happened was not
merely because Zinn was "the tall, rangy good-looking professor that many of
the girls at Spelman swooned over"—and was young, brilliant, funny, approachable, and dynamic—but also because "we were all in love with Howie. And he
loved all of us [laughs]. That was *new*. It was such a delightful *new thing* to have
a teacher who would put himself on the line with the rest of us. I just know that
attraction, love, these are things that happen whether you want them to or not.
. . . You know humanity shows itself. And I have no means of censuring him . . .
if something happened between him and a student."[245]

While it seems difficult to imagine that Zinn, who helped inspire and was a
key supporter of Spelman's proto-feminist student rebellion in 1963, might have
abused his authority as a faculty member by having an affair with a student,
such rumors cannot be completely dismissed. The student and faculty rumors
of such an affair, Zinn's later marital infidelities, and his generational location in
the prefeminist Old Left (whose sexual norms did not include a feminist power

critique of such unequal—that is, teacher-student—sexual relationships) leave this sexual question an open one.[246] There is no doubt that the arrest involving Roslyn Pope was completely distorted, falsely sexualized, and misused by Manley, Zinn's political nemesis, apparently to shock and intimidate Zinn into dropping the appeal of his firing. But the rumors of a subsequent Zinn affair at Spelman did not come from such hostile sources—and even Zinn's friends and admirers were divided as to whether such rumors merit credence.

Zinn's southern diary and correspondence, however, never even hint at such an affair. Nor do they indicate that he had a sexual interest in any of his students or colleagues at Spelman. But on the other hand, Zinn's diary rarely focused on his personal life and said nothing at all about his sexual relationships. So the diary cannot be said to prove that Zinn never had an affair with a student (or anyone else) at Spelman.

The diary, which is by far the lengthiest and most revealing source on Zinn's role as a Spelman faculty member, documents a personal closeness to his students, showing consistent characteristics of Zinn's relationship to his students, most notably his approachability toward, identification with, and concern for them. As the diary documents, Zinn was generous with his time, seeing his students day and night in his classrooms, his on-campus home, and at political, cultural, and intellectual events. He cared about their political development as much as their academic progress, and would let them use his car, his apartment, his typewriter, or his advice and encouragement if that would enhance their engagement in struggles for social justice and student rights.

While such proximity between a professor and his students would seem admirable to educational progressives, for an educational traditionalist like Manley—who believed in hierarchy and the teacher as authority figure—this proximity seemed suspicious. Indeed, as the Zinn diary reveals, even without the charge of sexual impropriety, and before Manley ever made that charge, Spelman's president thought Zinn had become far too close to his students, imagining that Zinn was not merely being supportive of students protesting the status quo at Spelman but was instigating those protests.[247] Manley was equally upset that Zinn passionately defended his students' rights, openly supported their protests, and carried their grievances to Spelman's president in toe-to-toe arguments, even when Manley had made it quite clear that he did not want to hear them. Manley's charge of sexual impropriety can even be seen as an extension of his earlier complaints that Zinn was guilty of political improprieties, with Zinn violating his professional ethos by being too embracing of his students, backing them even when they defied the Spelman administration's authority. Manley surely recognized, and was irritated, that some of Spelman's best students admired and even loved Zinn, whose eagerness to change Spelman so offended Manley.

Manley was not wrong in thinking Zinn had crossed at least one line that Spelman's president valued with regard to professionalism. Manley was concerned that excessive political activism could disrupt the education of Spelman students and thought it his duty and that of his faculty to push students to complete their studies or at least not overtly privilege activism over academics. Zinn was quite out of sync with Manley's traditionalist version of academic professionalism. In thinking back to how he approached these activism versus academics tensions at Spelman, Zinn explained,

> I wasn't encouraging students to leave college [to do civil rights work], but if it was a choice say between going to class and participating in a demonstration, I believed that people could learn more—far more—about the world and about the reality of the world and about society by participating in the social struggle of our time than by simply reading and going to class. And of course, I was teaching class, and didn't encourage my students to leave class, but when it came to one or the other there was no doubt in my mind what was more educational. And I know there are some people—in fact this has always been true when students participate in movements—who thought that most students would do better by sticking to their books and not getting involved with these things. But I just never believed that.[248]

If you reflect on this statement, it reveals Zinn's romantic radicalism and his progressive faith in experiential learning—a strong linkage between political activism and deep and meaningful education. For Zinn, a student skipping class to participate in a sit-in was seizing a great learning opportunity, a kind of action research or learning by doing, and a chance to promote democratic change. This reflected Zinn's ethos as both a radical and a scholar-activist. But Manley, an administrator, not a scholar—and a cautious paternalist, not a daring activist— saw political protests as a distraction from the education he was responsible for providing and an invitation to arrest and possible violence. Manley looked at the risks rather than the potential gains of such activism, worrying about the prospects of Spelman's young black women if their activism monopolized their time, led them to drop out of college without their degrees, and came out of school with an arrest record. Manley, as we have seen, was also concerned about what such arrests would do to Spelman's reputation, so there was some institutional and personal self-interest involved in his position as well. Zinn, on the other hand, cared little about such vocationalism, careerism, and institutional self-interest, prioritizing the education in citizenship students would receive on the picket line and the potential of the struggle for a society free of racial discrimination to open up a whole new world for them. Their two views of education and activism were not only incompatible, but representative of the conflicting calculations most of us make when we consider departing from our ordinary routines for risky forms of political activism—with Zinn stressing the benefits and Manley the costs of such activism.

Howard Zinn's southern diary carries one other important lesson for anyone seeking to understand the 1960s and the student movements that helped to define that turbulent decade: Faculty matter. Student movements are usually not solo acts, and as they seek to make history their success or failure is often linked to their ability to make allies among their teachers. Zinn was among the most active faculty in supporting the student movement, a key member of a core of like-minded activist professors and instructors in the AU Center whom student activists admired, learned from, and even took advice and inspiration from at times. No history of the Atlanta sit-in movement, SNCC, or the Spelman student rights rebellion is complete without an understanding of their faculty allies—and Zinn's southern diary offers an extensive and detailed look at these allies and their deep connections and interactions with this remarkable generation of student activists.

DEDICATION

To Dr. Howard Zinn, who came here with us when we were freshmen, and who has been an inspiration to the whole Spelman family since his arrival. We admire and appreciate you for your warm and friendly personality and your deeds of unselfish guidance.

We dedicate this book to you as a token of our affection.

Howard Zinn, as a Spelman professor, 1960. This photo and dedication appeared in the Spelman College yearbook, *Reflections*. The students had voted to dedicate the book to Zinn, a testament to his popularity as a teacher and mentor. (Photo courtesy of the Spelman College Archives)

Myla (Kabat-)Zinn and Jeff Zinn with Marian Wright
(Edelman), center, on the Spelman campus, 1958. Wright, a
Merrill scholar and Zinn student, would become a leader of
the Atlanta sit-in movement in 1960, a civil rights lawyer, and
founder of the Children's Defense Fund. (Photo courtesy of
the estate of Howard Zinn)

From left to right on the back row, Lenora Taitt (Magubane),
a student of Zinn's; Johnny Popwell, a Morehouse student; and
Roslyn Zinn in the AMS Players performance of *The King and
I*. On Howard Zinn's devotion to promoting racially integrated
theatre, see the January 24, 1963, entry of his Spelman diary.
Taitt participated in the Atlanta sit-in movement and was a
Freedom Rider in Albany, Georgia. (Photo courtesy of the
estate of Howard Zinn)

Spelman College student protester Marilyn Pryce, arrested with Atlanta student movement leader Lonnie King of Morehouse College and Martin Luther King Jr. at Rich's department store sit-in, Atlanta, October 1960. Though Spelman students played a prominent role in this nonviolent protest against segregation (more than a third of the arrestees were Spelman students, and Spelman student leader Herschelle Sullivan had together with Lonnie King contacted Martin Luther King Jr. to urge his participation in the sit-in), most news reporters, who were male, slighted this female student activism. Thus the caption that initially ran with this photo in the *Atlanta Constitution* failed even to identify Marilyn Pryce, terming her an "unidentified woman" arrested with Lonnie and Martin Luther King. (Photo by Charles D. Jackson, copyright *Atlanta Journal Constitution*, courtesy of Georgia State University)

Picketers protesting the refusal of Leb's delicatessen to
serve African Americans, 1963. Zinn, his students, and his
colleagues were among those who sat in at Leb's seeking to end
its Jim Crow policies. Leb's placement of the anti-integration
sign in the window is mentioned in the May 23, 1963, entry of
Zinn's diary. (Photo courtesy of the *New York World Telegram
and Sun* photograph collection, Library of Congress)

Marian Wright (Edelman), left, facing front, a Zinn student, and other Spelman students jailed for participating in a nonviolent sit-in against Jim Crow lunch counters, Atlanta, Georgia, March 1960. (Bettmann/Getty Images)

Albert E. Manley, Spelman College president, 1953–76. (Photo courtesy of the Spelman College Archives)

Zinn, teaching his seminar on China at Spelman, 1961. (Photo courtesy of the estate of Howard Zinn)

Howard Zinn and his student Herschelle Sullivan (Challenor), Spelman College campus, 1958. Sullivan became a leader of the Atlanta student movement and was arrested with her fellow students and Martin Luther King Jr. in the Rich's department store sit-in, October 1960. (Photo courtesy of the estate of Howard Zinn)

Howard Zinn and his students in the living room of the Zinn family apartment, Spelman campus, 1959. (Photo courtesy of the estate of Howard Zinn)

Zinn in Selma, Alabama, with James Baldwin, Freedom Day, October 1963. (Photo courtesy of the estate of Howard Zinn)

Zinn in Selma, Alabama, Freedom Day, October 1963. (Photo courtesy of the estate of Howard Zinn)

Zinn with his student, Spelman student government president
in 1963, Betty Stevens (Walker), who was active in the Atlanta
sit-in movement and the Spelman student rights struggle.
Walker would become the first Spelman alumna to graduate
from Harvard Law School. (Photo courtesy of Betty Stevens
Walker)

SPELMAN SPOTLIGHT

VOL. XXV, NO. 4   SPELMAN COLLEGE   ATLANTA, GEORGIA   December 17, 19

May the Peace of Christmas Be Yours

1964-65 Merrill Scholars Named

The Spotlight, along with all our Spelman sisters, takes pride in honoring the recipients of the Merrill Scholar awards for the year 1964-65. We extend our congratulations to Misses Marilyn Holt, Leronia Stokes, Alice Walker, and Josephine Dunbar. These four young ladies, all honor roll students, exemplify that which Spelman College attempts to inculcate in her students.

Marilyn Holt, a mathematics major from Atlanta, Georgia, is presently participating in an exchange program with Wellesley College in Wellesley, Massachusetts. She has distinguished herself academically by receiving the Orchid award for two semesters. This award is given to those students who receive straight A's. Indicative of her leadership capacity is her election to the office of president of her junior class before being selected for the Wellesley exchange program.

Leronia Stokes is a senior from Norfolk, Virginia. Her accomplishments and activities here at Spelman indicate that she will be successful in her aspirations to become a lawyer. As a result of her scholarship in her major, political science, she was asked to participate in the Social Science Honor Seminar. She was also a representative to the U.N. Assembly honoring Prime Minister Nehru.

Marilyn Holt   **Josephine Dunbar**

Alice Walker is also a participant in the Social Science Honor Seminar. A social science major, she is the president of the Social Science Club. During her junior year, she was among those students who initiated the residence of the French dormitory. Alice's home is in Elberton, Georgia.

Josephine Dunbar is a senior from Waycross, Georgia. Her achievements in her chosen field of mathematics are evidenced by the fact that she is teaching a course in mathematics this year. She has represented her fellow students and her school in various areas. She is treasurer of the SSCA, she was a Student Council representative to the NSA Congress in Indiana, and she participated in the Crossroads Africa program in 1962. These achievements have earned her listing in Who's Who in American Colleges and Universities, 1962-63.

Leronia Stokes   **Alice Walker**

This listing of accomplishments is indicative of the qualities of the Merrill scholar. However, we must not be so misled as to think that distinction is a direct result of following prescribed patterns. Each of these persons has distinguished herself as an individual.

Gladys Wells

SNCC News

Helena

On Nov. 16, Helena, Arkansas, located on the Mississippi River, experienced its first sit-in demonstrations. Three SNCC field secretaries and thirty o t h e r anti-segregation workers were arrested on charges of "vagrancy", "disturbing the peace", and "refusing to leave a public place".

Macon

Twenty-two-year-old Joni Rabinowitz, SNCC worker, was convicted on charges of perjury by a Federal Court Jury. Six others, representing the top leadership in Macon, were also charged with perjury and face trials soon. Her trial followed the investigation of the organization of a white store owner who served on a jury which denied damages in a Negro civil rights case. Sentence has not, as yet, been passed.

Americus

Donald Harris of N. Y., Ralph Allen of Melrose, Mass., and John Perdew of Denver, Colo., three SNCC field workers who faced death sentences under Georgia's insurrection and unlawful assembly statutes, were freed on Nov. 1 by a three-judge Federal panel. The court also prohibited further prosecution of the youth on the outlawed charges and ordered them set free on bail. This ruling marked the first time a Federal Court has halted prosecution in a civil rights case at the request of private citizens.

Atlanta

Rev. Ashton Bryant Jones of San Gabriel, California, is being held in Fulton County jail under $20,000 bail for his participation in an anti-regulation movement at the First Baptist Church here. Rev. Jones was on a hunger strike for one month. Attorneys for Rev. Jones will press motions for a new trial on Nov. 22.

Raleigh

On Nov. 20, a new SNCC voter registration project in Raleigh, N. C. was announced by SNCC Chairman, John Lewis. The Raleigh Citizens Association (RCA), a body of Negro organization in that city, requested SNCC's professional aid. The project is to be directed by Reginald Robinson, last stationed in Cambridge, Md.

Return To Pine Bluff

The Pine Bluff Movement has called for a nationwide protest against McDonald's Restaurant Chain. Un-
(Continued on page 3)

Who's Who Winners for 1964

Nelda King   **Beverly Whatley**   **Joyce Hawthorne**

Marilyn Holt   **Damaris J. Allen**   **Betty Stevens**

Annease Chaney   **Alice Walker**   **Josephine Dunbar**

Judy Tillman   **Ida Rose McCree**   **Aurelia Brazeal**

Thirteen Juniors and seniors were recently elected to membership in W h o ' s W h o. Among Students in American Colleges a n d Universities, an organization which nates students from approximately 775 colleges and universities. This year's group, elected by the student body and approved by the Committee on Admissions, Appeals and Scholarships is as follows:

Seniors—Annease Chaney, Josephine Dunbar, Margaret Hampton, Joyce Hawthorne, Nelda King, Ida Rose McCree, Betty Stevens, and Beverly Whatley.

Juniors—Damaris A l l e n, Aurelia Brazeal, Marilyn Holt, Judy Tillman, and Alice Walker.

These young women were nominated on the basis of scholarship, participation, and leadership in academic and extracurricular activities; citizenship and service to the school; and promise of future usefulness.

Each student who becomes a member receives a certificate and is recognized in the annual publication of the organization for the year.

Margaret Hampton

Yes, it's that time of year aga and the mad rush to buy prese and send cards has begun. With or a few shopping days left befo Christmas, we are crowding stor pushing and shoving at the "barga counters, and trying to keep up w young children who insist on wand ing away to the toy departments. get caught up in this rush every ye and every year we vow that the n year will be different.

When we sit down to write Chri mas cards we get our lists and se cards to people who sent them to last year. Next come the people expect to get cards from this ye We never stop to think that a p sonal with for a happy holiday often means more than an elaborat printed card.

Usually we never get a chan during the days before Christmas, sit down and think about the holic season itself. If we did we mig feel the warmth and cheerfulness Christmas, and the hope of the N mas Eve, when the tree is decorat and is ablaze with gay lights. P haps a fire crackles nearby in 1 fireplace on which the stockings hung, and we are surrounded by lov ones. This is the time we really f the spirit of the season and gl with an inner warmth.

We should all try to stop a wh during this season and capture moment like this for ourselves. can make a complete change in way we think about the holiday a son and can give us a new approa tion of our traditions. This mom can be something we cherish look back upon with fond memo and a warm heart.

Lucia Hollov

MUSICAL NOTES

Music Sets Mood For Christmas

On December 1, at 4:30 in afternoon Miss Jane Briggs, instruc of piano and theory, who joined Spelman faculty this year gave most enjoyable piano recital. I performed, with dexterity and expr siveness, works by Bach, Beethov Schumann, and Schubert.

The recital was well attended those who came were delighted hear the accomplished Miss Brig

The mood for the Christmas h day was really set by the beaut Christmas Carol Concert. The c cert has a marvelous reputation its lovely and varied music perform beautifully by the A-M-S cho Morehouse and Spelman College clubs. This year was no except to the wonderful tradition which an annual treat to hundreds. Al with such favorites as "March of Shepherds", "Feast of the B Kings", "Behold the Star", "Wasn't That A Mighty Day" chorus sang some new carols fr various parts of the world which cluded Lapland, the Far East Carols and a motet, "Hodie Christ composed by a contemporary Fre composer. Along with such favor as "Mary's Lullaby", and "Deo G cias" the Spelman College glee c performed a most delightful rou "Rejoice and Be Merry". The Mo house College glee club under direction of Mr. Wendell P. Whal who has returned to Morehouse a two years of study for his doctor performed wonderfully as his r dition. Among the songs which t sang were "Hodie Christus Na Est" by Sweelinck, "Veni Emm uel," and a contemporary rediti of "Lo, How a Rose E'er Blo ing."

Christmas Carol Concert—Impressive View of Majestic Decor of Sisters Chapel.

Spelman Spotlight, December 17, 1963. Alice Walker is pictured among the winners (second row, right, in the left column, and third row down, center, in the center panel) of the Merrill Scholarship at Spelman and as elected to *Who's Who among Students in American Colleges and Universities*. Walker, a Zinn student active in civil rights and student rights protests, would turn the scholarship down. She would transfer out of Spelman the semester after Zinn's firing, disillusioned by the limits on freedom at the school. Note the SNCC news column on this same front page of the campus newspaper, symbolic of the students' involvement and interest in the Black Freedom Movement. (Photo courtesy of the Spelman College Archives)

Roslyn Pope, a student of Zinn's, Merrill scholar, and student government president, who had studied music in Paris. Pope served as the prime author (with Julian Bond) of *The Appeal for Human Rights*, the founding manifesto of the Atlanta sit-in movement in 1960, and was arrested with Zinn by police in Atlanta. (Photo courtesy of the Spelman College Archives)

Spelman drama student Marie Thomas, opposite right, as
Miss Alma in Tennessee Williams's *Summer and Smoke*;
Atlanta University graduate student Ashton Spann, center, as
the father; and Spelman student Lois Weston as the mother.
The Spelman administration sought to postpone the cast
party that followed this play in December 1962. The refusal
of the Spelman students to abide this postponement led to
harsh disciplinary action that outraged Howard Zinn, who
discussed this in his diary, and led Thomas to become an
eloquent critic of the administration's paternalism. Thomas
would go on to a career in acting on screen and stage.
(Photo courtesy of Marie Thomas)

Historian Vincent Harding, Zinn's friend, a civil rights and antiwar activist, who headed Atlanta's Mennonite House and would succeed Zinn as chair of Spelman's History and Social Science Department. Harding would later draft Martin Luther King Jr.'s Riverside Church speech against the war in Vietnam. (Photo courtesy of the Spelman College Archives)

Alice Walker and Howard Zinn, 1992, former student and teacher, who would became lifelong friends and influential authors—Walker winning the Pulitzer Prize for *The Color Purple*, and Zinn attracting more than two million readers with his *People's History of the United States*. (Photo copyright © Jean Weisinger, 1992)

Howard Zinn meeting Spelman president Beverly Daniel
Tatum, 2005, when Spelman (forty-two years after Zinn's
firing) awarded him an honorary degree. (Photo courtesy of
the Spelman College Archives)

Howard Zinn, delivering the commencement address at
Spelman, 2005. (Photo courtesy of the Spelman College
Archives)

DIARY EDITOR'S NOTE

Although Howard Zinn was well aware of his southern diary's historical value—and used quotations and other material from it in several of his books and articles—he never edited the diary or prepared it for publication. Thus the diary is a kind of diamond in the rough, brimming with historical insight and political passion in prose that often sparkles in ways that call to mind his best-selling historical books; but unlike his books, the diary includes punctuation problems, misspellings, and other minor errors. To preserve the diary's historical authenticity, I have offered his journal much as Zinn wrote it, correcting spelling and punctuation problems (in brackets[ ]) only when those errors seemed sure to confuse readers or lead them away from his original meaning. Zinn's more common slips on punctuation in the diary—such as a failure to close parentheses or inconsistency in using quotation marks—rarely cause confusion. Nor does his occasional tendency to flip back and forth on dates—though dating errors are corrected in the footnotes. Some adjustments have had to be made regarding layout, of course, when converting a typed and handwritten diary for the printed page (handwritten entries are indicated with a bracketed "H" following the entry). For the reader's ease of reference, I standardized the placement of date headers (Zinn sometimes ran these in, sometimes set them off on their own line, sometimes spaced above them or indented them, sometimes did not) and the indenting of the line following them. I also standardized such mundane items as the length of and space around dashes and the space after periods. Outside of such items, however, I have attempted to preserve as much as possible the look of Zinn's diary by using his paragraph structure, indenting (or lack of it), and extra-large spacing between certain words or above and below certain lines, which meant leaving in place the diary's inconsistencies so long as this could be done without leading to confusion. Words in the diary are italicized for emphasis only when they reflect Zinn's emphasis (no emphasis is added by the editor).

The main exception to my mostly verbatim approach to the diary occurs in the rare instances when the diary covers deeply personal matters of a Zinn colleague or student, in which the identity of the person or the personal matter is of no historical significance. In those places, out of respect for the privacy of these individuals, I have deleted their names or the personal matter.

Since the diary was for his own use and he knew who, where, and what he was writing about, Zinn did not always introduce the people or events he discussed on his pages, which is why one of the key tasks of editing the diary was identifying as many of these as possible. This is done through footnotes, which are intended to be concise and unobtrusive. Zinn mentions works in a great variety of academic fields, including American politics, African American studies, European history, Russian literature, Asian history, and drama, among others. So I have also used the footnotes to identify any of those references that might seem likely to elude general readers.

Readers of the diary should consider approaching it much as you would approach getting to know a new friend. At the beginning of a friendship, when it is still in the acquaintanceship phase, the conversations are likely to be brief and the confidences limited; but both grow and deepen if you invest the time in the relationship. The same is true of the diary, which begins abruptly, and with brief, almost outline-type entries. But before long the diary entries get longer and deeper. So readers will find that if they are patient and read on well beyond the diary's opening, they will be rewarded and engaged by Zinn's increasingly vivid narrations of the events, causes, and people that so engaged him in his final months as a politically active faculty member at Spelman College.

Howard Zinn's Southern Diary

JOURNAL 1963

Zinn opens without offering an explanation of why he decided to keep a diary. But from its start, Zinn's diary entries focus on issues of race, class, democracy, and freedom that were of concern to him throughout his Atlanta years (1956–63) as he worked with his students and colleagues to battle Jim Crow in the Deep South and to promote educational reform at Spelman College. The diary's opening is also typical of Zinn's Deep South years in that the first voices he evokes are those of African Americans: an alumnus from neighboring Morehouse College (the historically black college that was Martin Luther King Jr.'s alma mater), a sociologist from that same college, and a reference to a classic work of African American social criticism of the black bourgeoisie and of historically black colleges and universities. —RC

Black bourgeoisie*
"First time I've gotten within 6 inches of a white person."†

---

* *Black Bourgeoisie* (1957) is a classic critique of the African American middle class and historically black colleges published by the eminent black sociologist E. Franklin Frazier, whose daring and brilliance Zinn admired and whose visit to Spelman he helped to host. But on the condescending and sexist view of black women in this Frazier book as well as in his *The Negro Family in the United States* (1939), see Johnnetta Betsch Cole and Beverly Guy-Sheftall, *Gender Talk: The Struggle for Women's Equality in African American Communities* (New York: Ballantine Books, 2003), xxviii, xxix, xxxii, xxxiii.

† This quote appeared in print almost verbatim two years after Zinn recorded it in his southern diary. The quote in its fullest form was published in "The Mysterious Negro" chapter of Zinn's book on race in the South, *The Southern Mystique* (1965; rprt., Cambridge, Mass.: South End Press, 2002): "A Morehouse alumnus, with a doctorate in physics, told me about his freshman year encounter with a white woman teacher. 'She was a great teacher,' he said 'and also a fine human being, so provocative as a thinker. But most of all, I learned from her—wordlessly—that there was nothing mysterious about whites. She was the first white person I had ever gotten within five inches of, I mean in any

Wed. Dec. 19, 1962

M[ore]h[ou]se sociology prof[essor] from Birmingham—30 years a teacher—worked his way thru college as a waiter & bus boy in white hotels—Rosenwald fund scholarships.[*]

Back in [the 19]30s supported a Union. One by one other faculty
     backed down. So he decided—"Won't ever stick my neck out
     again. From now on it's no. 1.["]
One teacher (Mrs. Rese Winfel[?]: she attacked the president—she
     attacked the college—[)]

[Quoting the same Morehouse sociology professor] "I won't boycott Sears—Rosenwald (owner) [of Sears] did too much for me.["]

[S]he took a carload of boys down to Koinonia[†]—she invited the pres[ident] to her ap[ar]t[ment] & had liquor there—she had students in her ap[ar]tment talking till 2AM—

     ("But two brilliant grads said she was a fantastically stimulating teacher, had opened up new worlds for them"). ["]Yes she may be all right—but if someone attacks me, I'm not going to sign their check, no sir.["]

(And white faculty—who a minute before had said ["]I'm no radical—but we need to protect radicals"—says ["]she has the right to do these things—but the pres[ident] has the right to fire her!["])

     "These boys come out of the cotton country in Miss[issippi], Alabama; you can't start teaching someone sociology—you got to civilize them first."[‡]

(Thought of Mary Francis: "He thinks we're savages")[§]

[H = handwritten diary entry; entire Dec. 19 diary entry = H]

---

important sense, and after a year in her class I just saw race in a way I'd never seen it before. That is, I saw it was *nothing*'" (107).

[*]   Julius Rosenwald, founder of Sears Roebuck, was a major philanthropist of African American education whose scholarships funded the higher education of many black students.

[†]   Koinonia was an interracial cooperative farm in Americus, Georgia.

[‡]   Though unattributed, this quote appears to have come from the Morehouse sociology professor whom Zinn discussed at the start of this diary entry.

[§]   The "savages" quote came from this Spelman student (Mary Francis Watt) in reaction to the campus administration's announcement of its new program to teach students table manners—with the student viewing this as evidence that the administration saw the students as savages in need of civilizing. The "he" in the quotation apparently refers to Spelman president Albert E. Manley. Zinn to Spelman College trustees et al., July 1963, 29, Howard Zinn papers, Tamiment Library, New York University (hereafter Zinn papers, Tam, NYU).

Friday Dec. 20[*]

Cerney[†] called[,] said he and Norman Rates[‡] [Rates was black and Cerney white] had been invited to—and had purchased tickets for—Yale Club luncheon—[to] take place today at Athletic Club downtown—he was sick—would I [agree to] take his place—I told him since it was invitational he'd better check to see if I could (I had a summer at Yale)—he was anxious that Norman not have to go alone since his reception would be uncertain.

Hour later I called him—he'd just finished talking to Erikson, pres[ident of the] Yale Club who said when he asked if I could replace him at lunch "We're not discussing a topic he'd be interested in. We don't have Negroes in the Club (or *they* don't allow Negroes in the Club)." Whereupon Cerney (breaking a cardinal rule of the integrationist handbook!) said "But Norman Rates, whom you invited, is a Negro." Erickson then fell all over himself in embarrassment, said he didn't know this, that Negroes were not allowed at the Athletic Club & he would visit Rates this AM to explain personally. I told Cerney & he agreed it would have been better if Norman had just gone down—then they would have had a harder time disposing of the issue—he said he would call Norman to let him know what happened.

I phoned Atlanta Athletic Club, to make sure it was *their* policy rather than Yale Club. Asked young man who answered if they rented club for luncheons, He said yes. Asked if they rented to groups which included some Negroes. He said you'll have to talk to the secretary, Miss Pullen. Miss Pullen said Yes, it's a rule [that blacks are barred]. I said does this apply to groups *renting* the place for lunch? She said Yes. I asked if she could tell me why. She said "I don't have time to talk to you about it." Then—["]you know we don't take Jews either.["] "Why?["] I asked—"We don't want Jews in the club membership." ["]What about Jews who are in groups that rent the place for lunch[?]["] "Well we can't check everybody coming in." "Do you agree with the policy?" "I don't care what they do. We just do not cater to colored & that's a rule of the club."

[Entire Dec. 20 diary entry = H]

Spelman
Just before Xmas holiday 1962

Students—five, including Marilyn Pryce (Merrill scholar) and Marie Thomas (honor student), both of whom were in Summer and Smoke,[§] after last performance Sat. nite (request for after-show party had been denied, so official cast part[y] set for

---

* The correct date is Dec. 21.
† Ed Cerney, a professor of art at Spelman who was a close friend of Zinn's and a fellow radical.
‡ Norman Rates was a professor of religion at Spelman and the college's minister.
§ *Summer and Smoke* is a play written by Tennessee Williams (1948).

next afternoon at 4) signed in a dorm little before midnight, went out to party at A-M-S* fellow's house, were brought back to dorm by Marie's mother after frantic phone-calling, House-mother-Dean-Burroughs-Mother. Dean of women spoke to each student next day, then brought matter to Judiciary Board, (7 or 8 students, one of whom serves as chairman, plus two faculty, plus Dean of Women), which voted, with Dean presenting case (no defense attorney, no right to call witnesses, no written statement of charges beforehand, no right of cross-examination—the accused called before the group to answer questions and make statement, then dismissed) 7–2 (two students—Betty Stevens and Adybelle Sampson dissenting). Then Board of Review reviewed Dean of Instruction, Dean of Women, four faculty—[(]all faculty appointed by president and pres-vice-pres plus 3 students) and approved decision (to suspend for semester).

Students called SSGA [Spelman Student Government Association] meeting, which was packed. Meeting directed Student Council to appeal to president, to try to get decision revoked, called attention to pressure on Judiciary Board members, lack of procedural rights in trial.

Council went to see President,† who saw them after they'd waited long time near his office. In meantime Dean had asked all suspended students to leave that day. President agreed at this confrontati[o]n with Council to let students stay on campus until final settlement. Agreed to have Jud. B[oar]d and B[oar]d [of] Review meet jointly next day (Tues.). This joint meeting agreed to let B[oar]d of Review review, which then did so (Wed AM) and decided first decision must stand. Then students wept, asked for mercy. B[oar]d of Rev[iew] then said, with president there, approving (or did he say) that it would allow students to return a week before final exam so as not to lose whole semester, but each one must write an appeal to the president.

Students wrote appeal, saw president. He said they should leave campus and he would consider appeal. Students decided they would not leave campus until he gave decision. So he approved appeal and they left Wed. (or Thurs.). Judiciary Board students in meantime had signed affidavits of improper procedures at trial and pressure on them by Dean before trial.

SSGA met again, decided not to press this particular issue any more, but to try to make basic changes in rules.

Faculty meeting Wed. am, informal, unofficial—20 faculty showed (no members Jud. B[oar]d, B[oar]d of Review)[,] agreed to present motion at official meeting Wed. eve for joint, elected, fac[ulty]-student committee of 6 to go over whole question of student life and government. When broached at faculty meeting, Manley said he couldn't accept this, that administration must be involved in any such thing. Lois

---

*   "A-M-S" refers to Atlanta University/Morehouse/Spelman.

†   Spelman president Albert E. Manley.

Moreland* asked if adm[inistration] represented would he then consider. He said he would think about it.

Sunday Dec. 23

Two college fellows with regards from Kathy [Cathy] Cade[†] (one from Carleton—one from Indiana U) hitchhiking thru South (John Mc Auliff & Ed Harmon) just out [of] Jackson on way to Albany[‡]—asked if any surprises—whites more moderate than expected in Miss[issippi].

[Entire Dec. 23 diary entry = H]

Mon[day] Dec. 24

Jim Forman,[§] as serious xmas eve as ever, asked me to be consultant to depth research into Black Belt counties by SNCC field people plus perhaps college students.[¶]

[Entire Dec. 24 diary entry = H]

Xmas week 1962

Brief coffee and egg-nog at the Mickelburys.[**] Drove the Chivers[††] home and he suddenly talked real radical, as if responding to the conversation we'd had at the Pearsalls[‡‡] a few days before.

Chivers invited us to their home Dec. 26.

Xmas Day, made rounds: Seatons,[§§] Maggie Long[¶¶] (where Bonds[***] were—Mag-

---

*   Lois Moreland was a Spelman political science professor.

†   Cathy Cade was a white exchange student from Carleton College, who in the last semester of her junior year enrolled at Spelman as part of an interracial exchange program that Zinn founded. She worked in the Atlanta SNCC office and was arrested while participating in civil rights protests in Albany, Georgia.

‡   Jackson, Mississippi and Albany, Georgia were centers of major black freedom movement struggles that SNCC helped to launch in the early 1960s.

§   James Forman in 1963 was SNCC's executive secretary who was that organization's most important administrator and one of its key strategists.

¶   This Black Belt organizing in Mississippi paved the way for the historic Freedom Summer voting rights crusade in 1964.

**   Mexico Hembree Mickelbury was a librarian at Spelman.

††   Naomi Reid Chivers was dean of women and a professor of education at Spelman.

‡‡   Robert B. Pearsall was chair of the English department and professor of English at Spelman. Marilyn Meyer Pearsall, his wife, was a lecturer in sociology at Spelman.

§§   Esta K. Seaton was a poet and a professor of English at Spelman, and a close friend of Zinn.

¶¶   Margaret (Maggie) Long was editor of *The New South*.

***   Family of SNCC leader Julian Bond.

gie called me a few days later to say how Julia Bond, Jane's* mother, was bitter—intelligent when she did talk, how she advised Cissy Long, wondering whether to finish at Sophie Newcombs[,]† Tulane: "Now Cissy, you should know by now—the world is made up of and run by stupid people, and if you don't want to be dominated by stupidity, you must go ahead, and get the degree these stupid people want you to get, so you can use it to fight your way out of their control"), Dunbars.‡

[Wed.] Dec. 26 at Chivers:

[O]ne of those unexpected bang up parties with ferocious discussion. Center of it was duel between remarkable A.U. [Atlanta University] sociology graduate student—Harold§ —— Harlem raised, not quite a Black Moslem but a black nationalist—much more clever and flexible and *right* than the Muslims, with wit and a ruthless argumentative style, merciless in slashing at Dr. McBay, prof. of chemistry at Morehouse,¶ not really a conservative, but a [member of the] ~~complacent~~ middle class ("That $80,000 house you'd like to buy," Harold taunted him with) critical of US but also able to glorify the way of life. No Southern-Negro humility or "respect" for the Ph.D. in Harold—even insulting at times, but drawing back skillfully just before explosion. Not really a black supremacist like Muslims ("I'll stand at the wall, Zinn, and I'll be good to *you*") but says this emphasis is needed as a corrective at this stage to end complacency. Believes in being tough [tough] & extreme in argument to draw out ideas. The liveliest bang-up discussion in a long time as a dozen people sat and stood around the living room table and mostly listened, occasionally threw something in to what was a 2–3–4 person business. Mrs. Chivers['s] children by first marriage are just great (so much more advanced—at least her son—than their gracious but conservative parents). Her son, a biology school teacher for 7 years in Virginia, now at Episcopal Seminary near Washington (Duke[]), most unusual seminarian. Entered discussion from other room just in time to hear someone make some comment on segregation, and he threw out loudly into the room "CRAP!" Intellectually alive. His sister teaches school [in] Baltimore, quiet, most attractive (Harold taunted her smiling on her red, straight, "good" hair).**

---

*   Jane Bond is Julian Bond's sister.
†   Zinn was referring to H. Sophie Newcomb Memorial College in New Orleans, a private women's coordinate college of Tulane University.
‡   Leslie Dunbar headed the Southern Regional Council, a moderate integrationst civil rights group.
§   Harold Bardinelli, who later co-led the Freedom Schools with Staughton Lynd during the Mississippi Freedom Summer.
¶   Henry Ransom Cecil McBay was a professor of chemistry at Morehouse college.
**   This is a mocking reference to a form of class colorism, the notion that "straight" hair is preferable because it is associated with whiteness.

[Fri.] Dec. 28

Invited Campbells, Seatons, Maggie Long, Helen Roberts to dinner. Five Chivers came later, and another not so wild but interesting evening, with Duke holding forth on education (bitterly), telling of keeping discipline in Lynchberg [Lynchburg] class with his fists, of his former student now in jail for rape, people advancing arguments on what is wrong with whole education thing—Mrs. Chivers, former dean of women, an "educationist" says[,] "We're doing research on that problem right now and we're making progress"—but when I suggested economic system—poverty—at root, and maybe revolution only thing that would do she agreed!

New Years Eve—

at Maloofs[.]* Bourbon, chatter, pleasant, Ted with his colored lights, music, playthings. Gloria sweet and efficient.

[Wed.] Jan. 2, 1963

Jennifer Ragwar,† Esta Bezhura‡ (Uganda, father an Anglican bishop)[,] and our one remaining official white student now that Carol Barker is gone (home. . . .), Anna Jo Weaver.§ Nice evening. Last few hours of it African folk songs, with Jeff¶ picking up from Esta and Jennifer on his guitar.

(Jeff did a painting yesterday I consider a work of genius—great sweeping curves forming a sort of man, with waistcoat and long buttons, and huge nose, red (only *color* in the whole thing) and jowls he calls it POMPOSITY). Did another great one (I mean brought them home, and shaded one [of] them in school these last few months) on MacVicar** building from front, removed everything he didn't want, just the building itself, splashes of flowers in front, and a huge tree [in] front of the building curving around it, and the driveway as a great arc curving to the left around it the other way.

---

* Gloria Maloof was an actress in the ensemble of the Southeastern Academy of Theater and Music, and her husband Ted was its photographer. Both Howard and Roslyn Zinn had a strong interest in theater, she as an actress and he later as a playwright.
† Jennifer Adhianbo Ragwar was a Spelman (class of 1963) student from Kenya. Zinn, as an avid supporter of international exchange programs, was close to almost all the African students at Spelman and was deeply impressed by their intellectuality and political sophistication.
‡ Esta Bezhura was a Spelman (class of 1965) student from Uganda.
§ Anna Jo Weaver was a white Spelman exchange student from Bethel College in Kansas. She was involved in the battle to desegregate Atlanta's hotels.
¶ Howard and Roslyn Zinn's son Jeff Zinn.
** MacVicar was Spelman's infirmary, and the campus building where the Zinn family apartment was located.

Tonight hope to take some students to Emory foreign-correspondent roundtable. First day of classes. Do tsarist background of revolution.

Earlier Jan. 2

Conference with Manley. Told him I sought conference because it was clear our relationship had deteriorated and I was bothered about this—that there was conflict between us which probably couldn't be completely overcome because we had such different views, but perhaps atmosphere could be less strained. He said this past year had been particularly bad in this regard—every time he was away and returned, he faced a crisis (last spring, with student petition, and AAUP* letters on salary and student newspaper) and this time, with 5 suspended students and student uprising (he said students talked of being engaged in a "revolution" and wondered if they got that in their classes. I said probably—that as a result of classes they did a lot of reading, and in reading bound to encounter revolution). Said he heard from some faculty that other faculty had helped students draw up petitions—I said he had false information that we had not, that all this arose out of intense student feeling and he should recognize this—he said we'd been supporting students—I said yes, I had, and would support them in matters where I thought they were right—he said I should consult faculty and take things up in faculty channels before expressing myself on these issues—I said I thought faculty members, and I, had right to express ourselves any time we wanted—he said he had made it clear to petitioners of last spring that some committee would be set—or that they should ask for this—to go over rules—but then they went ahead with petition, and it wasn't necessary—I said if students thought petition was necessary, that was up to them, and they had perfect right. He said he disagreed with my letter in student paper saying students had right to bypass channels like in sit-ins, that Spelman not like sit-in situation because no discrimination involved—I agreed no discrimination of that sort involved, but similar in questions of democracy—he said he was concerned about faculty members['] chief role as a scholar—I said I couldn't have [a] wall between myself as teacher in classroom and concern for student rights that my subject involved democracy, liberty[,] etc. and it would be meaningless to teach it in theory and ignore it right-round us in practice—he said we wanted to overturn the school—it had certain rules and regulations—I said I didn't advocate disobeying rules, but trying to get them changed, that Spelman mustn't be overturned, but must change to meet new times. He said Spelman a small private Christian college (I detected, am I too sensitive[?], an emphasis on Christian†) and it had to stick to its basic character. I

---

*   American Association of University Professors.

†   Zinn was referring here to his being Jewish and wondering if there was an anti-Semitic edge to Manley's phrasing, or whether his Jewish background simply made him overly sensitive, reading too much into Manley's "Christian" college emphasis. Spelman College's motto was "Our Whole School for Christ."

said it could stick to its basic character and still be a more liberal organization. He said he could find complaints about me too—I said I'd like to hear them—he said complaints on my being late to class last year (I had thought from his long harping on some secret complaints that something big was in his mind!). I said probably true, but many appointments in Non-Western program, beside[s] I always kept class overtime so they got their full time and more. He said he could create crises too—like when Esta, Staughton [and] I picketed on Cuba*—he didn't think anyone should embarrass national administration[,] he had phone calls on us—had thought of calling us in but desisted because we were in conflict at [the] time and we'd think him vindictive—but wanted us to be sure we were identifying us as individuals and not rep[resenting] College (I was relieved that *this* was basis of his concern and not challenging our right to picket and told him we made sure always to say we were individuals).

I suggested more representative committees, with both conservative, liberal people represented—he said he would give this thought.

Said he didn't object to a committee to go over all the rules, etc. (providing administration represented[)].

All in all friendly discussion, atmosphere better at end, even though disagreement remains.

Evening: Joan Browning calls—is about to be sec[retar]y in Ga. State philosophy office, had to sign loyalty thing with long list organizations including Atlanta Peace Council (which he used to take strong stand on Cuba, meets at Quaker House).

Thurs. eve—Jan. 3

Gordon Sugarman[†] called, I had called him yesterday on Myla's request to do something about Pat Linch, 22-year-old folk singer jailed New Years Eve for non-support of wife and two kids—he'd been here a few times, sang some wonderful things for us—thin sliver of a beatnik. Sugarman responded so nicely—went down to county jail today, spoke an hour with Pat and wife Barbara (who he says is fine mature girl works at Ga. Tech)—Pat needs job, will try—is on probation a year. Pat will call me tonight he said, but hasn't.

---

*   Refers to a protest that Zinn and his colleagues Staughton Lynd and Esta Seaton participated in in downtown Atlanta opposing President Kennedy's decision to blockade Cuba during the Cuban Missile Crisis in October 1962.

†   Gordon Sugarman was an Atlanta attorney.

Wed.—Jan. 2

Meeting with Dorothy Dawson,* Staughton, and Harvard fellow Robb Burlage, very bright guy interested in economics of South,† works with Tom Pettigrew‡ and Roger Hagan.§ Discussed training session of one month in Mississippi for college kids about to go into voter registration.

Thurs. Jan. 3

Instead of Tsarist Russia, which I started on, got off [in Russian history class] on Jews under Tsar, discussed evaluation of nations like Soviet Russia, different—possible, bases, all valid—one of these bases the past, so Tsarist Russia knowledge necessary. Bostic (heavy, tough fellow who works at Americana Motel) said how come all Jews rich—how come they stick together (admiringly, sort of), thinks they're specially ambitious—I talked about poor Jews, in Russia (told Sholom Aleichem story,)¶ in US (NYC factories, etc.), said groups do have diff[erent] characteristics, from hist[orical] experience, but no innate special mystical quality to a group which is independent of experience.

In US History [class], discussed 19th century, Haymarket Affair,** AFL,†† Debs,‡‡ labor, class, the poor as "invisible" men then and now, the aristocracy of labor today hiding the rest, the problem of justice as in Haymarket where all procedures prop-

---

* Dorothy Dawson, a civil rights activist at the University of Texas, was assistant director of the Voter Education Project.

† Robb Burlage was a civil rights worker at the University of Texas, and husband of Dorothy Dawson. Burlage contributed to the economics section of Students for a Democratic Society's (SDS) Port Huron Statement and also was the prime author of the founding document of its southern counterpart, the Southern Student Organizing Committee.

‡ Thomas Pettigrew was professor of social relations at Harvard University and served on the editorial board of *Phylon*, published by Atlanta University.

§ Roger Hagan was a Harvard historian and editor of the newsletter of the antinuclear Committee of Correspondence.

¶ Zinn was referring to Sholem Aleichem (Sholem Rabinovitz), a novelist, humorist, and key Yiddish literary figure, whose stories of Jewish life in tsarist Russia Zinn used in his Russian history and literature classes.

** The Haymarket affair in Chicago in 1886 began when workers gathered to protest antilabor violence against strikers as part of the eight-hour-day movement. A bomb went off at the demonstration killing eight, leading to a red scare and a wave of xenophobia, targeting immigrant anarchists who were blamed for the bombing, culminating in a rushed trial in which eight anarchists were convicted without evidence for the fatal bombing—and in 1887 four were hung and another committed suicide in a frame-up that became a cause célèbre for the international anarchist movement.

†† The American Federation of Labor was the most influential craft union federation in the early twentieth-century United States.

‡‡ Eugene V. Debs was leader of the American Railway Union, the Pullman rail strike, and the American Socialist Party, who ran as that party's candidate for president of the United States.

erly gone through (obvious, to some, I think, was analogy with recent judicial experience here).

Thurs. eve Jan. 3

Guy Carawan* called, just moved to Atlanta, wants to take one of my courses. Wife† and little boy. Has ap[artmen]t in Negro neighborhood.

Rakulski‡ [Rukalski] came in (Roz§ away at Emory)[,] glowing about Mexico. Brought us a bottle of coffee lique[u]r. How free, how natural, how unconventional people live there, he said. And no consciousness of color. "And then back in N[ew] Orleans on the limousine from the airport, I said to the driver 'New Orleans! A nice city.' And he said (Rakulski imitated the Southern accent!) "Yeah, except for the niggers." Rakulski's face & voice changed. "I wanted to smack the bastard in the face!" . . . "But, oh, Mexico, black and white & café au lait—who knows, who cares—wonderful!"

Also at Carawans met Dorothy Cotton¶ again—both of us had been asked to leave post office below federal courthouse in Albany** because "no loitering"—postmaster didn't like Negro-white talking together—it made him furious.

[The first two paragraphs of this second Thurs. evening Jan. 3 diary entry = H]

Fri. Jan. 4

Went to Andy Young's†† house to meet Guy Carawan, folksinger, wife and little boy. Bunch of people. Sang. Coincidence—met Charles Wingdale (now attending [Booker T.] Wash[ington High School] though at night, working for SNCC office in day)[,] the young fellow whose petition on the bulletin board of Lee County Training School James Mays had shown me, which got him expelled. Then joined SNCC in

---

*   Guy Carawan, folk singer and folklorist, was the music director of the Highlander Folk School. Along with Pete Seeger, he adapted and spread to the civil rights movement the song that would become its anthem, "We Shall Overcome."
†   Guy Carawan's wife, Candie Carawan, was a singer who performed and recorded with him.
‡   Zygmunt Rukalski was a professor of French at Spelman.
§   Roslyn (Roz) Zinn, wife of Howard Zinn.
¶   Dorothy Cotton was a civil rights activist who taught in the Southern Christian Leadership Conference's Citizenship Training School.
**   Zinn had spent time in Albany, Georgia documenting the freedom movement's battle against the local white supremacist power structure in a study for the Southern Regional Council. See, Howard Zinn, *Albany: A Study in National Responsibility* (Atlanta: Southern Regional Council, 1962).
††   Andrew Young, SCLC leader and adviser to Martin Luther King Jr. Later served as mayor of Atlanta and as U.S. ambassador to the United Nations.

voter registration [in] Lee and Terrell Counties.* "Hard to get people registered. Got to talk so long to each one. Lots of people didn't want to be seen with me." Went to Shreveport for SNCC, called in by FBI, they were nasty—he feels sure they tipped off others of his presence because he got threatening phone calls, etc. and people he was staying with had to ask him to leave. FBI man said[,] "You were mixed up in that voter registration mess weren't you?" (As if he'd done something awful.) He'd gone down to register in Leesburg & registrar said[,] "You been expelled from school—you can't register to vote." House was shot up same night as James Mays. Baby sister's head missed by inches. Folks moved to Florida right after.

[Entire Jan. 4 diary entry = H]

[Jan. 4 diary entry was written on the flip side of the following flyer from a previous year's Non-Western program lecture series, which is included here as it offers a window onto the kind of academic events Zinn was organizing in his late Spelman years. —RC]

[PLEASE POST
NON-WESTERN PROGRAM
(China, India, Africa)

Atlanta University
Clark College
Interdenominational Theological Center
Morehouse College
Morris Brown College
Spelman College

Mailing Address:
Non-Western Program
Spelman College
Atlanta 3, Georgia
Phone (9 A.M.–1 P.M.)
525-8700

VISITING LECTURERS—SPRING SEMESTER 1961–62
(All public lectures at Dean Sage Hall, Atlanta University, 8 P.M.)

---

*   Lee and Terrell counties, in southwest Georgia, were sites of major SNCC civil rights organizing in the early 1960s.

Tuesday, March 6 (Revised date)

PROF. JOHN K. FAIRBANK: Harvard University; author, *The United States and China, East Asia: The Great Tradition*, and many other works; lecturer at Tsing Hua University in Peiping, 1933–34; war-time American official in Chungking.

Subject: "Why the Communists Won in China"

Wednesday, April 18

PROF. PING-CHIA KUO: Southern Illinois University; former official of the Koumintang government; author of *China: New Age and New Outlook*.

Subject: "The Challenge of Red China"

Thursday, May 10 (Three participants in Town Hall Forum)

PROF. RICHARD WALKER: University of South Carolina; author of *China Under Communism, The Continuing Struggle*, and other works; lecturer at National War College in Washington.

MR. ALLEN S. WHITING: Department of State; formerly with Rand [RAND] Corporation; author of *China Crosses the Yalu, Sinkiang, Pawn or Pivot?*, and other books; recently in the Far East.

MR. WILLIAM WORTHY: correspondent, *Baltimore Afro-American*; visitor to Red China; Nieman Fellow at Harvard University.

Subject: "The United States and Red China"

Sat. Jan. 5

Betty Stevens* called. Prexy† summoned whole student council to meet this AM with him, Dean of Women, Ass't Dean, Registrar, and faculty members who are on B[oar]d of Re[view].& Judiciary Board. In general a calling down for recent student protests against suspension of five, particularly directed against Betty but without calling her name—talked about bad leadership, bad citizenship, criticized Betty saying to meeting she would not go to Blue & White Banquet‡ if Marie Thomas couldn't go. Said don't confuse democratic theory with situation here. Started with quotation read by Ass[istan]t Dean from book saying a private college supported by private funds could not have all the freedoms you have out in society or something like that, that students didn't pay enough at Spelman to warrant their assuming so much

---

* Betty Stevens (Walker) was a student (Spelman class of 1964) of Zinn's who played a leading role in the student government as well as in the protests against Jim Crow off campus and paternalistic social and political restrictions on Spelman students on campus.

† "Prexy" was a term used to refer to a college president—in this case, President Manley.

‡ This banquet was an annual Spelman tradition celebrating the achievements of its honor students.

preorogative [*sic*], said he was discussing the economics of it to set a tone for the discussion. Challenged students to tell right then and there of "corruption" they spoke about in administration, but they decided t[h]is wasn't place. Betty told them they couldn't tell this adequately to admin[istration] because it was the party involved. Manley said he hoped such things wouldn't happen again. Criticized editor [of Spelman's student] newspaper for only printing 400 copies when usual total was more (was he trying to get at her for printing my letter?).

Sat. [Jan. 5]

News of possible Fulbright to Finland.

Sun. eve. Jan. 6

Went to Callenwald (Candler Estate) for Druid Hills Arts Council Twelfth Nite—A monstrous, magnificent mansion set in the midst of a wooded area of Briarcliff Road, all built by Coco [*sic*] Cola! And the Emory University set dressed up for 12th Nite, some in costumes—all white—a combination of charming, protected children, ridiculous adults, nice people—all white, white (this is what happens, I guess, when you've been living in a Negro community, from being conscious of negroes present, you become conscious of their being absent). The young people were good in their little theatre pieces—Jeff as jester in Twelfth Nite, Myla as Kate in Taming of the Shrew.

Later, home, up to Lynds,* where Vincent & Rose Marie Harding[†] visiting with their new-born girl Rachel. Vincent had copy of Ga. State loyalty form with fantastically long list of subversive organizations, where even if your father, mother, step-sister was a member you must report it—on it is Atlanta Peace Council, of which Vincent & Staughton are members at Quaker House, but decided it must refer to some old Atlanta Peace Council since this one is of new vintage. Discussed Spelman situation; Vincent pointed out administration view of our girls as special, not like Vassar, Smith etc. is the segregationist argument.

---

* Zinn's colleague Staughton Lynd and his wife, Alice Lynd.
† Vincent Harding headed Atlanta's Mennonite House. He was a leading civil rights activist, adviser to Martin Luther King Jr. as well as an antiwar activist (who drafted King's historic Riverside Church speech against the Vietnam War). Harding was also a leading historian of black America, and a friend of Zinn's, who would succeed him as chair of Spelman's history department. Rose Marie Harding, his wife, shared his activist trajectory.

Mon. Jan. 7

Bacote* came over lunch-time. He is . . . [now] member of advisory Committee to Civil Rights Commission in Ga., also member of Congressional District Democratic Committee. Told us of Peter Zack Geer† (who'd encouraged violence at U of Ga‡) calling him, thru ch'n [chairman] of County Committee—close friend of Geer—in runoff with Maddox,§ trying to arrange meeting at Bacote's house—obviously trying to get Negro support in his run-off. Bacote didn't want word to get out that Geer was in his house (a reversal of the old business of the white wanting the Negro to come in the back door!), so switched to another place, and asked that Geer meet with group rather than just with him. Geer has met with new Negro Senator LeRoy Johnson,¶ long conference, cordial, promised him several committee posts and no gallery segregation. Bacote told of Charlayne Hunter** visiting Talmadge†† in Washington— most cordially received ("Anything I can do for you, let me know") whereas Russell‡‡ cold. Bacote says Talmadge will bend, privately tells Negroes "You know, I have to say those things for publication; I know segregation is on its way out."

Bacote reminisced as usual, of Ben Davis Jr. as young Atlanta lawyer out of Amherst and Harvard, being put behind stacks in state library, wrote protesting to Gov. Richard Russell, got back letter "Dear Ben, sorry, etc. It's rule, signed Richard Russell, Gov. State of Ga. Davis wrote letter "Dear Dick . . . protesting, etc. Signed Benjamin Davis Jr. Counsellor at Law". Told of Davis defending Herndon [in] 1932 at famous criminal anarchy case,§§ and smoking in court so held [in] contempt of court, fined

---

*   Clarence Bacote was an exchange professor of history from Atlanta University, who was teaching at Spelman in 1963.

†   Peter Zack Geer was Georgia's lieutenant governor.

‡   During the desegregation crisis at the University of Georgia in January 1961 Geer had praised the segregationist students who rioted outside the dormitory of Charlayne Hunter, the first African American female student to attend that university.

§   Lester Maddox, segregationist demagogue and future (1967–71) governor of Georgia.

¶   Leroy Johnson in 1963 became the first African American elected to the Georgia state senate since Reconstruction.

**   Charlayne Hunter, the University of Georgia's first African American student, who together with Hamilton Holmes, desegregated the University of Georgia in January 1961. Hunter(-Gault) would later become a prominent correspondent for the New York Times, PBS, and NPR.

††   Senator Herman Talmadge of Georgia, an avid segregationist.

‡‡   Richard Russell, Georgia's senior senator, a segregationist and leader of the U.S. Senate's powerful anti–civil rights faction.

§§   In 1932 Angelo Herndon, a young black Communist, was indicted under an archaic Georgia law against servile insurrection for leading a demonstration of Atlanta's unemployed. Davis and the International Labor Defense challenged both that law and the exclusion of blacks from the jury in Herndon's case. Herndon was convicted and sentenced to twenty years, but after four years the Supreme Court reversed the conviction and freed him.

$5, asked Bacote to lend him money to pay. Davis spoke two hours sit-in cases out of his head, lawyer for state had pile of books he consulted.[*]

Tues. Jan. 8

Jean Berrien told me last night Lana Taylor . . . may come back to finish at Spelman next year, says she wants us to go ahead on her "citizenship" problem.[†]

Last night Betty Stevens came over to tell of Dean calling in individual student council members, telling the first that she stood on shaky ground as regards citizenship and shouldn't talk of "corruption" in Dean's office.

This afternoon, US history class heard from Sandara [Sandra] Marshall[‡] and Loretta Mathews on Bellamy's Looking Backward.[§] Led to a wild, bang-up discussion, hard to control at times, on whether the girls would want to live in such a society, Demaris Allen[¶] saying vociferously it took all the romance out of life, Eileen Terry saying people would be mean no matter . . . [what], the two others defending the book, saying you couldn't tell from their report, but it was really a great society—they were both captivated by the book—Demaris got a picture of 1984, and perhaps Brave New World and 1984 have pushed out of the consciousness of this generation those old great utopias.[**] I talked about being culture-bound, not being able to envision totally new situations, and about whether "human nature" works against a society without fierce competition.

In evening, India Seminar with Prudence Meyer, expert on Indian art who showed beautiful slides but talked too much, I thought, about them. "Notice the curving off to the left, notice the intricate rich work at the base, notice the shape of the arms, the broadness of the shoulders . . . ." I may be over-cynical but I prefer to look silently and see what I see (maybe *some* pointing out, of things I wouldn['t] be likely to pay attention to, would be okay[)]—but words, words, words diminish the emotional effect of looking in silence—maybe musical background would be better.

Tues. AM Met Betty Darden,[††] agreed to go Monday to test out galleries at Senate[‡‡]

---

[*]   Davis, after his leading role in the Herndon case, became prominent in the Communist Party, and succeeded Adam Clayton Powell Jr. as Harlem's representative on the New York City Council.

[†]   Lana Taylor (Sims), a student of Zinn's, had lost her scholarship at Spelman because of her role in leading a student petition drive in 1962 on behalf of student rights, after the administration condemned that activism as "poor citizenship."

[‡]   Sandra Marshall, Spelman (class of 1965) student.

[§]   Edward Bellamy's Looking Backward (1888), a classic socialist utopian novel.

[¶]   Demaris Allen, Spelman student (class of 1964), who spent a year as a scholarship student in India.

[**]   The dystopian novels 1984 by George Orwell and Brave New World by Aldous Huxley.

[††]   Betty Darden, Spelman (class of 1965) student.

[‡‡]   Zinn and his students in 1957 and 1958 had visited the Georgia state legislature and defied the

on opening day with inauguration [of Leroy] Johnson [the first African American elected to the Georgia state senate since Reconstruction].

[Marginalia: to the left of this last Jan. 8 entry Zinn wrote "1963"]

Wed. nite Jan. 9

Went to Non-Western lecture, again Prudence Meyer of Tulane, slides on India, with interminable commentary on each one, perfect example of Zen complaint of Western verbosity, telling the audience exactly what they see, the words a great cloud in the way of the art. And arrogant in her descriptions of Indians "there are so many abnormal types in India."

Thurs. [Jan. 10] PM

In US Hist, discussed Progressive movement reforms, making point that TR[,] Taft[,] Wilson[*] were *re-acting* to pressures (of Populist heritage,[†] IWW,[‡] Socialists, strikes, muckrakers, etc.) —but they get credit, as Hartsfield[§] does, in history books, though Harstfield reacted to Negro upsurge. In Russian [history class], went over days between March & Nov. Lenin at Finland Station, Edmund Wilson,[¶] John Reed[**]—powerful role of Lenin, the confusion, the ordinariness, of a Revolution, (of Krupskaya[††] not wanting to catch the very next train [out] of Switzerland because she had to return some books to the library!).
Thurs. Ran into Ruby Doris Smith[‡‡]—she finishes school this semester, will do field work for SNCC thereafter. Told her [I] want to tape her experiences.[§§]

---

color line in its galleries, and were planning to do so again on the occasion of Leroy Johnson's inauguration in 1963 as the first African American state senator since Reconstruction.
* Presidents Theodore Roosevelt, William Howard Taft, and Woodrow Wilson.
† Populist heritage refers to the farmer's revolt in the late nineteenth-century United States.
‡ International Workers of the World, a revolutionary syndicalist labor union.
§ William B. Hartsfield was Atlanta's longest-serving mayor, whose tenure extended through five terms—1937–41, 1942–62. Zinn thought that Black Atlanta and its civil rights activists rather than Hartsfield deserved credit for the limited progress the city had made toward racial equality during his mayoralty.
¶ Literary critic Edmund Wilson's *To the Finland Station* (1940), a classic account of socialist and Communist thought from the French Revolution to the Bolshevik Revolution.
** John Reed, author of the classic eyewitness account of the Bolshevik Revolution, *Ten Days That Shook the World* (1919).
†† Nadezhda Krupskaya, Bolshevik revolutionary and politician, wife of Vladimir Lenin.
‡‡ Ruby Doris Smith Robinson, Spelman (class of 1962), was a key leader of early SNCC.
§§ Zinn did pioneering work in oral history, recording the memories of SNCC organizers such as Smith, and using them in his *SNCC: The New Abolitionists* (1964).

Thurs. eve. Town Hall meeting[.] Eugene Patterson,* Macon Mayor Ed Wilson (pleas-ant, mild, friendly, judicious "ineffectual" Roz says but I liked him) and Sam Williams.† Sam in usual form. After Patterson & Wilson (topic was "The South Ten Years Hence") gave rosy picture, he tore it to shreds (tokenism, the Peyton Road barricade,‡ the do-nothing moderates, lack of jobs for Negroes). Hit Patterson's emphasis on coming million-dollar plants, said it was moral attitude toward human beings which was the key thing in the South and this didn't look good because South hadn't yet come to say that men are equal. Question period: Sam Williams made hardest, most unequiv-ocal statement I've yet heard him make on South. That he studied church history, and church has Never been in forefront, has always followed, and we mustn't expect church to lead[,] its role is to sanctify what others have done. Patterson was better in question period (when asked did he disagree with Sam Williams said basically no, was uncomfortable at some things he said, but not real disagreement, Sam's view-point was a necessary and important one)—said he had faith in Southern white that when he turned would turn hard, pointed to Populists, told of Atl[anta] Const[itu-tion] compositors, printers, country-fellows, arch-segregationists, always voted for Jimmy Davis,§ but this time, on basis of Davis'[s] anti-labor stand, voted for Weltner.¶ Bread and butter over segregation. Both Sam and Patterson said at different poi[n]ts must change Southern white behavior before change his mind—squares exactly with what I've just been writing about. Later, at Sam Cook** reception after town hall, Sam again powerful on church, with Father Scott†† uncomfortable nearby, asking, then why are you in the church, and Sam said[,] "To me the church is Jesus Christ." Implication was, didn't believe in God but in Jesus, in the moral Jesus. Sam said was in church because it gave him a good platform, that church was incorrigible.

---

*   Eugene Patterson was editor of *The Atlanta Constitution*.

†   Sam Williams was professor and chair of the Morehouse College philosophy department, pres-ident of the Atlanta NAACP, pastor of Friendship Baptist Church, and active in the Southern Chris-tian Leadership Conference.

‡   In January 1963, under pressure from whites opposed to racially integrating their neighbor-hood, Atlanta mayor Ivan Allen Jr. authorized the erection of a wooden barricade separating the white and black sections of Atlanta's west end. Denounced as Atlanta's "Berlin Wall" by civil rights activists, the Peyton Road barricade was removed after the mayor agreed to do so under court order in March 1963.

§   James C. (Jimmy) Davis was a segregationist who served eight terms in Congress representing Georgia's 5th congressional district.

¶   Charles L. Weltner, a moderate, defeated Jimmy Davis in the 1964 Democratic primary. In Con-gress, Weltner was one of only eight southern House members to vote for the Civil Rights Act of 1964. He also voted for the Voting Rights Act in 1965.

**   Samuel DuBois Cook, professor of political science at Atlanta University and friend of Zinn's. Cook, a Morehouse classmate of Martin Luther King Jr., would later become the first black professor at a historically white southern university (Duke University).

††   Father Warren Scott of the Canterbury House (Episcopal) at Atlanta University, and acting Spelman minister.

Thurs. [L]unch at Canterbury House, QV Williamson* on Peyton Road, very interest-ing, articulate Southern-type speaker. Drew laughter again and again. Said he and Empire Realty didn't blockbust—that meant surreptitious and one block at a time[.] "We do it openly, and we encircle the area by a pincers movement and then move in and mop up[.]" Said first whites to sell sell at loss, first Negroes get bargain (because whites had had trouble selling, so finally sold to Negroes), but then Negroes pay 10–20% more, which is Negro market. Said Peyton Road houses $40–80,000 homes. Clinton Warner's $65,000 (Esta [Seaton], sitting across, gasped). Said more housing integration Atlanta in early [19]30's than now. Federal Govt. in early 30's imposed seg[regation] with public housing. Said no such thing as barrier to Negroes buying homes. When Westview cemetery put up as a barrier, hundreds of acres, they simply went around it. I asked if ever conflict between real estate profit and moral aim of in-tegration. He evaded. Said Mayor Allen not a politician, hence didn't handle Peyton barrier skillfully. Said once whites make an issue of Negroes coming in, it speeds up process of whites leaving!

Paper this morning announces Assembly galleries will be desegregated Monday! (Geer never answered my letter but this is good enough).†

[Final two sentences of the last Jan. 10 entry = H]

Fri. eve. Jan. 11

Monroe Berger, Princeton sociologist, came to spend 10 days or so [on] his project on the changing Negro community since WWII (also to inspect on Non-West[ern] program; he says he is expected to write a favorable report, since the Foundation wants these programs to expand). Lois and Charlie Moreland‡ came over in the eve-ning, and the five of us talked until one, about race, the Black Muslims, academic freedom (Berger wants to visit our classes, Lois once got into trouble with Manley because she invited Griffin[, author of] Black Like Me§ to her class and he was go-ing to write a book and she was supposed to ask administrative permission, I stood with Lois, Charlie for [not] asking permission, Berger talked about responsibility of teacher as well as freedom, said should ask administration in case like that Lois & I

*   Q. V. Williamson, black realtor, who in 1965 would be elected Atlanta's first black alderman since Reconstruction.

†   Zinn is referring to the galleries of the Georgia state legislature, which he had been working to desegregate since 1957. He had recently written to Lieutenant Governor Peter Zack Geer urging this desegregation, but had received no response from this segregationist state official.

‡   Lois Baldwin Moreland was a professor of political science and sociology at Spelman.

§   John Howard Griffin's Black Like Me (1961) was an account of this white author, who darkened his skin color so that we would be mistaken for an African American, and traveled across the South documenting the racism he encountered.

argued nothing secret about a class and teacher should decide for himself). Berger says Muslims won't commit violence, Lois says they will. Helped him draw up list of Atlanta Negroes to talk to. Discussed Spelman.

Even discussed (Berger had noted in Jet* Negro beauty measurements showed larger hips than bust) Negro hip measurements! He asked if Negroes ever deliberately excluded whites from an evening party because they wouldn't "fit"; Lois said she knew one faculty member who would, Charlie said he didn't think so. Charlie says more matter of individuals than color.

Saturday, Jan. 12

Visited Roslyn Pope Walker† & her husband in their new apt. New baby—beautiful.

[Entire Jan. 12 diary entry = H]

Sunday Jan. 13

Took Jeff to Quaker House. Great Books program—discuss Epictetus[.]‡
Evening: Monroe Berger interviewed *Julian Bond*§ in our living room.

Julian said at Nashville SNCC conference a leader said integration into *existing* white society not enough, need to change this society. Julian agrees.

Said he & others opposed Kennedy's blockade of Cuba.

Said non-violence only a tactic with him.

Told of start [of Atlanta] sit-in movement at Yates and Milton¶ a few days after Greensboro sit-in Feb[ruary] 1960. Another fellow** approached him about doing something—they divided up the store, talked to people, called a meeting.

---

*   *Jet* was a weekly magazine that reported on and for black America.
†   Roslyn Pope (Walker), was a Spelman (class of 1960) alumna. She had been a student of Zinn's, a Merrill scholar, president of the Spelman student body, and a leader of the Atlanta sit-in movement; she was also the primary author of that movement's founding statement, the Appeal for Human Rights. She was arrested at night in a car with Zinn in 1960 in Atlanta, an incident President Manley would use four years later to charge Zinn (falsely) with having an affair with Pope—in an effort to stave off Zinn's appeal of his firing. See pp. 67–73 of the introduction.
‡   Epictetus was a Stoic philosopher in ancient Greece.
§   Julian Bond, as a Morehouse student, was, along with Lonnie King, the initial organizer of the Atlanta student movement. He coauthored its Appeal for Human Rights with Roslyn Pope, became a key SNCC leader, and would later be elected to the Georgia legislature—which only seated him after a U.S. Supreme Court decision ruled it unconstitutional for him to have been denied his seat because of his opposition to the Vietnam War.
¶   Yates and Milton was a drugstore and a kind of coffeehouse on the corner of Fair and Chestnut streets that served as a meeting place for Atlanta University Center students.
**   Lonnie King, a Morehouse football star, and key organizer of the Atlanta sit-in movement.

Are Negroes diff[erent] than whites? Yes. As mothers & fathers—as friends to friends? No. Knows it's there but doesn't know how to define it—Greater sympathy for suffering? That's close to it but not it.

Do Black Muslims hurt the cause? No. They've done good things with people, made decent people out of alcoholics and perverts. Haven't seen them *starting* violence. Serve as gadfly to both whites & Negroes.

Negroes envy them—clean-cut, attractive people who say things other Negroes want to say. People admire Malcolm X's *ability* even if they know his *content* is wrong.

Their anti-Christianity doesn't bother Negroes.

Are you a Christian? Don't belong to church.

SNCC has 50 people—chairman is a Jew (Chuck McDew)—when he was at SC State* when white ministers showed up rel[igious] emp[hasis] week & only rabbi let him come to his church—read passage in Talmud[,] "If I am not for other men then who is for me?" He works out of NY raising funds. Chuck expelled from SC State. Now wants to go to Brandeis.

Core [CORE] got lots of money from Freedom Rides. They abandoned Freedom Rides at (where bus burned) Montgomery. Then Nashville [SNCC] kids & Freedom Ride Coordinating Committee went on to Jackson. (SDS 112 E. 19 St. NYC—Chuck McDew there).

Parents approve of what Julian is doing now but want him to support wife & child better.

What of *Negro* radio stations? First resented it. Now, why not[?] (One Atlanta station owned by whites.)

(As for Berger, Roz says, truly "an uninvolved person," the "objective" scholar—writes books, gets grants, doesn't really care, is interested, bemused, but not moved.)

[This entire Jan. 13 diary entry = H; at the top of the second page of this Jan. 13 diary entry Zinn had handwritten: "Julian cont[inued]."]

Sun. Jan. 13

Dotty Dawson called about some weekly discussion group, and also to inform me that in three separate instances somebody had referred to me as a Communist or something like that 1—in her presence at an intergroup meeting where couples discussed [plans] to lead summer voter projects and we were brought up [by] this tall handsome Negro woman from AFSC[†] in Philly said she heard from NAACP office

---

*   South Carolina State College in Orangeburg, a historically black college.

†   American Friends Service Committee, a Quaker peace and social justice organization.

in NY that I was controversial figure[,] 2—Wyatt Walker[*] heard this bruited about at SNCC conference in Nashville, and 3—Wyatt told Jane Bond who told Dotty that in Les Dunbar's office, guy from Anti-Defamation League (!) said I was a Communist, and Les (to put him off, perhaps, Dotty says) said he would "investigate"!

[Dotty Dawson = H]

Mon. Jan. 14   State leg[islature]

Roz & I and Betty Stevens & Betty Darden & Sandra Shorter[†] went to the opening session of the General Assembly to see Le Roy [Leroy] Johnson sworn in as Senator & to participate in the desegregation of the gallery. We did. Stares & all—but not like before. There was resigned resentful acceptance but not hate bordering on violence as in the three times before.[‡] Pat Watters looked up saw us chuckled.[§] Johnson & three white senators laid their left hands together on one Bible. One of the senators kept his hand off. Next to Betty a stiff white woman played musical chairs, moving away as Betty moved into the empty seat between them to get a better view of the Senate. Roz & Sandra used the restroom marked "white ladies only." Went to Stouffers for lunch after that. Girls told me two more instances of Spelmania:[¶] Manley telling Marie Thomas (one of the suspended five) to get off campus (she had come to get something out of her room). And the senior class, wanting to dedicate the yearbook to Irene Asbury,[**] told it wasn't good idea.

Letter from Leuchtenburg[††] saying nice things about Albany Report.[‡‡] Letter

---

[*]   Wyatt Tee Walker, executive director of the Southern Christian Leadership Conference.

[†]   Sandra Elaine Shorter was a Spelman (class of 1964) student.

[‡]   Zinn is referring here to the three previous attempts, dating back to 1957, that he and his students and colleagues made to challenge the racially segregated seating in the galleries of the Georgia state legislature.

[§]   Pat Watters was the city editor and columnist for the *Atlanta Journal*.

[¶]   "Spelmania" was a term coined by Zinn referring to what he saw as the mania of the Spelman administration about issuing and enforcing infantilizing social and political restrictions on students and punishing those who challenged or violated those restrictions.

[**]   Irene Asbury was the former dean of women at Spelman, who resigned from her deanship at Albany State after its president, William Dennis, refused to stand up to local racists and punished students and suspended their student government for supporting Albany's civil rights movement. As to exactly which of Dennis's antimovement actions precipitated her resignation, there are conflicting accounts. See n. 124 of the Introduction in this volume, *Howard Zinn's Southern Diary: Sit-ins, Civil Rights, and Black Women's Student Activism*, pp. 249–50.

[††]   Columbia University history professor William Leuchtenburg.

[‡‡]   Zinn's initial report for the Southern Regional Council on race and the freedom struggle in Albany, which was released in January 1962 and published in its final form later that year as *Albany: A Study in National Responsibility*.

from Chris Allen's two friends in England. Letter from Jeanne— is marrying Nigerian & will go there.

[Entire Jan. 14 diary entry = H]

[n.d.]

[A]n outstanding personality in society, while standing outside of it enough to be a sharp critic of it.
Einstein rather than a Teller[*]
Tolstoy a Thoreau a Steinbeck rather than a Herman Wouk or Ayn Rand[†]
James Baldwin[‡] rather than a hack
a generation of DuBois and King Jr.[§]

Tues. Jan. 15

AAUP[¶] lunch, discussing salary & teaching criteria demanded by AEM[**] as basis for raises; afterward, Rukalski said: "How timid people are, afraid to speak; there's an atmosphere of fear all around here."

Monroe Berger sat in on my class, lecture on Age of Jazz or Age of Blues? and discussion.

---

[*]   Edward Teller was a Hungarian-born American nuclear physicist, known as "the father of the hydrogen bomb." An ardent anti-Communist and Cold Warrior, Teller was a key proponent of the thermonuclear arms race. He testified against J. Robert Oppenheimer, the former director of the Manhattan Project who had become a critic of that arms race in hearings that took away Oppenheimer's security clearance. Zinn was contrasting Teller and his use of science for war with the pre-eminent physicist of the twentieth century, Albert Einstein, who was a Cold War critic and had cofounded the Emergency Committee of Atomic Scientists to curtail the usage of nuclear weapons.
[†]   Here Zinn is favorably contrasting progressive writers—Leo Tolstoy, a pacifist; Henry David Thoreau, a proponent of civil disobedience; and John Steinbeck, who in his early work romanticized the struggles of workers and poor farmers—with writers who lacked progressive politics, such as Ayn Rand, who fetishized the free market, and war novelist Herman Wouk.
[‡]   James Baldwin, the African American novelist and essayist, whose writings challenged America to confront its history of racism, most notably in his best-selling *The Fire Next Time* (1963), published to coincide with and reflect upon the 100th anniversary of emancipation.
[§]   Zinn is referring to the 1960s generation of student civil rights activists as being shaped by the antiracist thought and activism of W. E. B. Du Bois and Martin Luther King Jr.
[¶]   Spelman's American Association of University Professors (AAUP) chapter.
[**]   President Albert E. Manley.

Dinner with him and Non-West[ern] Committee. Then Seminar, with 5 Indians leading discussions on various topics—quite poor on their part with the result, lively discussion—one-sided presentation of Kashmir, incredibly ill-informed presentation of border dispute with China, & other things, including statement less juvenile delinquency in India because of strict discipline for children which was immediately challenged. Berger said afterward how interesting, that Negroes had jumped on that because they were sensitive about Negro part in juvenile delinquency—I'm not so sure—they jumped on others with Kashmir and China and economic growth too.

Roz went to WILPF* meeting tonight with Mrs. Manley & Alice Lynd to see film on Sobell.†

Wed. Jan. 16

Bacote came by to tell me about going to the Governor's Inaugural Ball at the Dinkler Plaza last night. He was one of four Negro couples—Leroy Johnson & wife, Col. Walden & wife, Dr. Yancey and wife. First time in recent history, perhaps in all Ga. History, Negroes were at Ball. Everything went well. Sanders‡ Inaugural Speech yesterday the first one clean of racism. Even Geer fairly moderate, talking of states['] rights rather than segregation, but also state "responsibility."

The students are talking about a new project of the administration to improve table manners of students—lessons once a week or some such thing. Rukalski says: ["] it's an insult.["] We are translating two of his French stories. He wants us to go abroad with him to teach at some university in Peru or Mexico or who knows where.

Evening: Called students in Russia class to watch hour TV program narrated by Ernest Simmons§ (whom we had seen at Agnes Scott), of Russian literature, excerpts from: The Cherry Orchard (magnificent, moving performance of Jo Ann [Jo Van] Fleet), The Overcoat (a gem, just perfect, with students laughing occasionally at references to bureaucracy which they immediately applied to Spelman), Fathers & Sons, the Grand Inquisitor, & Dr. Zhivago.¶ A marvelous evening, worth ten of my classes in Russian literature, and the students were obviously thrilled, having met

---

*   Women's International League for Peace and Freedom.

†   Morton Sobell was tried and convicted of espionage charges with Julius and Ethel Rosenberg in 1951.

‡   Carl Sanders, Georgia governor, 1963–67.

§   Ernest J. Simmons, a founder of Russian studies in the United States, biographer of Chekhov, Pushkin, and Tolstoy, was professor of Russian literature and chair of the department of Slavic Languages and Culture at Columbia University when Zinn was a doctoral student there.

¶   These are all classic works in Russian literature: The Cherry Orchard (1904) is the last play by Anton Chekhov, The Overcoat (1842) is a short story by Nikolai Gogol, Fathers and Sons (1862) is a novel by Ivan Turgenev, "The Grand Inquisitor" is a poem from Fyodor Dostoevsky's novel The Brothers Karmazov (1880), and Dr. Zhivago (1958) is Boris Pasternak's dissident novel.

Simmons in person, having read Chekhov and Gogol and done a paper on the Grand Inquisitor scene, and having talked about the nihilists. It all came to life.

Spoke to Mrs. Macomson* on phone. An unusual, complex woman. Conservative about Spelman tradition, advanced in her views on world affairs (a hint of past leftism). She said she was furious at news that NEA† was adopting "code of ethics" for teachers, including provision that teachers must not bring their institution "into disrepute" or something like that; she noted it as attack on academic freedom, obnoxious to her.

Fri. Jan. 18

Lunch with Les Dunbar. He said he didn't say he would "investigate" or anything like that. But told the ADL man (it all came from the national office of the Anti-Defamation League) that both my ideological and policy stances, from what Dunbar knew, precluded my being a Communist. I asked Les his position on Communists in a civil rights organization. His reply was terse[:] "I don't want them." I said my view was that the only basis for acting against a person was specific empirical data showing this person was acting in a harmful way. I told Les that this was all a very slippery business anyway—how can we *know* a person is a Communist unless 1) person admits it 2) FBI or HUAC‡ charges—so that one could be acting—in other cases than these—on suspicion. Les said there are degrees of suspicion & he just made his own judgment each time. (Example: SCLC guy had been accused at HUAC Atlanta hearings—Les didn't buy that, *but* it worried him that the man had changed his name.)

Les gave me example (unwittingly) of how dangerous whole business is by telling me Roy Wilkins§ called him up to charge someone in Atlanta civil rights work. When he saw Wilkins in NY it turned out Wilkins had gotten data from someone else—Les himself, knowing the person, disbelieved it. But what if Les hadn't known the person?

Told me incidentally, only opposition to SNCC joining Atlanta council of human relations groups came from ADL, AJC, & NAACP! SRC & SCLC for them.¶

[Entire Jan. 18 diary entry = H]

---

*   Elizabeth Jackson Macomson, a professor of history and geography at Spelman, where she had taught since 1939. She was also a Spelman alumna.

†   National Education Association.

‡   House Committee on Un-American Activities, anti-Communist investigative committee of U.S. House of Representatives.

§   Roy Wilkins was the NAACP's executive director.

¶   ADL (Anti-Defamation League), AJC (American Jewish Committee), NAACP (National Association for the Advancement of Colored People), SRC (Southern Regional Council), SCLC (Southern Christian Leadership Conference).

Sat. Jan. 19

Sterling Lord Agency[*] wrote yesterday, sending back Stop-Off at Ludlow[†] saying there is "much, very much" that is good in it, but needs revision; they would like to represent me in other writing.

Jackie Wilkes of YWCA called to ask if I could lead summer project in Atlanta. I said no. She still wants me to give two keynote addresses at Y conference in March, on world affairs, and race relations.

Letter from Father Scott of Canterbury House this morning to tell me annual Conference of Episcopal Chaplains in Eight Southern States will meet at ITC[‡] in May, with theme "In Unity & Godly Love" and he'd like me and Lonnie Newsom[§] to speak to them on Albany situation. "Besides the factual information that you will be able to give them, I would like our chaplains to get to know you as a person because you have so much to offer us in your whole attitude toward people and life."

(This and YWCA request kind of ironic along with charges of communism.)

Sat. Jan. 19

Lois' reaction to Berger[:] "Cold. Divorced from life." Roz too. I see a little more warmth than they do, even if only in his own awareness of detachment.

Monroe Berger came over for a last chat before departure for Princeton. He's been here a little over a week in concentrated talk with Negroes in all sorts of situations. He spoke with relief[,] "I'll be so glad to get home and away from this race issue. I need a rest. I never realized how overwhelming, how ever present it is. And this only after a week. I begin to understand now what it must be like to live with it all your life—or rather, I only get a glimmer of this understanding. It's vicious, it blocks everything you want to do in life, it gets in the way of every normal activity."

We disputed a little about the future. He sees, after legal desegregation, a plateau, no real improvement, with whites continued to be prejudiced and no indication of change. Said "If you'd heard some of the conversations of white salesmen in the hotel . . . ." My argument: yes, it seems strong, and it is at the moment, but it can change quickly—with contact. When housing and jobs become open, when white

---

[*]   Sterling Lord was a literary agency based in New York that represented leading authors—and would represent Zinn in his publication of *The Southern Mystique*.

[†]   A Zinn manuscript on the Colorado labor wars centering on the Ludlow massacre of coal miners in 1914. The Ludlow massacre had been the subject of Zinn's master's thesis in history at Columbia University in 1952, and Zinn would write about it again in his *A People's History of the United States* (1980) and in *Three Strikes* (2010).

[‡]   Interdenominational Theological Center, an affiliate of the Atlanta University Center.

[§]   Zinn was referring to Lonnie Newsome, who was a professor at Atlanta University and president of its AAUP chapter.

salesmen begin to have lunch—thru business necessity—with Negroes and stay at the same hotel with them, and so on—I cited my warehouse experience. Although his father was workingclass he himself has been in the academic world practically all his mature life, and Princeton is a hot-house community.

Evening: Maloofs over. Ted said impressed with intelligence and fairness of judges in Fulton County Superior Court. Explained Judge Pye's* ruling on Senate voting (a fanatic segregationist, he'd ruled voting for state Senate should be by districts within the county rather than county-wide, thus assuring a Negro in the 38th district. But it also, Ted said, assured three or four *rural* reps in Fulton County by letting outside-Atlanta districts elect their own. Esta interrupted and said that was my Harper's thesis of value hierarchy borne out.[†]

After most people left, Harold Bardinelli, the Maloofs, Staughton remained and a coat-on, at-the-door question by Harold led to about two more hours of talk, centered on Myla (Dave was there too, impressively intelligent). Harold had asked what to tell a Northern white teacher thinking of teaching at Atlanta Univ. and this got into the new integrated high schools. Myla was wonderfully honest, telling how the five Negroes at Brown[‡] sit at one table and everyone else sits at others in cafeteria, that she couldn't do anything about it. He was as indignant not only at the situation, but at her, as I have been in the past, and now I could see myself, the aroused, angry revolutionary, expecting from a 16-year-old girl what 99% of adults could not do. Myla said, "I know it['] s wrong. I'm not like you Staughton. I'm not a radical, a revolutionary, an organizer, a doer. I don't have the courage. And I'm all alone. Maybe if I had one more person. Just one more person with me."[§] Staughton softened.

Maloofs, leaving at 3 AM, said "A most interesting evening."

---

*   Judge Durwood T. Pye was a segregationist known for his stiff sentences against activists involved in civil rights protests.

†   Refers to Zinn's main argument in his *Harper's* magazine article, "A Fate Worse Than Integration" (August 1959), 53–56, which was that among most white southerners there was an "unconscious hierarchy of values," and in it "segregation does not hold the highest rank." Thus, for example, most white southerners highly valued public education and so would rather see public schools remain open on a racially integrated basis than closed down (as far-right extremists would) to prevent their integration.

‡   Brown High School in Atlanta, which had begun to desegregate in 1961.

§   Myla does not think this diary entry fully conveys her experience at her desegregating school. And that is because neither her father nor any of the adults thought to ask her what it was like to be in that school. The focus instead was on what they thought was her personal responsibility to contribute to the process of racial integration. The reality was that Myla, as a transplant from the North, was herself an outsider, who found the school's social environment difficult and didn't feel able to contribute to the acceptance of the new black students. Nor was it clear to her that the black students sitting together in the cafeteria would have wanted her to make overtures to them. In other words, the school situation, and her own, were complicated, but that was not brought out in the discussion narrated in this diary entry. It was not until Myla was interviewed by Robert Coles, the

Sun. AM—

argued with Jeff who takes position "be natural" with Negroes, don't treat them differently in any way, don't go out of your way to be nice, with me trying to explain that in certain situations which are themselves unnatural, only an unnatural act can lead back towards the state of nature, that there are situations requiring "special" treatment.

Sun. Jan. 20, 1963

Evening. Spoke to Emory Liberal Club on "Jingoistic Liberalism" with very good discussion afterward. Roz thought talk was great but felt I downgraded, in question period, effectualness of talk, meetings, petitions, etc., because I said in this unusual situation some incredibly imaginative step was needed to get us out of trouble. I think she's right—that we can also make it thru attrition and time, and in this every bit of change in the ideological atmosphere helps.

Right after to Harry & Daisy Adlee for goodbye party to Sam Cook, going to be visiting prof. at U. of Illinois spring semester. Sam said again [he] would entrust Town Hall* to no one but me, tho several people called him asking for it. I asked how it would go with Clement† (who had said to Sam a few months ago—"Zinn has a bad reputation" with Sam answering "I think he has a very good one") and Sam said he thinks Clement won't object because Clement knows I'll do a good job.

Nora McNiven‡ who last week told Roz a hair-raising story about dropping a Negro student at the bus stop and then being followed by a car with white kids who kept bumping her pushing her off on the curb (this morning paper reports woman killed by bumping which hurled her from car)—told of policeman giving her traffic ticket, usually 4.50 or so, asking for address, saying "oh that nigger college" and she told him it's a Negro university and people don't use "nigger" any more and she ended up with $17.50 ticket.

Harvard psychiatrist studying integration, that she got to discuss what the experience of being in an integrating southern school had meant to her—and for her that encounter was memorable because no one before had thought to ask.

While Myla admires her father's political courage, she noted that when he acted in civil rights protests he was not alone as she was at her school. She came to feel that there was something of a "double standard here," since she was being asked to do alone what he had done in a politically embracing activist community. She also felt that her father, living and working in the friendly Spelman enclave, an almost entirely black environment, did not really understand what it was like for her, and how difficult it was to attend a school with predominantly poor white southern teenagers who viewed her more or less as different and alien. Myla Kabat-Zinn telephone interview with the author, April 8, 2016, notes in author's possession; Myla Kabat-Zinn email to the author, September 11, 2017.

*   Town Halls were the Atlanta University Center's public affairs forums, which featured talks by leading academics.

†   Atlanta University president Rufus Clement.

‡   Nora McNiven, editorial assistant for *Phylon Magazine*, published by Atlanta University.

Dorothy Dawson called, said that in her meeting with Les just a few minutes before he went to lunch with me, where she and Connie* presented their plan for summer educational project in civil rights for college students, Les looked over list of teachers, where Staughton & my name appeared very often and said[,] "These are good men, but it's a loaded list, loaded towards 'non-violence'" which Dorothy took to mean "loaded towards the SNCC idea of direct action. Les suggested people like Dabbs† and other SRC men, saying "I have great respect for Howard Zinn's and Staughton Lynd's ability, but this list is loaded."

Mon. Jan. 21

At party last night for Sam Cook, Gerald Reed‡ told this story—when he first started practicing dentistry in Atlanta a Negro man came to him and said[,] "Do you fix colored teeth?' Gerald replied tersely[,] "All teeth are white." The man left & never showed up again—only later did Gerald realize the man thought it a rebuff.

[This first Jan. 21 diary entry = H]

Mon. Jan. 21

Saw Marie Thomas in snack shop. She told me she didn't sleep well for two weeks during the "crisis." She retold the story of her being ordered off campus by Manley, and it corroborated in every detail what had been said. She now just wants to get out as soon as possible. At the party for Sam the other night Sylvia told Roz: these girls on suspension were all gifted in some way, actresses, artists—the school makes no provision for people like this. Marie said she had told the committee after her performance she just couldn't go back to the dorm, it was emotionally impossible; they made fun of this.

Thurs. Jan. 24

Below-zero weather in Atlanta. Finished rough draft of second section (of book on Mystique)§ and said something toward end about the South being a great theater of the absurd, and then this afternoon something happened to bear it out.
Janice Rothschild (Rabbi Rothschild's¶ wife) wrote a little play sometime back based on the Abraham-Isaac sacrifice story, but modernized, with Negro couple discuss-

---

*   Constance Curry, a civil rights activist, was director of the Southern Student Human Relations Project of the National Student Association and a SNCC executive committee member. Later edited oral histories and memoirs on the civil rights movement, including *Silver Rights* (1996).

†   James McBride Dabbs, president of the Southern Regional Council.

‡   Ultraliberal Atlanta dentist Gerald Reed, who was for a time business partner of Julian Bond.

§   Zinn's *Southern Mystique* (1964).

¶   Janice Rothschild was the wife of Atlanta's outspoken rabbinical supporter of the civil rights

ing the "sacrifice." Beryl Goldberg, director of Theater Atlanta[,] called me to ask if I would read man's part in this before Hadassah[*] Monday morning. Not thinking, I said okay. Then, after hanging up, I remembered it was a Negro in the play. I called Janice Rothschild & told her I thought Negroes should play these roles. She said she agreed but someone in Hadassah connected with the affair for Monday was dubious about others agreeing, so Janice said she would read with Beryl. Janice said: "I know that girl has no objection herself. She's a Brandeis graduate. It's others." I said these are the people who are the biggest obstacles to progress, the "good" people who have no objection themselves. I said if she could work it out to have Negroes do it, I would promise to get the man and woman to read. I told her I thought this was a simple matter really, that a few telephone calls would do it, that surely the people in Hadassah would want this. She confirmed this, saying she had mentioned this to a past president [of] Hadassah who blew her top. I called Beryl, and he said, "Now I don't want to read it either." Janice called a few hours later, said she had spoken to pres. [of] Hadassah & everything was okay now. Roz pointed out irony that this play, designed to make a point about Negroes, should fare this way. Beryl has suggested maybe if we read it to group, even if whites read it, they would learn something thereby. I said I didn't think so, that people have a remarkable capacity to separate their own situation from a distant one that they tsk-tsk about. Anyway, it ended well.

Thurs. nite: Took Sam & Sylvia Cook out to Stouffers, spent the evening chatting. He is going off next week as visiting prof. U. of Illinois. I'll never forget his remarkable switch from letter to Const.[†] blasting UN demonstrators for Lumumba[‡] as un-American and then his blast at Richard Walker when Worthy was here,[§] and then his joint letter to Const. with me and Staughton on Cuban blockade.[¶]

---

movement, Jacob Rothschild, of the Hebrew Benevolent Congregation, whose temple was bombed by white supremacists.

[*]   Hadassah is a volunteer women's Zionist association.

[†]   *Atlanta Constitution.*

[‡]   Patrice Lumumba, Congolese nationalist and first prime minister of the Democratic Republic of the Congo.

[§]   This incident, in which a Town Hall forum on Communist China, featuring University of South Carolina professor Richard Walker (author of *China Under Communism*) and radical black journalist William Worthy (of the *Baltimore African American*), turned into a heated debate about race in the Jim Crow South, is discussed on pp. 10–11 of the Introduction in this volume.

[¶]   Zinn had been a critic of the Cuban blockade and President Kennedy's nuclear brinkmanship during the Cuban Missile Crisis.

Fri. Feb. 1

First week of classes, more Spelmania: lovely and intelligent senior named

Pat Smith, after signing up for student teaching in the fall (and perhaps after listening to prexy speeches in chapel urging students to think boldly, realize new opportunities exist in other fields, don't stick to the tried and true for Negro women college graduates, etc.) decided at the last minute she didn't want to spend her last semester in college this way. But: registrar told her she would get an F if she pulled out, so she went and did it for a week, then showed up at registration and told me this is not what she wants, she wants to prepare for grad school. I went to Dean Eagleson,* who is in charge, and who can withdraw her. No, he says, it would hurt the whole program, hurt Spelman's name with the state education people, therefore hurt a whole generation of Spelman student teachers if she withdrew. Next AM I called Mrs. Dempsey, in charge of "Negro" student teaching for Atlanta. She says, no it won't hurt Spelman, yes there are rules, but "we are flexible," tell Eagleson to call me and we'll withdraw her. Told Eagleson this; he said he'd call. I call him next day, he says, ["]no dice, It's my decision, I think it is to the best interests of the college["] to "force her—have her—stay in the program["] (a slip of the tongue). She came over last night to reiterate she wants out. I told her to call Eagleson, make her feelings very clear to him.

Dean of Women called meeting of student council, read them 12 page two-hour statement, then dismissed meeting, saying if any questions or discussion they will have to see her individually in her office. In her statement said: the student leaders have created a bad image by supporting rule breakers. Opportunism and personal advance have been motives. No, they could not get copy of her manuscript. College reserves right to put anybody out who's not in sympathy with its ideals. An articulate minority has been swaying the unthinking majority. Majority of faculty is with the administration. No student meeting must take place in future without presence of dean! President of college has right to approve or disapprove any action by student government.

Feb. 2 Sat. PM

Morehouse exchange [student] from Carleton came over—Ken Byalin of NY—unhappy at M'[ore]h[ou]se—didn't find intellectual excitement or social action he thought there'd be—new dorms kept [as] a showplace rather than for use—plaques on every door showing name of donor—air of philanthropic benevolence all around—fellows play whise [wise]. May go home, following suit on girl from Car-

---

*   Oran Wendell Eagleson was Spelman's dean of instruction and professor of psychology.

leton who just took French leave—(was tearful she was, was lonely, homesick, not what she expected, talk and atmosphere in dorms unsettling, etc.[).]

[Feb. 2 date = H]

Sun. Feb. 3

Jeff at Gt. Books reading Areopagitica.[*]
Evening—rousing discussion with Spelman students, a Ga. State member of SDS,[†] Bert Parks & Lois, supposed to start with Staughton & Harold Bardinelli on non-violence domestic & int'l, but got off completely different and stayed that way—because I started by playing record of Abernathy's[‡] Memphis talk—everybody liked it except, obviously, Harold and his criticism started and kept going the evening's discussion. It wasn't so much what Abernathy said—although this too, the playing on the old Negro church-type humor, etc. bothered him—but his immediate negative reaction to King-Abernathy, etc. His point they're still living on Montgomery[§] & sit-in glories, nothing doing now, no action, only a tiny pct. of Negroes have been affected by "progress" so far. People stayed till after midnight. Disagreement on all sides. Harold is nationalist, but with a difference. When he sees a Negro walking down the street he feels something for him special. When he sees a poor white, no. But don't we all—regardless of race—have certain miseries in common. Yes—but. And when you see a wealthy Negro real estate man walking down the street do you feel kinship with him? No. But "you people" have sat on us so long and now we've got to sit on you for a while to straighten things out. And at the tail end of this discussion Harold says, all this radical position of mine is to move all the rest of you closer to it.

[Feb. 3 date = H]

Tues. Feb. 5 Lunch at Canterbury House

(Took Yale Law Dean there after he'd met Betty Stevens—he obviously was not impressed by her in an excited way—yes he liked her, she was intelligent, but . . . Yale law? Well, don't know. I tried to make the point to him that over six years or so my faith in my old ability to appraise intellect has been shaken—that the old image I had of the "bright young Negro" had to be altered—there are young Negro people

---

[*]   *Areopagitica* (1644), John Milton's essay against government censorship of publications.
[†]   Students for a Democratic Society (SDS) was the largest and most influential New Left organization in 1960s America.
[‡]   Ralph David Abernathy was a key SCLC leader, closest friend of Martin Luther King Jr., and minister. Abernathy would succeed King as head of the SCLC after King was assassinated.
[§]   Referring to the Montgomery bus boycott of 1955–56, King's and Abernathy's one major victory until Birmingham in May 1963.

out of the South who don't overwhelm you as real sharp, intellectually impressive, and you need to spend time with them to catch every once in a while flashes of real brilliance and to see that there's something remarkable there that should be encouraged.* He suggested a summer at Harvard to see.)[†]

Rousing lunch discussion led by Ed Grider,[‡] who'd been bothered by QV Williamson's obvious gloating over being able to manipulate residential patterns. He spoke on "Poverty & Power in Atlanta[,]" said Negroes are coming into power, shouldn't use it as unwisely as whites have. People there might have taken to this point, but he used a bad example to illustrate it, pointing to the white man on the block into which all Negroes have been moved and QV Williamson saying easily, no, we don't give him any alternative. People there took this—and perhaps with some truth—as an indication of Ed Grider's own resistance to complete integration—but also there was misunderstanding. He called me Wed. AM to . . . [say] he'd expected Negro reaction but not the harsh one of the white women! I told him Newsom had said it was one of the best discussions ever at Canterbury House and this made him feel better because he'd obviously been bothered during and after the meeting. The Yale Dean was fascinated.

[Feb. 5 date = H]

Mon. Feb. 4

Betty Stevens came over late in the evening (after I'd taken Ken Byalin to Greyhound Bus back to Carleton) with Morehouse guy and Spelman girl. Her birthday—also girls. We all had a sip of wine, talked. She became depressed about Spelman, pressure on her, unending pressure; there were tears in her eyes as she left. She said if you ever leave, please tell me first, because I'll leave too.

(Few days ago received five-page letter from . . . the last of the 3 Albany State refugees[§] to go—in her case before her final semester—she poured her heart out—a document to go into the Spelman history, summing up as well as anything could how terrible it is for a sensitive, freedom-yearning girl to be cramped up here. "There are no more Spelman young ladies; there are just young ladies who go to Spelman.")

---

*   This was typical of the concern Zinn displayed and the energetic advocacy he waged on behalf of his students, championing them for graduate schools, fellowships, etc.

†   At Zinn's urging, philanthropist Charles Merrill would provide fellowship support for Betty Stevens to attend Harvard in the summer, and she would go on to earn a Harvard law degree.

‡   Ed Grider, a civil rights activist and minister, was active in the Albany movement.

§   These three "Albany State refugees" were among the dozens of students expelled by their college president, William Henry Dennis Jr., as reprisals for their activism in Albany's civil rights movement. Former Spelman dean Irene Asbury, who was a dean at Albany State and supporter of the movement, helped these three students gain admission to Spelman and Zinn arranged for them to get financial support to attend Spelman.

Tues. eve. Feb. 5

Chairman Emory YAF[*] called to ask me to speak or get someone else to—debate with Fulton Lewis III[†] on HUAC, Monday nite. Will probably do it.[‡]

"I was very depressed and I felt hemmed in.[§] I found myself losing the little inner peace that I had left. I have always been a very sensitive person and it seems that Spelman only increased my sensitivity. . . . I realize that I live in a small home town but the people, common as they may appear, are very, very wonderful. They are sincere and honest; some of them of course, but at Spelman I met some of the phoniest people I've ever seen. People who smile at you and try to take away all the individuality that you have. Little things count, and little things can grow into big things. I just got tired of being agitated and locked up. We have places we can go; but the movies get boring sometimes. I like the girls at Spelman, but I will never have any real love of the place, because it offers me nothing to love. Rules, some rules, are fine, but one's emotions are not easily controlled by rules. To me, college is a place where the student grows. Bu[t] how can anyone grow in an atmosphere where the issuance of demerits means more to the housemother than the students? How can one grow any way but warped when one lives under warped conditions? I don't expect to be self-governed. I realize the necessity for some discip[l]ine, but . . I feel that I am losing more than I am gaining. And nobody who can do something about the conditions really cares. That's one of the frustrations about it. I am interested in the things that count. I feel that I can adapt myself to situations that are not impossible.. . . Most students and working people look forward to the weekends, but not at Spelman. The mov[i]es are even out on the weekends. Therefore I didn't go anywhere. . . . Many nights I have stayed down in the basement by myself because I couldn't sleep.

---

*   Young Americans for Freedom, the leading national conservative student organization in the United States.

†   Fulton Lewis III was on the staff of the House Committee on Un-American Activities.

‡   Zinn would go on to debate Lewis on the question of whether HUAC should be abolished. Zinn discusses the debate in his February 11 diary entry. The text of his opening remarks at that debate is included in Appendix II of this volume, *Howard Zinn's Southern Diary: Sit-ins, Civil Rights, and Black Women's Student Activism*.

§   This line and those that follow relate back to Zinn's prior (February 4) diary entry, where he discusses receiving a "five page letter . . . from the last of the 3 Albany State refugees." He was referring to the students from Albany State College, who, after being expelled from that historically black college for participating in the Albany, Georgia civil rights movement, were—with Zinn's help— admitted and funded to attend Spelman. But these students found that its social restrictions and regimentation meant that Spelman too was unfree. And "the last" of these "3 Albany State refugees" had written Zinn a letter, excerpted here in this February 5 diary entry, that offered a powerful indictment of the lack of freedom at Spelman and how this had an unhealthy impact on students. Zinn was so moved by this letter that he would read it at the largest meeting protesting the lack of freedom at Spelman in 1963. Highlights from this "On Liberty at Spelman" meeting are excerpted in Appendix I of *Howard Zinn's Southern Diary: Civil Rights, Sit-ins, and Black Women's Student Activism*.

Sometimes one of my friends when she had late classes the following day would stay up with me as long as she could. . . . Spelman is missing the point, I feel, in many ways. . . . If the standards for Spelman are so very high, more students should pass the GRE, and less freshman [freshmen] should be planning on leaving because of grades. But these things go unnoticed seemingly except by a few. They should realize that there are no more Spelman young ladies. There are just young ladies who go to Spelman. . . . I was awakened one night at about 12:45 A.M. and questioned about some trash in the hall. My roommate and I were told we would be reported to the administration—long after room check hours, because my bed was unmade. It had been made, but I went back to bed. Demerits for loitering. . . . These are the things that are important—more important than the growth and development of the students and the school.

["]I had to leave for a while. I hope that I am making sense and not just raving about generalities. It's so hard to put one's feelings and frustrations into words, but I have tried to.["]

Thurs. Jan. 7*

First US history class on civil liberties. Handed out cards, asked students to copy down "I hereby affirm, as a member of this class, that I am not a member of an organization dedicated to the overthrow of the govt. by force and violence." Said: "And now, sign your name." I saw looks of consternation on a few faces, amazement on a few, many signed. In general the new students who didn't know me signed, my old students were suspicious and two of them blurted out[,] "I won't." Sarah Marshall said[,] "Mr. Zinn I'd like to discuss it"[;] I said, "Sorry, no discussion on this point." And then all sorts of excited comment back and forth broke out, arguments among the students about whether to or not to sign, arguments with me. After it all I made the point that civil liberties in the abstract is one thing; an actual situation faced by people, immediate, no preparation, with someone in authority expecting . . . [something] of them, makes it difficult to resist.

Sat. Jan. 9†

Young Amer[cans] for Freedom chairman Bill Eckbert called. Said they'd tried to get Mayor Hartsfield (out of town), Gene Patterson (prefers to write), lawyer Elliott Levitis (out of town that day)—so called me. Came over to bring tickets for my students. Medical student at Emory, very nice.

---

*   February 7 is the correct date of this diary entry.
†   February 9 is the correct date of this diary entry.

Mon. Feb. 11 Debate.

First they showed Film: Operation Abolition.* Nancy Perkins agreed yesterday to comment on it after the film. She was a little nervous up there—big crowd, perhaps three hundred—but did a marvelous job. Film itself was not as damaging to students as I had been led to believe. Unless one were already convinced of their guilt, they didn't look bad. Long, extended shots of men called Communists by commentator, orating into mike in rather unpleasant way, probably the most effective things in film from their point of view. Otherwise, the committee didn't look too good.

Fulton Lewis III came to my office earlier in the day to meet me, go over ground rules. Said he'd listened to tape of my WQXI broadcast—which meant he didn't get best picture of me because I wasn't too good that night.

The debate itself was a greater success than anything I anticipated. Lewis had been built up as a formidable opponent (has been all over the country speaking—debated 13 times with Michael Harrington† alone whom he described as greatest debater he's ever seen) but was hardly that. Intelligent, but saddled with a poor issue to defend, and more right-wing really than he would let on. Made a few remarkable concessions: that the committee "as it was in the earlier days . . . should have been abolished" but this committee was more "sophisticated" had improved procedure, etc. Also, at very end, admitted committee not following its enabling resolution, said if it were it should be abolished, said resolution was outdated. Concentrated on need for committee to avoid espionage, sabotage "250 Communists in Conelrad‡ stations." No question about who got more applause, both at end of main presentation and in course of evening. Excellent questions from floor. A great one by Staughton: "The great men in history who have been remembered have not been the members of inquisitorial committees but their victims: Galileo, Socrates, Jesus, Liliburne . . . .["] Interruption: what is your question. Staughton: "[T]hose statements are connected by semi-colons, I'm coming to my question. My question: Why is that?" Lewis tried to answer, but was inept. Often tried by flow of words to accomplish his purpose, by sheer quantity. I'm sure his definite followers liked him. As for people in-between I don't think he was too effective in winning them over.

---

*   *Operation Abolition* was a film produced by HUAC in an attempt to discredit its critics in the wake of the March 1960 student demonstrations against its hearings in San Francisco—which ended with students being washed (with high-powered fire hoses) down the steps of San Francisco City Hall. The film was so heavy handed and propagandistic in its depiction of the protesters as Communists and dupes that it became a recruiting tool for the New Left, helping to attract to its ranks students concerned about civil liberties and abolishing HUAC and other such vestiges of the McCarthy era.

†   Michael Harrington was a socialist intellectual and author of the influential expose of poverty in the Kennedy years, *The Other America* (1962).

‡   Conelrad was the emergency broadcasting system in Cold War America to be used in the event of a nuclear attack.

They made tape and will send me one.

P.M. Jim Forman and Victor Rabinowitz* came over to settle fact that I will be consultant for two year SNCC research project in BlackBelt counties.
Dorcas Boit,† Betty Stevens, Betty Darden, Constanc[e] Nabwire,‡ Marilyn Price, came to the debate, loved it. Jeff and Myla came. Myla was thrilled with what I'd done which made me feel good because she had been most critical of a talk she heard me give at Emory last year on Zen. Roz said it was the very best speech I'd ever made and she's heard me give a hundred.

Thurs. Feb. 14

Moot court in US history [class] on the Debs case 1919[.]§—Last week Demaris Allen was only one of the four to do a really good job—throwing herself into 1798 and the Alien & Sedition Laws¶ even tho she didn't believe in them herself. This week Ophelia Gilbert** was only one of four to do a similar thing on the Debs case, prosecuting Debs very vigorously, dramatically, convincingly tho she said later she was for Debs. What's frightening is the ease with which students are convinced that speech must be curtailed in times of trouble—a vote on the Sedition & Espionage Laws of 1917–18†† showed the class split close to even on them—I've been kind of neutral so far but I can't continue this way!

Thurs. nite—faculty meeting
Another stupid meeting—*grades* the subject—endless statistics on who got F's who got D's, Eagleson presenting the figures, his favorite word is *percentile*. Towards end of meeting Manley said he had problem to throw before us: staff of yearbook has voted to dedicate it to Irene Asbury—*but* he said, "several students are disturbed" over this—because—she'd only been with college two years, the yearbook has always been dedicated to someone who was either retired or still with the institution, etc, etc. Would the faculty help out with this decision? (I had been given a premo-

---

*   Victor Rabinowitz was one of the leading lawyers on the American Left, whose foundation provided critical financial support for SNCC in the early 1960s.
†   Dorcas Chempkenboi Boit was a Spelman (class of 1965) student from Kenya and a student government leader at Spelman.
‡   Constance Rose Nabwire was a Spelman (class of 1965) student from Uganda.
§   The Debs case was the prosecution and jailing of Socialist Party leader Eugene V. Debs for opposing World War I and U.S. conscription for that war.
¶   The Alien and Sedition Acts, enacted during the U.S. quasi war with France in 1798, were the earliest attempts of the U.S. government to outlaw antiwar dissent.
**   Ophelia Ann Gilbert was a Spelman (class of 1964) student.
††   The Sedition and Espionage Acts were used by the U.S. government to outlaw antiwar dissent after U.S. entry into World War I.

nition of this weeks ago—that staff and seniors wanted Irene Asbury but pressure being brought against—after all, she symbolizes liberalism, dynamism,* etc. It would be a slap at the present unpopular dean). Miss Simon[†] supported Manley—"we need to give the students guidance—it shouldn't be dedicated to someone who was only here two years—we've got to teach the students to make responsible decisions—it shouldn't be a sentimental act." I said: I always thought a dedication was precisely that, a sentimental act, a spontaneous expression of feeling, that it should be abhorrent to us to tell or even suggest to the students who it should be dedicated to, that whoever heard of *organizing* a dedication! Staughton said, how come administration now listens to students who are "disturbed" when in past students who were "disturbed" were met with rebuff saying, go thru channels—well here channels had been gone thru. Esta, talking on point Irene is gone, said—would we hesitate to honor someone from our hometown who'd gone off to become president of the US? Irene has gone to Albany and become a leader in that movement. The meeting didn't go as Manley expected—he didn't get the mandate he wanted—there was no consensus expect [except] that the students should decide themselves—perhaps by vote.

Sat. [Feb. 16]

Yearbook staff met . . . AM with Manley and he was quite mild, tho urging them to "reconsider." They will Sunday. One of the staff has been leading the battle for [former Spelman dean] Irene Asbury. As a freshman she [the Spelman student] "leading the battle" [to dedicate the college yearbook to Asbury] was about to be expelled by Manley because he saw her kissing a Morehouse student—but Irene Asbury came to her defense and students rose up in arms [objecting to the expulsion threat.]

We go in this whole stupid Spelman struggle, from days of hopelessness to days when we think Manley may begin to recognize reality.

Fri. Feb. 15

Cocktail-buffet at Billy & Harry Piffner. She is a big League of Women Voters person. British consul there, other League people, Dick Starr[‡] of Emory. All superficial chatter, flitting from one person to another, nothing consequential said, no meeting of people.

---

*   Zinn was referring here to Asbury's prominent role in championing student involvement in the Albany civil rights movement and her own leadership role in that movement.

†   Marguerite Frances Simon, instructor in physical education at Spelman. Note that Simon, like many faculty supporters of Manley, had been on the Spelman faculty for decades (she began teaching there in 1943) and was herself a Spelman graduate, a pillar of Spelman social traditions and conservatism that Zinn opposed.

‡   Historian and political scientist Richard Felix Staar, a Russia scholar, who later served in the Reagan administration's arms negotiation team and was an associate director of the Hoover Institution at Stanford.

Sat. Feb. 16

Another cocktail party—this more like fun. A much smaller group, at Burt Schorr who works for Wall St. Journal. He from NY, his wife from Mississippi, a lovely girl, new baby—Jon Johnston & Essel there. Jon was very happy about the Fulton Lewis debate said I won easily.

Sun. Feb. 17

Took five African students—Dorcas Boit (Kenya), Constance Nabwire (Uganda)[,] and three fellows from Tanganyika, S. Rhodesia, Nigeria respectively to Emory Liberal Club for them to give a talk. They did a marvelous job, corroborating our general impression of African students [as] mature, confident, relaxed, articulate, good-humored. Constance said when she came to Spelman one student asked her if in Africa they ate people raw or cooked. She responded: when your mother buys meat do you eat it raw or cooked? Answer: cooked. Well, she said, we do the same. Driving back in the car, discussed various things. They all hate Tshombe,* liked Lumumba. At the discussion in the car they took a very matter of fact attitude towards violence. Very pragmatic on that as in other things. The Mau Mau[†] had accomplished something they said that no entreaties could have.

Mon. Feb. 18

Fellow from Int'l Research Associates visited us to find out about library desegregation in Atlanta. They're doing nationwide survey for Amer. Library Assn.

Jackson Bailey[‡] phoned from Earlham to ask if I'll serve on committee for Ass[ociatio]n [for] Asian Studies—for Asian Studies in Undergraduate Education.

Tues. Feb. 19

Dept. lunch. Told others about great Howard Smith[§] program on poverty which pulled no punches on administration's[¶] lack of boldness. Mrs. Macomson told of sev-

---

* Moise Tshombe, Congolese political figure who—with covert backing from Belgium and white mercenaries—in 1960 led a secessionist rebellion against the new Democratic Republic of the Congo.

† Mau Mau, the militant Kenyan nationalist group that emerged in the 1950s and engaged in armed struggle to help topple British colonial rule.

‡ Jackson Bailey, a leading Japan scholar, was professor of Asian history and founder of the Institute for Education on Japan at Earlham College.

§ Howard K. Smith, prominent newscaster, ABC Television News.

¶ Zinn is referring here to the Kennedy administration, whose record on poverty and civil rights he criticized in his publications.

eral months ago helping white man in supermarket buy many cans of dog food, drove him home, found he was buying them not for dogs, but for his children.

Agenda was forgotten as meeting ended in tumultuous argument over student freedom, with Mrs. Macomson arguing they have enough ("Who heard of a college girl staying out on Sat. nite till 1AM? Why must they have dates on week-ends? Etc. Etc.) Lois Moreland disturbed, Staughton fuming silently, me doing most of the arguing, Marilyn Pearsall bewildered. Then, on subject of student democracy, college suppressing printing of petition, another hot argument, with Lois strong on this for freedom of press, with Marilyn getting excited, saying a college is different, same rules of freedom don't apply.

Class: very hot debate on Smith Act[*]—girl who had been sitting in back of class and who I was sure was really out of everything all semester really alive on this issue in her side of the debate—at one point she put her hands on her hips and shouted at her antagonist "Now, honey . . . !" It was moot court, and perhaps first time one attorney has called another "honey."

Wed. Feb. 20

Hear[d] Joseph Papp, found[er of the] Shakespeare Festival, talk at Clark.[†] Very engaging speaker, refreshing after so many formal, paper-reading performances. Direct, honest, good-humored, intelligent. Told of first Julius Caesar performance at E. River Drive, no notion of how it would turn out, and 2000 people showed up, in shirt sleeves "a baseball crowd." "When Caesar killed they yelled as if it were a home run." Told of great numbers of kids turning out to see Romeo & Juliet, jeering when her family wept over her death, explaining to him later "They had just turned her out. Now they're sorry. When she killed herself she showed them!" Told of being pulled behind Sanitation truck all over city. Spoke on behalf of subsidized theater—they get $100,000 of their $300,000 from NYC, no strings. Fought Moses,[‡] who wanted them to charge admission, successfully, by having lunch with Chief Justice Appeals Court, getting squeezed into calendar. Defended Shylock, a rich-warm character— no not anti-Semitic characterization, a human one.

10 PM, party thrown by Esther Jackson for Papp. JP[§] got drinking, talking grandiloquently of MacIver's great wasted talent, suddenly shouted to me, "Let's get Mac-

---

[*]   The Smith Act (1940) made it a federal crime to advocate the overthrow of the U.S. government or to belong to any organization that so advocated overthrow. Initially deployed by Washington against Trotskyists, the law was used in the Cold War era to suppress the Communist Party.

[†]   Clark College was one of the six higher-educational institutions affiliated with the Atlanta University Center.

[‡]   Robert Moses was New York's master builder and power broker, whose role as parks commissioner is likely the one that forced Papp to deal with him to establish the Shakespeare in the Park program.

[§]   "JP" is Dr. J. Preston Cochran, professor of drama and speech at Spelman and director of the AMS Players.

Iver."* Over Burrough[s]'s† disdainful objection. As we left the house with my car keys, JP said, "Burroughs doesn't care, no human concern; people are thrown away when they've outlived their usefulness. MacIver is fifty and he only has a few chances left. Papp must hear him." We drove crazily to MacIver's house ("Just next block"[).] Was two miles. It was midnight, his wife in pin curlers taken aback, telling JP thru door, ["] no MacIver asleep.["] I came from car to join JP standing outside the door. JP said "Oh you must wake him. We have a producer here from NY who wants him to read for him. It's a great opportunity!" The woman looked at me "how long you going to be in town" I said "I'm not the producer!" She came back again, said "He's been drinking, I can't wake him." I convinced JP it was no use, even if we woke him he'd make a bad impression. Sadly we returned, JP half-lit, talking about being boxed in here in Atlanta, saying "Sure MacIver drinks. Its ceiling zero for him, that's why. He can't go up, can't see anything for himself." When we returned, Papp had just gone, everybody else just about gone. Drove JP home.

7:30–9:30 Betty Stevens came over, for spaghetti & meatballs, and to discuss with me as her honors work, Cha[rle]s Frankel's The Case for Modern Man & EH Carr What is History. It was a good session. Discussed perfectability, empiricism, secularism, causation, objectivity, ultimate values, cultural relativism, Maritain,‡ Niebuhr,§ Mannheim,¶ Marx. At end she went off with a few clippings on capital punishment (somehow something I'd said about murder and absolute values led to that) saying students must take on a project in Ga. on this.

Thurs. Feb. 21

Class discussed Huck Finn & Merchant of Venice from standpoint: should they be barred as perpetuating stereotypes? General consensus seemed to be no. But when less literary, more extreme examples were posed, it was more difficult to decide.

Evening: Rushton Coulborn's** first lecture. Quite a lot of Spelman students there, more than have attended any other such thing since perhaps Frazier††—because we

---

*   Zinn was referring to Ray McIver, a Morehouse graduate, actor, and playwright who taught in the Atlanta public schools.
†   Baldwin Wesley Burroughs was a professor of drama at Spelman.
‡   Jacques Maritain was an influential twentieth-century French Catholic philosopher, Thomist, and leading interpreter of the thought of St. Thomas Aquinas.
§   Reinhold Niebuhr was a leading twentieth-century Protestant theologian and critic of liberal theology, who shifted from being a socialist to a critic of political utopianism.
¶   Karl Mannheim was a leading twentieth-century sociologist who pioneered the sociology of knowledge.
**   Rushton Coulborn was a historian who had published on the rise and fall of ancient Egyptian civilization and on feudalism. He was the former chair of the Atlanta University history department.
††   E. Franklin Frazier, whose talk on his iconoclastic critique of the African American middle class, Black Bourgeoisie, made him a huge draw when he spoke at Spelman.

worked on it. He spoke about his framework: civilized societies growing, decaying; the balance of power based on the existence of many sovereign nations. Our present civilized society starts with 9th century (decay of Greco-Roman Civ. Soc.). Civ. societies seem to start with ecclesiastical leadership. Towards the end of each the original nations which were core of the society lose power to large peripheral states (today, US & USSR). All in all, stimulating in the breadth of the subject matter, in the attempt to think philosophically about history. Disappointing in what seems to me a non-recognition of the fact that old cycles may be drastically altered in the 20th century. Staughton asked: doesn't nuclear war change patterns. Coulborn's answer: nations can recover remarkably well from wars.

After lecture, to Baldwin Burrough[s]'s place (he's living in Billie Thomas' home) with Coulborn, his new wife (a secret up to now because so close after Helen's death) Banks, Lynda, Billie's brother-in-law & wife.

Fri. Feb. 22

Betty Darden liked Coulborn's lecture. Alice Walker* & Damaris Allen said they found it a little dull, said he never defined civilized society clearly.

Cecile Ganpatsingh[†] over for dinner. Wants us to come to British Guiana. Says Spelman is "like a coffin. You have to fit it exactly either by stretching or shrinking. But nothing must stick out, a toe, a hand, a hair. And not a modern coffin. But an old wooden one. Says she feels her years here have been wasted."

Sat. Feb. 23

Get together at Rose's house, with Barksdales, Newsomes, Lynds, Boldens (a most intelligent, nice couple—she knows Loften Mitchell) and Esther Jackson, who told interesting story of how white theater patrons—Geo. Goodwin particularly—are trying to take Shakespeare group of Papp away from Clark [College] to downtown, because Clark is not "the right cultural setting." Are even working on Wagner to Allen[‡] communications to achieve this. Will be interesting to see what happens.

Sun. Feb. 24

Jeff & Tony Dunbar at Great Books, discussing The Federalist [Papers].

---

* Alice Walker was a Spelman student active in the Black Freedom Movement and the student rights movements at Spelman. She would go on to become a poet and novelist, the first African American woman to win the Pulitzer Prize in literature for her novel *The Color Purple*. Her Spelman experience is discussed on pp. 52–62 of the Introduction.

† Cecile Ganpatsingh was a Spelman student from British Guiana.

‡ New York City mayor Robert Wagner and Atlanta mayor Ivan Allen.

Mon. Feb. 25

Jennifer Ragwar approached me to give her Russian lessons again. Spent an hour with her that evening. Then to Renate Wolf's* to meet two Sarah Lawrence exchange students here for a week.

Tues. Feb. 26

Lunch at Canterbury House. (Roz noticed Sarah Lawrence girl—Roz was thinking about our Operation Etiquette[†] here on table manners—dunking pieces of bread with great gusto into gravy, thought this such a delightful contrast). Real Estate man, former pres. Bickers spoke. Ch'n Bd. Of Trustees at some church. Is it Sam Williams church, and is this why Sam was there, and why he was milder than usual toward the speaker? Just before coming there Roz—a remarkable coincidence—got into conversation with Mrs. Harvey, who cleans our house once a week for the college. Mrs. Harvey said: are you boycotting West End? I'm not. I wouldn't do anything for the Negro real estate men. I'm getting 55 cents an hour. You know how hard it is for you to make both ends meet. Imagine how it is for me. Well I tried to buy a house from Bickers, he wanted $2000 down. I told him I have a steady job, so has my husband, but no dice. A white man got us a house for $800 down. I have no use for the Negro real estate men. At the lunch, Bickers was assailed and had no answer on the fact that he and the real estate men are moving into white neighborhoods in a solid phalanx, thus creating larger segregated areas, rather than doing it checkerboard style, and, as Sam Williams suggested, make it impossible for a white to move anywhere away from Negroes without moving out of the city. Bickers said, we have immediate problem of housing shortage, must meet that.

In class: played Sacco Vanzetti record of Woodie [Woody] Guthrie.[‡] After one whole sider [side] over-about six songs thought they must be tired of it, said I wouldn't play any more. They protested, wanted to hear the other side. I told them they could leave if they wanted. Only 1 or 2 out of 25 left.

Evening: Rushton Coulborn: Russia a continuation of Tsarism but more effective: caesaro-papism, Byzantine bureaucracy. China too a continuation of traditional China. I questioned his statement US still vigorous: where is the vigor in economic

---

*   Renate C. Wolf was a professor of English at Spelman and friend of Zinn.

†   "Operation Etiquette" was Zinn's nickname for the administration's initiative—which he and his students viewed as insulting—to teach table manners to Spelman's students.

‡   Folk singer Woody Guthrie's song "Two Good Men" (1947), on the case of Nicola Sacco and Bartomelo Vanzetti, in which they were convicted in 1921 and executed in 1927 for armed robbery and murder. The trial that ended in the conviction of these two Italian-born anarchists was marred by an atmosphere of xenophobia and antiradical hysteria. Their case became a liberal and Left cause célèbre.

growth, in political flexibility, in ideology, in culture [?] His answer: we've given tremendous econ. aid to rest of world.

Wed. eve. Feb. 27

Last Coulborn lecture. The worst. He is brilliant, provocative, wide-ranging, but removed from human concerns, tied to old-fashioned historical extrapolation. Points: nuclear war is likely. But, going by Clausewitz,* defense against nuclear weapons will come, and if we can hold out 20 years, it will, probably be perfected by then. In any event, going by Liddell-Hart,† the world will be able to rec[o]nstruct swiftly after nuclear catastrophy [*sic*]. Young white visiting student in audience challenged his pessimism, said he was left depressed, said Coulborn underestimated liberalization in Russia. C. said yes, liberalization, but optimism due to youth. He . . . [in his youth] dreamed of socialist utopia, but understood realities now that he is older. I questioned his military-balance-of-power emphasis as self-fulfilling prophesy, suggested possibility of peaceful growing together of Soviet & Western worlds. He said he disagreed.

Letter from Merrill‡ saying yes on Betty Stevens' summer at Harvard. She wasn't in class so left message for her to call. Late that night we finally made contact. She was anxious for me to come to the dorm to show her the letter. She was thrilled.

And Betty Darden cheered by letter from Univ. Ibadan, Nigeria where she can study African languages. Merrill will help if no Whitney grant. Manley saw her in morning, said, I hear Merrill will help you; remember, it needs my approval.

Thurs. [Feb. 28] Class debate on Sacco-Vanzetti.

Good Russian class session on K's§ 1956 secret De-Stalinization Speech.
Dramatic enough for four students to come up on own afterward and ask me to order book of documents which contains speech.

Sunday, Mar. 3

Returned yesterday from weekend at Gatlinburg, Tenn, where YWCA brought together about 80 Negro and white college students from all over the South. This is the third time I have seen them in this sort of situation, and regardless of all the organizational nonsense associated with Y conferences, it is a revolutionary act—many

---

*   Carl von Clausewitz was a Prussian general and military theorist, author of the classic work on military strategy, *On War* (1832).

†   Liddell Hart was a twentieth-century British military historian.

‡   Philanthropist Charles Merrill.

§   Nikita Krushchev, Soviet premier, 1954–64.

of these white students have never been with Negroes before—those who have, have had this experience at a previous conference. I spoke to a girl from the Univ. of Alabama, who said she had first gone to one of these conferences pretty much as a casual thing, became involved, and now she's one of the leaders in inter-racial activities, etc. Three girls from Agnes Scott, one from S. Carolina, another from S. Georgia—all for first time. Really a marvelous thing to see. Two days of living together are worth two decades of reading or talking about "good race relations." Wish though they would spend their time hiking into the mountains rather than sitting and conferencing. They don't really need to *talk* about these things, just live them.[*] This point fits into the second of the two talks I gave. Fri. nite I spoke on national pride, then afterward sat around in lobby with a group of students with more questions more talk, one Negro woman taking down name after name of book[s] I suggested, continuing to ask "more titles, more titles!" Sat. AM on the Southern mystique. All in all, marvelous reception. These young people are so open to bold inquiry. They seem never to get it, keep getting Christian platitudes and whenever someone speaks to them sharply about something meaningful and expresses a radical viewpoint they find it terrifically stimulating. Anyway the whole reaction from everyone was enthusiastic. Met some marvelous people—Dan Dodson, head of NYU Human Relations Project, tall, lanky, very regular guy, a Southerner, most perceptive. Jim Callahan was my roommate, a former Methodist minister who left the church in disgust, is now chaplain at Womans College in Milledgeville, Ga. Young, dynamic, very earnest, born in Athens, Ga. Raised in Valdosta. Went out late Fri. nite for hot dogs with Bobbi Yancey and Mary King the twins who've been visiting various colleges in the South for the Y. They showed me a report they did on their experiences. Very good, very well written, intelligent, ardent. Gives the general picture of Southern colleges as lack of academic freedom. Negro colleges get attention. General picture (except for Tougaloo[†] which is pictured as a remarkable place) is lackadaisical faculty, arbitrary administration.

Sat. nite [March 2] at Estas

Young fellow Ray brought along a white co-worker who has always made anti-Negro remarks, because he knew Finley Campbell (with white Swiss wife.!) would be along. Finley didn't know this was an "experiment"—nor did the guy—after a while (the guy is interested in composing music, and Finley can talk all night on music) they were having a great time together.

---

[*]   This was a key argument Zinn made in his first book on race in the South, *The Southern Mystique*, where he—very optimistically—claimed that expanded and egalitarian personal contact between blacks and whites could diminish and then doom racist myths and white supremacy.

[†]   Tougaloo, a private historically black college in Mississippi that was a center of student civil rights activism in the 1960s.

Monday AM [March 4]

Betty Stevens on phone, says her roommate left college suddenly, will tell me more tonight.

Alice Morgan, editor of Spelman Spotlight* and straight A student last semester, left school, was unhappy all year, had been subject to much pressure as editor, distressed at pressures, restrictions, etc.

Talk with Betty in evening, now that she has Merrill okay for summer at Harvard, Manley called her in, very conciliatory, wants to reestablish good relations.

Russian lesson for Jennifer Ragwar & Alice Washington,[†] both persistent and earnest about learning Russian (then off with Roz to see the film David & Lisa).[‡]

Tues. Mar. 5

Norman Brown[§] at faculty seminar on origin sanctity of cow—not in Vedas[¶] he says, begins medieval times with jump from figurative use to actual use as inviolate thing, from Brahman's treasured thing to everybody's, and for economic reasons. But neither Vedic[**] nor ahimsa[††] source of it.
Acad. Freedom Comm. AAUP for lunch, me Staughton & Bob Pearsall, brought up case of Lana Taylor, Bob amazingly militant on it.

Wed. Mar. 6

Dinner at Lois with Norman Brown. At his lecture, Indian Mohanti short, thin, physicist, very excitable, got in dither about what he interpreted as Brown's imputing sutti[‡‡] and caste[§§] to Vedas. Brown knows Vedas in & out, showed Mohanti wrong by eight centuries on one point, etc. Have seen pattern of fierce, and unknowledgeable nationalism, by Indians here this year.

---

*   *Spelman Spotlight* was the college's student newspaper.
†   Alice Washington was a Spelman (class of 1964) student.
‡   *David and Lisa* was a feature film (1962) directed by Frank Perry, which won a Golden Globe award.
§   W. Norman Brown was a leading scholar of India, professor of Sanskrit at the University of Pennsylvania, and founder of the first department of South Asian studies in the United States.
¶   Vedas were the oldest Hindu and Sanskrit writings from ancient India.
**   Vedic was the period in ancient Indian history when the Vedas were written.
††   Ahisma is the ethical principle in Jainism, Hinduism, and Buddhism of doing no harm to other living beings.
‡‡   Sutti was the premodern Hindu custom in which widows were burned alive on their husbands' funeral pyres.
§§   Caste was the rigid social stratification system in premodern India,

Thurs. Mar. 7

Students put on Scopes trial[*] show, Jesus signs, monkeys hanging in courtroom, cross-exam by Darrow[†] of Bryan[‡] (by Jo Ann Groves[§] of Carmen Fennoy), near violence between them—all a delightful show. Perhaps short of content, which I tried to supply in charge to jury, but all in all worth it I felt. Damaris Allen and Alice Walker were most enthusiastic later, Esta Seaton not so.

For Russian class, played tape of Harvard grad students who'd been on exchange in USSR a year—remarkable effect comes across this tape, no one thing is outstanding, but the total impression is powerful, a different view—not an opposite view, but a different, complex, human view of Soviet Russia, and more convincing coming not from naiive [sic] pro-Soviet people but from sophisticated, hard-headed, very critical Harvard bright young men. At end, Robert Allen said: why aren't they in the administration[?] I told him they had said their experiences—unique as they were—were just forgotten about, not utilized by administration.

Fri. [March 8]

lunch Non-West. Adm. comm. Another battle Brisbane[¶]-Banks.[**]

Sat. [March 9] AM

AAUP morning to Oglethorpe[††]—with Lionel Newsome, a real guy—said he'd like to find a college with good president we could both teach at together.

PM   Surprise—Lana Taylor in Atlanta, spent evening with us, husband army captain in paramilitary warfare—might go to S. Vietnam—very bright, personable, capable guy. Says military offers him best deal, what could he do in civilian life—teach school? Says many capable young Negroes turn to army for same reason. Missed out on best scholarships and recommendations at Southern Univ. Baton Rouge[‡‡] (where

---

[*]   The trial in 1925 of John Scopes, a high school biology teacher, for teaching evolution and in so doing violating Tennessee state law.

[†]   Clarence Darrow, famed progressive lawyer, who defended John Scopes.

[‡]   William Jennings Byran, the former populist presidential candidate and former secretary of state who supported the prosecution of Scopes.

[§]   Jo Ann Groves was a Spelman (class of 1964) student.

[¶]   Robert Brisbane was a professor of political science at Morehouse College, who taught courses on India.

[**] Arthur Banks was a political science professor at Morehouse College.

[††] Oglethorpe University, liberal arts university in Atlanta.

[‡‡] Southern University in Baton Rouge, the largest historically black university in the 1960s.

Sam Cook & Newsome his heroes) because he fell afoul of administration. Got 331/3 demerits for questioning wisdom of Dean in one statement.

Lana wants us to go to bat for her scholarship. She got . . . [excellent grades] in each of her last two semesters here, was denied scholarship both times, last time on "citizenship." Thinks first time, which was before petition trouble with administration, might be because came back spring . . . announcing engagement. As husband Harold Sims put it, college doesn't like their pets being "taken away" by someone else, getting out from under their wing. Harold spoke bitterly about whole situation [in] Negro colleges, worse than segregationists in lack of faith in young Negroes, mistake lack of literacy for lack of intelligence, pointed out college is last chance for young Negro to get freedom to learn and act before going out in world.

Sun. Mar. 10

Tennis with Jon Johnston, Staughton, and the Youngbluts.* Then Pro Musica Antiqua, marvelous Renaissance music, then to Henry Grady[†] to pick up Peter Davison, to have dinner with us. He was much struck by Myla. Later, Pat & Cecil Watters came over, also the Campbells, the Seatons, Renate, Staughton. Told him about Rukalski —he said, noone's [no one's] interested in concentration camp stories. What a commentary. A great evening of conversation, up until 2 a.m. discussed publishing, literature, race, the Kennedys.

Monday evening, March 11.

At Abby Game Room, Social Science Club[‡] meeting "On liberty—At Spelman." Manley told Dorcas he had previous engagement, couldn't come. I went there at 7 on the dot with tape recorder, could hardly get into room—it was jampacked, every bit of floor space full, maybe 150 students (20–30 usually come to our meetings). Mrs. Brazeal[§] and Mrs. Curry[¶] there too, Mrs. Macomson, Mrs. Perry,** Miss Simon, Rukalski, Renate, Esta, Shirley McBay, Staughton, Ed Cerney, Mrs. Allen.[††] Soon Dean Johnson[‡‡]

---

*   John Youngblut, of the Quaker House in Atlanta.

†   Henry Grady hotel in Atlanta.

‡   Zinn had been faculty advisor to the Social Science Club since the 1950s, and with his encouragement it had become a center of social protest (engaging in desegregation work) as well as critical thought and study. Excerpts from this protest meeting, taped by Zinn (and which he saved and stored), can be found in Appendix I of this book.

§   Ernestine Erskine Brazeal was Spelman's Alumnae Secretary.

¶   Margaret Nabrit Curry was a professor of history at Spelman, and an alumna of the college who had been teaching at Spelman since 1925.

**   Grace Jason Perry was registrar of Spelman, and former assistant dean of women.

††   Sadie Sims Allen was assistant dean of women at Spelman.

‡‡   Mercile Johnson was dean of women at Spelman.

came along. A tremendous meeting, it's all on tape. Started with reading excerpts from Mary Francis Watt's letter[:] "Here you aren't made to feel dirty about what you do. Hope Spelman students don't stop pushing for a better campus existence no matter what." And . . . [from student attending Spelman after being expelled for civil rights activism at Albany State, her] letter[:] "There are no more Spelman young ladies—just young ladies who go to Spelman. . . . How can anyone grow any way but warped living in a warped environment?" Students spoke, dozens of them, boldly, movingly—even Esta & Renate, used to complaints, were astonished by some of the things they heard—intimidation, stupidity (girls who couldn't go to concert Sunday weren't allowed to sit on the porch or leave their room[)] . . . game room at Abby Locked up because new furniture there . . . girl had to leave movies at 11 before it was over to be back in time. Mrs. Brazeal said look at positive things too. Mrs. Curry made conciliatory statement about balancing liberty and authority. Dean Johnson evaded and obscured. Mrs. Macomson said the students were confused. Rukalski said, be specific. Renate said let[']s have few rules and simple ones. Lana Taylor affair came up and Dean Johnson slipped and slid all over it. Students challenged her. I spoke on it, got enthusiastic reaction. I said here we tell students have the courage to dissent in our commencement day orations, etc, and when one does we chop her head off. Mrs. Macomson said if this were so, all heads would be off. Staughton spoke, said he'd unknowingly said in an early lecture, about New England town meeting, "You know, just like your Dorm Councils, and the roof almost fell in." Students kept crowding in until must have been every student on campus there. The overwhelming thing about it was the total, unanimous, crushing evidence of discontent. Highlight was Marie Thomas'[s] letter—which I got as I walked in the meeting—she was at rehearsal and wanted me to read it. "I am an honors student, a winner of the Jerome Award, an Abby resident, a victim of circumstance; I am Marie Thomas." Told of three years while city student, everything fine. Then her time on campus, and she became a ["]criminal.["] Spoke of how to simply keep going people must become uncaught criminals. Said times have changed, and Spelman must change. Got terrific hand.

Now, will anything come of it? This is the year of change.

After meeting spoke long time with Shirley McBay, who told me her troubles.

Tues. Mar. 12

Spoke on academic freedom in US History class as a prelude to lively discussion: Should Communists Be Allowed to Teach?

Dinner with Mays,[*] Manley, Brisbane, Banks, Moreland, on Non-West Program. The presidents want Banks to spend summer in Africa. He said flatly no. Mays was ripping mad.

---

[*]   Benjamin Mays was president of Morehouse College.

Then to seminar. Lois & Grady Randolph (he's come so long a way!) on
  Gandhi. Saxena there, on guard for any anti-Indian remarks. When Lois, on Amritsar Massacre* said "hundreds were killed" he interrupted quietly "Thousands."
  Randolph had noted new Indian Constitution has provision for detention, without cause, for "dangerous" people, just like what the British had and Indians had
  protested. I asked Saxena about this—he said, well you know there are subver-
  sives, agitators, dangerous people.

Leaving seminar, passed big lecture hall in Chemistry Bldg, students were in circle
around the hall, holding hands, singing "We Shall Overcome." Walked home with
white girl exchange student and another student, and they told me plans for tomorrow morning. Five persons, including Anna Jo Weaver, have reserved rooms in
Henry Grady Hotel, whose manager is only one nnwilling [unwilling] to negotiate
desegregation (Will desegregate when World[']s Fair comes to Atlanta he says). They
have written guarantee of reservation, will insist, will sit in lobby with blankets if necessary, will go to jail if arrested, will picket both hotel and court if necessary.

Thurs. Mar. 14

Margaret Hampton, the little girl from Forsyth Ga. who has been chosen to go
abroad as Merrill Scholar next year, came into office to talk to me and Staughton,
clearly nervous, shaky, but trying to smile and act in control of the situation. She
had just been stopped on the campus by Eagleson and Manley and engaged in conversation for an hour. They said they'd heard that at the meeting she said she didn't
learn anything from her time at Spelman, and if this were so, perhaps the wrong
choice had been made for the Award. She tried to explain what she had said. They
said many people misunderstood you, perhaps you should go around and explain to
them. (Mrs. Brazeal at the meeting, had been heard saying, as Margaret was speaking, that perhaps a wrong choice had been made.)

  Lunch at Canterbury House, Horace Mann Bond[†] gave an impassioned talk on
slavery as the root cause of Negro backwardness in education, pointing to fact that
geneology [sic] of Negro PhD's shows them descended mostly from free Negroes.
Human beings are infinitely adaptable, he said. Their intellectual attainment is the
result of their background. Standard tests should not be given too much credence in
relation to Negroes. He said one medical school had note on its tests "Pay no attention to score if student is from a foreign culture," and said this is applicable to Negro.

---

* Amritsar Massacre (1919) in India, in which British and Gurkha troops fired on unarmed protesters, killing more than three hundred.

† Horace Mann Bond was the dean of education at Atlanta University and father of Julian Bond.

Our standard tests are excellent for testing *one thing*: the extent to which the taker of the test fits into, understands, the basic culture pattern of American civilization.

(In the midst of his talk, loudspeaker truck came by, urging students to assemble for march downtown. They marched—200 or so—to Mayor Allen's City Hall. He came out, spoke to them, friendly but vague. Picketing of Henry Grady will continue. Saw Anna Jo Weaver at end of day. She said others of Big Five* (Biltmore, Atlantan, Dinkler Plaza, ?) had agreed on desegregation by March 15, but only if all would do it, and Grady had held out).

US Hist Class: heard tape of Emory debate with Lewis III on HUAC. Class indicated that they (some of them) had heard references to one Spelman faculty member (not in history dept, they said) as a Communist. One of them said: I would trust my life with that man, and I don't know him very well. Another said, well, he's a nice person.

Faculty meeting: Spoke to Lois on phone before meeting about bringing up playing of tape of Soc. Sci. club meeting† to rest of faculty & Manley. She didn't want to bring it up herself, said it would only anger Manley, said private negotiations might work. I told her six years of private talks with him had brought nothing. She said I might bring recorder, play it for half hour in free period. But at last minute I decided against. When free period started, I told faculty about the meeting, noted large attendance, candid discussion, asked group if they would like a special meeting for everybody including president to hear it. President said he wouldn't have time, even if tape were cut down to an hour, that anybody who would want to hear it could, but indicated he wanted nothing to do with it. I asked if Dean Eagleson could send out notices for such a meeting. He said that's up to Dean. Staughton brought up tri-partite committee to discuss student govt, which Manley said 3 months ago he was considering. Manley's response was he had his regular committees to do this. Barnette Smith‡ spoke (just when things seemed about to end, saying it was his impression faculty members were stirring up the students). I suggested he listen to the tape and then make up his mind. Manley spoke, said he had prepared written statement, but hadn't brought it, now felt the need to talk. Said he wondered why (as Smith had wondered) why Soc. Sci. Club felt need to sponsor meeting, why not thru regular student govt. channels. Also felt faculty members were pushing things.§

---

*   The five biggest hotels in Atlanta.
†   Zinn is referring to the March 11 "On Liberty at Spelman" meeting, sponsored by the Social Science Club.
‡   Barnett Frissell Smith was professor of biology at Spelman, who had been teaching at the college since 1945. Here again was the pattern of older, mostly black faculty and administrators, partisans of Spelman's conservative, hierarchical social, political, and academic culture, aligning with Manley against Zinn.
§   These remarks were targeted against Zinn, as faculty adviser to the Social Science club, the implication being that the protest meeting had been organized by that club rather than the student government because the club was directed by Zinn to stir up trouble.

Yes, you could always assemble a great number of students for a gripe session, but there had been complaints since he came in 1953 and they were to be expected. The "proper channels" should be used in all cases rather than such meetings. I spoke at some length, saying the meeting was called to provide an opportunity for faculty, students, administration to get together in a free, honest discussion of things which were bothering students. Manley had said faculty members were sympathetic to students, and I said yes, of course. I said democracy required all forms of expression, going ou[t]side regular channels when these channels no longer allow free flow of ideas and action. I said const[itution] had been adopted seven years ago, and it needed the tri-partite commission to review the whole situation, make recommendations. Mrs. Chivers* spoke, hastily: "Dr. Zinn has spoken so long—it's one of his techniques[.]" Went on to say she hadn't gone to meeting because it was obviously loaded, what with faculty member reading letters from students at start of meeting, with tape recorder there. Besides, she had seen sign advertising meeting; it showed big picture of Liberty Bell with crack in it, which was a way of casting aspersions on the college. Students always griped; they looked for instructors who would give them a sympathetic ear. Young prim biology teacher spoke, then left room. Her statement vague, but in general with administration. Mrs. Chivers had spoken of things like Soc. Science Club meeting as "dangerous." Mrs. Mickelbury spoke, said all this pointed up what she had said: we needed discussion of basic purpose of college, philosophy etc. indicated also she was with administration. Miss (Senorita) Howard† spoke, said she hadn't wanted to get personal and direct like this but she must: some faculty members who were raising this fuss would not do this at Emory or Agnes Scott or some other institution, or Morehouse. (Shirley McBay‡ said after the meeting this was an unmistakable racial statement.) Manley spoke again briefly, said he had no time to listen to tape, would listen to things coming thru regular channels. Staughton & Renate had hands up and I called out "Dr. Manley." to say something but he stood up and started to leave, saying "That's all I have to say." The meeting was over. Shirley McBay confronted him as he was leaving, protesting his cutting off of discussion. She continued with him going out of door, telling him he kept putting off things, never getting to them. He finally, with her pushing, said angrily, okay, we'll discuss the salary question at next faculty meeting. Lois said, as meeting broke up, See, it's what I was afraid of; he got his back up and now we haven't accomplished anything. (What if she were appraising a white faculty member at a white college

---

*   Naomi Reid Chivers was professor of education and former dean of women at Spelman.

†   Camilla Louise Howard was professor of modern languages at Spelman, a Spelman graduate who had been teaching at the college since 1948.

‡   Shirley Mathis McBay was professor of mathematics at Spelman. The racial subtext here with regard to the Emory and Agnes Scott comparisons was that the kind of dissent being directed against Manley would not have been directed by white faculty against the head of a white university or college.

where president opposed segregation; would she also urge keeping quiet this way, not riling him by saying what you think? The problem of *transference* of values is so crucial, of being able to see beyond those things which affect you personally and about which you can easily get militant, to other problems affecting others.) Several of us—Staughton, Renate, Esta, Shirley—stood outside for a while afterward, with Rukalski. He pointed to his nose: "I have a nose for these things. I've been in concentration camps. It's no use. This faculty is against all this. When we were in our twenties we thought oh how much we could do to change things. But later it becomes clear we can't; this is the way the world is." (The essential irrelevance of race comes thru the whole meeting; tyranny is tyranny, whether whites over blacks, blacks over blacks, mixed over mixed, etc. Spelman is one big footnote to Frazier's Black Bourgeoisie.) Staughton walked me home. I was very depressed. He wondered if his coming to Spelman had made things more difficult for me; I said no of course not. But I told him I thought I had had my fill of the place. I love the students, but the administration, no—the faculty, no. Sad to see how silent they were. This is salary-judging time for the president, and everyone is conscious of it. A harsh sentence might be worth a few hundred dollars. I probably have lost a thousand already! It seems up to the students now. Shouldn't forget a basic point: the people most hard hit on any issue are the only ones you can depend on; sympathetic allies, no matter how potentially powerful don't have the inner incentive. Faculty might fight for themselves on certain occasions, but not for students. Last night, it was: stick up for the students, and lower your own salary. The choice was clear. I told Esta (silent, discouraged) that I was still optimistic, that all social change involves tension, temporary defeat, disappointment, conflict before surrender. (But I also told Staughton on way home that Spelman did not *have* to change. It could continue indefinitely petty and mediocre. Yet, I think it is close to change.)

Fri. March 15

Kiss me Kate,* by A-M-S Players.† Their usual great talent, verve, a delight to see and hear. Afterward Bert & Fran Schor (he, Wall St. Journal correspondent from NY, she sweet pretty girl from Mississippi), and Gordon & Betsy Sugarman (he had helped with Pat Lynch in jail), and Pat Watters (we just listened to his tape before he came, his prologue to novel, the specific language not the greatest but the total effect, atmospheric, moving, effective). And Maxine Yalowitz, an Atlanta painter (naturally the person named Yalowitz would have the deepest Southern accent in the group. She's a nice person). Talked about Kiss Me Kate, Al-benny [i.e., the Albany, Georgia civil

---

*   *Kiss Me Kate* (1953) was a musical by Bella and Sam Spewack, music and lyrics by Cole Porter.
†   Atlanta University-Morehouse-Spelman Players, a drama group.

rights struggle], the latest ballistics disclosures on the Preston Cobb case.[*] (Called State Dept. on Fulbright. No news.)

Sat. March 16

In morning, Marie Thomas came over with three other girls who were at rehearsal during Soc. Sci. Club meeting—to hear tape of meeting. They sat around on floor, drinking coffee, reacting as the students did at the meeting, with all their emotions. Marie is so sensitive to all this. She's upset now because Dean has called her in for next week: to discuss her letter at the meeting? (While they were here Damaris Allen & Sadie Beasley[†] came in, got letter from warden turning down request to see Morton Sobell to prepare them for moot court in class.) Took Marie home, she told of sick girl forced to walk over to infirmary because nurse insisted over phone she was well enough to do so.

Jeff to Sebbas to spend weekend with John. Myla to her actors lab, to go to Catholic Mass tomorrow morning to get in mood for next play.

Jennifer Ragwar came over to give Roz Swahili lesson, stayed for dinner.

Quiet evening at home, baroque music combined with typewriter clatter from time to time. After 11, with Kiss Me Kate ending, group came from it to visit us: Ann Ford & husband Eugene Harris (a sort of fabulous guy, a jazz pianist losing use of his hands due to some disease, his father a converted Jew from Gary Indiana, he does sets with AMS players and occasionally "heavy" roles as in Kiss Me Kate, a handsome, soft-spoken intelligent fellow). Also Lenore Taitt,[‡] back from field work in Washington, ebullient as usual. And Harold Bardonelli, with Desiree Jett.[§] We sat around until four, over beer and bourbon at first, then waffles and coffee. Real fun. Harold was less Black Muslim tonight, more with funny stories about Rufus Clement, A.U. bureaucracy, etc. Eugene told of May[']s pettiness, dictatorship at Morehouse. The picture now builds up—it's not just Spelman—tho Spelman is the worst—it's the whole Negro college set-up. Ann was pushed out of Spelman after three and a half years, a semester to go to graduation, because she married Eugene without telling administration—they require 30 days notice or some such thing. Now, after two years she wants to finish, can't even get Manley to agree to see her. They told of him skulking around campus after dances, him catching girl kissing, throwing her out, and relent-

---

[*]   The Preston Cobb case drew protests nationally and internationally, after an all-white Jasper County jury—deliberating for just 45 minutes—convicted Cobb, a fifteen-year-old African American, of murdering a white farmer. Cobb was sentenced to death, the youngest person ever to be so sentenced in Georgia's history.

[†]   Sadye Maria Beasley was a Spelman (class of 1964) student.

[‡]   Lenora Taitt was a Spelman alumna (class of 1960), a former Zinn student, who had helped lead the Atlanta sit-in movement and was a freedom rider arrested in the Albany movement.

[§]   Desiree Jett was a Spelman alumna (class of 1961) who was arrested during the Atlanta sit-ins.

ing only after mass student protest, march on his home. Apocryphal story about him hiding in shadows of Giles and Morehouse man announcing loudly he would take a leak there, and him jumping out.

Sun. March 17

Visited Esta to get duplicate tape made. We agreed biggest problem is not our "rashness" but tendency to get immersed in the idiocy, lose perspective and begin to live with it. To retain a sanity based on the way things should be, we must say things that seem outlandish to the lunatics in this setup. (She said Jean Smith[*] told her a student said: how about that, it's the white teachers who are on our side!)

Mon. Mar. 18

Mendy Samstein,[†] at Morehouse for this semester to teach Eur. hist, then back to U of Chi[cago] to finish PHD over for dinner and evening. Very intelligent, good person. Brandeis student. Marcuse[‡] his god. Comes from 6 St. & Ave. A NYC![§] Told about his arguments with conservative Morehouse faculty about various things. Gave most convincing argument for Kennedy blockade of Cuba I've heard—from the standpoint of a peace movement man therefore very impressive. Said it was just right, not too provocative, but got missiles out, which moves things back toward more peaceful situation. My main argument—it turned out right, but is there guarantee in risky business like that, that it will. What if there is cumulation of dares, dares? Can it get out of hand? Choose between risks.

Dorcas called: Saw Manley Saturday. They had agreed she would inform him on results of meeting. She asked him to hear tape. He said he didn't want to be bothered by details. Wanted written statement from Club on what was wanted. Dorcas: isn't this a sign of disinterest[?] Then he said didn't have time. Said students were not thinking for themselves, someone stirring them up. Dorcas: was this true of meeting too? He said he hadn't decided. Students being manipulated, he said. Statement drawn up by SS Club[¶] should be written by students, not anyone else, he said. Said channels should be used for grievances. Dorcas didn't agree. Said would never feel limited to channels. They agreed on improving SSGA,[**] and she said this was a

---

*   Jean Blackshear Smith was an instructor in English and education at Spelman.
†   Mendy Samstein was a SNCC worker who helped organize the Mississippi Freedom Summer voting rights and education crusade.
‡   Frankfurt School philosopher Herbert Marcuse was a key critical theorist admired by the New Left. He was the author of *Eros and Civilization* (1955) and *One-Dimensional Man* (1964).
§   This was on New York City's Lower East Side, where Zinn and his family lived before moving to Atlanta.
¶   Social Science Club.
**   Spelman Student Government Association.

way to stimulate it (by SS Club meeting). AEM* said some students didn't like atmosphere of meeting—a gripe session. He said again background of students at Spelman didn't permit freedom. Spelman student had not been exposed to same things as students in other areas—they were interested primarily in social activities. Dorcas: are you saying none of the things we ask for are valid—is this the end—will our statement be ignored? Manley—will first see if anything in statement is valid—that *he* had right to decide what was valid and what should therefore go to student council! Said can't go too fast. Said if this kind of thing continues—meeting outside student govt—will divide faculty members, bring chaos.

Dorcas said Mrs. Perry told her she liked the meeting, gave students a chance to express themselves, said perhaps I was not kept busy enough by my teaching duties, hence involved in student affairs. Dorcas said she was in my class last year, and no teacher she ever had worked harder. Mrs. Perry said wasn't questioning my ability as teacher, but . . .

Tues. Mar. 19

. . . . Yearbook editor in office said she almost had a nervous breakdown this year, had been taking pills on doctor's prescription. After Yearbook staff voted to dedicate Book to Irene Asbury Wright (admittedly with some students not knowing her, & Nancy Fessen plumping for her).

Dr. Manley called her in, asked her to hold up on the selection. Then, she was called in by Mrs. Brazael who spoke of all the long-term people on faculty & staff who deserved dedication, implying she was one of them (her daughter Ernestine had come to a meeting of the staff & submitted her mother's name but no one else had voted for her) & saying couldn't understand how they picked Mrs. Asbury (this is first time, as far as anyone knows, that a staff selection was challenged[)]. Then Dean Johnson called her in, said faculty members were protesting selection of Irene Asbury. Mr. Caruthers said it was not the thing to do, violated usual procedure of picking long-term person. Finally, vote was taken again, after much discussion, after . . . [yearbook editor] told staff how she had been called in & placed in awkward position, secret ballot taken—Asbury replaced by mothers.†

[The first Mar. 19 diary entry = H]

---

*   Spelman President Albert E. Manley.
†   So due to this administration pressure, Spelman's yearbook in 1963 was dedicated not to Asbury but to the mothers of Spelman's graduates.

Tues. Mar. 19

Class US Hist: Moot court on Barenblatt Case.* Near end, I threw question: Barenblatt has been found guilty of contempt of congress, sentenced, conviction upheld by Sup. Ct., serves time in jail, now wants back at Vassar. You are Bd. of Trustees—will you rehire him? Most said yes. Two strong holdouts for doctrine: the welfare of the college comes first, and the college needs the support of the community and money to grow on—so, no to Barenblatt. I posed another problem: small private white college in South, Negro applies. To admit him would outrage community, lose its support, money, etc.—same verdict? To maintain consistency, both said yes, same verdict—angering a few other students!
Edw. Dimock of Chicago U. over for dinner, very nice guy—Sanskritist with training in Bengali, translates Bengali literature into English—Banks and Brisbane brawl again. At seminar he discusses translation problems.

Wed. Mar. 20

Dimock discusses Tagore.† Then bunch come over here for coffee and talk.

Thurs. Mar. 21

Class discusses Albany Movement vs. Pritchett‡—signs on blackboard "Colored sit to the rear." Student does perfect mime job on Southern lawyer defending Pritchett. Evening, Town Hall meeting—good turnout, Staughton does brilliant job on US-Cuba policy, very well researched, well-presented, ending "If this (welfare, jobs, health, etc.) be socialism—let capitalism profit by the example." Got rousing hand. Brisbane moved over quite a bit to meet the assault, much more moderate than usual, admitted invasion wrong, should leave Guantanamo, should have a nuclear weaponless world, *but* must face *realities*. There's no moral code in int'l affairs, so why act as if there is. When someone brought up race Brisbane insisted it had no

---

*   *Barenblatt v. U.S.* (1959) was a civil liberties case in which a divided U.S. Supreme Court decided (5–4) that HUAC had not violated Professor Lloyd Barenblatt's First Amendment rights by inquiring into his affiliations with the Communist Party. Barenblatt had refused on First Amendment grounds to answer HUAC's questions concerning his political beliefs, and had been cited for contempt of Congress, a citation the Court's decision upheld.

†   Rabindranath Tagore was a Bengali poet, novelist, essayist, short story writer, dance and musical dramatist, and the first non-European to win the Nobel Prize in Literature (1913).

‡   Albany, Georgia, police chief Laurie Pritchett was the nemesis of Martin Luther King Jr. and the black freedom movement there. By instructing his police force to avoid public acts of violence, Pritchett denied King and the movement the kind of catalytic media events—the televised mass police brutality—that helped King to emerge victorious in the Birmingham and Selma struggles. That strategy contributed to the failure of King and the movement to win any clear victory in the Albany struggle in 1961–62.

place "Negroes are Americans—they fought for this country, will do again." Lively discussion. Strange thing—no strong right-wing expressions from audience. General audience mood seemed to be pro-Lynd. Three African students who spoke all very critical of US policy. Carolyn Nicol* (Sierra Leone) in her inimitable singing voice: "Who does the US think she is—charge d'affairs for the Western Hemisphere?" A priest and student sitting in front, I thought might be critical of the whole thing, but afterward he spoke very strongly in favor of the things had been said against US policy.

Fri. Mar. 22

Carolyn came to office to listen to tape of meeting, loved it, expressed her own strong feelings. (Yesterday, AAUP meeting lunch, Lana Taylor case again, the conservatives seem to be staying away. Lois wants to mediate.) Spelman Spotlight out today, with two powerful letters, one by little Evelyn Terry,† the other Marie Thomas' beautiful letter. Under Marie's letter a few lines had been inked out. Carolyn told me what they were. Mrs. Chivers, adviser to paper, had without consulting staff put in that Marie had been suspended for breaking rules. Staff crossed it. Now waiting for reactions!

Wed. [March 27]

Damaris Allen & Sandra Marshall over after Staughton's seminar (stayed till 11:30 talking, were campused‡). Damaris said Mrs. Manley once asked her to put on apron to serve guests, she said had to study, Mrs. Manley said she was at Spelman on scholarship and should be cooperative. Sandra also said scholarships are thrown at students—gratitude wanted.

Sun to Wed. Mar. 24–37 [27]

In Philly for Assn Asian Studies. Needed badly to get away too. on Sat. night Zygmunt had stayed till three a.m. telling me I was pushing trying too hard for students. Wrong tactics. Need to go easy. Antagonizing faculty. Cooled off, regained perspective in Philly, told Lois there at breakfast one day what I think: that tactically, if the power structure doesn't at first recognize extent of dissatisfaction and negotiate, only course is to continue pressure, even with antagonism, recrimination, angry re-

---

*   Caroline Sylvia Nicol was a Spelman (class of 1964) student from Sierra Leone.
†   Evelyn Terry was a Spelman (class of 1964) student.
‡   "Campused" was a verb at Spelman which meant being grounded, such as a student being barred from leaving campus as punishment for some violation of campus rules—especially evening curfews.

actions, etc. and if continued there will be results—and after victory, the antagonism will fade and the powers will say—this is what we wanted to give you all along.

Thurs. Mar. 28

US Hist this PM, Damaris Allen spoke about Sobell Case. In Soviet course read excerpts from Eng-lang. textbooks used in Soviet schools and discussed kind and extent of indoctrination.

Stopped on lawn for long talk with Betty Stevens—they've got a student govt. meeting in chapel hour in the morning and will try to put thru a bunch of reforms then. Committee on Appeal[*] will meet with Mayor Allen this afternoon on various desegregation problems in Atlanta. After dinner, Mendy Samstein came over, he's spent last four days with SNCC and Committee on Appeal, is worried about overstress on negotiation with no direct action backing. A very earnest, nice guy. Said at Brandeis and in high school rather apolitical—the humor mag. at Brandeis was banned, then he became an editor it was okay—in high school was a trimmer[†]—went to Cornell for grad school and realized they were trying to make a professional scholar out of him, moved to U of Chicago. Chicago dead, full of problems, most segregated city, no social action. Decided to make a leap out of his life, hence this semester in Atlanta.

While he was here, Betty Stevens called, with her customary conspiratorial coolness[:] "Dr. Zinn, may I come over to fill out those forms? I'll be write [sic] over." Five minutes later, she was here, with Margaret Hampton[‡] and the president of the Junior Class, Annease Cheney. (Margaret Hampton looked worried in class today, and in general has been nervous ever since the administration began to harry her about her complaint at the Soc. Science Club meeting. She told me she called home after her talk with Manley-Eagleson to say don't be surprised if I lose my scholarship. Her grandmother told her don't get into trouble. Her father—a brickmason (she said proudly), told her, stick up for your rights, don't give in.) The three wanted me to go over draft for tomorrow morning—bill of student rights and responsibilities at Spelman. I told Betty biggest problem would be procedural, getting it on the floor and to a vote, with a cold chairman. Annease was casual, Margaret serious, intense, Bettye [Betty] was Bettye [Betty], strong, cool. Had to call the housemother to say—ten more minutes, Betty will be back. She went out the door, saying (she had just said, remember, we weren't here) in her inimitable cool, arch way[:] "Thanks—for nothin'!"

---

[*]   The Committee on Appeal for Human Rights was the organizing body for the student sit-ins of the Atlanta student movement.

[†]   A trimmer is a person who adapts his or her political views to the dominant trends. On the Left this was a pejorative term for someone who compromises their principles opportunistically for the sake of popularity.

[‡]   Margaret Hampton was a Spelman (class of 1965) student, Merrill scholar.

Betty told me Manley tried to get Burroughs to get Marie Thomas to straighten out, dangling scholarships in front of her.

[Mar. 28 date = H]

Fri. Mar. 29

Students demonstrated this afternoon (I went down, but had been misdirected to old post office instead of new one) in front of Justice Dept office with coffin representing the Constitution, protesting Mississippi events of last few days (ten SNCC field men, including Bob Moses[*] and Jim Forman) arrested leading group Negroes to register in Greenwood, Miss. Charge: inciting to riot.

In chapel this AM, the student president made announcements about Founders Day until 8:30—time for end of program—then put on Betty, who had time to read part of statement, that's all. Now problem is, how to call enough meetings fast enough to get things thru.

Evening: Constance Nabwire and Esta (from Sierra Leone)[†] came over to ask Jeff to join them in the African song he learned, for an African shindig next weak. Both fed up with Spelman. Esta wants to go elsewhere next year. Constance is going to Columbia Univ. this summer and wants to make it permanent. Told of African student who left last year. Constance told of how in Africa students wouldn't take so much junk—in her high school, where headmaster suspended a student, the boys surrounded the headmaster[']s house until the police came, called a strike—they stayed out of school three months until the headmaster relented. Later Margaret called, to borrow Sacco & Vanzetti record for her and Dorcas to listen to. They came over afterward bringing it back and we chatted.

April 1 to April 5 (Mon to Fri)

Fred Gardner our guest—the best we ever had, Roz says. A fantastic person. Roz knew him as the stage manager in Caucasian Chalk Circle at Harvard who would put up all sorts of witty-meaningful notices on the walls. An editor of the Crimson[‡]—it turns out he wrote that long editorial on "The Zinn Report."[§] Coming down for spring break to "look around." Major in biochemistry, but wants to be a writer. Calmly came in Monday night and told us of stopping off in Hazard Kentucky to have a hearing before a judge for filling a guy full of shot (72 pieces or so). He had driven a truck-

---

[*]   Bob Moses was the leader of SNCC's voting rights crusade and Mississippi Freedom Summer.

[†]   Constance Nabwire was from Sierra Leone; Esta Bezhura was from Uganda.

[‡]   *Harvard Crimson* was the student newspaper at Harvard University.

[§]   Zinn's initial Albany report for the SRC. The final version was *Albany: A Study in National Responsibility.*

full of food to Hazard because he is sort of working for the Teamsters who want to replace the UMW there and because he's concerned about the terrible situation there—and was staying in a house full of miners' guns (sounds like 1913!)* when a guy approached to set fire to the house—so he and another fellow fired at the fellow, wounded him. But the judge was okay he says so no trouble. Also announced that two weeks ago he sold novel to Random House. Also had two plays produced at Harvard. (Also seems to like Myla!) Spent his time here walking [to] SNCC office, (Myla often with him), talking to students, to Mays, to McGill—wants to bridge gap between small professional SNCC people and large fairly inert mass students.

[Sat.–Sun.] April 6–7

In NY for Committee T† meetings. Impressed with John Millett, ch'n Miami University Ohio. Depressed with several other presidents, including one of NYU. But just about everybody—presidents and faculty—take for granted what we don't have here— like faculty knowing about budget (Millett consults with faculty beforehand), like faculty-elected committees. Impressed with Fidler, Southern-speaking, intelligent head of AAUP. Met at Sat. meeting pres of Texas Southern, Marg. Curry's brother, Sam Nabrit, who seems nice, told of hiring [a] man who'd been fired on academic freedom case elsewhere, needed a few years to retire.

[Mon.] April 8

More Spelmania of the past few days:
1) Cecile Genpatsingh scheduled to deliver the Founders Day luncheon little speech, approached by Mrs. Brazeal to submit speech to her in advance. Cecile declined. Mrs. Brazeal said "I hope it will be a good speech. Remember, it's no occasion for grievances." Also if it's nice it will be put in the *Messenger*‡ & send it to all your friends.
2) Caroline Nicole approached by housemother Priscilla Rowe to run for president§ vs Betty Stevens. Caroline declined.
3) AEM called Bettye [Betty] in said he saw Merrill in Boston, told Merrill of Betty's poor citizenship, that as vice pres. she had been uncooperative has worked to defeat

---

*   The 1913 reference is to the Colorado mine labor wars that in 1914 would culminate in one of the worst episodes of anti-union violence in American history, the Ludlow massacre, which Zinn wrote his master's thesis on and which he was planning to write a book about.
†   AAUP Committee T on the Place and Function of Faculty in University Governance and Administration.
‡   *The Messenger* was the official Spelman news magazine published by the administration.
§   President of the Spelman student government.

Spelman's goals, but AEM said Merrill should give her summer grant anyway! (How interesting the *real* conversation must have been!)

[Entire Apr. 8 diary entry = H]

Tues. Apr. 9

Conference with Manley. I had asked for it to try to generate some cordiality in face to face encounter after tension of last meeting. No cordiality, perhaps slight easing of tension, but absolutely no agreement on anything. On the Social Science Club meeting. "You should have cleared it with me first." I said that was "intolerable"—that on a democratic campus any group should be able to meet any time on any subject without clearing it with anyone. He said—as he kept saying throughout—"that's where we disagree." Why did we have to have such a meeting, he asked, why wasn't it handled by student govt. I said student govt. had all year to have such a meeting, didn't. I didn't bring up again why he refused to listen to tape of meeting. He said, when I spoke of tension, he didn't do anything to produce it. I said, yes, you did. I mentioned Lana Taylor. He reiterated: she "undermined" the president of the student body, hence bad citizenship, hence scholarship not granted. Are you aware the facts are in dispute, I asked? He said, he didn't know that. I said, why didn't you try to find out. I said, how could you in fact, find out anything since the letter was sent to her over the summer. I asked how a student could have poor citizenship and be sent away on exchange, win the prize of her department, be elected president of senior class. He stuck to insistence he acted right—then said the committee on scholarships made the decision. I said I'd talked to members of the committee and it was his decision. He said he would have to check his files on that, but anyway it was a correct decision.

Most meaningful statement: he said at one point. "I have never been a crusader and I am not now." At the end of the meeting I said, you put your finger on the heart of it when you said you aren't a crusader. Perhaps I am somewhat. But whatever we are, shouldn't we want to turn out students who have something of the crusader in them? No response.

He said, why do you keep bringing up these things, Why aren't you interested in other things. I asked the faculty to be interested in: students cheating on exams, students stealing in dormitories, things missing all the time. Aren't you interested in these things? Not very much I said. Yes, I said, I'm interested in everything, but some things are more important.

He pointed to progress. I reminded him it was like white south on eve of desegregation pointing to progress.

He brought up Merrill, said he'd told faculty early in year that if they had scholarship recommendations to bring them before faculty committee. I told him I assumed this referred to Spelman scholarships. These were for summer and post-graduate, given by someone else. I asked him do you have any objections to these girls getting scholarships?" He said: in one case, yes. Betty Stevens, and I told her so.

At one time I told him Lana Taylor had more citizenship more character than 90% students, and also faculty and administration.

I asked him again and again, since we cannot agree, to submit issues to someone from outside. Not necessary. Or to have a small group of faculty and administration meet informally, regularly or irregularly, to thrash out some of these things, act as a safety valve to relieve tensions. Not necessary. We have all the machinery, we have the channels we need.

Wed. Apr. 10

Staughton & I are both talking about next year being our last. He says Renate says the same. We would like somehow to let trustees know situation here before we leave.

[Thurs.] Apr. 11

Founders Day,* after which four of us sat in our living room (Ralph Moore Morehouse student from Fitzgerald Georgia, former chairman, still active in the Committee on Appeal for Human Rights, tall, thin, personable; Mendy Samstein, Brandeis & U of Chi. guy from Lower East side, now teaching this semester at Morehouse, new discoverer of student movement, anxious for "direct action"; Finley Campbell,† who shows bursts of activism—is it his wife Jackie's influence—(he astonished us by showing up on that Cuba picket line—tall, skinny, Gandhiish, bespectacled, brilliant; and me.) Negotiations with restaurant owners assn have foundred [foundered]—they keep stalling,‡ so Ralph & Mendy came over the other night with suggestion for a quiet sit-in, at Lebs. The suggestion appealed to me—Passover—pastrami at Lebs—two Jews taking two Negroes to [get a] taste of Jewish food, even if not kosher for Pesach,§ on Passover. We discussed whether to get arrested, decided not to—with students on vacation, no immediate impact. Now stop short of arrest, later if necessary

---

* Founders Day is a Spelman commemorative tradition, held in early spring each year, honoring graduating seniors who don their commencement caps and gowns, where first-year students come to Sisters Chapel in white dresses, academic goals and challenges are articulated, and Spelman alumnae return to campus.

† Finley Campbell was a professor of English at Morehouse College.

‡ These negotiations were initiated by Zinn and other civil rights activists to press Atlanta restaurants to serve African Americans. The initial waves of sit-ins in 1960–61 had led to an agreement among Atlanta's large stores and the Chamber of Commerce to desegregate but many restaurants still clung to their Jim Crow traditions in 1963.

§ "Pesach" is the Hebrew word for the Jewish holiday, Passover.

follow up with more sit-ins, perhaps arrests. Mendy was anxious for arrest, but relented. Ralph seemed anxious too, but after discussion seemed happy with decision because then he can see his girl tonight. We drove downtown. I walked past alone first to see if empty tables and easy entrance. Then the four of us briskly walked past cashier, through roped entrance, to a table, sat down. The manager came over, a Mr. Goldberg, forty-ish, concerned. Said his own thoughts were his own thoughts but he had a job to do and he had a wife and kids and he couldn't serve us. A former school athlete, from New York, only three months on this job, wanted to keep it. Would he do the same to Jews? If his job, yes. Wasn't this like the people under Hitler doing their job? Let's not talk politics. We chatted, joked, told how we hungered for hot pastrami. Said he'd be glad to wrap up some beautiful pastrami sandwiches for us to take out. But he had to work by his orders. We asked to talk to Leb himself. He said perhaps Leb in Las Vegas. He didn't know where he was. Finally left. We got hungrier. Decided we'd made a tactical error sitting down at a table where no plate of pickles. One right near us. Mendy debated whether to reach over and grab them. Suggested we switch tables. This rejected by group as crass opportunism. Soon a man unmistakable as Mr. Leb* appeared, short, fatty, balding, a delicatessen owner without doubt. With him two plainclothesmen. They came over. One of the plainclothesmen I recognized from the Cuba picket line. They remained silent while Leb made a big deal over fact we'd come in on the side of the rope marked exit, therefore we were trespassing, therefore we should walk out and come back again: I said "Be honest, Mr. Leb, you want us out because there are Negroes in this group." He replied excitedly, "I didn't say that. You won't get me to say that." They left, walked away, the plainclothesmen stood around quite a while, talking to Leb. Then uniformed policeman came, hung around. Three guys passed the window, one motioned for Mendy to come outside, clenching his fist. Meanwhile the restaurant filling up, people coming in to eat, most not noticing us, a few curious looks, one apparently hostile look. But no one leaving. A Negro bus boy came by, shoved four glasses of water on the table—for a moment there [w]as a feeling of triumph, they had decided to serve us: but then he said, "Wish I could do more" and went away. The water tasted good. Fifteen minutes later Leb came to the table, swept the half-finished glasses off, saying "These are mine!" We decided to stay till eight—we'd been there two hours—then decided on another fifteen minutes when we saw more people coming in. The three mean ones came into the restaurant, looking at us, sat down at the counter. We thought they'd follow us when we left, but they didn't. Outside, a paddy wagon stood. Had been there all the time apparently. We went to Paschals† to feed our starved bodies, decided Ralph would call Leb to see if he would change his mind.

---

*   Charles Lebedin was the owner of Leb's delicatessen in Atlanta who, along with other local restaurant owners, resisted integrating his restaurant.

†   Paschal's restaurant and lodge was a central meeting (and dining) place for Atlanta civil rights

[Marginalia: At the top of this entry Zinn wrote "Lebs" [Leb's], perhaps planning to use this part of the diary to publish an account of this attempt to desegregate Leb's delicatessen]

[Fri.–Sat.] April 12–13

SNCC Conference on old Gammon campus.[*] About three hundred students, observers, etc. Big delegations from Greenwood, Miss. and Southwest Georgia—and Friday night each group stood on stage for a while and told about experiences. Saturday morning, tremendous singing. I spoke at full assembly after that—hard to follow. I had prepared roughly, but it went over well. My point: SNCC has done, and should continue to maintain centers of power outside the existing political structure, should not be deluded that registration to vote will solve everything, that people voting are coming into a basically undemocratic political structure. When Negroes begin to vote they will achieve as much power thereby as the rest of us have—which is very little.

Sunday morning, Dick Gregory[†] who'd spent six days in Greenwood marching to courthouse with movement—they'd arrested his writer but refused to arrest him, held forth for maybe two hours. A tremendous session. Drank gallons of ice water while talking so maybe had a hangover. He destroys a stereotype by using it to death. In Greenwood called white police "nigger." Maybe this is a great weapon—make an epithet meaningless by overuse. Many of his jokes directed at black bourgeoisie. "The Negro committee came to sit when we had moved into the neighborhood—to tell us how to do right." He made mockery of the switchblade bit by carrying it to its ultimate "I cut eighty-one people last week." He mocked the Negro chosen for moon-flight. We can now sit in front of the bus, and go to the moon. But how about all those things in between? He told of visiting Bobby Kennedy,[‡] and the map on his wall of race incidents—colored pins everywhere. This was the extent of his activity—everything [i.e., every time] something happened, another colored pin.. He imit[at]ed the FBI man taking notes while people [civil rights workers were] getting beat up [by white supremacists].

Missed Bob Moses Saturday afternoon telling of Greenwood,[§] because Ralph called Lebs and got an appointment for 2:30 at his office at the Kings Inn. On the

---

activists, located on West Hunter Street (now, Martin Luther King Jr. Drive) and famed for its southern cooking—especially its greaseless fried chicken.
[*]   Gammon Theological Center, Atlanta.
[†]   Dick Gregory was a leading black comedian and civil rights activist and fundraiser.
[‡]   Robert F. Kennedy was U.S. attorney general in 1963 and was frequently criticized by civil rights activists for doing too little to challenge Jim Crow or to protect civil right workers.
[§]   Greenwood, Mississippi was a violent white supremacist stronghold and a center of SNCC organizing.

phone Leb was very apologetic—said "I was unreasonable—you were so reasonable—bring that fellow along who mentioned passover["] (when he took the water away I had said—"That's the Passover spirit!")—I want to tell him he drank from a non-kosher glass! His office at the Kings Inn (Ralph & Mendy and I went) was small but packed with wine, champagne. Offered us a drink which we declined. Affable, with fits of nervousness and anger; back to affability. Why pick on me? I'm sixty-one, what can I do if I go out of business? Will you give me security? No, I can't take the risk. Yes, I have a few restaurants, but I have no money. I wish I could sell, but no one will buy. Everyone in town says Charlie Leb is a millionaire. But it's all tied up in the restaurants. When we told him he wasn't first—what of J Stouffers, Rich's,[*] etc.—he said, oh they're big corporations, I'm an individual restaurateur. First get other individual restaurants in my area. Told us resentfully of newspaper treatment of him after Belafonte incident (during summer NAACP convention he'd turned away [Harry] Belafonte[†] from Kings Inn) had a desk full of clippings, letters from all over the country and world calling him names—Japan etc. Professors from Ga. State had called him, called him a Hitler. Grand Kleagle of Klan called him, said he was a good American made an appointment to see him. Three Klansmen came, praised him. He said do you know I'm a Jew? They said: there are good Jews and bad Jews. We left, after having some bourbon, with no decision. We told him to think it over, posed what we called small risk of integrating quietly (we pointed to diffidence of his customers the night of our sitin) as opposed to more sit-ins. He said, I know it's right, I know it's coming, but I can't take the chance myself. We left, decided we will sit-in Herrin's perhaps Ship Ahoy, then back to Leb. (Mendy & Ralph were fed at Davis Brothers right after our Leb failure—a surprise.)

[Marginalia: To the left of this final paragraph Zinn wrote "Lebs"]

Monday evening. April 14[‡]

Stayed up late talking to . . . [the wife of a colleague]. How are you so optimistic she asked me? Then she started to cry. At Cambridge people ask "What do you do?" Her father thought she would be an ace in everything. She feels she's accomplished nothing. We talked of human decency vs. accomplishment. She said she wonders if she's really a good person.

---

*   Stoufer's restaurant and Rich's department store ended their Jim Crow policies in the wake of the first round of Atlanta sit-ins of 1960–61.

†   Harry Belafonte was a popular black singer and civil rights movement fundraiser.

‡   The proper date of this diary entry is April 15.

Sunday April 14

Clancy Sigal approached me at SNCC conference after my speech, said he wanted to talk to me. Came Sunday for dinner, he I Mendy Roz spoke for about four hours. Fascinating conversation. He's written two novels—Weekend in Dinlock—Going Away—writes for Encounter,* etc. has lived in England seven years—is a minor literary celebrity there (his words) will stay there—returned to see what US is like (was Hollywood minor writer here and travelling radical before he left) finds it qualitatively worse. Except for Negroes in South, finds country in decay. We talked about everything. Thinks Negroes *are* different and we argued that. Very intelligent, articulate. Roz liked him a lot. Near end almost cried out when I said I didn't believe in death wish—he said "Then we're a million miles apart!" Furthermore, I said, I didn't think it important whether anyone believed in the death wish.

The Seatons brought Pat West from the airport while Clancy & Mendy were here. Clancy said he was going to Albany. Danny said (in his usual dour manner) the Negroes won't receive you hospitably there. Myla embarrassed Danny by asking "Have you been in Albany?" We argued that for a while. Danny thinks there is a racial barrier which is impassable—he pointed to Spelman faculty—I pointed to Spelman students. Mendy said he knew six Spelman students who said they would leave if I left the college. Danny took to Clancy—they drove him back to his hotel.

[April 14 date = H]

Monday April 15:

Roz and I drove up into the Appalachian trial [trail] to Neel's Gap to pick up Jeff and John Sebba who'd spent four days in the mountains. We had pretended not to be worried, but we were a *little* concerned. When we got to the lodge at Neels Gap there [*sic*] packs were on the porch. They'd arrived there the night before, their last shelter having been without water so they couldn't cook. They had visions of eating steak at the lodge but it wasn't open for the season, so they bought dozens of candies and ate them for supper. Then they slept out on the hill in their bags. They looked good, reddened from the sun. They had seen no wildlife except eight deer, and only two other hikers in four days plus one lonely tower man whom they'd promised to send some books.

The Spelman paper has come out—the most angry edition ever—they didn't show the letters to Mrs. Chivers† first—"Letter from a Junior" by Anna Jo Weaver—the Bethel exchange student who stayed on permanent—talks of: "Disgusted, sickened

---

and revolted by the hypocrisy, the under-handed dealings, the evasive answers and lies, the deceit, the glaring discrepancies, the treachery—in short, disgusted, sickened and revolted by the corrupt state of this school, Spelman College, as exposed by the victims under its intimidation and threats that various persons are now enduring as a result of their forthrightness in exercising their freedom of speech in discussing liberty at Spelman." Etc. Etc. a marvelous courageous letter from this quiet girl who's been in the thick of the student movement since she came. Another, less literate but strong letter from a student who details the silly rules, etc. says "little girls behind a prison fence." "Spelman is nothing and will continue to be nothing until the administration recognizes that we are mature young ladies with minds and ideas of our own." And a long account of the Social Science Club discussion. And a strong, firm, quiet editorial from Dot Myers* the new editor (the old one left in mid-year, a very good student, disgusted with conditions) saying the editors were now constituted as a board. "This board decides what is to be published and what is not be published. Any and all policy is either made by this board or must be presented to this board before it can be accepted. Our faculty advisor, Mrs. Naomi Chivers, is of course always present to give us the benefit of her experience through her well thought out advice. The final decision rests in the hands of this newly established editorial board." We're waiting to see administrative reaction on this issue. If our protest over the censorship last spring has allowed this degree of freedom it's a great victory.

[Apr. 15 date = H]

Tues. April 16

Spoke in Clark College chapel on Death of a Salesman,[†] which opens tonight with Frederick O'Neal[‡] as Willy Loman. My theme: there is Willy's dream—and ours—represented by the opening flute music, telling of grass and trees and the horizon, and there is the other dream, represented by Uncle Ben. Our civilization is the business civilization of Willy Loman and Ben is its hero. This is the time for a Negro production, as it is the time for Frazier's Black Bourgeoisie, because now we know Negroes are being admitted to the world of Willy Loman—[James] Baldwin's point about Negroes getting onto a burning ship. But Biff rebels—he is the Misfit ([Arthur] Miller I suddenly realized, has been writing about Misfits, John Proctor, etc and the Marilyn Monroe movie he wrote). I quoted "Screw the business world," as something we must say. Our problem is to survive and rebel at the same time. We must pretend to

---

*   Dorothy Mae Myers was a Spelman (class of 1963) student.

†   *Death of a Salesman*, a play by Arthur Miller that won the Pulitzer Prize in Drama and the Tony Award for best play in 1949.

‡   Frederick O'Neal was an actor, theater producer, TV director, and founder of the American Negro Theater.

go along (but not pretend too hard or the pretense will become reality) but defy it all at crucial moments . . . .

At night saw it. A tremendous job. Frederick O'Neal better than the Broadway guy.[*] More affecting than what we saw on Broadway—though poor acting roles by Linda Loman and a few others. Very moving to Roz. (But: the line by Biff changed—"Damn the business world") Uncle Ben a different interpretation but good. Not cold, but seductive, a chilling smile.

Wed. Apr. 17

At seven a.M. drove out south for an eight am appointment with Sen. Herman Talmadge, made by Kay Hocking. She, resonant-voiced John Youngblut—southern-tongued Ruth Boozer, and I. Past colts and horses, a white, 1850 house ("Sherman didn't get this one," Talmadge said). Talmadge in short sleeves, no tie ("I'm up at four-five, best time to work"). Affable, opinionated. H's views (we'd come on Senate support of nuclear test ban treaty) the views of Mr. Joe who reads the morning paper. ["]The Russians are out to conquer the world. They can't be trusted. We've got to arm to the teeth. Any treaty must be iron clad.["] Said he had no information but what he got from newspapers on tests and disarmament, would use his judgement [*sic*] when issue came up. Twenty minutes of nothing. Then we left, he came out to the car, shook hands. "Glad you came, Brother Zinn." Write to me, he said to us, your views. Put it in 3rd grade language.

Thurs. April 18

Class US Hist—discussed WWI & the blind rush to war—Guns of August—All Quiet . . . Johnny Got His Gun.[†]

  Evening—Town Meeting on Academic Freedom.

    Jack Nelson[‡]

    Morehouse senior David Satcher did a *brilliant job*.

  Dinner with British historian Plumb[§]—says was at White House, frightened by mechanist style of Kennedy admin—no moral fervor.

[Entire Apr. 18 diary entry = H]

---

[*]   The "Broadway guy" Zinn referred to is Lee Cobb, the actor who played Willy Loman in the original Broadway production of *Death of a Salesman*.

[†]   Classic works on World War I: Barbara Tuchman's Pulitzer Prize–winning history of the origins of that war, *The Guns of August* (1962); German antiwar novel, *All Quiet on the Western Front* (1929), by Erich Maria Remarque; American antiwar novel, *Johnny Got His Gun* (1938) by Dalton Trumbo.

[‡]   Jack Nelson was a Pulitzer Prize–winning reporter for the *Atlanta Constitution*.

[§]   J. H. Plumb was a British historian and professor at Cambridge University, best known for his scholarship on eighteenth-century England.

Fri. Apr. 19

Spoke in Agnes Scott chapel this morning, on eve of UN Model Assembly. Yesterday, strong anti-UN speaker spoke. I discussed national sovereignty as the basic cause of war, national pride as propping it up, poked at our pride by citing historical record of our expansion, said democratic internal structure didn't guarantee sweet disposition externally, said S[oviet]U[nion] not a slave society, not total good vs. total evil, mustn't accept stereotypes, can't divide good and evil people in the world by drawing lines across face of earth, ended with picture Bridge on the River Kwai scene. Afterward, Agnes Scott president, Dr. Wallace Alston said "That hurt, but thanks for coming" and a few outsiders (rather than students) including one physician regaled me about various things.

Evening: Guy Carawan, wife, and kid came over.

Also Myla's two redheaded sister school chums.

Wed. Apr. 24

Lunch at Emory with Shemone Gottschalk and Horace Kallen[*] & his wife he is visiting prof. at Emory this quarter—has taught at New School for Social Research since 1919—was founded by Beard, Robinson,[†] etc. idea was something like Knowledge for What?—continuous use of social sciences to meet current world needs. Kallen teaches "on liberty"—is a libertarian in . . . [a] way, deplored Anti-Defamation League red-baiting in civil rights movement, while Shemone seemed a little bewildered at this.

Fri. Apr. 26

Three long-distance calls: from Nat, on summer camp; from Dean Runyon[‡] inviting me to Yale Law School next week; from Louie Howland of Sterling Lord convincing me to withdraw mss on Exclusiveness from Knopf, telling me David Donald[§] has read my mss. on Mystique for McGraw-Hill, likes it, disagrees with it strongly, will send along critique of mystique.

[Charles] Merrill made opportunity to meet Betty Stevens at bkfast at Manleys today. He gave a rousing speech in chapel urging students to be "troublemakers," told Manley scholarships for two Bettys were private arrangement between him and me, made appointment with Betty for later afternoon. After he saw her he dropped in at our place and we chatted over usual Merrill repast—wine. He feels need to mod-

---

*   Horace Kallen was a philosopher and the leading theorist of cultural pluralism.

†   Historians Charles Beard and James Harvey Robinson.

‡   Charles Runyon was assistant dean of Yale Law School.

§   David Herbert Donald was a leading southern historian and biographer of Abraham Lincoln.

erate between Manley and Me. Wants to use me as extra nominator so that girls who think differently than Manley can have a chance but feels Manley should have theoretical veto power as president. Said he made it clear to Manley he wanted girls of varying ideas to have chance for scholarship. Merrill and I walked over to dining hall at six (Merrill said, should I walk with you? joking—also "will they put you at a table by yourself?") for 10th year testimonial to Manley. Series of dull platitudes, except for Ch'n of Bd of Trustees Lawrence McGregor [MacGregor], a Jersey banker, who said: "A president is like a gardener—he must make sure things grow in their place—and if anything grows where its not supposed to grow—he must get rid of it." Also: "There are times when a president must do like the father whose little boy at the museum kept plying him with questions, and as Ring Lardner[*] put it: "Shut up!" he explained." Manley himself in dull acceptance speech quoted Trevor Arnett[†] on himself: "He's a quiet man, doesn't seem aggressive, but he won't allow himself to be pushed around."

Millie Jordan,[‡] sitting at our table, told us she resigned in letter ten days ago (still unanswered) saying: "For 8 years I have been working at minimum rank, minimum salary, with a maximum workload. I see no future for me At Spelman, so I must resign." Jean Smith is leaving too to join her husband in California—a great girl a tremendous mimic of Mrs Curry & everyone.

Sat. Apr. 27

At theatre Atlanta, for first time, annual prizes for best actors and actresses. On Thursday someone from Theatre Atlanta called Roz, said "make sure Myla is there Sat. nite"—so we were pretty sure. Myla went to see Ondine[§] with Jeff and a friend, after which the awards were to be given. They saved Best Actress for last—then she got it. A real thrill. Topped, as we were leaving the theater by a blazing two-alarm fire in an abandoned building across from the theater.

Sun. Apr. 28

Got up 8:30 AM to transport Spelman students to NAACP organizing drive, but no one showed. Need real exciting issue to get students to act.

Dave Baker at noon brought over Ernie Marrs, Woody-Guthrie-type 34-year old writer of several thousand topical folk songs—born Oklahoma, moved all around the country ("Whether it's a recession or depression depends on whether you or

---

* Ring Lardner was a famed early twentieth-century American satirist and sportswriter.
† Trevor Arnett was a leading administrator for philanthropies supporting African American education, as president of the General Education Board in the early twentieth century.
‡ Millicent Dobbs Jordan was an instructor in English, Spelman.
§ *Ondine* (1938) is a play by French dramatist Jean Giraudoux.

the other fella is out of a job"), came to Atlanta two years ago, gets by as brickma-son or mostly selling newspapers. Friend of Pete Seeger, will turn out three songs one morning, two more in the afternoon. Sang us a few of his songs—I liked par-ticularly one about Jim Brown, how they kept putting him on a list, on a blue baby list when he was born, then classified as a white when he went to school, then on a blacklist when he complained about low wages, then as a red when he said "work-ers of the world arise"—this "red, white, black & blue Jim Brown"—but he's just Jim Brown to me.

Mendy came over to tell us about the 11 students yesterday who sat in at half dozen places including Lebs (Leb barred the door). No arrests. We discussed tactics from now on.

Saw a copy of Emory Alumni Magazine (Richard Hocking* on cover, holding up a huge book called Academic Freedom)—great article in it by Pat Watters saying if teachers don't use their academic freedom to battle the live issues of society—cor-rupt politics, segregation, world affairs—then it is only academic.

[Marginalia: To the left of the closing paragraph Zinn wrote the name of his journalist friend Pat Watters]

Tues. Apr. 30

At Canterbury House lunch Mary King & Bobby Yancey held forth on student ac-ademic freedom to a distinctly cool crowd—Mrs. Manley was there—they didn't know 1) she was wife of Spelman president† and 2) she is a wheel on national YWCA which pays their salary, and Mary said in response to a question of what she'd heard about Spelman[,] "The students say going to Spelman is like going to jail." The Chiv-ers were there, also Kennedy, who said something about the "background" of stu-dents right after Mary King said faculty members cited "background" of students as rationale for denying them freedom. And Brisbane said his daughter was going to Spelman and he didn't want her to decide for herself what parties she should go to. On other hand, Mitzie Akellrad spoke of Europe, that kids 18 were old enough to go off on weekends, do things on their own. And Newsome spoke up. And Alice Lynd pointed to punishment of students who protested. And Saxena said quietly at end (everybody had been saying, well at Atlanta Univ. colleges it's different, we're okay—Sam Williams also implied that—his stance remarkably reticent, conservative) that not real freedom at A.U. either.

During class, car with loudspeaker (Jeff later pointed out it was Mendy's car) toured campus announcing all students turn out at four at courthouse for hearing of

---

*   Richard Boyle O'Reilly Hocking was professor of philosophy at Emory University.

†   Dorothy Shepherd Manley was Albert E. Manley's first wife.

eight students arrested this morning on trespass law for sitting in at Davis Bros and Ship Ahoy restaurants. Ralph Moore at the mike and I leaned out the window and asked him the details, him answering thru the mike. Then six students borrowed my car (I had my Russian class) to go to the hearing. It was held over for two weeks. Mass student meeting at seven was to plan more action.

At faculty meeting, report on Spelman "philosophy" by Miss Howard, a repeat of a chapel talk she gave 9 years ago when Manley came in. One of her points: students don't have time for full discussion & decision making, hence must have part democracy and part autocracy to be realistic. I suggested if philosophy expresses aim—like 1st amendment & 14th must express it as absolute even if reality will bend it.

After faculty meeting at coffee hour, Shirley McBay told me a few faculty members s[a]id they believed dissidence comes from a white group, that she is being "used" by this group, that Lois was used but now is being tossed aside, that it is all part of conspiracy to replace Manley with me as president! and that communism in the backgrounds of one or more of these conspirators is a factor. Well! She asked them if they thought these people had planned in advance to come to Spelman and do this; they said, no, it probably developed after we came!

[Marginalia: To the left of the Apr. 30 paragraph on the sit-ins Zinn wrote "arrests"]

Wed. May 1

At four Mendy called from Comm[ittee] on Appeal [For Human Rights] office, needed car to take bunch to hearing city court for Frank Holloway (Big Frank). I took them down. Frank can't get out on bond, is on probation from previous charge, snatching purse. This time, charge is using "opprobrious language" on phone to white girl. She showed in court, a come-on blonde in tight clothes, said she was 15 (looked 17–18) from Sylvan High. Needed 4:30 hearing she said to give her time to come from school. But couldn't make a Tues. hearing because she would be "out of town." So set for next Thurs. Detectives came to Hunter St. this morning, in a car, grabbed Frank, threw him into car on this charge. All very vague. His attorney doesn't even know exactly what they're accusing him of.

More sit-inners arrested today, but right out. Yesterday's arrested out, saw girl from Bethel, pale from night in prison, out on Chestnut St.

Dave & Ernie came for dinner. Then to Town Meeting, where [Rufus] Clement defended Kennedy Admin. vs. Finley Campbell who did his usual brilliant job. Clement was a horror. Defended appointment [of] segregationist judges in South ("Wasn't Black[")]* a KKK member. Can't tell how they'll turn out. Got to appoint people "from all over the country" whatever that means). Question from Saxena—what has Ken-

---

*   U.S. Supreme Court justice Hugo Black.

nedy done for peace, to ease int'l tensions. Answer. He's built up our missiles? Qu[es-tion]. What about 5 million unemployed? We're bound to have unemployed all the time. The audience was remarkably lethargic, easy-going on Clement. Bunch of fat cats, Roz says, Dem. committeeman Bacote lapping up what Clement said, others not daring to hit. No real indignation. Of course the Snick [SNCC] people are out *doing* tonight—they weren't there.

Herschelle called from Wash. tonite, got John Hay*.

Yesterday: no on Finland†—we're adjusting to next year in Atlanta. Why? Some mumbo-jumbo about it was an alternate lectureship from the beginning. But last time I called they indicated outlook was "most favorable." So?

Thurs. May 2

Left with Melvin Kennedy for New Haven at Yale Law School invitation. Didn't get to Yale till 3 AM because someone switched bags with Kennedy at West Side Terminal in NYC. (Kennedy's son drove us to airport in new Olds—K. said proudly "this boy's going to be a millionaire": he's studying business adm. at M'hse). Dean Chas. Runyon at Yale treated us thruout like visiting dignitaries—seem real anxious to est. contact with Negro colleges to get bright students, to have exchanges of faculty-students. He waited at Yale Police HQ till 1 AM for us, then left word to wake him when we ar-rived. Guest suite—young bright Yale Law man waking us in the morning to take us to breakfast. At breakfast, Marian Wright‡ (first time she'd come to breakfast at Law School in years!). Then Marian who was "assigned" to me, walked around with me—a beautiful day—a long time—we talked—she's been doing less speech-making this year, is finishing up all right, will go to DC to pass the bar early part of the summer, then will work at NAACP NY a year, then to Mississippi. Her eye is on Bob Moses. She took me to the Coffins§ for a bit. Lunch for a dozen or so had been arranged at some famous little Yale club. Sat next to very nice guy named George Springer—a Ph.D. linguist, got out of Slovakia just before Hitler came—had seen me at 16 Dunster St. Cambridge—now in admissions office at Yale, will help Herschelle get in if Columbia says no. Sat in on law class PM, fellow named Moore, expert on Federal Procedure, very entertaining also informative class. Met interracial couple, Jean and—Cahn (he's son of Edw. Cahn of Moral Decision at NYU) very good couple. (Marian says his father gave trouble about the marriage. He a very bright guy—PHD in philosophy now at

---

* The John Hay Whitney Fellowship.

† Turned down for a Fulbright scholarship to go to Finland.

‡ Marian Wright (Edelman) was a Spelman (class of 1960) alumna, sit-in leader, Merrill scholar, Zinn student, Yale law student in 1963, who would later become a civil rights attorney in Mississippi and founder of the Children's Defense Fund.

§ William Sloan Coffin Jr. was the Yale chaplain and a civil rights and antiwar activist. His wife was Eva Ann Rubinstein, daughter of pianist Arthur Rubinstein.

law school, she doing unusual law work in poor neighborhood—along with social worker—Ford F[ou]nd[ation] help.[)] Cocktail party on lawn, spoke to them again. Both convinced me Yale Law School is special—socially oriented—students get less of the technique and facts but wide-ranging social-philosophical background and stress on civil lib. civil rights. 2nd cocktail party right after—talked to Thomas Emerson,* small, white-haired quiet—a good man (in his office is cartoon presented to him by Nat'l Lawyers Guild of which he was president, showing Tom Emerson with bomb in hand and near him the slogan "For Yale, for God, for Country"). His wife much younger, very nice. Then supper at Dean Rostows.† He very affable—said plainly his view of a law school is a place to teach reform of the law. Unusual. Charles Black, from Texas, a most interesting guy (Henry Luce Chair of Jurisprudence is his and Rostow says Luce set it up as opp. to McCarthy). When Rostow at one point told of his being accused of socialism and someone defended him saying he wasn't, Black said, why should you have made a point of saying you're not—I'm not sure I'm not. (But Rostow is sure). Generally excellent impression of the atmosphere of the school. Whatever Rostow is, a libertarian certainly.

Sat. [May 4] am—

ret. to Atlanta. This PM Spring Festival at Callenwald—the stiff place (Sandler Coca Cola & all) is beginning to proletarianize and inter-racialize—Roz on committee, arranged for Guy Carawn to sing, for Marilyn Price & Bunny Foster & Brenda Boyd to do opening scene Antigone‡, Marilyn doing it in French—most impressive. Guy on way to Birmingham, has convinced Joan Baez§ to sing at mass meeting there, and in Greenwood, in interstices of her Southern tour.

All things breaking loose: the freedom march for Moore thru N. Georgia (Pat Watters and Claude Sitton¶ along)—arrested in Alabama. Birmingham in tremendous turmoil. And Atlanta sit-ins rising to crescendo—40 arrested today at various restaurants—including Mendy—Anna Jo Weaver & Satcher for 2nd time. (Charlie Leb—Be a Mensch!** is our next slogan).

Sun. [May 5]

to prison today to play tennis with their team.
Betty Stevens elected pres. student body over administration candidate.

[Final sentence of May 5 diary entry = H]

---

*   Thomas Emerson was a Yale Law professor and leading civil liberties scholar and litigator.
†   Yale Law School dean Eugene Rostow.
‡   *Antigone* is an ancient Greek play by Sophocles.
§   Joan Baez, popular pacifist folksinger who was active in the civil rights and antiwar movements.
¶   Claude Sitton, a Georgia native, was the famed civil rights reporter for the *New York Times*.
**   "Mensch" is Yiddish for a good and honorable person, a person with great integrity.

Mon. May 6

40 Saturday sit-inners have hearing today. Parade of students downtown to city court. Roz went to rally on green, but I had to take Jeff to his track meet. Then I took Roz down to city court, but place was packed and we couldn't get in. Meantime students had gone downtown to bother the restaurants. No arrests.

Evening, Ralph Moore called, for me to bring car to county jail at 8:30. Forty had been bound over to county. Needed to take them home. When I got there, Sam Williams, Finley Campbell there. Also a white bondsman who was very friendly, who is partners with a Negro bondsman—office across the street from county jail (a brand new structure—reminds me of our colleges—new buildings, old contents). Ralph Moore was there, also Willie Paul Berrien,* and Finley's brother Russell who seems to have become one of the leaders. A little lady, maybe sixty, was sitting there too, real Southern—sweet-faced, white hair, little hat on head—then I saw her talking friendly to Ralph Moore. He introduced me. Mrs. Hume. Turned out her daughter was in jail with the sit-inners. Her daughter teaches English at Morehouse (I'd seen her around, dark-haired girl in late twenties)—had gone to Randolph-Macon, getting Ph.D. from Yale, Chaucer scholar. "I'm proud of my daughter," the lady said. Born in Alabama, social worker in Atlanta (works with alcoholics) since 1922. Daughter raised in Atlanta. Wonderfully patient, sat in county jail from 8:30 to 1:30 until daughter came. First 38 came, but Anna Jo Weaver and her daughter missing. Then round of phone calls to find out where they were. Benj. Mays called to push things.[†] City jail said they weren't there. County jail said they weren't there. For several hours it was a Kafka-like thing. Meantime, Mendy Samstein was out with the rest and we talked. We went to Paschals to pick up box lunches for Anna Jo and Miss Hume (direct descendant of David Hume's[‡] brother!) and Willie Paul. The 38 were eating in the backroom tho Paschals was closed. Ralph Moore was talking to them, "Okay you cats. We give them until Friday to negotiate on the restaurants. If nothing Friday we hit them on Saturday with everything." Everyone seemed too intent on their chicken. David Satcher and Anna Jo had gone on hunger strike Saturday—another reason for our wanting to get them out fast. Mendy and I went back to the county jail. At city jail guard had tried to egg on drunks in jail with Mendy. But didn't take. Here, in county jail, put in cell with eight or so others. They asked him charge. He was evasive: "Disorderly conduct." But when he and I were sitting there, two of his cellmates got out on bond and as they walked past, one of them looked at Mendy and said to his buddy "Hey, that Freedom Rider's out!" After hours of exasperation, someone walked over to the window for the fifteenth time to ask if they were sure the two girls weren't here. The guy behind said calmly—"Yeah, they're here. We're processing

---

*   Willie Paul Berrien was a SNCC organizer.

†   Benjamin Mays was the president of Morehouse College.

‡   David Hume was an eighteenth-century Scottish philosopher.

them now." But then more delay. Another hour. Asked why the delay. Again calm reply. "No bond has been made." But of course bond had been made. Willie Paul ran across the street to get the bondsman, a gangling blonde Southern boy is kind of errand boy for the Negro and white partner bondsmen. He ambled back, shoved thru the door to do his duty, returned a few minutes later, Anna Jo and Miss Hume came out. I took Anna Jo back to dorm after taking Humes to where their car was parked downtown. Housemother was asleep, but she called to a window where a light was on and a student came down and opened the door.

[Marginalia: To the left of the second paragraph of this May 6 diary entry Zinn wrote "Jail"]

Wed. May 8

Spoke to Episcopal chaplains at Southern Colleges with Lonnie Newsom[e], on Albany. A lively bunch. At Paschal's.

Ran into Ralph Moore on way out. Mayor Allen has asked please hold off demonstrations until May 15 vote on bond issue & promise restaurant owners meeting on May 16. Students will accept.

[Entire May 8 diary entry = H]

Thurs. May 9

David McReynolds[*] of FOR[†] visiting Staughton so he visited our class. Spoke to my Russian class on lawn, on disarmament. Realized at one point how many members of this 12 person class *involved*. Guy and Candy Carawan just back from Birmingham jail. Anna Jo Weaver just out of Fulton Cy. Jail. Betty S. a veteran of 14 days in jail. One fourth of [the] class.

[Entire May 9 diary entry = H]

Fri. May 10

An unprecedented meeting, from about noon to about 4 PM, took place today out on the Emory [University] quadrangle. A few Liberal Club students called it, to dis-

---

[*]   David McReynolds is a leading pacifist, antiwar organizer, and writer, active in the War Resisters League, the American Socialist Party, and an editor of *Liberation Magazine*. He would later become the first openly gay candidate to run for president of the United States (on the Socialist Party ticket).

[†]   Founded in 1915, the Fellowship of Reconciliation is the largest and oldest interfaith peace organization in the United States.

cuss informally, with no specific program of action, the events in Birmingham and elsewhere in connection with integration. About ten of our students went, including Anna Jo Weaver, Davis Satcher, Dot Myer, Robt Allen. Ralph Moore spoke at length. They had expected some trouble but there was none. Antagonistic questions, but nothing approaching violence. At one time 150–200 students were sitting on the grass listening. All in all, far more successful than anyone had anticipated. And Emory Univ. officials made no move to break it up. After it was over a faculty couple invited the Negroes home, followed by a score of white students. They brought in a keg of beer and had a ball.

Jeff gave an oral report in his class on Thoreau's Walden. His teacher gave him an A plus, asked him to repeat it at her 11th grade class. The 11th graders gave him grades and comments on it—almost all A's and praising it. One girl gave him an F, saying "No eighth-grader could read Walden and understand it. I don't believe you read that book."

Myla's English teacher told the class to write on "something I care deeply about." Most wrote on integration—something that wouldn't have happened two years ago (maybe not even two weeks ago—maybe the headlines have had this effect). Most against. But four or five for, and very bold. One girl said: "If I had Martin Luther King here I'd shoot him, and a few paragraphs on spoke of Negroes committing murder and said 'Don't they know the Bible says Thou Shalt Not Kill.[']" The class snickered at her obvious inconsistency, and the teacher called attention to it too.

Jeff's math teacher mentioned I'd been quoted in Newsweek, got into ~~dispute~~ discussion with Jeff on integration. Turned out she's from Albany, Georgia.

["discussion" in last sentence = H]

Sat. May 11

Mendy came over. Attended Frank Holloway's trial Thurs. Same judge—Jones—that he had seen last week binding over Negro man for $5000 bail after woman had accused him of purse-snatching, asked to identify him, said she wasn't sure; and mo[m]ent later two girls accused of shoplifting out on $100 bond. Mendy disgusted with Howard Moore's* handling of trial. The shapely blonde girl who is accusing Frank of "opprobrious language" (certainly not her phrase) and had asked postponement trial because she "had school," Sylvan High, it turned out hadn't gone to school for two years, and Moore didn't do anything with this. Charge was man had called her offering job as prostitute. She went down to Hunter St. to "meet" him after calling police. Frank walked out of Kitty Cat Lounge (being built, not even open, he always

---

*   Howard Moore was a prominent civil rights lawyer who worked in the black law firm Hollowell and Ward. He was one of only ten black lawyers in Georgia in the early 1960s. He later represented Julian Bond and Angela Davis and did work for the NAACP Legal Defense Fund.

goes there to watch construction, Mendy says), approached by girl who said "Are you Tony[?]" He said no. She said, are you sure[?]. He said no I'm not. Girl told all this in court, of his repeated denials. Said also man on phone had said he'd be wearing blue suit, white tie, but Frank not wearing this. Moore didn't do anything with this either. (Mendy noted white criminal lawyers all got their people off on fairly easy bail.) Then finally she said Frank said he was Tony, said he had job for her. Then, she said, he turned to go away, but police now came and grabbed him. Moore did not concentrate on simple fact no proof he was same person that made the call. Judge bound Frank over to county court. (Frank is on probation on 3–5 years for larceny, purse-snatching.)

Evening, Lois & Charlie here to picnic with Lynds. We sat around talking. Lois told incredible story of a faculty member who is resigning telling Manley that she would get at him thru Rockefeller's valet, whom her husband knew well, and Manley started to cry!

Staughton upset over Manley's blithely telling faculty last meeting no word on next year's salary until June. Faculty submissively sat and took it. If no rebellion on this, then on what?

At Savannah state, student body walked out of classes on dismissal Econ. prof.

Sat. May 11

Clark College student asked me to introduce Theodore Bikel[*] this morning. He's giving a concert in Atlanta tonite (a high school in a Jewish area, few Negroes will go) and has agreed to talk at Clark. Haskell Ward[†] who was once on Town Meeting with me, asked me, and we went together to pick up Bikel at Peachtree Manor (only integrated hotel in Atlanta, though Negroes are rarely there). Bikel turned out to be much more regular and pleasant than he has looked on TV, where his personality was a little irritating. Riding down, we talked about "the movement"—he's been one of the show people regularly helping Core [CORE] and SNCC he said. He arrived last night, got together with Guy & Candy Caraw[a]n and Jim Forman and six others, said proudly "Everyone in that room had been in jail at one time or other." At Clark about 100 turned out to hear him. He gave a good talk: spoke of artist as a participant in social struggle, spoke of the artist as a laborer requiring an organization (he's on governing board of Actors' Equity, and in fact got to talk at Clark thru intercession of Frederick O'Neal, who did Death of a Salesman's Willy Loman at Clark last month and

---

[*]   Theodore Bikel was a folksinger and screen, TV, and theater actor, nominated for Tony Awards in 1958 and 1960, and was a cofounder with Pete Seeger of the Newport Folk Festival.

[†]   Haskell Sears Ward, a student at Clark College, would later hold positions in the Peace Corps and the Ford Foundation; in the Carter administration he would become the first African American on the policy staff of the state department.

who is on Actors' Equity Board too). He was one who fought in Actors' Equity for that rule saying no performance before segregated group.

Sun. May 12

Lynds, Vincent & Rose-Marie Harding, and us invited for evening to Ed Grider (Young, southern white ass't minister at Central Presbyterian Church opposite state capital [sic], grad. Yale Divinity, at whose home the Albany prisoner-ministers stayed on way back home, who had arranged with me for some of Spelman students to join some young adults at his church to visit Juvenile Detention Home together one afternoon). We went to pick up Hardings at Mennonite House in Atlanta, which he started when he came to Atlanta two years ago with wife—she has a newborn little girl. Vincent is a remarkable guy—middle-height, thick set, huge head, glasses, dark-brown, intelligent, sober, like a rock, non-violence with him a philosophy a way of life, one of the few civil rights leaders very strong on int'l peace and civil liberties; gets into thick of any conflict and acts as a pacifier-negotiator but without losing powerful moral resolve. He was just back from Birmingham where he'd been in on negotiating meetings with B'ham businessmen, said here Burke Marshall* & D[epartment] of Justice had done a lot to bring reps of national firms to the meeting. Vincent said behind the bombings—disorder etc. was great accomplishment, firm agreements from businessmen on deseg. downtown lunch counters, employment opportunities, setting up bi-racial commission. At Mennonite House was Septima Clark,† veteran of Sea Islands & Highlander Folk school, also a white couple with baby living there, a few other people, white & Negro. It is only place in town where white and Negro families live together in a common house-kitchen, sharing everything. On to Ed Griders. Ed is strong jawed, blonde, very handsome, and still very Southern but trying very very hard. Said he'd been told Nigro was preferable to Negro, I told him story of Maggie Long and her trouble with Nigra, and of the segregationist who'd orated at Negro state college and been greeted with footstomping whenever he said Nigra, until his accent changed by end of speech. We talked about B'ham, housing sit[uation] in Atlanta, about which Ed is very concerned—his church is in slum area, with lots of Negroes moving in.

Tues. May 14

Blue & White Banquet for Honors Students. Don Hollowell‡ was guest speaker, and

---

*   Burke Marshall was the assistant attorney general for civil rights in the Kennedy administration.
†   Septima Clark, civil rights activist and educator, served as citizenship education director of the Highlander Folk School and education director for the SCLC.
‡   Donald Hollowell was a prominent civil rights attorney whose clients included Martin Luther

without judge to control him he was at his hammiest (he can be great, forceful, direct as cross-examiner, but also is given to florid language). Literally hammiest, because he spoke of The Ham. (Birmingham) and went on & on with endless metaphor about how the juices of the ham were spilling over the streets of America, and sizzling in the minds of the world, and sputtering in the hearts of mankind, etc., etc. And how he was happy to be here with these beautiful charming lovely delightful enchanting young Spelman ladies who represented *excellence*. Luckily I was at table with the arch (and arch-radical) Betty Stevens (just elected student body pres. over chagrin of Pres. Manley) & smiling little Alice Walker, best writer I've run into at Spelman, & others.

Thurs. May 16

Faculty meeting (also last day of classes, nice session with US history class on foreign policy, broad-ranging questions on everything; and Russia class discussed Neal's pamphlet on US-Soviet relations with various disagreements). The faculty meeting was routine: Willis James* reading off the list of prizes to students for this year. After that Staughton brought up what AAUP had discussed that noon at lunch meeting: the college notifying us earlier of our salary for next year; he made a motion on it. Manley coldly said motion not necessary, would put it on agenda for next fall. Then before closing meeting, he said Mrs. Toomer (retired High School Eng. teacher who joined Spelman faculty last year)† had a statement to make. Said he didn't know what was in her statement or that she was going to make one but here it was. Mrs. Toomer now spoke: she had touched Spelman at three generations of college presidents—was a child when Mrs. Tapley‡ was president, a student under Mrs. Read,§ a faculty member now under Dr. Manley; it has always been a marvelous school, has prepared its students well, turned out fine young women; students keep coming to the school in great numbers, proving its philosophy is good; when a student she too had thought it was restrictive but later realized that the restrictions, the disciplines, the controls were necessary; students had always complained, would always complain; faculty members—*some* faculty members, were lighting fires under the students; if parents didn't want to send their students to Spelman they didn't have to; and likewise, if faculty members didn't like the philosophy of the school, they didn't have to remain. When Mrs. Toomer finished, Manley said: I didn't know what Mrs. Toomer was going to say, but I want to say I agree with her. At this point I raised

---

King Jr. He had also represented Zinn and his student Roslyn Pope when they were arrested by racist police in Atlanta in 1960 (see Introduction, pp. 67–68).

*   Willis Laurence James was professor of music at Spelman.

†   Juanita Toomer was an instructor in English at Spelman.

‡   Lucy Tapley was president of Spelman, 1910–27.

§   Florence Matilda Read was president of Spelman, 1927–53.

my hand and said, "Dr. Manley . . . ." He got up from his chair and said the meeting is over, and started to walk away. I said, "Dr. Manley I would like to respond to Mrs. Toomer's statement." He kept walking quickly towards the door. I said, "Dr. Manley, this is a *faculty* meeting." His face was contorted, he didn't respond, but walked to the door and out. The faculty slowly filed out of the building, murmuring to one another, gathering in knots outside. Renate Wolf, tiny, pale, said to me, obviously shaken: "Well, this is it. I'm going to resign at the first faculty meeting in the fall." Lois [Moreland], more moderate with each week, her capacity for indignation almost dried up by now, could only say, "See, you have been going about it the wrong way." Rakulski [Rukalski] shrugged his shoulders and kept saying to me, "Zabud, Zabud!" (Forget it! Forget it!) "Nichevo" (Nothing can be done). Esta told me Jean Smith (young, intelligent, irrepressible, on her way from Spelman to California for good this summer) sent her a note while Mrs. Toomer was talking, which read[,] "This is a paid political announcement." Mrs. Macomson & Mrs. Curry told Esta that while they probably would have disagreed with what I was going to say, they thought it outrageous I hadn't been allowed to talk. In general, the faculty is timid, scared, wondering if the president will raise them $100 or $200 or $400 this June for next year, not accustomed to acting like a faculty, accustomed to being treated like children by a matriarch or a patriarch of a president. Staughton was furious, came back to house with Zygmunt for shot of bourbon to calm down.

At ten, Emory students (four of them) came over, Ronald Turner among them. He'd been jailed in afternoon sit-in, would have to stop now because parents, in Marietta Ga. were aroused. They are planning Emory meeting next week to talk and begin to do things, want me to speak there. Robert Allen was with them, brought Master Plan for tomorrow of the Committee on Appeal (Comm[ittee] on Appeal for Human Rights, the Atlanta student movement), with awesome directions: "First wave downtown at one; second wave at two; third wave; fourth wave: all to converge on city hall after sit[-]ins and arrests, etc.etc." But I fly to NY in early morning. Allen will drive me to airport.

[Marginalia: Zinn wrote "sit-in" to the left of the final paragraph]

Fri. May 17

To NY. My going to NY is an act of defiance in itself. I called Bob Brisbane Thurs. morning, said since I'm going to Washington anyway, & since we have little time left and we've been worried about Non-Western Program plans for after Africa year, and Ford Foundation grant, and since I know Geo. Beckmann of Ford F[ou]nd[atio]n quite well by now (we spoke on panel together in Miami, and worked on forming Assn for Asian Studies Comm. on Undergraduate Educ. in Philly recently), why not visit him and discuss informally what we might begin to plan for after Africa year. Bob said fine, said he would tell John Coe[*] to advance me expenses for Wash to NY and back. That was about 10 AM. I phoned Ford F[ou]nd[atio]n in NY to make sure Beckmann would be in on Friday. He was out at the moment, but sec[retar]y said he would be in Friday—I left name. At three-thirty, between my classes, I walked into Coe's office to pick up advance for trip—this procedure has been routine for two years, the director authorizing expenses, Coe drawing a check, Manley counter signing it. Coe said to me: Pres. Manley didn't approve the advance. He's discussing it with Pres. Mays. I went home to phone Manley. Not in. I phoned Mays. It was obvious Manley['s] idea with which he got Mays to concur. Mays said: Mr. Manley and I thought no one should go until all six of us—comm. of four and presidents—meet and discuss it. I said, but time is short, and this will just be informal talk, and I will be so close to NY. He repeated what he said. I was angry, because it was a clear case of Manley being personally vindictive, but I said okay. At five-thirty I came home from class & Roz was home. She said Geo. Beckmann had called, and he was expecting me in NY tomorrow, wanted very much to see me! This decided me. I called Bob Brisbane, told him what had happened, said I thought I should go, He agreed. Admin. comm. runs the non-western program and the presidents are consultants but they act is if it[']s theirs. Said I should check with Banks & Lois and if they say okay to go. Banks on phone said definitely yes. Lois at faculty meeting nodded yes. When I got home after faculty meeting I tried to contact Mays by phone twice at home, but not home.

On same plane to NY was Jeanette Hume, gal from Randolph Macon College, about to get Yale Ph.D. in Eng. Lit. (Chaucer), for whom I waited with her mother two weeks ago at the county jail after she was arrested in sit-in. We sat together and talked. She plans to stay at Morehouse.

In NY, saw Geo. Beckmann, had nice cordial, useful chat. He is submitting plan to Ford Trustees, expects it will be approved: for 100 colleges, money for people to spend a year away studying a non-western area, released time for a man to develop a course, library, new faculty. Wants me to phone him in Sept. to make sure these guidelines are approved, then we can go ahead draw up plans.

To Wash. by shuttle from Newark, plane delayed landing over an hour because Wash. in clouds and rain. Finally in, to lavish Int'l Inn, where the Capital Press Club had made a reservation for me (great dome over swimming pool, removable in good weather). Called Herschelle Sullivan, took cab to her place. She looks fine but worried about acceptance at Columbia for Ph.D. in Public Law & Govt. Getting her MA at Johns Hopkins. Introd. me to her roommate, Barbara Alperowitz, slim blonde girl with little cute baby girl wearing horn-rimmed glasses (the baby). Herschelle went out with me to Chinese restaurant, and we talked long. She tried to arouse Hopkins students over Birmingham, found terrible academic objectivity, diffidence, coldness—yet things beginning to stir.

---

[*]   John L. Coe was the assistant treasurer of Spelman.

Phoned Roz to find out what happened to great plans in Atlanta today. Small student turnout on lawn (finals near). Marched downtown, met on bridge by Mayor Allen himself who asked them to turn back, said didn't want them arrested. They went on to restaurants. No arrests. Decided to sit in at city hall. But when they got there Allen invited them to eat at city hall as his guests. They did.

Sat. May 18

Myla's birthday   Roz has bought her record of Corelli singing Pagliacci.[*] She heard him at Fox Theater in Atlanta few weeks ago and loved him.

Made the most of my Capital Press Club paying my hotel bill: had my suit pressed while I ate breakfast in my room and thought about what I would say at panel. Zen is coming thru to me—don't treat travel as a pain—make the most of it—relax: Live it up if they force you to: Non-violent resistance to luxury.

The panel was held in the Senate Room of the Int'l Inn. A hundred or so *Washingtonians*, mostly Negro, quite a few pressmen, some white liberal or Democ. Committee type men and women around. Photographers all over snapping pictures. Carl Holman[†] there to chair (he was resp. for inviting me, said later he did so because he knew I would say what he would have said if he were perfectly free to do so and not working for Civil Rights Commission). On panel: Lerone Bennett, editor of Ebony, young[,] slim, handsome, intelligent, much more militant in words than his magazine; you'd never suspect he edited something like that. Berl Bernhardt, staff director of civil rights Commission, dark, good-looking, smiling, chosen one of ten young men of year by Jr. Chamber of Commerce—at end said "he must respond to my criticism of fed. govt.["] Said FBI was producing many good reports, that Kennedy *had* taken stand on moral issue. Herblock, middle-aged, very pleasant, sat next to me.[‡] Topic: "What is Future of the Negro." Bennett's prediction[:] "Eyeball to eyeball confrontations coming up in South." Bernhardt: Things will get worse, then better. I said immediate future would be like present in Birmingham: tremendous Negro energy going into wide end of funnel, tiny bit of national action coming out other end. I said president was hesitant, vice-pres. was diffident (I was partic. anxious to get this in because Capital Press Club, as second feature of its celebration of May 17th anniversary [of the Brown decision], was honoring Vice-Pres. [Lyndon] Johnson at dinner tonight), atty-gen. [Robert F. Kennedy] was callous, and FBI was incompetent in area of civil rights. As for farther future, I saw Negro becoming part of miserable white society, and only hope for him to avoid fate of present whites was to use leverage

---

*   Italian tenor Franco Corelli singing the opera *Pagliacci* by Ruggero Leoncavallo.
†   Carl Holman was the founding editor of the *Atlanta Inquirer,* and professor of English and humanities at Clark College.
‡   Herbert Block (Herblock) was a liberal Pulitzer Prize–winning political cartoonist.

of his present militancy to overturn this society, non-violently, but to bring revolution in the national political structure, the economy, the social structure. Afterward, Herblock leaned over, said he was glad I hit Johnson, that he deserved it. A young Washington minister questioned me on my adjectives for the administration. I went into detail for each one. Plenty of questions, comments from audience. Lasted 10:30 to 1:30. Then beer and cold-cuts in adjoining room. Herschelle, Barbara & little girl were at the panel, the little girl astoundingly silent through three hours of jabber.

On planes this trip read David Bazelon's *The Paper Economy* to review it for Pat Watters' book page in Atlanta Const. A tremendous book. Wonderful style, wit, cuts through nonsense on profit motive, competition, private property with a cheese knife. No cliches, yet devastating. Better than Galbraith or Heilbroner or anyone.[*]

Home Sat. 6 PM in time to take Roz & Myla to Stouffer's (one of few integrated restaurants in Atlanta) for Myla's birthday. Jeff wanted to go early to Joan Baez concert, get in his usual front row seat. Almost—cap[a]city crowd at concert (while we were at Stouffers Betty Darden came in with Bill Scott of Atl. Daily World[†] and young official from Haute-Volta whom Betty had met on Crossroads[‡] last summer). Mostly white Emory kids, few Spelman & Morehouse. Ralph McGill[§] there, introd. me to visiting Mrs. Ignazio Silone—a surprise!—Silone[¶] himself sick in hotel room (read next day Silone said to reporter change must come slow and gradual in South—shades of Fontemara!).[**] Joan's voice was pure and beautiful—got tremendous reception. And had these white kids singing We Shall Overcome—not as loud as Negro audience but pretty good. Sang moving song about Emmett Till.[††] And: What Have they Done to the Rain. And a new song written by Bob Dylan, powerful, bitter about the wars our country has fought, always with God on our Side, and Germans, now our friends, killed 6 million Jews, but God is on their side now. Wow.

---

[*]   Economist Robert L. Heilbroner had written a best-selling history of economic thought, *The Worldly Philosophers* (1953); economist John Kenneth Galbraith had written a best-selling critique of consumer society and its inequities, *The Affluent Society* (1958).

[†]   *Atlanta Daily World* was the city's more conservative black newspaper; it opposed the sit-in movement.

[‡]   Operation Crossroads, Africa was a forerunner of the Peace Corps, established by Rev. James Robinson of New York City to build bridges between African and U.S. students.

[§]   Ralph McGill was the editor and publisher of the *Atlanta Constitution*, whose pro-integration commentary won him a Pulitzer Prize.

[¶]   Ignazio Silone, pen name of Secondino Tranquilli, was a leading twentieth-century Italian novelist, famed in his time for his antifascist politics. Later (in the 1990s) he was found to have been an informant for the fascists.

[**]   *Fontamara* (1933) was one of Silone's antifascist novels.

[††]   Emmett Till was a fourteen-year-old African American from Chicago brutally murdered in Mississippi in 1955 by white supremacists for allegedly flirting verbally with a white woman. The murderers were quickly acquitted by an all-white jury, and the case became a symbol of southern racism and injustice.

Sat. May 18 (cont.)   A long night: Somehow, thru Guy Carawan, who's known Joan for years thru his folk-singing tours and Highlander and whatnot, and thru Clark Foreman of Emerg. Civ. Lib. Comm [ECLC]. (Joan was giving concert for benefit of SNCC and ECLC) who was at concert, and thru Manny Greenhill, Joan's manager, whom we had known in Boston thru his son who came to give Jeff guitar lessons and see Myla, it was arranged for Joan to come to our place. We invited a few Spelman students, and those Emory students who'd been working on the movement, but somehow word got around and when we made our way to our house we found the road packed with people and cars on the way to our house. When we got inside it was jampacked and people outside not able to get in. We sent a lot of people out in back on the grass—it was a beautiful night. Joan came, went into the kitchen, had a banana, then went out on grass, people gathering round her, sang and sang and on into the night. Must have been a hundred Emory students, some Spelman some SNCC people. Manny Greenhill drank Scotch, Jack Patterson (of Business Week) drank Bourbon, Jim Forman drank milk for his ulcers, the Spelman students sneaked in a few drops of scotch, the Haute Volta fellow drank beer, and everyone else cokes. As the singing went out on the campus at midnight, housemothers called up for their girls, but some of them said they would take their chances. Girls in a nearby dorm came out on the fire escapes in their pajamas to listen. Mr. Little (huge, incredibly muscular, militant but unorganized in his protests against the terrible wages, hours, conditions of the buildings and grounds people) came by on his night watchman tour, came in for drink and food. We cut Myla's birthday cake and it went fast. Joan left about 1:30 or 2 [AM], and a group followed her along road, halfway to Manley's house, then formed circle around her, everyone linking arms like in the protest meetings and singing verse after verse of We Shall Overcome. An eerie and thrilling scene. Damaris Allen whispered to me, "Nothing like this ever happened in the history of Spelman! I always dreamed something like this might happen where I was!" Mr. Little came along again, joined the circle, thrilled to death, singing with the rest. What a birthday for Myla! She and Jeff stayed up to the end. Inside, guitar playing until 3 or so.

Sometime in evening Jim Forman told me SNCC had elected me to Exec. Comm.—me and Ella Baker* the two adults allowed on exec. comm.

Mendy told me he and a Morehouse student tried to sit in at Pickrick† earlier Saturday, were bodily thrown out. Man pulled knife. [Lester] Maddox (Atlanta's leading hate man, has lost again and again trying for mayor, l[ieutenan]t gov[ernor] every-

---

*   Ella Baker was a former organizer for the NAACP who later ran the voter registration campaign of the SCLC. She was a key mentor for SNCC, who organized its founding meeting and introduced its leaders to the idea of group-centered nonhierarchical leadership.

†   Pickrick was the restaurant owned by white supremacist (and future Georgia governor) Lester

thing else, runs ads every Sat. in *The Atlanta Const[itution]* adv[ertising] fried chicken and segregation[,]) tried to get Negro help to throw them out, but no one budged. But they decided to leave rather then get help fired.

Sun. May 19

Perfect, quiet, peaceful day after the storm. Tennis with Mendy and Roz. About 2 PM looked outside & there was Joan Baez lying on grass behind the house, alone! Myla went out to talk to her. Her manager Manny Greenhill came along. We all went out, talked. She told of her of her two month stint at Perkins School for blind. Very intelligent & articulate girl. Then newsmen came around to take pictures, ask questions of her out back under tree. She's very impressive. Said most important thing what kind of person, not how well they sing. Hence Pete Seeger the greatest. Asked, would she be conscientious objector if a man, said, Yes. Fended question about God, said wasn't sure.

Mr. Little came by, talked about his wife's recent operation, cost $500. They are not covered by medical insurance with college, as faculty is. They get one week vacation a year! And little sick leave! And a dollar an hour.

Mon. May 20

Mendy came over AM to pick up copy for leaflet to be dist. at Lebs today. At noon went over to student HQ. Word came in on Sup. Ct. sit-in decision[*] and Ralph Moore excited for a while. But we called paper and from wording of decision seems doesn't affect Atlanta because only voids arrests where local seg. ordinances exist. Carful [Car full] of us went to picket Lebs. I had called earlier Ted Maloof to check on existence city ordinance req. permit to hand out leaflets. He couldn't find any, said he'd be available if any trouble. I agreed to hand out the leaflets, carry it as far as jail if necessary to test the right. Anna Jo Weaver & Liz Heath were [the] only Spelman students down (reading period—it['] is illegal), plus several Morehouse students. We were there about three and a half hours. Leb was foul mouthed, nasty, nervous, tried to get cop to arrest me for stepping over line, but Capt. Mosely old hand at this, shook his head. Hostile comments: "White Niggers! Bunch of Commies! Back to Khrushchev!" One fellow to me: "You look Italian. Why don't you go back to Russia?" But also: several people with encouraging remarks, one fellow gave card and phone number to call him for help. Friends passed by. (Learned later in week Esta

---

Maddox, who gained notoriety by wielding pick handles and guns to keep black patrons out of his restaurant.

[*]   *Peterson v. City of Greenville*, South Carolina sit-in case, in which the U.S. Supreme Court on May 20, 1963 reversed the conviction of protesters arrested for defying a local segregations ordinance in their sit-in.

was trapped in Lebs by picket line, saw us out there suddenly, and they skipped out back way!)

[Marginalia: Zinn wrote "Lebs" in the margin to the left of this May 20 diary entry]

Wed. [May 22]

Noon. Non-West. committee met, agreed to stand together on showdown with presidents over my going to NY to see Ford.

4 PM Horace Kallen of New School came over with wife, met Betty Stevens, Alice Walker, Dorcas Boit. Staughton Lynd too. Queried students on academic freedom at Spelman and Betty spoke articulately interestingly at length.

730 PM To Emory for meeting. About 100 Emory students, handful of ours. Panel of me, Ralph Moore, Emory Dean of Students Zeller—a very impressive, good person, and an Emory minister—both these guys unfortunately leaving next year. Lots of questions—good spirit. Many Emory students signed up as interested in the movement. Ten signed up to picket tomorrow. Highlight of evening. Rev. Ashton Jones, 65 or so, born near Albany Ga. jailed thirty times, beaten kidnapped, has spent last 32 years walking, riding around country with message, all men are brothers—with wife. Real old South in looks, speech, manner. Wonderful disposition, inspiring speaker. Mostly easy humor then suddenly a burst of passion for a moment or so, carrying you with him in a surge of emotion, then back again to gentle, amusing story.

Thurs. [May 23]

Mendy came over to say Emory students showed up to picket. Ashton Jones, four Emory students, four Morehouse men, arrested sitting in Ship Ahoy. Left all-white picket line at Lebs, first time in sit-in history here. Newsreels ground away. Hundred viewers around. Lebs has huge signs in his window now "I serve whom I please" "I must protect my investment" etc.

[Marginalia: Zinn wrote "Lebs" in the margin to the left of this May 23 diary entry]

Fri. May 24

Roz decided to come picketing with us today. We drove down about noon to the Rush Memorial Church, where the Committee on Appeal (COAHR—Committee on Appeal for Human Rights) [which was the organizing committee of the Atlanta sit-in movement], has its rough little two-room H Q. On the wall was a placard saying "This is Headquarters for All Radical, Communist-Inspired, Outside Agitators." Ralph Moore was on phone, trying to get a trustee of the Committee's defense fund to release

$1000 of it for day-to-day expenses of the Committee. A few Morehouse students were around. Only girl was Eliz. Heath the white exchange student from Bethel. Mendy came after a while. SNCC had run off a bunch of leaflets. We grabbed some picket signs, piled into my car and another, with our car for Lebs and the other for Ship Ahoy (where Ashton Jones arrested yesterday). Emory students called in meantime, said about five of them around, would meet us at the picketing. Walking up from the parking lot along Luckie St. we passed Hong Kong again; again Chinese manager or owner standing outside at the door, fearful that we would try to get in. We did look formidable—interracial group, students, carrying signs under arms—an unusual sight for downtown Atlanta. Deciding to make him more at ease I walked over to him and asked gently if some of us could eat in Hong Kong. He shook his head, said, almost inaudible, with strong accent: ["]When others do.["] We passed by Herrens and manager was at that door too. I spoke to him; he was friendly, said when the others did he would too. We went to Lebs, formed the line; we only had four pickets. Roz and I handed out leaflets. Charlie Leb wasn't around today, but the starers and hecklers were. Soon bunch of Emory students came—ten, twelve. Small group broke off to picket Ship Ahoy. At one point all-white picket line. Roz, I, two Negro students, white girl from Emory, white Emory fellow (from Georgia mountains) left line for a while to get a sandwich at the five and dime. Wonderfully friendly waitress as we sat squeezed together in booth (white). Back on line. Young white fellow stopped to talk to me: just out of marines, raised in South, now in Atlanta to publicize coming of movie Cleopatra, is in New Orleans much of time. Said "I have tremendous respect for you people." We talked. He wanted SNCC's address. Was just wide-eyed at whole thing. Young, tough looking Southern fellow stopped to talk with Roz for a long time, went away, came back and talked again. She told me later he said[,] "You're right. I just don't have the courage to do what you're doing." One man came by and whispered in my ear, in a strong Southern accent: "I'm with you!" One young guy stood two feet away and just stared, with hate in his eyes. Roz and I left to pick up the kids, and young pretty Emory girl freshman took the leaflets from us to distribute. On our way to parking lot we saw picket line at Ship Ahoy and another one at Hong Kong. Those Emory students really made it today.

Ashton Jones still in jail, doesn't want to come out.

Evening: went to see Myla and her group in Shadow and Substance.[*] They all did … [a] remarkable job. (At Callenwald) After that Roz and I went to Waluhaje,[†] guests of Jim and Gwen Wilson, where her school was having a dance. We sat at table with

---

[*]   *Shadow and Substance* (1937) an award-winning Irish play by Paul Vincent Carroll.

[†]   The Waluhaje was a black-owned luxury apartment complex with a ballroom where touring jazz groups played. It was one of the few such venues in Atlanta where musicians could play to integrated audiences in the Jim Crow era.

Wilsons and their group, danced some, met various old friends (prison probation officer John Boone, actor-writer Ray McIver, former Spelman actress Christine Jaffer Bonner). We were [the] only whites there for a while, then one other white couple came.

[Marginalia: Zinn wrote "Lebs" in the margin to the left of the first paragraph of this May 24 diary entry]

Tues. May 28

Letter from Forum Service (Cong. for Cult. Freedom) in England asking story on Birmingham, for dist. to newspapers in Africa, Asia.

Finished Section 4 of Southern Mystique.

Was typing up my translation of Zygmunt's "Le Ligne de Marc-Aurele" when he came in. I said "How are you Zygmunt" and he burst into tears like a child. "I lost my aunt . . . ." Roz and kids were away at movies. I made tea for him, and we sat together, he weeping intermittently, telling me of his aunt, 70 years old, whom he last saw in Vienna where she lives [lived] in 1948, & always meant to see her again but never quite made it. Said, shrugging his shoulders, tearful[,] "I always thought—someday if I had a family, and I had a home I would take her in with us—and now . . ."

It seems that it was her husband with whom Zygmunt had left Warsaw as the Nazis arrived, to get into Russian Poland, hoping to get out of Europe from there. Her husband was blond and Nordic, and the hope was he and Zygmunt would get thru the Nazi lines easily and across the border, and then Zygmunt's parents would follow. But they were arrested by the Russians when they crossed the border, slapped into jail in Bialystok, spent nine months in jail there—then the German invasion of Russia and the jail opened up—only to have them bottled up in the Bialystok ghetto for two years by the Nazis. Then the Final Solution, shipped on the train from Bialystok, thinking they were going to the death camp at Treblinka. When train stopped for light, Zygmunt said to uncle—Let's jump off. Uncle said no, let's wait and see. Zygmunt jumped, laid on tracks until train passed—it was nighttime (then he got into Warsaw, joined underground, had operation on his penis to destroy circumcision, then arrested and thrown into Auschwitz). This aunt was not Jewish, so she was not expelled from Vienna as he was. Nazis took her property, said they would return half if she divorced her husband. She refused, remained faithful to him until the end. He never returned from Auschwitz. (Yes, he went into the gas chambers, and up in smoke out of the ovens, Zygmunt said in tears.) "What a woman[,]" Zygmunt kept saying. "What a fine woman. A woman of principles, an old-fashioned woman of ideals—not like the people you see today. And now she's gone." At first, my reaction had been one of surprise—who weeps violently over the death of a 70-year-old aunt?

And then, as he told about her, about her husband and what he and Zygmunt had been through together—it became comprehensible.

Wed. May 29

Went to SRC [Southern Regional Council] to do research on Birmingham article. Then lunch with [SRC leaders] Les Dunbar & Staige Blackford. Staige talked of my doing possible study of Jackson, Mississippi. All three of us expressed desire to go to Mississippi. Maggie Long loaned me book by Dick Gregory on promise I would review it for New South.

Evening: Dinner at Renate with Lynds, then Cecile Genpatsingh & Sadie Beasley (off to Ethiopia in summer on Crossroads) came over.

Thurs. May 30

Non-West Committee meeting at ten am. Bob Brisbane showed us his year-end report, and we discussed it. Now Banks takes over, on Africa. Manley left abruptly at eleven, saying he had appointment, and we hadn't gotten to the crucial point that our committee had prepared for confrontation with Mays-Manley over my going to NY (the committee, in a meeting a few days earlier decided they would back me completely). Bob mentioned, now with Manley gone, that I would report on my trip to NY. Mays' face clouded over. He said, I had no idea Zinn went to NY. I said, let me explain, and I did. Mays listened, then said quietly, "all right," and it was done. What would have happened if Manley had been there, we don't know.

Friday. May 31

The Atlanta Chamber of Commerce has unanimously passed resolution calling on businesses to desegregate. Richard Rich* among them. Hope is now that restaurant owners will act, but probably they won't write [right] away. Ran into Carl (Morehouse student) on campus. Said he and Ashton Jones were going down to Lebs at two to test and see if Charlie will now relent. (Read later Ashton Jones was arrested, sentenced 30 days work gang on old statute making it crime to enter city with express purpose of breaking the law.)

10:30 Faculty meeting. Annual reading of list of graduates. Lois called me last night to ask my support for student left off the list, because she didn't pass swim-

---

* Richard Rich was the president and chairman of the board of Rich's department store, the largest in the southeast and the most prestigious in Atlanta. His store was a prime target of the Atlanta sit-in movement.

ming test. She spoke up, swimming teacher answered, then I spoke. But we made mistake not making specific motion to add her to list—instead it ended wishy-washy with notion she would march in procession but without degree and with opportunity this summer to make it up and get her degree. Shirley McBay asked Mrs. Perry important question: why last year did she (Mrs. Perry) bring up case of Minnie Riley (the administration's favorite) who lacked two points but who wanted to graduate anyway—and this year didn't even mention this student[?] Mrs. Perry said quietly: Last year I was told to bring it up—this year I was not. No more was said. Everyone knew *who* told her.

During "announcements"—Renate said: I would like to take this opportunity to reply to Mrs. Toomer's statement at [the] last faculty meeting. (She wrote Manley ten days ago asking opportunity to reply at this meeting, but got no answer, so went ahead and mimeographed a reply, in case she would not get a chance to reply orally.) Manley said he would give her five minutes later. I then raised my hand and said, "I would like four minutes to reply to Mrs. Toomer." Manley coldly said—"I allowed Dr. Wolf five minutes—we're pressed for time . . . ." I said[,] "Dr. Manley, I would like *two* minutes to reply, *please*." (If I had fought it out on four minutes, don't know what would have happened, this way I think he found it difficult—it would have seemed ridiculous that he couldn't spare two minutes—tho four of course was just as ridiculous, but who knows?[)] He said, reluctantly, all right. Then the time came, Renate made her statement, a mild but firm statement that everything changes, that Spelman *had* done a good job, but could do a better one, and that we should have the right to advocate changes. I spoke then, said I was speaking against the spirit of intolerance in Mrs. Toomer's remarks—that her attitude was a proprietary one—that Spelman College belonged to no person—whether he was of high or low rank in the college officialdom—it did not belong to her—or to anyone else. That the Spirit of her remarks was like that of Ross Barnett[*]—if you don't like it here, go back to where you came from, that this was a terrible thing—that people should have the right to speak up, to criticize the practices and policies of any institution or place where they are, that I hoped the spirit of tolerance would prevail at Spelman. I spoke mildly, aimed at the common denominator of the right of free speech. The meeting ended, and we all (the libertarians) felt very good. We had said something important—it had not been topped by any angry reply. (Mrs. Toomer had replied—Manley said he would give her three or four minutes—said that "personal aggrandizement" was behind the demands for change of some faculty members—that she "felt" this, and that "feelings" sometime were true guides.)

---

[*]   Ross Barnett was the segregationist governor of Mississippi whose resistance to the desegregation of the University of Mississippi in 1962 paved the way for the deadly segregationist riot that followed James Meredith's court-ordered admission to that university.

After meeting, Staughton, Esta, Lois Moreland, Shirley McBay, Zelma Payne* all went to Paschals for lunch. A good spirit pervaded. But Shirley won't be at Spelman next year. Zelma may leave. She is disgusted.

Alice Walker wrote a poem for me. I wrote one for her in return.

Evening: Went with Sid Davis and Mary Davis (a marvel she is, from Jesup, Georgia, quiet, long blonde tresses, studied literature at Emory, works with Peace Council—lovely demeanor) way out to new rented country home of Maloofs, on banks of Chattahoochie.

[Marginalia: Zinn placed a line in the margin highlighting the first paragraph of this May 31 diary entry]

Sat. June 1

Took Myla for her driving test. She got 100% in written test, in her usual serene test-taking magnificence, then passed driving test—and she now has her license—two weeks after she was 16.

Mail this morning: Yale law student Oscar Chase sent me paper he did on federal use of injunctive power to help civil rights—and prospectus for series of articles on this—he wants help from SRC—and I'm going to try to help him get it. A great need and he seems just the guy.

Sat. June 1

Jennifer Ragwar was over—left us a beautiful picture of herself, and a nice letter to us on back of it. Will return to Kenya this summer.

She wrote two beautiful poems—one about missing home—in the Spelman literary magazine. Told us about her Spelman situation: for three years she's been working as a desk girl—at no pay—why? "to show her appreciation" for what Spelman is doing for her. Under agreement with Mboya† etc. these colleges are paying tuition and giving spending money to these students. So—she is *given* a job and *told* this is to show her appreciation. She gets seven dollars a month for all her personal expenses. Once asked raise to ten dollars a month—told this would be too much. Has just asked college to buy footlocker to ship her stuff—she went out and priced it—came to $20.00 or so. Manley said, too much, go back and get a price for a smaller one! (And we are spending $750,000 to build a Fine Arts Building!)

Letter this morning from Leila Sussman—no longer at Wellesley—now editor of a

---

*   Zelma Payne was a professor of home economics at Spelman.

†   Tom Joseph Odhiambo Mboya was a Kenyan nationalist and cabinet minister.

new journal Sociology of Education under auspices of Amer. Soc. Society (no, Amer. Soc. *Assn*—otherwise would spell ASS!).

Noon, Tues. June 4, 1963

We were supposed to leave for New York this morning, but things have happened to delay us. First, the last two days have been terrible ones because of Lee Lynd's accident. On Sunday early afternoon a woman called from Grady hospital to say that Lee had fallen out of a second story window at Quaker House and was hurt badly. I drove over to the hospital. Lee was lying on a cot just outside the Xray room. Alice & Staughton were near him. He was sleeping, his face serene, his breathing slight, the back of his head showing splotches of blood through the skin. The x-ray showed his skull fractured, but no depression, no fracture on his leg which was cut and sewed up. Staughton pale, Alice by turns very calm and tearful. After a while a doctor came and examined Lee, and then said, ominously—"He's not as safe as when he came in." A neuro-surgeon had been called in the meantime and was on his way over to St. Joseph[']s Hospital, where he was connected. An ambulance arrived to take Lee to St. Joseph, plasma going into his arm meanwhile. I took Lee's clothes into the car, phoned Roz (baccalaureate [*sic*] service was on!) then went to St. Joseph[']s. The neurosurgeon examined Lee, then told Staughton, with me and John Youngblut listening: He had a bad crack, jagged all over the back of his skull—a crucial place— with a deep fissure, the whole thing indicating internal hemorrhaging, which was dangerous—and that it would be "nip and tuck." Lee had a fifty-fifty chance of living; he seemed to be saying. A few minutes later apparently he decided to operate, for exploratory purposes. Staughton and Alice waited. I went down for coffee & soup for them and everybody waiting in Lee's room. Then I went to pick up Barbara at Jon Johnston's and take her home to eat and spend the night with us. Staughton called in the evening to say that the operation had been successful—there was a blood clot in the brain which would have been fatal soon and which the doctor removed, there was a severed artery and a severed vein which apparently the doctor was able to fix up—they'd given Lee six pints of blood during the operation. He was resting quietly now. Staughton had breakfast with us Monday morning before returning to the hospital. I went to commencement, of which the only decent note was Vincent Harding praying 1) for Lee[,] 2) for the porters, maids, janitors on campus (He was thinking of what Staughton & I had said about them he told us later)[,] 3) spoke about thinking beyond "budgets and buildings." In the evening I went to the hospital to see Lee. He was in his oxygen tent, being fed intravenously, but looking rosy-faced. He'd been waking up from time to time, moving, saying things, responding. All in all, by Tues[day] morning, things were looking good for the first time.

Then: this morning, remembering Manley's promise that our six-week-delayed salary letters for next year would be in the mail this morning, I went to the mail room

and got this letter: "June 1. Dear Mr. Zinn: Your present five-year term as a Professor ends at the close of the 1963–1964 academic year. The College does not intend
to renew your employment at the end of your present term, and you are hereby
notified of that fact. Further, the College has decided that your services will not be
required during the 1963–1964 academic year; therefore the College has decided to
pay you now as termination pay your salary for the coming year, and to dispense
with your services after June 30, 1963. Accordingly, you are relieved of all duties with
the College after June 30, 1963, and you will be expected to vacate your apartment
by June 30, 1963. The College's check for your termination pay is enclosed. Sincerely
yours, A. E. Manley." (check for $7005.68 enclosed—$8000 less income tax—no TIAA
payment.) No health insurance!

Back at the house for breakfast, I took Roz, Myla & Jeff out back on the lawn where
we had coffee and I told them. Myla (who's been campaigning for us to leave Atlanta
for years) burst out[,] "We won't go. We'll refuse to go!" Roz was hit hard. Jeff always
takes things easily, humorously. I went to my office to look up the employment rules
and regulations. They indicate that either I have permanent tenure or if I am on five-
year tenure next year will be my *fourth*. Betty Stevens came into the office while I
was poring over the files. I showed her the letter. She burst into tears. When she composed herself, she said[,] "I won't do anything now. First chapel program . . . ." Betty
must leave the dorm by noon, so I took her there to pick up her things and bring
them back to our place. I dropped in on Dean Eagleson. I said, "When I handed you
yesterday the teaching schedule for my dept. for next year did you know I wouldn't
be here?" He said, no. I said, you didn't know I was being released? He said no, not
until you told me just now. I asked him were you consulted on this. He said no. I said
do you have anything critical to say about my teaching ability. He said no. I have
always imagined that you were a very good teacher. I went into Mrs. Perry's office.
She said, well, I was fired twice from Hampton.* Since then (it is now six or seven), the
phone has been ringing all day, faculty members dropping, Renate bringing wine,
Staughton, Esta, Carney, Pearsall. I called Lois. She was shocked, said she would call
Curry & Macomson. Millie Jordan called; I've never heard her so outraged, so angry.
She said[,] "What about the community—what Roz & Myla have done in the theater,
what you have done for the student movement?" Walter Love called from Emory.
"What can I do?" Lionel Newsome called—he'll be over at nine tomorrow morning,
to get the facts, then to call Fidler at Washington AAUP. We decided to delay depar-
ture until tomorrow morning. Staughton has been roaring in and out all day, despite
Lee's condition (which is better). I phoned Merrill to ask if he had place in Common-
wealth School for Myla & Jeff. He said yes—said if we needed living space he would
make room on the fourth floor of the school, said Manley's act was "irresponsible."
Betty Darden called Roz from the station, on her way home to Montgomery, broke

---

*   The Hampton Institute was a historically black college in Hampton, Virginia.

down weeping, later she phoned me again when she was composed. I said goodbye to Betty Stevens on the phone too. Dottie Miller* and Casey Hayden† called from SNCC, they want to send telegram, letter to Manley, protesting, saying I'm needed here by SNCC. Robert Manse called from the student committee on Appeal—the quiet, very impressive guy who picketed with us, had lunch with us at Woolworths, with whom Mendy was so impressed—rarely talked—now he exploded—said he wants to picket Manley tomorrow! Reporter from Atlanta Inquirer‡ called asked if it were true, I said yes. I went over to see Don Hollowell, on way ran into Ralph Moore also (surprise) Carl Holman who said ("the son of a bitch!"), and Ashton Jones, out of jail, who smiled broadly and said "Congratulations!" and shook my hand, said[,] "Come to California with me—there's plenty for you to do there." Up to Don's§ office—he looked over the letter, rules, said[,] "The college is in a bad way legally—looks like you have permanent tenure." Suggested I write Manley a letter giving him chance to retract, saying I was holding check in escrow—so I can say I exhausted administrative responsibilities. As for eviction that's complex, but he says if Manley moves my furniture I can sue for damages, also might enjoin eviction. Won't decide on taking case until I get a response from Manley—I asked him if his personal relationship with Manley was such that he would hesitate to take case. He said no. Esta and Danny over at night—she got no raise, not a cent.

[Last sentence of second paragraph = H]

Wed. June 5 (new departure date)

Les Dunbar called
Called Pat Watters
Constance Nabwire
Mrs. Rates¶

[Entire June 5 diary entry = H]

---

* Dottie Miller (Zellner) was a SNCC staffer and coeditor of the SNCC newsletter, *The Student Voice*.

† Sandra "Casey" Cason Hayden was a civil rights activist from the University of Texas who worked for SNCC in Atlanta and was part of the SNCC planning group that organized the Mississippi Freedom Summer.

‡ *The Atlanta Inquirer* was a black newspaper established in 1960 as a pro-movement alternative to the more conservative black paper, *The Atlanta Daily World*. The *Inquirer* was the voice of the Atlanta freedom movement's student wing.

§ Attorney Donald Hollowell.

¶ Laura Rates was the wife of Norman Rates, professor of religion, and college minister at Spelman.

Fri. June 7 At AAUP in Washington

1) No legal waver

2) Hold up legal

3) clear case, strong

4) a censure situation, after investigation

5) by both AAUP & college, have tenure

6) will battle on 1) suspension

2) tenure

3) 5 yr not the 64–5

4) Health & TIAA

[H]

Arriv. of evening

NY messages from Lenore

[Entire June 7 diary entry = H]

Sat [June 8]

Letter from Betty [Stevens]—beautiful thing.

Called Lenore—Herschelle [Sullivan] had called her.

Herschelle called.

Carl called—Westefield int

Operator in NI—Do you find them any different?

What do you think / own?

Malcolm X "He'll tell them off"

Called Staughton:

[Benjamin] Mays' cool

Ga. Allen

Grace Hamilton*

Vincent H[arding] & John Youngblut

[Richard] Hocking

PM—Herschelle says she & Marian [Wright] and Carl will have "planning session" in Washington.

Harold Bardinelli & Ann Beilby came to see us.

[Entire June 8 diary entry = H]

---

* Grace Towns Hamilton was the executive director of the Atlanta Urban League. In 1965 she would be the first black woman ever elected to the Georgia state legislature.

Thurs. June 20

Saw Harry Carman[*] late this afternoon, in a suite on the 19th floor with the most magnificent view of New York I've every [ever] seen—the Hudson wide, below to the left,
and whole N.Y. skyline stretching far in the distance to the right, and directly in front
of the window the huge, magnificent, ornamented face of the Riverside Church.

Carman was wonderfully warm, friendly, concerned, anxious to do things. He
said it was a terrible mistake, over and over again. He said plainly that Manley had
become rigid, dogmatic, that he simply could not see the winds of change blowing
through students today. Said very vigorously that it was the students who would
lose the most, and for them it was important to win. Felt Manley under the strong
influence of Lawrence MacGregor,[†] whom he described as a "very, very conservative
man, with a closed, tight mind." As for Rufus Clement, he said he and MacGregor are
like "peas in the pod." He believes Tuttle[‡] will be very good, knows Tuttle well, and
will call him. Will also contact Chauncey Waddell[§] whom he described as a fighter,
and Charles Merrill. Said John Alexander[¶] was anxious to do something, that Alexander had asked Carman what he, as a trustee could do, and Carman said as a
trustee he was entrusted with the education of the students, and that if he felt the
education of the students was being hurt by something that had happened, he was
entitled to inquire into it and do something about it. He said MacGregor had taken
the chairmanship supposedly temporarily but had stuck in it. Said people at the
Whitney Foundation were talking about what had happened—said the Negro secretaries there ascribed it to the narrow background of southern Negro college presidents who are insecure, who feel threatened very easily. Carman doubts Manley can
change much, feels sad about what he's become. Said [Benjamin] Mays came thru
and he asked Mays what happened. Mays said that in every controversy bet[ween]
the admin[istration] and the students, Zinn took the side of the students, and it was
terrible that this had to happen but . . . Said about Clement[,] "He and MacGregor
are two peas in a pod. . . . People think he's liberal but he's far from that." Asked if I
would be interested in either of two jobs at CW Post College, Long Island—a deanship or head of social science dept. both paying minimum of $10,000. I said no, I was
committed to working on my book in Boston next year—besides, I needed to find a

---

[*]   Harry Carman was a Columbia University history professor who had connections with the
Spelman board of trustees.

[†]   Lawrence MacGregor was a New Jersey banker and chair of Spelman's board of trustees.

[‡]   Elbert Parr Tuttle as a judge for the Fifth U.S. District Court played a key role in some of the
most pro–civil rights decisions in the South during the 1950s and 1960s. In 1961 he became the chief
judge of that court. He was also a member of Spelman's board of trustees.

[§]   Chauncey L. Waddell was an investment banker and philanthropist who served on the boards
of trustees at Spelman and Morehouse.

[¶]   John Alexander was acting dean of Columbia College, at Columbia University, and a member of
the Spelman board of trustees.

job that closely suited my interests. He put his hand on my shoulder and said with a remarkable amount of emotion, "I know. I know. Your heart's down there with those students." Said Clement wants to unify A.U. Center under his presidency.

Conversation with [Lawrence] MacGregor Fri. July 5, 1963

Repeatedly: "It's in the president's hands. It's completely in the president's hands. The president is in charge of all that. I place confidence in the presidential decision." Apparently no formal vote of Exec. Comm. of Bd. but he—and perhaps Clement; gave Manley go-ahead[:] "I reviewed that with Dr. Manley. It's in his hands."

Zinn: Can I appeal to the Board?

Mac: That is your right.

Zinn: What will happen then?

Mac: The Board will then turn the matter over to the President.

Zinn: Do you mean to tell me that when I appeal a presidential decision to the Board they will then turn the matter back to the person whose decision I appealed in the first place?

Mac: That's right.

Zinn: What are the chances of my getting a hearing before the Board (as opposed to a simple statement of appeal)?

Mac: That is extremely unlikely.

Zinn: Can't I discuss the matter with you, as chairman of the Board?

Mac: That would be out of order.

Earlier that day with Mrs. John Davis.[*] She said MacGregor has the real power in the Board. Said it would be different if Mrs. Waddell were still alive. Mrs. Waddell once told her "I hope that Zinn never leaves Spelman."

Wed. July 10

Spoke to Staughton on phone. He saw Mrs. Mays[†] this morning, who'd been telling people "moral questions" were involved in my dismissal (the Roslyn Pope incident[‡]). When Staughton questioned her, she said after relating the whole incident in detail as it is generally known, that Dr. Manley had defended me, had assured her at the

---

*   Ethel McGhee Davis was a member of Spelman's board of trustees. Her husband, John Davis, was the former president of West Virginia State College and worked for the NAACP's Legal Defense Fund and its scholarship program for black undergraduates and law students.

†   Sadie (Gray) Mays was the wife of Morehouse president Benjamin Mays.

‡   The Roslyn Pope incident was the arrest of Pope, a Spelman student, and her teacher, Zinn, in January 1960. This arrest of the two for sitting black and white together in a car at night was used by President Manley against Zinn when he appealed his firing, with Manley claiming (falsely) that Zinn had had an affair with Pope. For a discussion of this incident and the ensuing controversy, see pp. 67–74 of the Introduction.

time there was no question of morals involved. She told Staughton she herself did not think there was connection between my dismissal and any "moral" question.

Sat. July 13

Staughton called from Atlanta. 40-minute conversation with Manley this morning. Manley's tone incredibly different, mild, conciliatory, asked why I didn't try to see him in June (!), why I had to take it to the AAUP, why I had to publicize it. Staughton suggested this year be considered a leave of absence, a cooling off period, and meanwhile faculty-administration-student committee work out reforms. Manley said he would take a few days to think this over.

Sun. July 14

Betty Darden phoned. Will go to Ibadan in Sept. Wrote three letters to Manley, no reply. Called him (after second letter) from Atlanta airport at midnight, spoke to Mrs. Manley said she wanted to ask what happened with her two letters. Mrs. Manley said Mr. Manley asleep, would give him message, was quite brusque.

◻ ◻ ◻

Why did Howard Zinn end his diary so soon after his final semester at Spelman? We don't know for certain since Zinn left no specific answer to this question. But it seems evident that since his firing removed him from Spelman and the South in the summer of 1963, the chapter in his life that he'd been writing about daily was over. So the need (and opportunity) for a diary tracking the student sit-in movement and the Spelman student rights struggles had ended, and that likely brought the diary-writing to a close. It signaled that a new phase in Zinn's and his family's life was starting in their move to Boston.

But though no longer based in the South, Zinn continued his involvement with the black freedom struggle there. He returned to the South in the fall of 1963 as part of the voting rights struggle in Selma, traveled South for SNCC meetings, and spent a memorable summer in Mississippi working in the movement's freedom schools in 1964. Zinn remained not only politically but also intellectually engaged with the movement for racial equality, using his year of severance pay from his firing at Spelman to complete two books—*The Southern Mystique* and *SNCC: The New Abolitionists*—that brought all he'd learned and researched about the southern racial revolution to a national readership.[*]

---

[*]   On Zinn's continuing activism in and scholarship on the South's black freedom struggle, see Howard Zinn, *You Can't Be Neutral on a Moving Train: A Personal History of Our Times* (Boston:

So the diary's end does not signal an end to Zinn's engagement with the South. Nor does it mark the end of the influence that his presence there had over those he had befriended in his southern years. This was especially true of the generations of Spelman students he had taught. As the late Vincent Harding (Zinn's friend, fellow activist, and successor as chair of Spelman's history department) explained: "For many of those students, especially the most politically oriented and world citizenship–oriented, they continued throughout their lives to talk about how important it was to have had the opportunity not just to study with Howard . . . but to be befriended by [him]. . . . And that continuing sense of how important a person like him was to their lives strikes me whenever I go and I meet a lot of young women who say the same kind of thing." —RC

Beacon Press, 1994), 56–84; Martin Duberman, *Howard Zinn: A Life on the Left* (New York: New Press, 2012), 95–127.

*   Vincent Harding telephone interview with the author, May 12, 2013.

EPILOGUE

Howard Zinn's Spelman years and his southern diary ended with his firing by President Albert E. Manley just after the spring 1963 semester had come to a close. Forty-two years later a very different president of Spelman, Beverly Daniel Tatum (Spelman's third African American female president), honored Howard Zinn, then eighty-two years old, at the college's 2005 commencement ceremony by conferring upon him an honorary degree and introducing him as the keynote commencement speaker. In her introductory remarks, President Tatum noted that 2005 was the fortieth anniversary of the Voting Rights Act, historic civil rights legislation "that was the result of years of protest and struggle by African Americans and their white allies." She praised Zinn as "one of those allies" who "continues" to work for racial equality and social justice. Tatum noted that Zinn was "known worldwide as the author of *A People's History of the United States*, a book that has sold more than a million copies," and that in "the Spelman community" Zinn had a very special kind of notoriety "as that dynamic professor who came to *teach* and inspired his students to *act*" in the 1950s and early 1960s.[1] The action Tatum was referring to here, was, of course, in the black freedom movement, helping to make Spelman a center of the student wing of that movement. She stressed that as a Spelman professor "Dr. Zinn played an active role in mentoring and supporting Spelman students who worked in the civil rights movement in Atlanta and across the South . . . students [who became prominent in the movement] such as Marian Wright Edelman . . . Bernice Johnson Reagon, Alice Walker, Roslyn Pope to mention a few." Zinn had, in Tatum's words, helped "inspire" the civil rights generation of "Spelman women" in their "fight against segregation."[2]

It is rare for a professor fired by a college to later be honored by that same college, as Zinn was by Spelman. And since Zinn by 2005 was not only the author of the best-selling radical history of the United States but also a playwright, former newspaper columnist, professor emeritus at Boston University, and one of the most famous figures on the American Left—a veteran of the civil rights and antiwar movements who had written influential books on both—his honoring by Spelman drew media attention.[3] Indeed, a few weeks before receiving the honorary degree and delivering his commencement address at Spelman, National Public Radio's Amy Goodman, on her *Democracy Now* show, asked Zinn about his firing and the decision of the college to honor him. Of his firing, Zinn explained that

> at Spelman I got involved with my students in the actions that were going on in the South, the sit-ins, the demonstrations, the picket lines. I was supporting my students, and this . . . [offended Albert Manley,] the first black president of Spelman, [who headed] a very conservative institution. He wasn't happy about me joining the students in all of these things, wasn't happy about a lot of things that they did. But he couldn't do anything about it, but when . . . the students came back from . . . jail, and then rebelled against the campus regulations and restrictions on them, and I supported them, that was too much. . . . He was very unhappy with the fact that I was supporting the students who were rebelling against the paternalism and the authoritarianism on that campus, [and that the movement] . . . brought . . . these black women students . . . out of this little sort of convent-like atmosphere of Spelman and out into the world.[4]

As to why a little more than "40 years after I was fired I am invited back" to Spelman, Zinn credited the college's "new president, a very progressive African American woman, Beverly Tatum, a scholar of race relations in this country." Tatum, Zinn explained, "sent me an invitation to give me an honorary degree and to deliver the commencement address, and she wrote at the bottom of the letter 'it's about time.' That was nice."[5]

Zinn was right to credit Tatum and her progressive politics for his being honored by Spelman. President Tatum initiated the process of awarding Zinn an honorary degree and inviting him to serve as the commencement speaker. The idea of honoring Zinn originated in 2003, and its roots were connected both to progressive scholarship and to student activism at Spelman. A convocation was held in October 2003 at Spelman in connection with the imminent release of Spelman sociology professor Harry Lefever's book, *Undaunted by the Fight*, a pioneering chronicle of Spelman students' role in the civil rights movement.[6] The convocation came amid the Iraq War, which Spelman student and faculty activists had opposed, and a war that Howard Zinn had denounced in print and on national television and radio. Zinn also figured prominently, of course, in the Spelman civil rights activism studied in Lefever's book. So Zinn was invited to address the convocation—cosponsored by the Spelman Women's Research and Resource Center, an institution promoting feminist scholarship and progressive student activism—on "War, Terrorism and the Lessons of History" and to comment on the 1960s student activism featured in Lefever's study.[7]

In his convocation remarks Zinn sought to convince Spelman students of the value of history for understanding the roots of imperialist military aggression and of student activism as a way to resist unjust wars and to battle for peace and for a more humane and democratic society. History, in Zinn's words, "was a matter of life and death" because it enables one to dig beneath the flowery justifications for war used by the White House and to explore how greed and nationalism land the United States in such wars as the one then raging in Iraq.[8] Zinn cited the civil rights activism of Spelman students in the 1960s, covered in Lefever's study, as a stunning example of how the young could make a difference in building a better world once they became politically active.

With anecdotes both moving and humorous, Zinn's reflections on Spelman's history at the convocation recreated the social and political atmosphere of his years at the college in the 1950s and early 1960s. Seeking to explain to the students how "very different" the free atmosphere of twenty-first-century Spelman was from the Spelman he had taught at in the mid-twentieth century, Zinn focused on the regimentation of religious life at the college centered on "Sisters Chapel, where students were expected to come six days a week, no six mornings a week, which was even worse . . . [for] compulsory chapel. Attendance was taken. You had to be in a certain seat. If you didn't sit in that seat BOOM! I don't know what happened to you. People were never seen again. (*Laughter*). You've heard of the disappeared of Argentina. The disappeared of Spelman College."[9]

Noting that his firing at Spelman for "insubordination" had been mentioned in the schedule he was given for the convocation, Zinn reflected on its meaning and connections to the activism of his Spelman students. Zinn explained that though he was a tenured full professor and had been department chair for seven years the administration did not initially offer any explanation for his firing. But later President Manley told people that he'd fired Zinn for "insubordination." Rather than objecting to this, Zinn told the audience that it was true: he had been insubordinate. And that when he learned of this charge of insubordination "it made me feel good. . . . Insubordination. We should all be guilty of that. What happened in the '60s was that people who had been subordinate became insubordinate," including his own students, Spelman activists in the black freedom movement, who had decided they "were not going to be subordinate any more to racism in Atlanta," and so they planned and were arrested in sit-ins that helped end Jim Crowism in the restaurants and stores downtown. And then when these student activists came back to campus they were no longer willing to accept Spelman being run like a "convent" where "you can't go here, you can't go there. Sign out here, sign out there. Compulsory chapel." So they rebelled against the administration, "and I decided yes, I wasn't going to stay in my classes . . . pretending to give lessons on liberty and democracy. So . . . I joined them in their rebellion against the administration. And that was it"—this shared insubordination got him fired.[10]

The crucial lesson from this story, "the important thing" that Zinn sought to impart to this new generation of Spelman students, was not that getting fired was sad or a mistake, but that being insubordinate in the cause of freedom "was worth it," even though it cost him his job. Being cautious in order to promote your career may seem smart, but, as Zinn explained, "it's not enough for a life that makes you feel that you have really lived." He urged students to read Tolstoy's novella *The Death of Ivan Ilyich* about the "successful judge on his deathbed who thinks back 'I've done everything right in my life. I've become prosperous, successful, and people recognized me and so forth. Then why is it now that I'm dying I don't feel good about my life?'" He asked students to consider that contributing to social movements devoted to making the world freer and more just could make their lives more rewarding and meaningful—which is why, as Zinn explained, at SNCC reunions even battle-scarred veterans of the black freedom movement looked back on their activist years as the best in their lives, despite all the violence they encountered. This sense of common purpose and working for the common good with like-minded activists was not only personally fulfilling and meaningful, it was, Zinn concluded, fun, "more fun than working for General Motors, more fun than working with the National Security Council advising the President—much more."[11]

Whatever its impact on the students, this Spelman convocation had an important impact on President Tatum. In introducing Zinn at the convocation Professor Lefever not only mentioned Zinn's firing in 1963—and offered quotes from President Manley's letter terminating Zinn—but observed that this 2003 convocation was "the first time" Zinn had "been invited to speak to the Spelman family" in the four decades since his firing. "It's sad," said Lefever, "that it's taken so long. Dr. Zinn, welcome home."[12] Since Tatum had, at Lefever's invitation, written the foreword to Lefever's book *Undaunted by the Fight: Spelman College and the Civil Rights Movement*, she attended this Spelman convocation. As Tatum recalls, she was startled to learn that "it was the first time that he'd been back at the campus in forty years, which, of course, in 2003 was forty years after he was fired."[13]

Though she had long admired Zinn's historical writing, Tatum had only recently—through the Lefever book—learned of Zinn's role in Spelman's civil rights protests and of his firing. Thus in attending this book event, Tatum reflected on how shabbily Spelman had treated this influential historian and mentor to Spelman's civil rights activists in firing him and not inviting him back to campus after all these years: "So actually while he [Zinn] was there I had the idea, you know, how terrible it was that he'd been treated that way, and what an important role he'd played and all that. And so I thought, 'Wouldn't it be great if we could fix that in some way?' I don't know if I had the idea [for the honorary degree] right at that moment. But certainly in this window of time I got the idea that we should nominate him for an honorary degree."[14] Spelman student activists shared Tatum's enthusiasm about Zinn. In fact one such activist, Sarah Thompson, who had organized the Atlanta University (AU) Center antiwar coalition during the Iraq War, served as the student who helped introduce Zinn at the convocation—and, crediting Zinn's *A People's History of the United States* with "opening my mind and my heart," she also nominated him for an honorary degree.[15]

Clearly, then, Tatum, as one of Spelman's first African American women presidents and as a progressive, was a *very* different kind of president than the paternalistic Albert Manley. And it showed in her decision to honor Zinn, the radical historian and activist who Manley had fired. But this still leaves us with the deeper historical question of how and why Spelman, which, as Zinn noted, had been for so long "a very conservative institution,"[16] was transformed into the kind of college that would elevate to its presidency not only the progressive Tatum (who took office in 2002) but four consecutive female African American presidents, beginning with the distinguished feminist scholar Johnnetta Betsch Cole in 1987. It is no overstatement to see the elevation of such progressive black women as Cole and Tatum to the Spelman presidency as an extension, or final stage, of the aborted proto-feminist rebellion that Zinn's students launched back in 1963—and which, as a result, led to his getting fired for supporting the students.

As Zinn's diary ended, that revolt on behalf of self-determination by young African American women students—demanding their rights against the rigid, paternalistic, and sexist social restrictions and censorship overseen by Albert Manley—had been stifled. Manley in 1963 effectively resisted all the changes the protesters advocated for Spelman, and then he banished Zinn as the revolt's most outspoken faculty champion—sparking an exodus by other progressive faculty as well. So to take the Spelman story beyond the end of Zinn's diary, we need to know when and how the transformation that Zinn's students had battled for unsuccessfully in 1963—the vision of a new, more progressive, liberated, and activist Spelman, in which African American women student voices and agency were recognized and heeded—was finally realized. And we also need to recognize when those old restrictions on student life and expression were toppled. Once we see how this important step beyond paternalism was finally made, we can then explore how Spelman as an institution at last made the move to black female leadership at the presidential level and became the kind of college that would honor Howard Zinn.

Were Zinn, the people's historian, alive today to tell this story of Spelman's transformation, he'd undoubtedly be delighted because, in both cases (the ending of the paternalistic rules that had maintained a "convent-like" atmosphere at Spelman and the elevation of black women to Spelman's presidency), change came primarily from the bottom up. That is, Spelman's student revolts played a pivotal role in sparking the transformation of Spelman, the liberation of its student body from the old paternalism, and the making of Spelman into a college that would choose to be led by progressive black women presidents.

This is not to say, however, that such changes came overnight or easily. Spelman was a college that was both socially and institutionally conservative. This was not merely a reflection of Albert Manley's regime but also involved the school's Christian roots, its conservative trustees, and the calcified politics of race and gender in the Jim Crow South. There were convictions held by powerful administrators, some faculty, and alumnae that the college's traditions had served its students well and ought to be preserved. So demands for change in Spelman's traditions met with resistance, and there was a lag time of years between when such demands for change were first articulated and when those changes were finally adopted.

The strength of this resistance to change is evident in Zinn's diary, as we have seen, with President Manley and his administrative subordinates and faculty allies opposing the liberalization of campus rules advocated by the student protesters whom Zinn was supporting. And Zinn's firing was not merely further evidence of the resistance to change but also a major setback for the protesters. After all, if a full professor and department chair could be fired for advocating liberalization, what chance did students have of winning such changes? With Zinn's firing the students lost their most vocal faculty ally, and the student movement to liberalize Spelman stalled and for a time declined after his departure.[17]

The endurance of the old order at Spelman was still crystal clear at the end of the 1966 academic year, and evidently former colleagues and newer faculty at Spelman kept Zinn informed about this, even though he had moved on to a professorship in the department of government at Boston University. Thus there is in the Zinn papers an extraordinarily revealing letter, written by historian F. J. Ingersoll of the Spelman history department (that Zinn had formerly chaired), attesting that the college's paternalism and rigid regimentation of student life had not changed in the three years since Zinn's firing.

Ingersoll had been asked to comment on a required freshman orientation course, and he responded in mid-August 1966 by sending the administration's coordinator of freshman orientation a devastating critique of both the course and the traditionalist Spelman mindset it embodied. Sounding very much as Zinn had three years earlier, Ingersoll objected to the stress on "etiquette for college students" and to "adjusting" students "to the Spelman tradition" via their compliance with the campus's rules and restrictions. "I know from many sources," Ingersoll explained, that Spelman "housemothers such as the one in Packard Hall can make their own rules and impose an utterly stultifying Victorian atmosphere." He thought it infantilizing for students to be told by "the secretary to the Dean of Women . . . that Spelman students have no business concerning themselves with the war in Vietnam while they're still only college students." With students bombarded with such messages, Ingersoll wondered "how we, as teachers can complain about passive, unresponsive students who can't think. Let's face it if they *did* think, we might have our hands full."[18] He found the orientation's flaws emblematic of

> a basic paradox at Spelman that we haven't faced up to. On the one hand, we talk about developing a free, inquiring, independent spirit in our students. But we still aren't willing to face the consequences of such a resolution. For on the other hand, Spelman strives at turning out, through much discipline and supervision, a socially acceptable and eminently respectable product. And here, I think the school contravenes the basic purpose of an institution of higher learning. Its [rigid oversight of the student body's social] . . . sphere tends to hamper the creation of a strongly intellectual, vigorous argumentative and challenging atmosphere that is crucial to the growth of young minds.[19]

In the dissident tradition of Zinn and his students, Ingersoll in 1966 was objecting to the cost of imposed social conformity to Spelman students, questioning the basic premises of the old regime's policing of student life. Indeed, Ingersoll decided that he could play no role in a freshman orientation course designed as a bulwark of the campus's traditionalism and regimentation. The course's "real intent," he wrote, was indefensible since it consisted of getting

> girls to adjust to Spelman. Why must they? Isn't it true that some of the most brilliant Spelman graduates, the ones to whom we point with pride, refused to adjust? Aren't too many people too well adjusted already? Is history—and change, and progress—made by well adjusted people? Are they the seekers after truth? Perhaps instead of forcing incoming freshmen to take this course, we should arrange one for the faculty and the administration and stress the obverse: that of Spelman College adjusting to the new student of the 1960s and to the critical pass to which American life—right outside our campus gates, even—has come? Shouldn't we be reading books like Paul Goodman's *Growing Up Absurd* and Z. Edgar [Edgar Z.] Friedenberg's *The Vanishing Adolescent* and [Paul] Jacobs and [Saul] Landau's *The New Radicals*, and articles like Howard Zinn's recent piece on the Negro College? Perhaps even Claude Brown's *Manchild in the Promised Land*? (They'll read it anyway; why don't we read it with them?)[20]

The Zinn article that Ingersoll mentioned attested that, though exiled from

Spelman, Zinn in 1966 had lost neither his interest in historically black colleges nor his passion for seeing them (and especially Spelman) renewed, reformed, even revolutionized. Zinn's article, "New Directions for Negro Colleges," was part of a special issue of *Harper's Magazine* on "The Changing Campus," devoted to the state of American higher education in the wake of the new student activism of the 1960s.[21] Drawing on his knowledge of Spelman and the history of African American education, as well as on interviews with faculty, students, and administrators at other historically black colleges, Zinn candidly confronted the problems of these colleges: underfunding, administration authoritarianism, excessive vocationalism, and "how to repair the blight of a century of segregation and impoverishment without taking on the worst characteristics of most American colleges and universities."[22] In spite of these problems, Zinn did not share the pessimism of those who held that with the death of Jim Crow historically black colleges would lose their raison d'être and become extraneous since black students could finally attend desegregated colleges and universities that had once excluded them. Zinn argued that "Negro colleges are hardly likely to be integrated out of existence" because their cultural affinity, low cost, and contrast with the alienating campus world of predominantly white colleges continued to make them attractive to black students, which was why, as Zinn reported, "of the 200,000 Negroes in college, half are in all-Negro or predominantly Negro institutions in the South."[23]

Not surprisingly, Zinn rejected the notion that to survive black colleges ought to play "catch up," emulating their white counterparts in a race for riches and academic entrepreneurship. Instead he called upon the black colleges to institutionalize a Third World consciousness and public service ethos that their student activists had embodied when they ended segregation at lunch counters in the sit-in movement in the early 1960s and founded the Student Nonviolent Coordinating Committee (SNCC). He urged black colleges

> to concentrate on their unique . . . overlooked. . . . supreme advantage over other American schools. . . . they are the nearest this country has to a racial microcosm of the world outside the United States, a world largely non-white, developing, and filled with the tensions of bourgeois emulation and radical protest. And with more white students and foreign students entering, Negro universities might become our first massively integrated, truly international educational centers. . . . If the United States is a white, affluent, middle-aged stranger in a dark-skinned, poverty-stricken revolutionary world, then a predominantly Negro university which attracts students from all countries can become uniquely effective as an educational center for young Americans.[24]

Zinn argued that historically black colleges should see themselves not as refuges from ghetto life or centers of bourgeois aspiration but as institutions deeply engaged with addressing the problems of the poor. Toward this end he recommended establishing work-study programs in which "students spend half their time in the poor communities that surround most of these colleges, and half the year in school studying the problems of poverty. Work in the social sciences, the natural sciences, and art could all be directed toward transforming the lives of the poor." Were this done it would distinguish black colleges from their predominantly white counterparts since no leading university or college "has yet directed all of its reserves of knowledge and ingenuity toward both studying and changing the conditions of life nearby. So the slums grow up around them while the students inside ponder social problems as abstract exercises."[25]

Zinn realized that there would need to be profound changes in the way colleges such as Spelman were governed if his cosmopolitan and egalitarian educational vision was to take hold. They must shed their finishing school ethos where students, as Zinn noted, were introduced to college with rules about "what a young lady may not *wear.*"[26] Such concerns were, as one student Zinn quoted put it, "so superficial, it makes me sick." And, quoting his friend and former colleague, AU political theorist Samuel DuBois Cook, black campuses needed administrative democratization, which meant "basic internal reforms. . . . Negro institutions cry out for an internal revolution that shakes, transforms, and purifies the very foundation of their existence. . . . [This involves] more faculty and student participation in policy making . . . and cessation of the glorification of orthodoxy, false piety, conformity, sentimentality, and authoritarianism."[27]

Although interracial in character, the educational vision Zinn articulated for Spelman and other historically black colleges in this 1966 *Harper's* article anticipated the egalitarian community service ethos that would be championed by black nationalist and black power advocates on those campuses in the late 1960s. When African American student activists and radical faculty spoke of creating a black university their stress, as with Zinn's article, was on building bridges to the larger black community off campus, having colleges and universities serve the poor and address ghetto problems. The upsurge of black nationalism, especially following Martin Luther King Jr.'s assassination in 1968, heralded a new wave of black student activism,[28] and it was amid this resurgent activism at Spelman that the social restrictions Zinn's students had rallied against in 1963 would again become a primary target—and in 1968 most of those restrictions would finally be toppled.

Actually, the idea that Zinn's students had promoted of a Spelman student body freed of the campus's traditional social restrictions never died at Spelman. Criticisms of those restrictions persisted, and the senior class in 1967 lobbied effectively for liberalization of the daytime sign-out policies—so that with parental consent students could finally leave campus during the day without having to get permission from a housemother.[29] Not until the fall semester of 1968, however, would a militant student protest movement emerge with the political leverage to pressure the Manley administration to make sweeping and fundamental changes. That political pressure emanated from the alignment of Spelman's student government and the Spelman students' black nationalist group, Sisters in Blackness, with the black power movement that was taking hold in the AU Center and nationally on black campuses and among African American activists at predominantly white colleges and universities.

Black power advocates eroded and, at some colleges, fractured the familial quality of the relationship between students and administrators on leading black campuses. Tactically, they broke with priorities of their early 1960s predecessors, the integrationist civil right activists on black campuses, who had displayed a certain empathy for their college administrators as black elders maintaining the black community's leading educational institutions in a hostile white world, and so accorded them some deference—or at least did not target them, as they did the movement's white segregationist enemies, with mass civil disobedience campaigns of resistance. Where in the early 1960s black student activists used civil disobedience only to attack segregationists off campus, the late 1960s generation of black power student activists proved willing to use mass civil disobedience—building takeovers and sit-ins—on campus against the administrators of their historically black colleges.[30] This shift came because black nationalist students had developed a critique of historically black colleges, holding that these were not truly black institutions serving the larger African American community but corrupted institutions dependent upon white money, white trustees, and white politicians and involved in acculturating black bourgeois youth to the values of white capitalist America.

This meant that black nationalist students tended to view college administrators on their historically black campuses as Uncle Toms, witting or unwitting agents of white America's intellectual and political oppression, who deserved not deference but pressure to change or get out of the way so black educational institutions would finally serve the black community. This critical perspective was one that late-1960s Spelman activists shared with their counterparts on all the AU campuses. It is also reflected in their October 1968 "Proposal of the Ad-Hoc Committee for a Black University," which asserted that "the so-called predominantly Negro colleges, with the Atlanta University system high on the list, continue to function as one of the main tools used by our oppressors to perpetrate the cruel colonization of Africans in America."[31] As Spelman's Sisters in Blackness explained, the old Spelman needed to go and be replaced with "a Black University," which the Sisters termed a "revolutionary . . . concept" that emerged

> out of the frustrations of black students, educators and artists, activists and community leaders who recognize that present institutions of higher learn-

ing have no real relevance to the total black community and who realize the contradictions of allowing themselves to be acculturated into a society which debilitates black people. We seek to build through education, a new social structure for black people in which they will be offered a valid, reasonable, and beneficial alternative to the status quo. . . . Ultimately, our hope is to include the beauty of our neglected culture and ethnic background into every course offered on Spelman's campus.[32]

Framed by this black nationalist perspective and fired by its militant spirit, Spelman student activists in mid-October 1968 sent President Manley a list of eleven proposals, which included lifting most of the social restrictions that Zinn's students had been organizing to end back in 1963. But though those same restrictions were opposed by both generations of Spelman student activists, the 1968 protesters used black nationalist ideology and terminology to give this cause of greater student freedom a new rationale. Thus in calling for an end to curfews on Spelman students, the Spelman movement of 1968 argued that

the control of social conduct on "Negro" college campuses by the Administration is in direct imitation of those same "puritanical" values which have for so long antagonized and ultimately oppressed Black people. Moreover, during a time when major "white" universities are discarding these values to achieve social freedom it is obvious to us that enforced curfews are another tool used by our oppressors to enslave the minds of Black students while socially separating them from their brothers and sisters in the community.[33]

The protesters used similar reasoning to oppose compulsory chapel—arguing that the time spent in chapel could be better used to connect Spelman students to the black community off campus and to student activists on other AU campuses—and that dress codes, which aped formal western fashions, barred "native African dress."[34] In addition, the students demanded representation on all Spelman committees impacting student life.

Given his past resistance to student protest, it should come as no surprise that President Manley was unhappy with this new student movement. Initially, he pushed back, questioning whether the protesters were interested in "dialogue" as opposed to their own "monologue."[35] Much as he had done with Spelman's Social Science Club in 1963, when—under Zinn's guidance as faculty adviser—it aired student grievances and asked the administration to liberalize campus rules, Manley argued again in 1968 that the student protesters had not gone through "proper channels," meaning the official student government.[36] But when the Spelman student government in October 1968 backed the proposals for change, the administration also rejected that government's claim that student government officers had the authority to terminate unilaterally curfews, compulsory chapel, and dress restrictions.[37]

Within a matter of weeks, however, Manley, under intense pressure from the student movement, began to make concessions. He agreed to suspend classes for two days so that students could hold a "speak out" to discuss their grievances. And after the student body voted overwhelmingly to support the movement's agenda for change, the administration was in an even weaker position. Manley was clearly fearful that the movement's tactics could escalate, since the AU Ad Hoc Committee for a Black University had threatened that unless the administration was responsive to their protests, direct action would result.[38] This was reflected in Manley's warning to the protesters of the consequences if they "blocked entrances to any building or damaged any property."[39]

The two-day speak-out made it evident that the students were not going to be satisfied with this break in classes to let off steam. Thus protest leader Christine Singleton insisted "students would not compromise, did not want forums, but rather wanted an immediate granting of the privileges they were asking for."[40] The students resolved to follow up the speak out with mass protest since their demands had not been met, and they announced a midnight "sleep out" at Giles Hall, inviting students to bring pillows, blankets, and food. Finding that Giles Hall had been locked in the afternoon, the protesters announced they would move the "sleep out to Morgan Dining Hall."[41]

An hour before the "sleep out" was to begin, Spelman's student government announced that the protest would no longer be necessary because the Manley administration—clearly worried about the escalating protests and likely aware that liberalizing Spelman's archaic social regulations was the easiest of the demands of protesters to meet—acceded to the movement's central proposals regarding campus regulations: "Second semester freshmen through seniors would be allowed unlimited curfew with parental permission. First semester freshmen, at the recommendation of the student leaders would have a 12:00 curfew. . . . Non-compulsory sign out and dress was granted to all students."[42] Manley also promised to explore ways of following up on the movement's ideas about a more black-oriented curriculum as well as some of the protesters' other proposals.

The protesters took this news as a great victory and began celebrating: "With an overwhelming amount of enthusiasm, the students recalled their civil rights struggle and applied the tune used then to their present struggle. All over the campus the young ladies could be heard singing 'We Shall Not Be Moved' and 'We Shall Overcome' from the steps of Howe Hall. Upon entering Howe Hall the students began vibrantly belting out 'Woke Up This Morning With My Mind Set on Victory' accompanied by clapping and stomping."[43] Spelman's student newspaper pronounced the protesters' victory "a peaceful and successful revolution."[44]

Although the black power ideals of the 1968 protesters were new at Spelman and the demands were made primarily in terms of racial self-determination,

these younger rebels shared with their 1963 predecessors (Zinn's students) a re-
vulsion against regimentation and compulsion in college life. The students of
1968 were in this sense speaking for both generations when they declared that
"all elements of compulsion deny the individual the right of choice. We believe
in the rights of students to choose those activities which they wish to attend, the
places where they want to go, and what they choose to wear."[45]

Since the Spelman protesters of 1968 framed their demands primarily around
black power and race rather than gender, they—like their predecessors in
1963—did not call themselves "feminists."[46] But as with the rebellion of 1963, the
Spelman movement of 1968 can be said to have been proto-feminist, with these
'68 rebels asserting their rights and abilities as black women. This can be seen
in the language they used to reject compulsory chapel and curfews: "As mature
Black women we feel we should not be *forced* to participate in religious activities
on or off campus. . . . With curfews. . . . We feel that the Spelman women are just
as capable as women at Bryn Mawr College, Vassar College, Mount Holyoke, or
any . . . Ivy League Colleges and we seek the same privileges."[47]

The move toward a more explicit feminism came to Spelman student politics
in the 1970s, the decade when second-wave feminism was surging. Though historians tend to equate militant student protest with the 1960s, the most militant
student revolt in Spelman's history would not occur until 1976—which is the
first time Spelman protesters engaged in civil disobedience *on Spelman's campus.* The issue here, representing a black feminist ethos, was that with Albert
Manley leaving the college presidency it was long past time for Spelman, a black
women's college—founded in 1881—to have its first black woman president.
Throughout the presidential search process, Spelman students worked with
like-minded faculty and administrators in the Ad Hoc Committee for a Black
Woman President, pushing for student representation on the board of trustees
and its search committee. Spelman's student government petitioned the trustees
for a black woman president and held a referendum in which the student body
overwhelmingly endorsed this goal.[48]

Students were thus incensed when, in April 1976, they learned that Spelman's
board of trustees had narrowed the finalists for the presidency of the college to
a man. Demanding that an African American woman be elevated to the presidency, a small group of students, as one protester put it, "to make the trustees
believe that Spelman women mean business," blocked the doors of the conference room where the board of trustees were meeting on April 22, 1976.[49] The
blockade, which came to be known as "the lock-in," lasted twenty-six hours,
and during that time Spelman's trustees were not even allowed to exit to the
restrooms.[50] The protest drew an impressive display of solidarity from the Spelman student body, as activists spent all night in the corridors outside the room
where the board of trustees had been meeting. Support for the protesters' de-

mand was also visible among Spelman faculty, one of whom explained to the *New York Times* that Spelman "has been dedicated to training young women for leadership for 95 years. . . . To say there are no qualified black women to be president: well you might as well close our doors."[51]

Though the "lock-in" failed to dissuade the trustees from elevating Donald Mitchell Stewart to the college's presidency, the protest did result in an understanding among the trustees and the Spelman community that Stewart would be Spelman's last male president, and that the next president of the college would be an African American woman. Thus the student protest in 1976 paved the way for Johnnetta Betsch Cole to become Stewart's successor in 1987.[52] It was not merely that Cole was a black woman that made the appointment so historic but also that she was an influential feminist scholar and a radical who believed in faculty governance, and so would establish a faculty council and promote a democratic ethos at Spelman. Cole's appointment also had a connection to the Spelman student movement of Zinn's time at the college in that her key champion on the divided board that elevated her to the presidency was Marian Wright Edelman (Spelman class of 1960), a leader of the Atlanta sit-ins who had been a student of Zinn's. All three presidents who followed Cole (Audrey Forbes Manley, Beverly Tatum, and Mary Schmidt Campbell) would also be African American women. So the Spelman of 2005 was free of the paternalistic authoritarianism that Zinn's students had rebelled against—a rebellion that he got fired for supporting—and had become a campus led by African American women, at least in part because of the protests organized by the young black women who had attended Spelman in the late 1960s and 1970s. These generations of student rebels can be said, then, to have helped in transforming Spelman into the kind of progressive college whose administration, faculty, and students would choose to honor its exiled former professor, that mentor of Spelman rebels, Howard Zinn.

Seen in this context, the rebellion that Zinn was fired for promoting in 1963 seems less like the failed movement for change, as it appeared to be at the time of Zinn's ouster, and more like an early clarion call for the new Spelman—a Spelman whose students would be accorded the respect and the rights of young women. This new Spelman was a place where student and faculty political activism would be pointed to with pride as a valued tradition of the college in promoting a commitment to engaged citizenship and public service.[53] It was a Spelman where President Tatum could bestow an honorary degree on Howard Zinn in 2005, and where her successor, Mary Schmidt Campbell, Spelman's current president, could write in 2016 that the college "is now exceedingly proud of our students' activism and Zinn's role in that activism."[54]

Nor is this activism merely a relic of the 1960s and 1970s; it is an ongoing tradition on a campus that takes pride in its role in producing leaders in the Atlanta sit-in movement and the larger black freedom movement of the 1960s. Indeed, the students attending that graduation ceremony Zinn addressed at Spelman in 2005 had earlier generated national media attention protesting against the extreme misogyny of the hip-hop video "Tip Drill" by the rap artist Nelly. They challenged him to engage in a dialogue about his sexism during a scheduled campus visit (a challenge Nelly ducked by canceling his Spelman visit).[55] Such students at Spelman were, as on most campuses, an activist minority, but one that—unlike in the 1950s and early 1960s—receives public praise from the college's administration. As Tatum explains, "Today we say 'Coming to Spelman is a choice to change the world.' This idea that Spelman women make a difference wherever they are. It is a critical piece of what it means to be a student at Spelman."[56]

As in the late 1950s and early 1960s with Zinn, so in the early twenty-first century at Spelman the student activist tradition has been sustained by politically engaged faculty, most notably professor Beverly Guy-Sheftall, who in 1981 founded and continues to head the campus's Women's Research and Resource Center and is a pioneering scholar of black feminism. Guy-Sheftall's progressive politics date back to the Zinn years, when she was a student at Spelman (class of 1966). Back then she had close friends at Spelman active in the sit-ins and SNCC, did coursework with Zinn's radical protégé Staughton Lynd, and had already developed an egalitarian sensibility that led her as a sixteen-year-old undergraduate to resent the contrast between Spelman's rigid dress code and curfew and the freer campus world of Morehouse men.[57] In 1996, Professor Guy-Sheftall led Spelman into becoming the first historically black college to establish a women's studies major, and her women's studies classes have inspired generations of Spelman students toward feminism and activism. Indeed, the protests against Nelly's misogyny originated with discussions in her women's studies course. Guy-Sheftall had recently published with Johnnetta Cole the pathbreaking study *Gender Talk: The Struggle for Women's Equality in African American Communities* (2003), which included a chapter critiquing musical misogyny, "No Respect: Gender Politics and Hip-Hop." The initial organizing of the protest occurred through the Women's Research and Resource Center.[58]

This is not to say that all traces of the old social conservatism have vanished. Vestiges of the conservative past live on in the minds of some older alumnae, who, for example, welcomed Johnnetta Cole's departure from the presidency—considering her an outsider and a radical—and spoke of "wanting our school back." They were relieved that the president who followed her, Audrey Forbes Manley, was a Spelman alumna who, as the wife of Albert E. Manley, might seem a less radical break from the old Spelman.[59] That traditionalism was also visible when, in preparation for Beverly Tatum's visit to Spelman for her final interview for the presidency, a Spelman alumna advised her to dress conservatively: "wear your best skirt suit." But Tatum, a woman "who wears pants most of the time," decided to wear pants since she thought that "if they really need someone who wears skirts all the time they probably don't want me." And when she did come to the interview in pants, someone came up to her remarking about her being so daring as to defy Spelman's conservatism about dress and praising her as a "great spirit."[60] Similarly, in the college's Founder's Day ceremonies—despite the objections of feminists—the first-year students still march in white dresses. And lesbian students continue to feel a tension on campus due to the college's Christian roots and ongoing religious influence.[61]

Moreover, though Albert Manley's presidency ended in 1976, its afterlife was still discernible on the day Zinn received his honorary degree at Spelman. Out of deference to admirers of Manley and his second wife, Audrey, whose term as president of Spelman (1999–2002) had ended only recently, President Tatum in her otherwise eloquent introduction to Zinn avoided mentioning that his years at Spelman had ended with his firing.[62] This, of course, did not detract from the honor Spelman accorded to Zinn, but it did mean that the college had still not undergone a public reckoning or even an open acknowledgment of this repressive side of its past. Most of the graduating students in the audience would have had no idea that, in honoring Zinn, Spelman's President Tatum was seeking to right an old wrong.

Though in terms of historical accountability this silence about Zinn's firing is problematic, the honorary degree nonetheless was thrilling and had great meaning for those who had been close to Zinn during his Spelman years. Betty Stevens Walker and other Zinn students saw the occasion as a blessing—that after all these years at last their beloved teacher and mentor was finally being recognized by Spelman. Stevens Walker wrote Zinn that his appearance at Spelman to be so honored was "a sacred moment of reconciliation and grace."[63] Samuel DuBois Cook, who had been one of Zinn's best faculty friends in the AU Center, and who in 2005 was president emeritus of Dillard University, wrote Zinn reflecting euphorically on Spelman's decision to honor him and how it contrasted in his own mind with the painful memories of Zinn's firing. "My immediate reason for writing," Cook explained to Zinn,

> has to do with a redemptive dimension of history and poetic element of justice in the moral universe: your being the Commencement speaker at Spelman and the recipient of an honorary degree. *Praise de Lawd!* The gods, in their terrible judgment, ethical integrity, prophetic power, and luminous vision, must join the celebration. I have a slight idea of your inner feelings. Oh, what reflections, recollections, and mediations must have crowded your mind. I shall never forget the letter, day, shock, and pain.[64]

As to Zinn himself, the return to Spelman was a grand one in part because of the way President Tatum had arranged the graduation week. By having his return coincide with the anniversary of the Voting Rights Act, Tatum ensured that many of Zinn's students, including civil rights movement veterans such as Marian Wright Edelman—who was serving as the baccalaureate speaker—would be there for the ceremonies, making it a joyous reunion.[65] Reflecting on the occasion in a letter to one of his former Spelman students, Zinn would write that for him and his wife, Roslyn, "our return to Spelman was like one long, warm embrace."[66] Politically, true to form, in his 2005 Spelman commencement address "Against Discouragement," Zinn paid tribute to the students he had taught at Spelman and who devoted themselves to the cause of social justice in the black freedom movement, remarking that "I learned more from my students than they learned from me." He credited their activism with helping to create the electric political atmosphere that would make his "years at Spelman the most exciting of my life, the most educational certainly."[67]

Zinn urged the class of 2005 to consider an unconventional definition of success and an openness to creative rule-breaking on behalf of progressive social change. He expressed the

> hope that you will not be content just to be successful in the way our society measures success; that you will not obey the rules when the rules are unjust, that you will act out the courage that I know is in you. . . . You can help to break down barriers, of race certainly, but also of nationalism; that you do what you can—you don't have to do something heroic, just something, to join with millions of others who will just do something, because all of those somethings, at certain points in history, come together, and make the world better.[68]

Zinn never seems to have reflected upon the political meaning that Spelman's honoring of him had for the college itself. But regarding his own political and personal relationship to Spelman, Zinn had long since looked upon his role there far more in terms of what he and his students had learned from one another, and what they had done together on behalf of freedom, rather than dwelling upon his firing. So he did not need an honorary degree to feel good about his Spelman years or to cherish his memories of them. Thus when asked by NPR's Amy Goodman on *Democracy Now* whether the honorary degree left him feeling vindicated, Zinn replied, "Well, I felt vindicated one minute after I was fired. But this [honoring by Spelman] is good. It's a good feeling, yes."[69]

"On Liberty at Spelman," March 11, 1963

While Howard Zinn's southern diary is the single best and most detailed guide to the Spelman student rights revolt of 1963, Zinn also left us a remarkable historical source that goes beyond the printed page in bringing that revolt to life: the audio recording he made of the largest and most important student rights protest meeting of the 1962–63 academic year. This meeting, called "On Liberty at Spelman," was held on the evening of March 11, 1963 and organized by the Social Science Club (with Zinn as its faculty sponsor). The meeting, which lasted over two hours, aimed to air student grievances against the social and political restrictions on campus maintained by the Spelman administration; it drew some 150 students, or about 25 percent of the entire student body. The recording of the meeting, which had been on old and inaccessible reel-to-reel tapes, has been digitized by NYU's Tamiment Library, where they are stored among Zinn's papers. And so for the first time in a half-century one can literally hear the voices of the student protesters, Zinn, and other faculty along with administrators opposed to their protests. Zinn did offer a brief and insightful summary of the meeting in his diary. But the audio recording allows one to hear the meeting from start to finish and to observe Zinn, and the student movement in action, interacting and also get a sense of the level of emotion in that meeting as critics confronted the administration.

Shortly after his firing, Zinn looked back on this meeting as a great moment of liberation, observing that "there had never been a meeting like this on the Spelman campus, where so many students spoke their minds so freely. What was made crushingly clear was the depth of discontent at the college, and the overwhelming unanimity with which students resented administrative controls. When the meeting ended, there was a hopeful feeling that perhaps it might lead to change."[1]

Coming through loud and clear on the audio recording is Zinn's skillful style of political mentorship. As the meeting opens we hear Zinn setting its tone, yet doing so in a way that fosters and highlights the students' sense of agency. He began by reading excerpts from letters former Spelman students had sent him that bemoaned the lack of freedom on campus and urged students to continue to struggle for freedom. These excerpts spotlighted the need for action and established that at the meeting students should feel free to air their grievances (despite the presence of Spelman administrators, which might otherwise intimidate students from expressing criticism of the campus environment).

Having established this meeting as a free political space where students could speak candidly, Zinn handed over the meeting to the students, whose catalogue of complaints was extensive, damning, and often expressed passionately and eloquently. One can detect an air of exhilaration as students, in the presence of administrators, blasted conditions they found oppressive. These included rigid dress codes, restrictions on their social lives, and abuse of authority by campus officials—especially by dormitory housemothers, who were accused of spying on students and punishing them in inappropriate ways for the most innocent acts (e.g., confining students to their rooms when they failed to attend a campus concert).

There were lighthearted moments as students mocked the way their campus lives were regimented. Thus the packed room full of students burst into laughter as one student questioned why they were forbidden to wear slacks except at breakfast on Sunday morning, noting that most students did not look any better or more ladylike in the wrinkled "breakfast dresses" they wore to the cafeteria during the week.

The moments of highest tension came as students objected to the intimidation tactics used by the Spelman administration—especially its taking away the scholarship of a leading student critic of the administration. Though not mentioning the name of this student, everyone knew who it was (Lana Taylor), and they pushed the administrators present to justify their action. When a dean sought to do so by claiming that this student had exhibited "bad citizenship," several students pressed for a definition of that term and asked whether the administration used it to stifle honest and much-needed dissent. Students with firsthand knowledge of this case refuted the charges made against Taylor. During this exchange Zinn, ever protective of the students' right to dissent, jumped in. Zinn said that while it was possible to subject Taylor's specific actions to conflicting interpretations, what was indisputable was the larger context of this case—that despite its claims to liberalism, the administration "chopped the heads off" of students who dared to challenge its authority.

As Zinn noted in his diary, students greeted his remarks with applause (as well as joyful laughter). And this was only one of several times when Zinn spoke critically of the administration and took issue with what administrators were saying at the meeting. Toward the end of the meeting, Zinn read another student's letter, which offered a scathing assessment of the regimentation of student life at Spelman. Perhaps because he was so focused on the students and so admiring of their courage in expressing their grievances (and delighted at being able to support them), Zinn failed to note in his diary how irate some of the administrators and their faculty allies present at the meeting were over his biting criticism of the Manley administration. This could not have been an easy meeting for these representatives of the administration, who labored to defend a paternalistic campus regime whose excesses were being documented and denounced by student after student as well as Zinn.

Zinn was the most vocal and critical, but he was not the only professor at this meeting to support the students' quest for greater freedom. Zinn's faculty friends Renate Wolf and Staughton Lynd also advocated for a freer campus. Lynd, whose remarks near the end of the meeting are included below, was especially eloquent on how Spelman had become a house divided, beset by tension between the social regimentation of student life and the free intellectual and political atmosphere that faculty and students desired and valued. But the fact that only these two other faculty openly sided with the student rights cause at this meeting is a testament to how isolated Zinn was among his colleagues—and how vulnerable he would become—in taking such a forthright stance on behalf of the administration's angry student critics.

As reflected in his diary entries, Zinn repeatedly sought to get President Manley to hear the students' complaints. First he invited him to the "On Liberty at Spelman" meeting; then, after Manley refused to attend, Zinn asked him on several occasions to listen to the tape of the meeting. This too Manley refused. Zinn was so impressed by this student protest and eager to convey its message to Manley that he seemed oblivious to the way his role at that protest meeting jeopardized his own future at Spelman—something he was not concerned with because his status as a full professor and department chair gave him a false sense of security.

The tone of key administrators at the "On Liberty" meeting and their ire at Zinn strongly suggests that Manley did not need to attend the meeting or listen to a tape of it because his outraged subordinates had reported on it to him. And with Zinn opening and closing the meeting by reading student letters critical of the administration, accusing the administration of politically decapitating dissident students, and encouraging them to believe that they and not the president had the final authority over campus rules, it is little wonder that Manley and his allies viewed Zinn's behavior at this meeting as insubordinate. Or that Zinn's friend and colleague from Atlanta University, Samuel DuBois Cook, would later learn from Benjamin Mays that for Manley this meeting was "the straw that broke the camel's back," leading Spelman's president to culminate his feud with Zinn by firing him.[2]

At the "On Liberty" meeting, Zinn proved himself to be the kind of fearless faculty ally that student activists dream of but rarely encounter. Still, the line between courage and recklessness was a porous one, and Zinn unknowingly may have crossed it. The support of this dedicated and beloved student movement ally proved to be transient, because soon he would be purged.

Readers of the following excerpts can form their own judgments on Zinn's handling of this fateful meeting and learn of how Spelman's young women students defied their paternalistic campus regime and spoke up eloquently for their rights. The excerpts here are from key moments of the "On Liberty at Spelman" meeting.[3]

PROFESSOR HOWARD ZINN: When we first talked about having this meeting, we were considering what the format should be. We thought at first that we would . . . have a panel, which is the usual thing. And then we thought that a panel might cut down on the amount of time for discussion from the floor. And so we thought that rather than have a panel the meeting would consist almost entirely of just discussion from the floor, give and take. And we thought that to stimulate this discussion that I would read a few excerpts.

And these excerpts are from three different sources. The first two are from letters that I received some time in the past few months. And I guess I'm reading them without identifying the writer, and with the permission of the writer, because they're provocative in their own way. And we hope they'll help stimulate discussion.

The first letter, or the first excerpt, is from a letter sent to me by a Spelman graduate who is now in one of the leading graduate schools in the country. I might say that both these letters were unsolicited. By that I mean I hadn't written to them—I'm a poor letter writer—I hadn't written to either of these students, but they wrote these to me. This student said, among other things,

> I'm interested in knowing how things are shaping up at Spelman this year. Well I simply hope the students do not stop pushing for a better campus existence no matter what. I can't tell you how good it is to be able to
> (1) Walk across acres and acres of grass without feeling criminal (*laughter*).
> (2) Smoke cigarettes and wear slacks in front of sophisticated teachers and alumnae without feeling vulgar.
> One is never made to feel dirty about what one does. There is a very natural living pace. No rules for graduates. Freshmen can stay out, no sign out, till 2:00 a.m. These freedoms help keep them from developing negative attitudes, which so far I've noticed in no one here.

The other letter is from a student who left Spelman. It says, among other things,

> It seems as though no one can make sense out of the reasons why I said I was leaving. Maybe my values are perverted, but as I see it now they aren't.

I was very depressed. And I felt hemmed in. I found myself losing the little inner peace that I had left. I've always been a very sensitive person, and it seems to me that Spelman only increased my sensitivity. Little things count. And little things can grow into big things. I just got tired of being agitated and locked up. There are places we can go, but the movies get boring sometimes. I like the girls at Spelman, but I will never have any real love of the place because it offered me nothing to love. I intend to come back but in a different situation. Rules, some rules are fine. But one's emotions are not easily controlled by rules. To me college is a place where the student grows. But how can one grow any way but warped when one lives under warped conditions? I don't expect to be self-governed. I realize the necessity for some discipline, but I feel I'm losing more than I'm gaining. And nobody who can do something about the conditions really cares. That's one of the frustrations about it.

Most students and working people look forward to the weekend. But not at Spelman. The movies are even out on the weekends. I didn't go anywhere. Many nights I stayed in the basement by myself because I couldn't sleep. Sometimes one of my friends, when she had late classes the following day, would stay up with me as long as she could. Spelman is missing the point I feel in many ways. If the standards for Spelman are so very high more students should pass the Graduate Record Exam. Less students should be planning on leaving because of grades. But these things go unnoticed seemingly except by a few. They should realize that there are no more Spelman young ladies. There are just young ladies who go to Spelman (*laughter*).

The third excerpt, and I'm reading this, this is not a personal letter, I'm reading this to perhaps bring the situation into larger perspective, and to point out that the problems that we think, or that we may think, only exist at Spelman are regional problems and perhaps in a certain sense national problems. But certainly they're problems that exist throughout the South. And what I'm reading to you now was given to me by two young women who traveled through the South on a special project for the YWCA going to various colleges—Negro and white—they're called the special human relations staff of the national student YWCA for the southern region. One of these two is a Negro; the other is a white. And they both got together in drawing up this report of their observations in southern institutions. This is just a part of the report:

Any work in human relations among southern students must necessarily revolve around academic freedom because it is concerned with the right to protest. The task in the south is as clear-cut as the system of segregation itself. The very basic need of southern students is to understand their right to protest, a right they have simply because they are human beings, apart from their position as students and irrespective of their race. The first strike against the southern student, both Negro and white, is that his growth is stunted by the insularity of the region. He's nurtured in a climate which has kept him from exploring the world that lays beyond his gaze. The social atmosphere is one of distrust for the different. And classroom learning only more deeply entrenches parental attitudes rather than freeing youth to protest and form its own system of beliefs. This is true for both the Negro and the white.

One of the areas in which the ravages of segregation are most evident and also most ironic is in the Negro college in the area of faculty-student relationships. Administration controls schools with an iron will, which can be altered by none, except the state and maybe the trustees. The faculty sees students as youngsters who must be cajoled and bribed into accumulating an acceptable amount of "knowledge." The result in some cases had been the acquisition of social rather than academic degrees.

Then they [the two special human relations staff members of the national student YWCA for the southern region] mention a Harvard PhD in sociology at a Negro college they visited who spent the class joking around, telling stories, gave very little material of value. A student at the school said, "We're tired of classes where instructors are just jiving around." The professor mentioned above discussed students as being products of generally broken homes, and went on to say they have to be approached on a level to which they have been accustomed. Rather than stimulating further exploration, the faculty stifle a vision of the future by constantly holding up personal backgrounds to the students.

The problems of faculty-student communications are further aggravated by improper communication between faculty and administrations. The faculty members feel they will jeopardize their position by taking very definite stands on any number of issues. When students are seen as enjoying privileges rather than having rights, the vehicle of the student press is naturally infringed upon. It is very frustrating to note that a discussion of academic freedom on most Negro campuses must begin at the level of curfews and minor privileges. Instructors generally feel that since this is the first experience away from home for most of the students they're quite content with things as they exist. The young person visiting the campus is quickly informed of the widespread discontent, however. The infringements upon academic freedom faced by most southern Negro college students seemed glaring. They're perpetuated through a lack of communication between administration, faculty, and students. Walls have been erected, shutting each group off from the other. An awareness of current opinions among the three is nil. Administrators spoke of how content the students were. Faculty members spoke of how apathetic students were. Students spoke of discontent with instructors who were just jiving around.

Well these are the three statements, and somebody handed me a few moments ago something [a letter by Marie Thomas], which I suppose a student wrote because she couldn't be here. And I don't know what's in it but I'll give it to some student to read for her I suppose. I'd like to turn things over now to the chairman, Dorcas Boit.

CHAIRMAN DORCAS BOIT:[4] Before we go further I would like to make a few statements, because on the part of students there is a feeling that if they speak out in places like this somebody is going to get back and ask them about it, and they are afraid of repercussions, because some of us have witnessed these already. But I wish to appeal to our teachers and administrative officials here to help this, because we are discontented, there is no question about it; there is discontent among students, and we're hoping that this will serve as a beginning, to bring us together, because this is not a healthy atmosphere in a college. It doesn't have to be this way. And there is a lack of communication in all these areas. So let's make this useful and let's have something that may help us in restoring a healthy atmosphere. And for this record player, I mean tape recorder, let's not worry that it's going to be held against anybody. It's really for the Social Science Club, their own discussions. . . . Don't be afraid. And please students, let's use this opportunity. Thank you. Now I will open the discussion.

STUDENT LEADER BETTY STEVENS (WALKER): My statements will include material from a book on freedom and responsibility prepared by a nationally recognized organization of college students. And some of the statements, of course, are my own. The American student has grown up. We recognize the responsibility of every student to devote himself to increasing his knowledge and understanding of the world around him in preparation for the fulfillment of himself as a human being. We recognize the responsibility of every student to respect the rights of the faculty, the administration, and fellow students. We recognize the responsibility of every student to make himself cognizant of and to comply with the regulations pertaining to the educational and cocurricular policies that govern the institution of his choice. We recognize the responsibility of every student to uphold the academic integrity of his institution.

We feel very strongly, however, that freedoms must not be restricted, freedoms which are prerequisites of a fully democratic social order and personal development. The vision towards which we strive is that of a democratic university in which we share certain rights of participation in matters of common concern, and a freedom of inquiry, association, and development. And where paternalism is replaced by the fellowship in the company of scholars.

We feel very strongly here that rules, regulations are necessary. Certainly we do not feel that this is not so. We recognize that all forms of university-imposed discipline are not of a paternalistic nature. However, we feel very strongly that there are some [that are paternalistic]. We, I, have looked at the situation. I am not an analyst, I'm not the most intelligent girl in the world but I pride myself on being reasonably intelligent. And this is what I have come up with. Here I think we operate under the philosophy of in loco parentis, a Latin phrase, which literally translated means "in place of parents." And this philosophy, or any school operating under this philosophy, mind you I'd say that sometimes, I don't mean that this is always, but enough to draw your attention to the fact, has certain effects. Paternalism in any form induces or reinforces immaturity, conformity, and disinterest among those whose imagination, critical talents, and capacity for integrity and growth should be encouraged and given opportunity to develop. Removal of responsibility for personal decision making from the individual student distorts and weakens a significant phase of the educational process. The unexamined acceptance of authority which is often appropriate to the child-parent relationship must be replaced in the universities by the dialectical and critical exchange between the student and his community. The range of inquiry within and beyond the classroom must not be restricted out of parental considerations, but must be opened, out of educational ones.

Here at Spelman, as Dorcas said, there *is widespread discontent*. There is chronic complaining. This is not the same complaining or discontent that is found everywhere. This is discontent of a deeper nature. I think we are fooling ourselves and we are actually obstructing progress when we maintain an attitude of holier-than-thou and superior-than-thou and not look at ourselves realistically, see what is wrong, and see what we can do.

Reinhold Niebuhr, in his book *Moral Man and Immoral Society*, makes the point that the feeble-minded have a difficult time distinguishing between constructive and destructive criticism. I hope that we will not be feeble-minded here tonight, and I hope that that we can really look at ourselves, work on our problems, and get on toward a better Spelman. Thank you (*loud and sustained applause*).

ANOTHER STUDENT: I want to throw out some things that I really can't see the logic in. And some of the things I can't see the logic in are: Say if you go to the dining hall on Sunday you can wear slacks. Now during the week you can't wear slacks to the dining hall. Now the thing that I can't logically see is that on Sunday you go to the dining hall and you see the same people . . . in the dining hall but Monday through Saturday you cannot wear slacks to the dining hall. Now I feel that since you encounter the same situations Monday through Saturday . . . so that [if] you wear slacks on Sunday I feel that you should be able to wear them on Monday through Saturday. Now the thing that I object to most of all is that Monday through Thursday when you go in dresses people look worse, they look much worse Monday through Thursday than they do on Sunday—because of the fact that many people have something that's called a breakfast dress (*loud and sustained laughter*). Now a breakfast dress is something that you wear to breakfast every day (*laughter*). . . . People come down the hall and they take the rollers out of their hair . . . now this is Monday through Saturday. Then on Sunday, everybody, usually, you don't get to wear your slacks anyway because the fact is there aren't too many things that you can wear slacks to so usually everybody has little slack suits that . . . they haven't had an opportunity to wear. . . . So you get out and you put on a nice-looking slacks suit, and then you decide, "Well I'll comb my hair." So you comb your hair and you put on some socks, and you look very decent when you go to breakfast on a Sunday.

Now one other point that I would like to make is this. They say that when you go to the dining hall you can't wear a scarf. Now, I don't feel that everyone should wear a hat to the dining hall. But there are some people who take swimming and they come out of swimming in the afternoon say and their head is wet. Now I know that I have had people stop me on the campus outside and say, "Put something on your hair so you won't catch a cold." And so I feel that if you're in the dining hall walking around with your hair wet you look horrible (*laughter*). No girl wants anyone to see her with her hair in its natural state (*sustained laughter*). Therefore if you put a scarf on your head it enhances your looks. You look much better. These are some things that I feel actually there is no logic behind. Just like the slacks, going every day and . . . [only] Sundays wearing slacks. I see no logic in this. That's all I can think of right now (*laughter*).

DORCAS BOIT: Please try to get to your explanation so there is time to give everybody an opportunity [to speak]. And may I just say it depends on where you are about your natural hair because I am used to seeing people in their natural state.

ALUMNAE SECRETARY ERNESTINE BRAZEAL: May I ask Betty if she would be specific. She said that there was unrest and what not. Could she . . . [specify] what is the cause of the unrest?

BETTY STEVENS (WALKER): An answer to Mrs. Brazeal's question will come out in the general discussion . . . and if this is not satisfactory I will [elaborate].

DORCAS BOIT: Somebody down there.

ANOTHER STUDENT: I don't live on campus but I have talked to a great many campus women with respect to freshmen this year. And one of the major complaints I have been aware of is that the students would like as nearly as possible for the dean's office to completely outline the duties of housemothers really (*sustained applause*). Now I can't testify to this but I believe [things] people have told me are reliable and I have heard it too many times to doubt it. But I have been informed that there are situations where housemothers actually [go] into students' rooms, go into their closets and eavesdrop on conversations (*laughter*). . . . There are housemothers who say that if you do not attend this function that you cannot go to that function, which the college does not stipulate but the housemother takes it upon herself to do this. And there is this type of a context between even the students and the housemother because there is a constant battle. . . . So the students would like for some office in a very detailed form [an] outline [of] the duties of housemothers so that if there is a conflict they would have some recourse.

DORCAS BOIT: Thank you. May I call on somebody [from the administration to respond?] Because we can talk about discontent and I think we will continue to do that. But can we speak to some of these things—why we have to have, why we cannot wear slacks . . . why we have to cover our hair? Can somebody speak to this please?

ADMINISTRATOR: It appears that at all times in a day you wouldn't permit yourself to go about in slacks. We recognize the fact that all of us don't look very good in slacks (*laughter*). Surely if you . . . have the privilege of going to breakfast on Sunday morning in slacks . . . this is the same as being in your home and you casually get up and have your breakfast. But if you're having dinner at 1:00 with young men present then you're not going to have curlers in your hair and pants on. You're going to dress up. . . . On Sundays you can wear pants in the morning but not at dinner (*students respond by saying "no" in unison*). What she is speaking to is wearing pants . . . .

STUDENT: Monday through Saturday.

ADMINISTRATOR: What about the students who cross the campus to go to breakfast? (*Students jeer.*)

ADMINISTRATOR: It's still a matter of good appearance because the campus is an open campus. It's just like leaving home to go to a restaurant. You don't know who you will encounter on the way. (*Students speaking to one another loudly.*)

DORCAS BOIT: Just a minute before you go on. Let's have order in here. Don't get emotionally involved. . . . Please let's be sensible.

ADMINISTRATOR: We can get bogged down in something small like this. But the point about something like this is that if you decide a change like that is to be made it is simply a matter of making that as a recommendation through your channels, to make recommendations. I would not like to see us get bogged down with the question of whether or not we can wear pants at breakfast Monday through Friday. I think that in the reasonable outline that Dr. Zinn gave we have more important matters to discuss. And this can merely become a matter of recommendations.

DORCAS BOIT: You've heard that you can recommend things so maybe we can get some good [recommendations].

PROFESSOR RENATE WOLF: [On student] discontent. . . . Whenever you try to find out what's the matter you get this answer—"rules.". . . . I would like to ask who makes the rules? Who is the one?

DORCAS BOIT:Dean Curry?

FORMER DEAN OF WOMEN MARGARET CURRY: I was about to say that most of these that you have now are based on the constitution that the students themselves made some years ago (*loud student murmuring*). Now you I know what I'm talking about girls so you may as well be quiet (*laughter*).

DORCAS BOIT: Can we have order please?

MARGARET CURRY: It's based on the constitution that they themselves drew up, along with I suppose faculty members and members of the administration. But it was very carefully done so that most of them [the rules] so far as I know, and I don't know about all of the rules there are some few percent that have been added. I'm sure there have been. . . . But basically the rules they have now. I believe all the ones . . . [came] from that constitution that was drawn up by the students and the faculty. They worked very hard in doing that and the students themselves put in it what they wanted in it, realizing that a democracy is the sort of society where rules change and conditions change, and you change with conditions. So that I think that the constitution was supposed to function just on a temporary basis, and from time to time changes would be made in it. And I don't know what changes have been made since.

ANOTHER STUDENT: I wanted to know if anyone here knows the last time that the constitution has been changed. When was the constitution made? (*Loud student murmuring.*)

HOWARD ZINN: I can't answer this fully. I can only answer to the best of my knowledge; but it was adopted as the whole student government set-up was adopted shortly after I came to Spelman which was in the fall of '56. And the constitution was adopted then. I remember the faculty considering it as well as the administration. The faculty did not consider the rules. The rules were not adopted by the faculty. As a matter of fact the rules are not part of the constitution. The rules are something separate from the constitution. And the rules, according to the constitution, can be changed by the SSGA [the Spelman Student Government Association]. Now, in other words, any meeting of the SSGA has the right to change the rules. And when students have come to me complaining about rules I have very often told them that "the power is in your hands." If you're timorous, if you're timid about exerting this power that's your own problem. But you have the power to change things and you ought to exert it.

Now the constitution probably has not been changed because it is not easy to change the constitution. And because—well this is a general difficulty with constitutions—and I suppose there hasn't been enough initiative forthcoming. But the rules are something that require no constitutional amendment, that require students to come to an SSGA meeting, and to vote.

I might say this, there is a provision—I was looking through this constitution (one of my jobs is to read constitutions occasionally), and I was looking through this constitution and I noticed that the student council has the right to legislate between meetings of the SSGA, which means that the student council can change the rules at a meeting between SSGA meetings. Student council decisions are subject to approval by the Board of Review. However, according to this constitution as I read it this is not true of decisions passed by the SSGA. At least it doesn't stipulate so in the constitution. It says in talking about the powers of the Board of Review, "the Board of Review may at its discretion review decisions passed by the student council and recommend reconsideration of such decisions of the student council." But it says nothing about reviewing decisions passed by the SSGA, which is the supreme legislative body. So I would suggest to you that if you are concerned, and that if you have an SSGA, come to meetings and do something.

DORCAS BOIT: Could we have a response?

STUDENT: Recently, particularly, I have questioned the ability of the SSGA to make changes in rules. And I was told that you can make *recommendations* for rules to be changed, however, you have to get the approval of the deans and the president of the college. And this is the sort of thing that we're interested in changing since it will be almost impossible for us to get those approvals.

DORCAS BOIT: Mrs. Allen, is this true? We have to get . . .

ASSISTANT DEAN OF STUDENTS SADIE ALLEN: No. You make your recommendations through your student council. You elect members to the student council. If we had attendance like this at SSGA meetings when they meet you could talk about these things just like you're talking about them here. This could be SSGA but unfortunately we don't have attendance like this at SSGA. But you make your recommendations to your student council, members who you elect, and they in turn bring those recommendations in the spring of every year before the administration.

DORCAS BOIT: A point has been raised about our attendance at SSGA and our general interest in the student government. . . . Is there a reason why we don't attend [its meetings?] . . . . Something has been said here which is very basic to many of our, to a lot of us our, discontent. So I'd like a response from the students about this.

STUDENT: I have a very good friend who made a point in SSGA meeting about the housemothers eavesdropping in the room. Within a short time she was called in by this particular housemother and threatened that if she ever got up and made another statement like that in SSGA meeting she was going to the Dean. . . . I have heard of similar threats from a couple of other girls that any time they make a point of protest they are threatened. I don't know if she got it from an administration official but it was passed around that if you wanted to keep your job and your scholarship it was wise not to participate in demonstrations, and protest movements, and what not. I believe this holds down quite a few girls, because a scholarship is a dear thing (*laughter*).

ANOTHER STUDENT: I'd like to say as a freshman upon getting here and hearing about the SSGA I recall the first meeting of this year that there were a lot of us there. And upon getting in the meeting it was this air about it, I don't know if I can explain it. It . . . seemed as if it was just a body with a name, I mean in name only. This is the feeling that I got. We went there and we saw nothing was said. Every, the whole atmosphere about the meeting was one of unrest. I don't know, but nobody would just get up and bring to the floor what the unrest was all about. And I think the freshmen felt that this is just a waste of time. Nothing constructive is being done. So they dropped off, you know the attendance dropped off among the freshmen. I believe this is what happens every year. The freshmen come in and they are all up in the air about it, and then they see that their upper class, you know the sisters are saying that this is just a body in name only. And every year it just drops off. There is no enthusiasm.

ADMINISTRATOR: I'd like to ask this. Do you have an orientation period conducted by the upperclassmen so that the freshmen will understand the constitution, what they can do to change rules and regulations? Or is it that you act out of ignorance because you do not take the *time* to really *study* the constitution. And you know it is just human nature that when you do not understand anything you are not interested in it. It seems to me one of your solutions would be to have such a time at the beginning of the year when you would have maybe a faculty member if you cannot tell it on your own, the upperclassman to just study the constitution and understand what it's all about. Then move from there. Because I think, as I listen to you, that there are ways to bring about change. And the fact that you feel disgruntled should not be just kept within. I think you ought to have healthy discussions, and that you ought to not only point out the negative things, but *certainly* in an institution of this kind there are some positive things, and I shall sit and wait for a few of those tonight along with the blight.

STUDENT: But it is possible for the SSGA to change the rules? . . . Let's hear it again. I would like to hear from Miss Johnson if this is so.

HOWARD ZINN: Well according to the constitution of the Spelman Student Government Association article III, section II, Powers: "The Spelman Students Association shall have legislative power in the following areas: campus and off campus student regulations dealing with calling hours, all sign out privileges, house rules, cultural and recreational privileges, and all questions of honesty, student association funds, student association publications, chartering student campus organizations, relations with other student governments, and campus social activities. . . ." And then this is the legislative power of the Spelman Student Association, which is composed of all of the students assembled in meetings. . . . "Every student in Spelman college is a member of the Spelman Student Association." This means that the Spelman Student Association, which has those powers that I read to you, consists of the total Spelman student body. . . . I think it is pertinent that any legislative action taken by the Spelman Student Association then goes to the administration. The question is then what happens then. And a Board of Review is set up in article VI, which consists of the Dean of Instruction, the Dean of Women, four faculty or staff members appointed by the president of the college, the president and vice president of the student council, plus three other members of the student council. And then in section II, "the Board of Review may at its discretion review decisions passed by the student council and recommend reconsideration of such decisions to the student council." I think the point I made before was that there are two groups that have legislative authority: one is the Spelman Students Association, which is the total membership, the other is the student council, which is a smaller, representative body. Each of these have legislative power. According to the constitution, when the student council acts this is subject to review by the Board of Review. There is no provision in section II, article 6 for review by the Board of Review of decisions made by the Spelman Students Association at its meetings. Therefore, according to the constitution as I read it, you have a meeting and you legislate over those areas about which I read to you that legislation should hold.

STUDENT: And that is just a majority of the student body?

HOWARD ZINN: The majority constitutes a quorum in order for a meeting to take place.

STUDENT: What about for voting?

HOWARD ZINN: Voting would naturally be by parliamentary procedure.

STUDENT: There would be 100% attendance . . . if we had the power to solve our problems then we all would be coming to student government meetings. I think this is the point.

MARGARET CURRY: On page 36 of the handbook on the powers of the [student] council, "A prompt report of all legislation passed by the SSA"—that's the entire students' association—"and by the council shall be made to the Board of Review," which means legislation passed by both of these is reviewed by the Board.

HOWARD ZINN: It says "a prompt report shall be made," it doesn't say that they shall be subject to review by the Board of Review.

ADMINISTRATOR: The procedure which we have used here is that *all* actions taken either by the Student Council or by the SSA certainly is reviewed by the Board of Review and is sent to the president [of Spelman] for his approval or disapproval. The president has ultimate *approval* or *disapproval* of *any policy* to put into effect by *any group.*

HOWARD ZINN: All I'm saying is that there is nothing in the constitution to justify review by the Board of Review of decisions passed by the Spelman Students Association.

ADMINISTRATOR: That is the procedure employed.

HOWARD ZINN: I guess we disagree about the interpretation of the constitution.

STUDENT: I'd like to say that going back to the reason students do not attend the SSGA meetings. . . . You go to an SSGA meeting and the president gives you, reads off of her agenda about a dance, what you should wear, walking on the grass, not signing in and out, or loitering in front of the dormitories, etc. So why bother going to SSGA meetings?

STUDENT: This is about attendance at SSGA meeting and the [last year's student rights and academic reforms] petition. I think one of the reasons . . . is mainly lack of motivation. You don't want to hear the same thing [at student government meetings] year after year. We have to be motivated. It's like a student movement. If there is no cause. If we felt we could go there and change some of the rules. We know we can't change all the rules, the president can't change all the rules, the trustees ultimately have to change, I think. . . . We know that if we go there [to student government meetings] and say certain things we'll get repercussions. This petition. We have gotten one or two of the academic things, none of the social things we got. I don't feel that we should have to ask for them again because we were very strongly behind this from the start. And people got, I don't know if this is true or not, but I heard that one student lost her scholarship because of "citizenship," because of this petition, and people are afraid—there are some of us who have to graduate—we are afraid that if we sign anything we won't graduate. There are people who have scholarships who if they don't have scholarships are leaving. You're afraid to say something. You're afraid that somebody might call you in.

STUDENT: There was a point raised and I would like to pursue, that a girl's scholarship was taken away . . . I cannot believe this and would certainly like . . . some clarification.

DORCAS BOIT: Could we have some official [response on] this question of citizenship and loss of scholarship because of citizenship? Is this true?

ADMINISTRATOR: My understanding is that the procedure followed . . . was not through your regular governing body. That this was a revolt or a mutiny or something like that.

STUDENT: The question I'd like to ask is how does Spelman define citizenship? What does citizenship mean on this campus?

DEAN OF WOMEN: Good citizenship is concerned primarily with a student respecting the rules and regulations as they are set up at this institution. I imagine it would include one's attitude in general and this type of thing. It is what kind of citizen is the person really, that is being considered.

STUDENT: If you protest or wish to change them [the rules and regulations] then you are not being a good citizen because you are not following the rules and regulations?

ALUMNAE SECRETARY ERNESTINE BRAZEAL: I think it's perfectly all right for you to protest and what not, that is not the reason these things happen to you, but it is the *manner* in which you go *about* doing this.

DORCAS BOIT: In what manner did this student [Lana Taylor (Sims)] lose her scholarship if she lost it because of her [citizenship]?

ERNESTINE BRAZEAL: I don't know what you're talking about, but I only was speaking generally, and I would like to say this: That citizenship at Spelman would be the same as citizenship in a community, in a church, in any organization.

STUDENT: I'd like to know if the person involved, the person in question, lost her scholarship because of being involved in a revolt, a protest . . . this constituted poor citizenship on her part. Why were there no other people who were involved punished? Or was it that they had no scholarships to take away? Also this particular person received a letter, along with other people when scholarships were decided, that she too was informed that she was being denied her . . . scholarship because of insufficient funds. Then later she was sent a letter saying she was denied a scholarship on the basis of poor citizenship, and no explanation at all was made. And I would like to ask my original question again. What was it about *her* citizenship that made *her* be punished in the manner that she was punished, and no one else involved was punished at all? Was it that they had no scholarship to be taken away?

DORCAS BOIT: Could you speak to that?

DEAN OF STUDENTS MERCILE JOHNSON: To some extent. I won't say that I have full information on the student in question. But I believe that in this particular case that this student perhaps *assumed* the kind of responsibility that was not assumed on the part of other students who were active in the protest. Certainly, as Mrs. Brazeal has pointed out, no scholarship was denied because a person protests, or because a person disagrees or anything of this sort. But in this particular case there was some misrepresentation on the part of this individual in relation to the president of the student body. The president of the student body was misrepresented in a public meeting. To the extent there was considerable feeling that there should have been a public apology on the part of the person who assumed such a leadership role. It was also stated that the president of the SSGA did not attend certain meetings because of a lack of interest when it was fully determined later on that the president of the SSGA knew nothing about the meeting. And there had been some maneuverings to keep this information from her. So I know that this kind of thing was taken into consideration. And perhaps there is much more of this, and perhaps some magnifications even on this. But it was this kind of thing in general. It was not a matter of being involved in a protest or petitioning, or anything else. But there was misrepresentation on the part of some person regarding the president of the student body.

DORCAS BOIT: What do you mean by misrepresentations, Miss Johnson? I am not sure.

DEAN MERCILE JOHNSON: Positions that were taken, why meetings were not attended, you see when in actuality she knew nothing about the meeting at all, and it was stated that she chose not to be at the meeting. This kind of thing. And I must say, that the person in question admitted that this was done, and offered to make an apology both to the person and publicly.

DORCAS BOIT: The person in question, also, and I know this, approached the president of SSGA about this meeting and the president of SSGA did not come. As to whether she knew about it or not, she did know about it.

DEAN MERCILE JOHNSON: Let me say this. I believe we can resolve little by talking about two persons in particular who happen *not* to be here and who *cannot speak for themselves now*. But as this was *discussed last year* the person whom you are questioning *accepted* responsibility in the line, the general line, that I have mentioned here because I think she realized that in the final analysis that she had *not* brought the kind of leadership to this situation that she should have brought, and that she did misrepresent the president of the student body and even apologized, according to my information, to the president [of the student body], and agreed to make a public apology if this were necessary. And I think there were some persons here who were aware of this and who even suggested . . . a public apology. . . . These are some of the things. I am not saying that this is all that was considered because the denial of a scholarship goes through a committee and then has final approval by the president.

PROFESSOR RENATE WOLF: If it was felt that a public apology was necessary, and if the student offered to make the apology why then was she not allowed to make it—have done with it? Why was the scholarship taken away from her?

DORCAS BOIT: Did you want to speak, Mr. Zinn?

HOWARD ZINN: I wanted to speak about the situation of this student because I would feel wrong sitting here hearing people talking about this from various angles without saying something that I have felt deeply about for some time. It's important, not as a personal matter with this student or between those two students. And I think it goes far beyond that. It really doesn't matter to me very much whether this student at this meeting said that this person did not attend, did not want to attend, the meeting, that she really did want to attend the meeting. Now this may be a case that if you want to call it misrepresentation, which is giving a fancy word to a rather ordinary act, and one which is subject to a great deal of interpretation. If you want to do that, all right. But I don't think this is really crucial because I think this one incident has to be seen in the context of the larger situation that existed in Spelman College at that time, and with this student. And the point that I'm trying to make is this: It seems highly surprising to me—I'm trying to be mild in my language—that a student who had been recognized in many ways as one of the outstanding students in the college, who had had very high grades, grades high enough to rate a scholarship, who had been sent away on exchange—which is evidence of something or other—who had been elected to a high student post, which is evidence of her standing among students, who won an award in her department for being the outstanding student in her department, it seems *remarkable* to me that a student who showed such leadership and scholarship qualities would be denied her scholarship on the basis of one incident that took place, and which in itself is of questionable validity. This leads me to believe, and I know this is an inference, and I know when you are dealing with problems of intimidation you're dealing with very subtle questions because intimidation cannot be proved very often in black and white; but I would say that I, looking at this situation, looking at all the evidence, would conclude that this student was punished because of her protest activity.

Now if somebody can bring forth evidence that can shake this conclusion from my mind I would welcome it. But I've *asked* for this evidence and I haven't seen it. And I persist in thinking that this was the case in this instance. And what is *really* important to me is that this is indicative of a larger situation in the college: That students are afraid to speak out. That students are afraid to express their views. Maybe it's because they have been slapped down too many times. This is a thing I am very much concerned with because here we teach the social sciences. We teach American history. We teach the suppression of liberty. We teach about the South and its oppression of the abolitionists. We teach about the right of dissent. We make commencement addresses or listen to commencement addresses about the kind of values we should have: "Don't go with the mob, don't accept authority all the time. Be different. Protest if you think something is wrong." And then the minute somebody protests their head is chopped off. This is a terrible thing. And it's a kind of spirit, the kind of situation, that should be changed at Spelman College (*sustained applause*).

QUESTION FROM THE FLOOR: Is that why the young lady isn't here? The scholarship kept her from coming back?

HOWARD ZINN: No, I don't think the scholarship was the main reason. The girl got married. But to me that's not the most important thing—whether it was the lack of scholarship or not. The fact is that she was denied it for that reason.

PROFESSOR ELIZABETH MACOMSON: I have also, after that rousing applause for Dr. Zinn I suppose we should just adjourn. As I have sat here and listened to this I have come to feel we are just as the world is, we are very confused. We are part of the world. . . . There is no perfect place. And . . . we want to establish a perfect place, and also . . . we have these high ideals. And I'm very happy about that. However, I think as Dr. Zinn spoke, if that were the case that we have our heads chopped off whenever we protest, or whenever we're against something, or whenever we complain, I dare say that there would be an immediate exodus from the campus and none of us would be here. Because that is definitely not the truth. So I think that as social scientists, if you are social scientists, that you should listen, and that you should have an open mind, as anyone else has. So that when you take one example and set that up as the *entire* situation I think that we are being very unrealistic. And when we say that when one head falls that everyone does, that everyone falls, that is not the case because none of us would be here because I am sure there is not a soul in here who has not protested, nor complained, nor set up should we say all kinds of negative attitudes. And that is true. And I think Dr. Zinn would have to agree that everyone who has disagreed, complained or protested has *not* had his or her head chopped off. And I think he will have to say that that is the case. Isn't it. Yes.

HOWARD ZINN: (*interrupting*) I think we—

ELIZABETH MACOMSON: You are making a point. And I think—

HOWARD ZINN: —need some students left at the college (*laughter and sustained applause*).

ELIZABETH MACOMSON: All I'm saying is that we came here for a purpose and we're apt to be bogged down. Now he said there are some students. I did not exclude *anyone* from my statement. I said that hardly any of us would be here because all of us have protested many things. And I think that he would recognize that. But I want to ask us if we cannot get back [to the point of the meeting]. We are setting ourselves up as a court, and I didn't think that we had come here for *that* purpose either. Now we are asking to make decisions without any information, any full information. Now if we're going to set ourselves up as a court , young women, it would seem to me that we would have to have briefs, and we would have to have full facts. And I didn't think that we were here for that. I thought that we were here to discuss Spelman, other things, and I would like to have that clarified.

DORCAS BOIT: Excuse me Miss Macomson, but if we cover anything here, the purpose of this meeting was to have students air their views, their discontent, and this matter of scholarships has been something that has been worrying students. For instance, making this a court. This is just part of our discontent, it's either social or academic, or anything.

ELIZABETH MACOMSON: Well first let me ask you this madam chairman, do you have documented—and if you are social scientists you want documents—do you have documented evidence of how many scholarships have been taken from you for protesting? (*Murmuring*.) I think that is something that we should take into account.

STUDENT: None of us have documented evidence. But I'd like to make two observations here. There is no evidence that we can bring and set before you now and say this is what happened. But as an *eyewitness* I know that the president of the student body was asked from the *very beginning* to come to these meetings that were held last year. A second observation is that every year since I've been here for the last four years we have had some type of uprising or revolt and nothing has ever come of any of it.

ELIZABETH MACOMSON: What you are saying is that you have no documented evidence (*loud murmuring*).

STUDENT: You can't document *people's feelings*! All I'm saying is this. Then let's state that this is our opinion.

STUDENT: I think that this problem with what has happened to this student about her scholarship is a good example of *passing* the buck along and somewhere down the line someone puts the buck in his pocket and then it comes up again and nobody is able to tell you just what has happened.

RENATE WOLF: There may not be evidence that intimidation is taking place. But I think there is evidence that students are intimidated. It may be all in their heads, but they are obviously afraid to speak up. . . . Tonight somebody said a girl who had spoken up at an SSGA meeting about her housemother's eavesdropping was threatened to be reported to the dean. What I would like to know is why would this constitute a threat? . . . If she is speaking the truth why would she be afraid of taking it before the dean? What would happen?

DORCAS BOIT: Would you like to speak to this? You are the victim (*laughter*).

STUDENT: I would like to state that I can verify the statement because it happened to me. I went to SSGA meeting and I asked, brought the question up as to whether or not a head resident, a housemother of another kid's residence, had the authority to eavesdrop on students who were not in her dormitory, whether she had authority to do that. And the question wasn't answered. They told me that they would find out, or they didn't think so. But there was no real answer given to me. Well the next day, when I came from class I was brought into the office by this head resident of whom I'm speaking and told that if I mentioned anything about it she would go to the dean personally, and that if I *ever* brought her name up again in any public circumstances that she would go to the dean *personally*, and see what could be done about the situation. And she sat there and wrote down everything she told me. And she said if I hear it again, I'll know where it came from (*loud murmuring*).

DORCAS BOIT: Miss Johnson?

DEAN MERCILE JOHNSON: I'd like to make one statement here. That if what the student says is true . . . then what would be the objection to making a statement before the dean, the president, or anybody else? I don't think there should be a feeling engendered here that if you say something you're going to be, your head's going to be chopped off, or there is a threat. But if you know what you're saying is the truth what difference does it matter where it has . . . to be said?

STUDENT: It's the principle, the principle behind the thing. . . . If I have something to say I don't mind telling anyone or who it goes before. But it is the principle behind the thing. I don't want anyone to *threaten* me and tell me I dare not to say it or I will be brought up for some reason. I feel that I should say something, it may be true, but I don't want to be threatened or called in or have my position threatened. I should have the right to say what I want without any repercussions or calling in, there may not be any actually saying "you can't say this" but I still feel that you should not have to be called in or threatened. You should be able to say what you have to say.

STUDENT: I was not here last year at this time. I was away on exchange. So I received notice . . . of the [student rights] petition that was drawn up last year. But when I came back I was *eager* to read the petition because I wanted to know all about it. I wanted to see it for myself. All right. I understand that the . . . editor last year was to publish this petition, it was to go in the newspaper, the *Spelman Spotlight*, the students' newspaper, the voice of the students. But I understand, I heard rather, that one of the administrators threw out this page *entirely*. This page, let's see I think it was page 3 and 4. It was missing from the paper. In the *Spotlight* we had [pages] l, 2, 5, and 6 (*laughter*). The page that contained this petition was gone. Since I've been back I have been trying to get a copy of the petition. I have not seen it.

I have also heard that one of our administrators said: if you don't like the conditions around here, *get out*. What kind of attitude is this? Suppose we don't like segregation in the South? What are we supposed to do, go to the North, or go to another country? If we don't like conditions, don't we have the right to *attempt* to better them? And if this was said by one of the administrators I wish that some other person could tell me right here and now that this was said to them, "If you don't like it here, get out." Why was it against college policy ? . . . [What] caused this petition to be thrown out of the newspaper?

DORCAS BOIT: Did you ask the reasons why it wasn't published? If so, were you told any reasons why it was not?

STUDENT: Here's what I heard. Now I don't know. This is just hearsay that [Spelman President] Dr. Manley said this could not be published. And that's it.

DORCAS BOIT: Miss Johnson?

DEAN MERCILE JOHNSON: I believe the students who met with Dr. Manley regarding this petition [would attest that] . . . he did not say it could not be published, but he raised questions with the editor regarding and understanding or conditions or three facts, three or four facts, that he had agreed upon with her and the adviser that these things should be met before *any* article was published, and he raised questions as to whether or not this petition satisfied these three facts, and if they did not then should it not be withheld until such a time as these questions could be answered.

DORCOS BOIT: Miss Brazeal, who can speak to this point?

ERNESTINE BRAZEAL: Well I was at the meeting as Dean Johnson said but the three conditions were it should not set Spelman in an unfavorable light, and misrepresent [the] attitude of Spelman, and what was the other?

ADMINISTRATOR: The other one was that she [the editor of the student newspaper] would confer with him [President Manley] before publishing anything of this nature. . . . And these three things, the attitude toward Spelman, after the meeting the page [with the petition] . . . did not appear in the paper.

STUDENT: I have heard since sitting here that the students here are confused tonight, and that's why we're here to understand. I have also heard that we're searching for high ideas . . . and I've heard that little things that we think [matter]. Now the administration, the faculty members don't understand because they're not on this campus. They can leave *whenever* they want to but *we* are the ones who are tied up on this campus. . . .

They say if you can't say something good about a thing don't say anything. We have a snack shop over there and that's good, but we get tired of hot dogs and hamburgers. We want to feel as though we can go to Paschal's sometime to get off a meal. We can go to Paschal's sometime in the evening and return by 7:00 . . . I want to feel as though I can go to Paschal's at *9:00* if I want something to eat. . . . That's all we're asking for. This library, we have a library, that's good. There is a library downtown . . . we have to return to school before 6:00. All of these are *petty things*. We ought to do these things. We are entitled to them.

STUDENT: We have unwritten rules. . . . We receive these rule books two days before we leave. . . . Some people didn't receive them at all. . . . And they're supposed to read these rule books. And they say "if you don't like it you got the rule books, you knew what it was like before you came so *leave* if you don't like it.".... The rules in those rule books are sugar coated. They don't have *half* the rules ... I have encountered about fifty additional rules since I have been here. There was an incident Sunday, when they had the concert. Some girls did not feel like going to the concert. And I don't think that we were *forced* to go to this one (*laughter*).... We were told that we could not leave the dormitory and sit outside in the beautiful sunshine.... We were told we could not sit on our porches. We were told we had to stay in our rooms. Some girls in my dormitory even wanted to go into the lounge and play the piano and sing ... but no, we had to go back in the room. *Dr. Manley sent a notice* to my *housemother* saying we had to stay cooped up in the dormitory. This is what she told us. And so many other rules. It would take hours and hours to stand here and tell you the additional things that we have to do that are *not* in these rule books.

DORCAS BOIT: May I ask the students here if this is general in all the dormitories?

(*Crowd shouts out "YES!"*)

STUDENT: Another thing ... I'd like to say on compulsory chapel. We come from sundry religious backgrounds. If we feel that we don't want to go to chapel I don't think that we should be compelled to go.

   I was somewhat astonished when two weeks ago I went in to sign my resident [book] that I was going to town, and I really thought that as freshmen we could go to town once a week, and I was told that I did not come in to tell her that I was going to town and came in here to ask her could I go into town. Now I feel I'm old enough to know when I've got to go into town (*laughter*).... I feel I don't have any privileges that I had before I came here.... We're denied so many *personal* freedoms. ... I'm in the dormitory that she mentioned. We couldn't go outdoors Sunday because I didn't go to the musical program because I didn't feel I wanted to go, and I think that's everybody's right.... I never did believe that I would come to college and somebody would tell me "you can't go outdoors and walk around because there is a program going on campus." I just don't understand this.

STUDENT: Take a look at the beautiful new furniture.... We're able to enjoy this now because you're here. You see, during the day and at night this room is locked. Now when we had the old furniture ... the room was open all times of night. You could come here day and night and do anything that you want to because, you see, we come from homes where we're used to *old furniture*. But when we get *new furniture* we don't know how to treat it, we might mess it up.... One Sunday morning I wanted to study.... I brought my books down and I was sitting on a white sofa over in a corner with my book ... and I was informed that the orders from the administrative office said we could not use this room for study. In fact, it must be locked until it is decided what it is to be used for (*laughter*).

STUDENT: All these things people are saying tonight, I think—we who are subject to administration wishes and we have to prove ourselves to get the things we want [to be treated as] individuals. We're tired of being treated as irrational, unthinking children. . . . We have rights because we are what we are. We want Spelman to do things because *we* want to do them. . . . We're tired of trying to be made into the Spelman image.

RENATE WOLF: What you do with your time, where you go on a Sunday afternoon, what you wear and so forth . . . I don't think [for that] there should be any rules (*sustained applause*).

PROFESSOR STAUGHTON LYND: I'd like to explain how I became interested in this question of rules and what not. Last fall when I was a freshman here (*laughter*) I was asked to give a speech at the initiation of dorm council officers in one of the dormitories. We had a lovely occasion and the girls held lighted candles, and I made my speech very quickly so they wouldn't get burned (*laughter*). And I even offered up a prayer as part of the occasion. And then about three weeks later or four weeks later in my American history class we were talking about the New England town meeting, where all of the citizens of the community came together to make decisions about their town affairs. And I, trying desperately to make the New England town meeting interesting, said, "you know, like in your dorm councils" (*laughter*). Laughter started to come down [from the students].

I did not, I think, agitate to produce this information. In all innocence I made an analogy which I had assumed was valid. When I heard from these students how invalid the analogy apparently was I felt that some way I had been made use of. That I had participated in something that was hypocritical. But I had been a part of something which was designed to produce a certain external appearance. . . .

My own feeling now about the thing that we have been talking about all evening is that, it seems to me that, there are two atmospheres. And atmospheres may seem vague but they're also real. I suppose heaven and hell are atmospheres. The difference between the two atmospheres, it seems to me, is that in the one atmosphere the attitude of the teacher or the administrator is that he knows what is right for the student to become, what is right for the student to learn. The other atmosphere, it seems to me, is one where the teacher or the administrator feels that he does not know what is right for the student to become, he does not know those things which the student should learn, but he will try to encourage the student in striking out on the course of action which seems right to him, and in learning those ideas which interest him. At the same time trying to offer whatever criticism that his greater experience suggests.

Now I believe that liberal arts education takes place in the second way. I think you can teach how to paint a wall in an authoritarian manner. . . . I don't think you can teach the nature of truth or the obligation of the citizen or what the true, the beautiful, and the good are in this way. These are things which students have to learn for themselves. I'm not saying there should be no rules. I'm not saying there should, that there should be no direction from the teacher. It does seem to me that a girl's college experience, a student's college experience, ought to unfold, outward from within herself, and should basically be guided by her own interests and her own individual needs.

And while I certainly don't feel that I can speak as an authority on what administrations there should be at a woman's college—not wearing curlers and always wearing pants (*laughter*)—nevertheless I do think I can say as a teacher there is a conflict between an authoritarian and paternalistic atmosphere of doing things . . . and between the acquiring of knowledge in the liberal arts way that I've explained. . . . That being so, if I'm right, then it seems to me that in the long run Spelman, which is now a house divided, will, as Lincoln said, have to tend to become more all of one thing or more all of the other. That is to say, either the education will have to be made more routine and mediocre and conform to the social atmosphere or else the social atmosphere will have to be liberalized to make possible a better education (*sustained applause*).

STUDENT: Long time ago the question was raised about why the newspaper was not allowed to print the middle section. . . . It was brought up that it had to conform to certain standards. And I just wanted to know who decides? . . . If a person decides "I want you to do what is right" and he decides what is "right," then it is nothing short of dictatorship, and I just think that's our basic problem—one person is doing all the deciding. . . . That's our biggest problem.

Shortly before the meeting ended Howard Zinn read a letter to the crowd from Marie Thomas, the honor student in drama who had been suspended in December, who did not attend the meeting. An excerpt from her letter describing the difference between her three liberating years as a city student, and her final year living on campus when she was subject to overbearing administration authority, is excerpted in the introduction to the Zinn diary (pp. 51–52).

◻ ◻ ◻

In reflecting on the clashes between Zinn and the administrators at this meeting and even the title of the meeting, ironies abound. Here was a meeting on liberty at Spelman where administrators and their allies denied Zinn's charge that dissenters at the college were punished and purged. And yet Zinn would be fired for just such dissent and for expressing it in this very meeting. Here too were college officials denying student claims of political intimidation, and yet, as Zinn later noted, one of the students who spoke at the "On Liberty at Spelman" meeting would be subject to just such intimidation for speaking critically about Spelman at that meeting.

According to Zinn, just three days after the meeting,

> a student who had made a point in the meeting about not having enough time to go to the library because of running from class to class (why not have less class meetings? she asked) walked into the office. She was one of my best students, a very intelligent and sensitive girl from a small town in Georgia. She had recently won a Merrill Scholarship to spend the next year in Vienna. And she was obviously upset. She had just encountered the president and dean on campus. They brought up to her a statement she had made at the meeting that "I haven't learned a thing at Spelman" (a statement which her audience knew she made metaphorically). One of them said that in view of this statement perhaps they had made a mistake awarding the Merrill Scholarship to her.
>
> She is an outspoken and courageous girl but she was shaken by that encounter. It was all a terrible vindication of so much that had been said at the meeting. Neither the president nor the dean had been at the meeting, and therefore did not have a clear idea of the context in which her statement was made. In any event, it seemed a cruel thing to say to her."[5]

Such intimidation and Zinn's firing were true to the old paternalistic Spelman, but the fact that a meeting like this was held at all attests that change was on the horizon. This was one of those startling occasions in the 1960s where old patterns of hierarchy and autocracy were challenged and when daring young students and their faculty allies made a reality of the cliché of speaking truth to power. It was not merely a thrilling moment of democratic dissent but a precursor of the new and freer Spelman that would be born in the wake of the black power and feminist movements.

Debate on Abolishing the House Committee on Un-American
Activities: Howard Zinn's Opening Statement in Support of
Abolition, Emory University, February 11, 1963

This final document offers us a view of Zinn at the top of his form as a historian
and social critic in his Spelman years. It comes from the transcript of another
recently digitized Zinn recording that had not been accessible for decades: old
reel-to-reel tapes of a debate on whether the House Committee on Un-American Activities (HUAC) ought to be abolished. This event, sponsored by Emory
University's Young Americans for Freedom chapter (a conservative student organization), attested to Zinn's growing reputation as a speaker and his contacts
at Emory, where, as we have seen, he brought Spelman students to political and
social events as he sought to challenge the academic color line. Here Zinn debated HUAC staffer Fulton Lewis III.

The debate followed a screening and discussion of the controversial film
Operation Abolition, a classic cinematic venture in red-baiting, produced by
HUAC. The film distorted and demonized the student protests against HUAC at
San Francisco City Hall during its hearings in 1960, insinuating they were based
on a nefarious Communist plot. Those protests had made national headlines
when they culminated in a sit-in, dispersed with high-powered fire hoses that
were deployed to wash students down the steps of City Hall. The HUAC debate,
described in Zinn's southern diary, was, according to Roslyn Zinn, his wife and
most discerning critic, Zinn's best podium performance yet.

Studying this Zinn debate opening is valuable because it not only enables
us to see how in the early 1960s he reflected upon HUAC's red-hunting, a legacy of the 1950s (which I. F. Stone aptly dubbed "the haunted 50s"—haunted by
the specter of McCarthyism), but also allows us to observe Zinn outside of his
mentoring role at Spelman. As a teacher, mentor, and political adviser at Spelman, Zinn placed his students at center stage, and so while helping to guide,
support, and protect them he stressed that they should speak for themselves.
At this HUAC debate, however, Zinn was at center stage, and we see him, in
his opening statement below, going full throttle as a critic, an activist, and a po-

litically engaged scholar. Zinn's HUAC statement also offers a useful reminder that, though his political life in 1963 centered on the black freedom struggle, his activism and criticism were not confined to the battle for racial justice. He was deeply concerned with the corrosive impact that the Cold War and its domestic counterpart, red-baiting, were having on civil liberties and dissent. Zinn's eloquence, humor, and mastery of history, displayed so impressively in this debate, were qualities that would increasingly draw national attention to him during the mid- and late 1960s, when he achieved fame at the podium and on television as a leading voice of the antiwar movement during the Vietnam era (and in subsequent U.S. wars).

Though this debate about HUAC may seem more a national rather than a southern or Spelman issue, focused on an anachronistic congressional committee left over from the Cold War/McCarthy era of the 1950s, HUAC was in fact very much alive in the 1960s—and was still impacting the lives and careers of radicals, ex-radicals, and liberals on campus, including at Spelman. In fact, shortly after his firing, Zinn noted that in the early 1960s a colleague of his at Spelman nearly lost his job because of his refusal to cooperate with HUAC. According to Zinn:

> In December of 1961, Staughton Lynd and I learned from a faculty member that he was in danger of being dismissed by Spelman College. Over the summer, a letter from a student's mother to President Manley had called attention to a House Un-American Activities Committee hearing where someone had accused this faculty member of being a Communist. The President had then demanded that the faculty member disclose any Communist affiliation or lack of it, and when he refused on the ground that his political beliefs and associations were a private matter, the President and a small committee of the Board of Trustees pressed him further on the issue. Staughton Lynd and I both felt that this was a serious violation of academic freedom. Dr. Lynd called the national office of the A.A.U.P., which told him that in its opinion a newspaper article was [a] very flimsy basis—certainly an insufficient one—for demanding a political testament from a faculty member.
>
> Dr. Lynd and I went to see President Manley and argued that this action of his was very much in the spirit of McCarthyism. We asked him to reconsider. We said that if this faculty member were fired for this reason, both of us would resign. The President was unmoved. It was apparently worthwhile for him to lose two members of the history department in order to get rid of a popular and competent faculty member who had been accused of Communism before a committee whose procedures and philosophy have been sharply criticized by scholars in the field of civil liberties and constitutional law. As the result of the intercession of a distinguished educator, we were able to win a

compromise on the matter, with the faculty member making a private denial of affiliation with organizations committed to force and violence but at the same time affirming his right of belief and association. The whole affair left the feeling that the Spelman administration would rush to capitulate to the first wave of hysteria on the Communist issue, rather than stand up courageously, as many first-rate universities have done, in defense of academic freedom.[1]

SPELMAN COLLEGE PROFESSOR HOWARD ZINN: I only have thirty minutes so I thought I would begin with the Stone Age. Mankind has gone through the age of stone and the age of bronze, and today we live in the age of irony (*laughter*). Probably in the twentieth century the ironies are more monumental than ever. But I am not going to pick one of these stupendous ironies nor one of the petty ones. Let's call it a middle-level irony. And it goes something like this. We the American people do not want to live in a Communist state. The reason for this is not so much that we object to a planned economy, although many of us do. Not so much that we object to socialized medicine, there's some controversy about this, this may be a factor. Certainly not because we're afraid that if we live in a Communist society Coca-Cola will be replaced by borscht (*laughter*) or that we have anything against the Bolshoi Ballet or vodka, that's not it. We don't want to live in a Communist society because we don't want to live in a situation in which the government or some agency of government is supervising our ideas and our associations to make sure that we hold no idea, believe in no political ideology, which is contrary to the official dogma. We don't want to live in a Communist state because we don't want any government agency inspecting what we say, what we think, the associations we have, the paintings we paint, the writings we write, the books we read, the meetings we go to, the organizations we join. We don't want to be in a situation where people around us are watching us and may inform on what we say or where we go, or the petitions we sign. We don't want to live in a situation where opposing the official credo may result in going to prison, where disagreeing with this governmental agency will send somebody to jail.

And so in order to avoid all this we set up a [House] Committee [on Un-American Activities]. And this committee in order to *prevent* us from experiencing this inspects what we read, looks at who we associate with, checks up on the things we write, the books we read, the associations we have, the meetings we go to, the wife that we married. It also employs paid informers to keep track of what people do, what they say, where they go. It also sends people to jail for disagreeing with the committee. Now the premise of this irony is that we don't really mind if our freedoms are taken away from us so long as it's done by Americans (*laughter*). And also that it is all right to take our freedoms away from us today because this will strengthen us to meet the trials of tomorrow.

The House Committee on Un-American Activities was founded in 1938. It had two predecessors, the Overman Committee of 1919 [and] the Fish Committee of 1930. They had roughly the same object. In 1938 the House Un-American Activities Committee was created as an ad hoc committee. The chairman, well I don't think I'm being unfair when I say that the chairman, Martin Dies, was not selected from among the most brilliant members of the House. The chairman was Martin Dies of Texas; this became known as the Dies Committee. And you all perhaps know, well it's not necessary to say anything about the Dies Committee. It saved our country (*laughter*). It investigated Brooklyn College, which everybody knows is the *seat* of subversion in this nation (*laughter*). It investigated the Federal Writers Project, and writers are among the most dangerous people in this country. It investigated the Farmer-Labor Party of Minnesota. And well, all you have to do is look on a map and see the strategic location of Minnesota. It is right next to Iowa (*laughter*). And not far away from Wisconsin, and then there's the Schlitz Brewery Company (*laughter*) which is right near. If the Communists got control of the Schlitz Brewery Company (*laughter*), well . . . .

This committee became a permanent committee in 1945. The man most responsible for making it permanent was another one of our great congressmen, John Rankin of Mississippi. As an example of Mr. Rankin's incisive comments on Communism, of which he was one of the nation's most assiduous students, July 18, 1945, on the floor of the House, John Rankin speaking: "These alien-minded Communistic enemies of Christianity and their stooges are trying to get control of the press of the country. Many of our great daily newspapers have now changed hands and gone over to them. They're trying to take over the radio. Listen to their lying broadcasts in broken English" (*laughter*). It's clear that the committee fulfilled its function. I listened to the radio yesterday for a while. I heard no broken English. All I heard were things like "I'm crazy about you, baby, cause you're so sweet" or something like that. The radio has been cleared of Communist propaganda, it seems to me, very effectively (*laughter*).

Now since then the IQ of the committee, since those days, since the days of Rankin, has gone up. But the values remain the same. It's important to take a look at the enabling resolution passed by Congress which gives the committee its legal power. It's important to know this because this is the legal foundation upon which the committee operates. This is what the committee is supposed to be doing. And this resolution says that the committee is authorized to conduct investigations "into the extent, character, and objects of un-American propaganda activities in the United States." And too, "the diffusion within the United States of subversive and un-American propaganda that attacks the principle of the form of government as guaranteed by our Constitution." I want you to note that both requirements are that propaganda be investigated.

No one on the committee, incidentally, as far as I can see, has given a very satisfactory answer to the question of exactly what is un-American propaganda. What is American propaganda? What is subversive, what is un-subversive propaganda? Dies, in the good old days, said that if you didn't believe in God this was an example of un-American thinking, and if you believed in a planned economy this was an example of un-American thinking. The most recent definition I've seen was given by the chairman Congressman [Francis E.] Walter in 1961 . . . (this was on [the] "Youth Wants to Know" television program), [who, in response to a] question from a young student, [said]: "Sir for our own information could you tell us just what is considered un-American by your committee?" Walter: "Well any activity that strikes at the basic concept of our republic." That's a good clear answer, isn't it? (*Laughter*.)

"Any activity that strikes at the basic concept of our republic." What is the basic concept of our republic? Well, I will offer my own answer. The basic concept of our republic, I think, is that no government agency has the right to say what is the basic concept of our republic because the principles of American democracy are changing things. They are hammered out on the anvil of experience. They are debated and redebated and they engage in a kind of dynamic process of reverberation of opinion and atmosphere of freedom. And they're not subject to the kind of vague or ultraspecific definition which the House Un-American Activities Committee enjoys giving.

Now let's look at the committee as it has actually worked. In 1947, and I hope you realize that I need to select out of *voluminous* masses of hearings and reports, this is the writingest, I didn't say the most literate, but the writingest committee; it compiled the most books, has heard the most testimony. In 1947 it issued a report on the Southern Conference for Human Welfare. I would urge you, if you get a chance, to read in *The Harvard Law Review* of October 1947 an article by Walter Gellhorn, professor of law at Columbia University, who writes in that issue of *The Harvard Law Review* an article called "A Report on the Report of the House Un-American Activities Committee" in which he dissects this HUAC report and finds in it distortions and occasionally a falsehood. And in general concludes that this report is lacking in a certain amount of intellectual honesty. The report refers to Frank Graham, who I think is one of our more distinguished people in this country, head of the University of North Carolina and governor of the state, as "one of those liberals who 'show a predilection for affiliation to various Communist-inspired front organizations.'" Now play with that and figure out what that means. "One of those liberals who 'show a predilection for affiliation to various Communist-inspired front organizations.'" Gellhorn notes the kind of items the committee uses: "Susan Reed a singer was named because she was employed by Café Society, which was owned by a man whose brother was a Communist" (*laughter*). Well, it's damning, damning (*laughter*).

In 1947 the 80th Congress issued a series of reports on activities in Hollywood. Back in 1945 John Rankin had laid the basis for this. He said, "One of the most dangerous plots ever instigated for the overthrow of this government has its headquarters in Hollywood. This is the greatest hotbed of subversive activities in the United States. We're on the trail of the tarantula now, and we're going to follow through." Well in '47 a subcommittee of the HUAC met in executive session, which is another way of saying secret session, heard witnesses, issued a report. And in this report said the Communists have "employed subtle techniques in pictures glorifying the Communist system, degrading our own system of government and institutions." "Pictures glorifying the Communist system." Now, some of you, I think, have seen movies for a number of years. I have. If you didn't see them on the screen in 19[45] around that time you are now seeing them on television, what was produced on the screen in those years. And I ask you to search and find a picture glorifying the Communist system.

Here is some of the testimony from those hearings. A Mr. [R. J.] Strickland, an investigator for the committee interrogating one of the nation's leading experts on Communism, Mrs. Lela Rogers, the mother of Ginger Rogers, who is also her daughter's manager. "'Mr. Strickland: 'Mrs. Rogers as your daughter's manager so to speak have you or your daughter ever objected to or turned down scripts because you felt there were lines in there for her to speak which you felt were un-American or Communist propaganda?' 'Mrs. Rogers: 'Yes sir. We turned down Sister Carrie by Theodore Dreiser.'" (*Laughter.*) Here she is again discussing that well-known Communist film *None but the Lonely Heart*, based on a novel by Richard Llewellyn. She says, she is demonstrating how Communist propaganda is inserted into films. "I can't quote the lines of the play exactly, but I can give you the sense of them. A Communist is very careful, very clever, very devious in the way he sets the film. I will tell you of one line. The mother in the story runs a secondhand store. The son says to her, 'You are not going to get me to work here and squeeze pennies out of little people poorer than I am.'" End of the passage.

Gary Cooper testifying, another friendly witness, another expert on Communism. If you had to hunt for Communists wouldn't you call on Gary Cooper? (*Laughter.*) He said to the committee, "I have turned down quite a few scripts because I thought they were tinged with Communist ideas." "Strickland: 'Can you name any of those scripts?'" "Cooper: 'I don't think I could because most of those scripts I read at night.'" (*Laughter.*) I won't discuss the interrogation of Bertolt Brecht by the House Un-American Activities Committee, except that someone said it was like a zoologist being cross-examined by apes. (*Laughter.*)

But we turn from comedy to dishonesty. March 1, 1948 the House Un-American Activities Committee issued—a subcommittee of it—issued a report called "Our National Security." And in this report they named in a very unfavorable way Dr. Edward Condon who was head of the National Bureau of Standards. And in their report they quoted a letter which J. Edgar Hoover had sent to Secretary of Commerce [W. Averell] Harriman the year before, and the letter—as quoted in the report—from Hoover to Harriman said the following: "The files of the Bureau reflect that Dr. Edward B. Condon has been in contact as late as 1947 with an individual alleged to have engaged in espionage activities. Mr. and Mrs. Condon associated with several individuals connected with the Polish embassy in Washington, D.C." Well this alarmed people. Condon was one of the nation's most respected scientists, I think. He was considered one of the world's leading authorities on quantum mechanics and microwave electronics, radioactivity, a few other things I don't know anything about. But it was discovered that the committee, in reporting this letter, had left out a sentence from that original letter sent by Hoover to Harriman. And that sentence read as follows: "There is no evidence to show that contacts between this individual and Dr. Condon were related to this individual's espionage activities." Not only did the House Committee, subcommittee in its report leave out this sentence, but they left out any indication that the sentence had been omitted.

Let's follow the committee through the years. In 1948 the committee did something which it has never let the nation forget about. And that is it opened up that whole [Whittaker] Chambers–[Elizabeth] Bentley–[Alger] Hiss business which led to Hiss being indicted for perjury, sent him to jail for a number of years. I won't argue the merits of that case. There is still debate over whether Hiss was guilty or innocent, and frankly I don't know. I just think that the sending of Hiss to jail for a few years is a mighty small contribution to the American nation for twenty-five years of assault on American intelligence and democracy.

In 1950 this committee, which was set up, as all investigating committees are, to produce legislation, in 1950 this committee, after twelve years of labor, finally gave birth to an important piece of legislation. And what was born was a monster. This was the Internal Security Act of 1950. I don't have time to go into it. Very complex. But I invite everyone to go through the provisions of the Internal Security Act of 1950, which your congressman or senator will send you, and then decide for yourself . . . whether this legislation is more likely to be found in a democratic state or in a totalitarian state.

More House Un-American Activities Committee doings, June 1949. At this time the chairman is John Wood of Georgia. He sends out letters to seventy-one schools, boards of education, asking them to turn over lists of their textbooks to the committee so the committee can inspect them to see if there is any Communist propaganda in them.

In 1954 the committee cites for contempt a faculty member at Antioch College because he told about being in a Marxist study group nine years before and he refused to name who were the other people in that study group nine years ago. So they cited him for contempt. The Court disagreed. Also Antioch College disagreed and kept him on. And I suppose there is a basic question to be asked—aside from the length of time and the little things you can argue about. And that is, in a free nation does a person have the right to join a Marxist study group?

In 1956 hearings in Youngstown, Ohio, Congressman [Harold] Velde, interrogating a witness: "Velde: 'Whose side are you on?'" This was at the time of the Hungarian rebellion against the Soviet Union. "'Whose side are you on in the revolt? The Soviet Union's or the rebels'?'" "Witness: 'I am on the rebels' side.'" Velde later on in the hearing "'From the witnesses' appearance and demeanor before this committee I am satisfied that he bears watching by the duly constituted authorities. I do not think he is on the side of the rebels. I think he is on the side of Moscow, the Soviets.'"

In 1952 Velde, interrogating a newspaper editor named Tom O'Connor. "Velde: 'Are you a member of the Communist Party now?' 'No sir.' 'Were you a year ago?' 'No sir.' 'Were you five years ago?' 'No sir.' 'Were you ten years ago?' 'No sir.' Velde a little later: '"I personally can draw only one inference. That you are not only a past member of the Communist Party, but that you continue to be a member of the Communist Party, and that you are an extreme danger to the security of the country as the managing editor of a large New York newspaper.'"

June 1959, well a prelude to the events on film [*Operation Abolition*], you saw 110 teachers in the San Francisco area were subpoenaed. There was a lot of opposition to the committee by Communist groups like the Methodist Church and the Episcopal Church, and the *San Francisco Chronicle* and people like that. And finally the committee left. It said it would come back but it didn't. But before it left it made sure that the little files it had on each one of these 110 teachers—and I don't know what was in the files, you know one signed a petition on this, and one did that, and one attended this meeting, and one belonged to that organization. You can pretty much guess. It turned over this information to the state superintendent of education. And then when his attorney general told him that there was not much he could do with that really, legally, they made sure it got into the hands of local county officials who were in charge of hiring and firing these teachers. However, even these apparently would not cooperate too much because they said that "well, the statements in the materials turned over to them by the HUAC didn't indicate where the information came from, who were the accusers," and so on so they didn't see how they could do very much with this.

Let me say a word about the personnel of the committee. Robert Carr, a law professor at Dartmouth, did the definitive scholarly study of the House Un-American Activities Committee. And I think people should read this because it tells a lot more than I can possibly tell in the short time I have. He has a chapter on personnel. He says: "The Un-American Activities Committee has not been famed among congressional committees for the high quality of its membership." This, in typical professorial fashion, is a bit of an understatement. Here is J. Parnell Thomas. Now I am not claiming that J. Parnell Thomas is a typical member of the committee. All that I am saying is that he is one member of the committee, or was. He served on it for ten years. He was a charter member. He was chairman for a while. He participated in some of its most important hearings. If you picked up the newspaper, December 8, 1949, the dispatch from Washington, D.C., *New York Daily News*: "J. Parnell Thomas was sentenced to a 6- to 18-month term in prison and fined $10,000 for defrauding the government by padding his office payroll. Earlier the 54-year-old former chairman of HUAC withdrew his pleas of not guilty, threw himself on the mercy of the court, resigned as Republican congressman from New Jersey, January 2. His attractive wife Amelia promptly announced that she will seek Thomas's congressional seat to continue 'his struggle against subversive influences."

In 1954–55, now I am not claiming, and I mean this, because there is a problem in selection, and in selection there is the possibility of coloring other evidence, and Parnell Thomas certainly is not typical in this sense of the other members of the committee. I'm certainly not imputing crime to the other members of the committee. All I'm imputing is incompetence, ignorance, and a totalitarian frame of mind (*laughter*). In 1954–55 the committee was plagued by a rash of recantations by witnesses who—it suddenly was exposed—had perjured themselves. Harvey Matusow, who had been providing hundreds of names of Communists, after two years of doing this suddenly said that he had been lying. That he'd name people he didn't even know. Wrote a book about it, called *False Witness*. Then he was indicted for perjury. Not for the lies he had told the first time but for lying the second time when he said he lied (*laughter*).

In 1955 Mrs. Mildred Matby, another paid informer, said she has lied about the supposed Communism of some applicant for an SEC license. In 1955 a man named David Brown, in a hearing before the Subversive Activities Control Board on the Civil Rights Congress, said he'd lied for four years to the FBI about organizations, about this particular organization. He'd received $5,000 in the course of this time. In June 1955 a fellow named Matthew Cvetic, he'd appeared as witness in 300 cases. He became the hero of the film *I Was a Communist for the FBI*. It turned out he was suffering from alcoholism and psychic disorders. In 1955 a government official named William Henry Taylor, defending himself from the charges of Elizabeth Bentley, went through her testimony and found about thirty-seven discrepancies. I haven't checked them [all] to see if they really were discrepancies. I just saw one or two in it, well I had some faith after looking at these two that there were probably others—I'm not sure. In 1956 the solicitor general himself in a petition to the Supreme Court recited a list of perjuries by a man named Joseph Mazie, who for twelve years had been an FBI undercover man. In December 1961, this appeared on a certiorari petition to the Supreme Court in the Killian case, an FBI agent named Adreica testified, no . . . his testimony appeared in the petition, that he had been an informer for the FBI for five years, and in this time he has married a member of the Communist Party, she had bore him three children, and all this time he kept reporting to the FBI on her party activities but didn't tell her.

Zacharia Chafee, the Harvard Law School professor, who is author of the classic *Free Speech in the United States*, has some things to say about the *use* of professionals, of spies and informers in proceedings. He says that they don't *always* lie and maybe they don't lie most of the time. But there's a predisposition on the part of some people to begin to muddy the truth with lies when they're being paid for it.

Now the thing I think that is the most terrible about the House Un-American Activities committee is not so much the specific damage it has done to I don't know how many hundreds of people throughout the country, thousands perhaps that it has named, that it has sent to jail for various reasons—although in a society that prides itself on respect for the individual and on belief that the individual is important, I think, even a few hundred people, whether they are teachers or writers or newspapermen deserve consideration, their lives mean something.

But I think more important than this is the poisonous fallout that has been the result of the committee's work. I mean the effect on everybody else. The effect on the whole country. And I don't have to document this because you have *seen* this. You have seen petty bureaucrats on school boards here and there and throughout the country searching for textbooks. You have seen politicians who don't know the first thing about Communism searching for Communists everywhere. You have seen all sorts of ridiculous things going on: The request that *Robin Hood* be taken out of the library because it is Communist propaganda. The removal of a mural from a New York University wall because the artist seemed to have put something Communist in that painting. The removal of Charlie Chaplin's films because of his political beliefs. The barring of lecturers from college campuses because of the fear that they might have subversive connections. All of these things.

This sometimes gets to the point of hysteria and murder. In 1961 a crazed man broke into the offices of a University of California professor, with a double-barreled shotgun in one hand and a Bible in the other. I don't know, maybe this is a picture of modern civilization. But he fired away, killing instantly a graduate student who was there and shooting off the jaw of the professor. They found in his briefcase a note saying, "Death to Communists."

Now of course the House Un-American Activities Committee is not directly responsible for this kind of thing. All I'm saying is that the kind of activities conducted by the committee create the kind of atmosphere which encourages the attacks on civil liberties that we've seen these past twenty-five years.

Let me say just one or two more things. I think I have two minutes. What we have done. We have taken a group of fairly mediocre congressmen. We've given them a lot of money and a lot of power. And we have said to them, "Save us from Communism." I wonder if it really makes sense that this group of men, bloated as they are with their own sense of self-importance, buried under the weight of the volumes of testimony that they have accumulated over the years, embarrassed by the caliber of their members, plagued by the reports of perjured testimony, I wonder if this group is really capable of handling the most subtle, the most complex problem of this century—and that is the relation of Communism to the dynamics of a world in rapid change. I want to end by quoting this from Justice Robert Jackson's statement when he delivered the decision in *West Virginia Board of Education vs. Barnett* in 1943. He said that "if there is any fixed star in our constitutional constellation it is that no individual high or petty may proscribe what shall be orthodox in matters of politics, nationalism, religion, or other matters of opinion. Or force any citizen to confess by word or deed their faith therein." If there are any circumstances which create an exception, I am now paraphrasing, if there are any circumstances which create an exception, we do not know of this now. If you believe that statement, I believe that you must also logically believe in the discontinuance of the House Un-American Activities committee (*sustained applause*).

NOTES

Mentor to the Movement

1. Tomiko Brown-Nagin, *Courage to Dissent: Atlanta and the Long History of the Civil Rights Movement* (New York: Oxford University Press, 2011); Winston A. Grady-Willis, *Challenging US Apartheid: Atlanta and Black Struggles for Human Rights, 1960–1977* (Durham: Duke University Press, 2006); David J. Garrow, ed., *Atlanta, Georgia, 1960–1961: Sit-ins and Student Activism* (Brooklyn: Carlson Publishing, 1989); David Andrew Harmon, *Beneath the Image of the Civil Rights Movement and Race Relations, Atlanta, 1946–1981* (New York: Garland, 1996); Stephen G. N. Tuck, *Beyond Atlanta: The Struggle for Racial Equality in Georgia, 1940–1980* (Athens: University of Georgia Press, 2001); Harry G. Lefever, *Undaunted by the Fight: Spelman College and the Civil Rights Movement, 1957–1967* (Macon: Mercer University Press, 2005). City of Atlanta oral histories of Atlanta student movement leaders, https://www.atlantaga.gov/visitors/history/atlanta-student-movement (Lonnie King, Roslyn Pope, Herschelle Sullivan Challenor, and Julian Bond interviews). On JFK's phone call to Coretta Scott King and King's release from prison following his Atlanta sit-in arrest, see Clifford M. Kuhn, "'There's a Footnote to History': History, Memory, and the History of Martin Luther King's October 1960 Arrest and Its Aftermath," *Journal of American History* (September 1997): 583–95.

2. Howard Zinn, "Finishing School for Pickets," reprinted in Howard Zinn, *The Zinn Reader: Writings on Disobedience and Democracy* (New York: Seven Stories Press, 2009), 40–46. On Spelman's early history, see Yolanda L. Watson and Sheila T. Gregory, *Daring to Educate: The Legacy of the Early Spelman College Presidents* (Sterling, Va.: Stylus Publishing, 2005).

3. Zinn, "Finishing School for Pickets," 41–44. Martin Luther King Jr. would express admiration for the "intrepid courage" of the female African American students who were arrested with him at the Atlanta sit-ins in October 1960. See King to female inmates, October 24, 1960, in Clayborne Carson, ed., *The Papers of Martin Luther King, Jr.*, vol. 5: *Threshold of a New Decade, January 1959–December 1960* (Berkeley: University of California Press, 2005), 528. At least twenty-one of the fifty-one protesters arrested with Martin Luther King Jr. at the Rich's sit-in were Spelman students (see Lefever, *Undaunted by the Fight*, 63–64).

4. Zinn, "Finishing School for Pickets," 41–44.

5. Ibid.

6. Ibid., 45–46. Zinn was correct that interracial exchange programs (which sent and received visiting students from predominantly white colleges and universities) were on the rise at historically black colleges. And this may very well have contributed, as Zinn suggested, to the decline of deference toward white authority on such campuses as Spelman, Morehouse, Fisk, and Tougaloo, which had such programs and became leading centers of black student protest in the sit-in era. However, one needs to be cautious about generalizing from these leading historically black colleges and universities (HBCUs) to the larger HBCU community. Earl J. McGrath's data suggest that such programs were not as widespread as Zinn implied. McGrath found that in the 1963–64 academic year only twenty-seven HBCUs had such interracial exchange programs out of the approximately fourteen hundred HBCUs. Earl J. McGrath, *The Predominantly Negro Colleges and Universities in Transition* (New York: Institute for Higher Education, Teachers College, 1965), 102.

7. Zinn, "Finishing School for Pickets," 45–46. An example of the way international exchange programs fostered student activism can be seen in the case of Roslyn Pope. After having spent time in Paris on a scholarship, Pope returned to Atlanta eager to make the South as free of segregation as was France. Pope telephone interview with the author, April 16, 2016, transcript in author's possession (hereafter Roslyn Pope telephone interview with the author). Also see Vincent D. Fort, "The Atlanta Sit-in Movement, 1960–1961: An Oral Study," in Garrow, ed., *Atlanta, Georgia, 1960–1961*, 124–25.

Though Zinn did not stress this in his initial *Nation* article, he at other times noted that the new student consciousness among Spelman students in the late 1950s and early 1960s had also been powerfully shaped by the black freedom movement itself. In fact, as early as 1958 Zinn had written that "the movements for desegregation have created a new spirit among Negro young women of college age." Zinn to Albert E. Manley, January 1958, quoted in Howard Zinn to Members of the Board of Trustees of Spelman College, the Spelman faculty, students, alumni, President Manley, and others interested in the future of the college, July 1963, Howard Zinn papers, Tamiment Library, New York University (hereafter Zinn papers, Tam, NYU).

8. Howard Zinn, *You Can't Be Neutral on a Moving Train: A Personal History of Our Times* (Boston: Beacon Press, 1994), 22. Zinn's fullest account of this library desegregation struggle and victory, "A Quiet Case of Social Change," appeared in the NAACP's *Crisis* magazine in October 1959 and is reprinted in *Zinn Reader*, 31–39. Zinn's files reveal that he had taken an interest in ending the color line in southern libraries soon after he moved to Atlanta to teach at Spelman. By February 1957, Zinn was already keeping clippings on attempts to desegregate public libraries in Virginia and North Carolina. See Zinn clipping file: *Washington Post*, March 5, 1957; *Chattanooga Times*, July 16, 1957; *Washington Evening Star*, February 22, 1957; *Raleigh News and Observer*, October 22, 1957. Zinn also kept detailed files on the Atlanta library desegregation struggle. See especially Zinn's notes from the attempts by Spelman students and faculty and Morehouse students to use Atlanta's (white) Carnegie Library, March 6, April 3, April 23, 1959; and Zinn's notes from his meeting with Whitney Young, May 19, 1959, when he learned that the library's leadership, prodded by the threat of a lawsuit, had agreed to desegrega-

tion. All in Howard Zinn [civil rights] papers, Wisconsin Historical Society, Madison, Wisconsin (hereafter Zinn papers, WHS). The files suggest that when he moved to the South, Zinn had become a civil rights activist even before he began mentoring student activists at Spelman.

9. Zinn, *You Can't Be Neutral on a Moving Train*, 27–30; Martin Duberman, *Howard Zinn: A Life on the Left* (New York: New Press, 2012), 37–40. Note that Zinn had this wrong in his memoir—it was not Pope but Bond who typed the Appeal (after Pope drafted it by hand). Roslyn Pope telephone interview with the author. The Atlanta student movement's Appeal for Human Rights is arguably the most impressive document generated by the entire southern sit-in movement in that it focused not merely on desegregating lunch counters but also on racial discrimination in education, employment, jobs, voting, health care, and recreation. The Appeal can be found at http://www.crmvet.org/docs/aa4hr.htm. Zinn's role as a key faculty supporter of the Atlanta sit-in movement was acknowledged formally when he was one of only two nonstudents elected to the founding committee of the Appeal for Human Rights. Howard Zinn to the Trustees of Spelman College, Spelman faculty, students, alumni, President Manley, and others interested in the future of the college, July 1963, Zinn papers, Tam, NYU.

10. Zinn was not, of course, a movement "insider" in the same sense that his activist students were since he was not black and had never experienced the discrimination that they did and that they were organizing to challenge. He also was a professor, not a student, and in that sense too could not be a movement insider in the same way students in the student sit-in movement were. But relative to the larger public Zinn certainly would be considered a movement insider, whom students in the Atlanta movement and in SNCC trusted, confided in, and accepted advice from. He understood the movement's interior life, ideals, and tactics as few nonstudents did and had warm relationships with its activists, which is why he was elected to its executive boards, was invited to undertake important tasks for the movement, and was supported in his oral history work on SNCC. For an example of how Spelman sit-in leaders confided in Zinn, see Herschelle Sullivan to Howie [Zinn], April 13, 1961, Zinn papers, WHS.

11. Howard Zinn, *The Southern Mystique* (New York: Knopf, 1964); Howard Zinn, *Albany: A Study in National Responsibility* (Atlanta: Southern Regional Council, 1962); Howard Zinn, *SNCC: The New Abolitionists* (Boston: Beacon Press, 1964).

12. Zinn, *You Can't Be Neutral on a Moving Train*, 15–45.

13. Duberman, *Howard Zinn: A Life on the Left*, 76–93; Staughton Lynd, *Doing History from the Bottom Up: On E. P. Thompson, Howard Zinn, and the Rebuilding of the Labor Movement from Below* (Chicago: Haymarket Books, 2014), 25–29.

14. Roslyn Zinn to Ernie and Marilyn Young, n.d.—ca. November 1961, Marilyn Young papers, copy in author's possession (hereafter Young papers).

15. Zinn, *You Can't Be Neutral on a Moving Train*, 1–114; Duberman, *Howard Zinn: A Life on the Left*, 129–54, 215–38.

16. On Spelman's conservatism and the struggle of progressive students and faculty there to break free of its traditionalism, see Howard Zinn to Members of the Spelman Board of Trustees et al., July 1963; Beverly Guy-Sheftall telephone interview with the author, March 26. 2016, tape in author's possession.

17. See, for example, Garrow, *Atlanta, Georgia, 1960–1961*. But there is some coverage of post-1960–61 Atlanta student civil rights protest in Grady-Willis, *Challenging U.S. Apartheid*, 33–58; and in Lefever, *Undaunted by the Fight*, 149–60, 170–91.

18. This desegregation agreement, made in March 1961, was itself controversial among student activists because it delayed lunch counter desegregation until Atlanta's public schools desegregated the following fall. The battle over restaurant, store, and hotel desegregation would continue well after Zinn's Spelman years ended. In fact, a second boycott threat pressured the Atlanta Chamber of Commerce to publicly urge the city's recalcitrant downtown businesses to desegregate in November 1963. See Tuck, *Beyond Atlanta*, 123–27; Ronald Bayor, *Race and the Shaping of Twentieth-Century Atlanta* (Chapel Hill: University of North Carolina Press, 1996), 34–35.

19. The importance of the on-campus revolt at Spelman against administration paternalism has been overshadowed and even obscured by scholars who focus on the students' off-campus struggle against racial segregation. For example, Lefever's *Undaunted by the Fight*, a pioneering chronicle of Spelman student activism, is so centered on the civil rights protests that it offers not a single chapter on the antipaternalist protests on campus. The same is true of the documentary film on Spelman student activism, *Foot Soldiers, Class of 1964: An Atlanta Story That Changed the World* (Alvelyn Sanders Production, 2012). But Zinn himself understood that Spelman student activists, including Alice Walker, were by 1963 engaged in protest on "two fronts: the struggle against racial segregation in the deep South; the rebellion of Spelman young women against the strangling conservatism of the college administration," Zinn, "Alice [Walker] at Spelman," unpublished mss. 3, Zinn papers, Tam, NYU.

20. Molly Blank, "Birth of Consciousness: Activism at Spelman Colleges, 1953–1965," unpublished paper, Tufts University, 1998, 105, Zinn papers, Tam, NYU.

21. Ibid., 107.

22. This unwillingness of students at HBCUs to use civil disobedience on campus was characteristic not only of Spelman but also of other centers of black student activism in the early 1960s—which derived from both the perceived fragility of these black educational institutions in the Jim Crow South and the familial quality of the administration-student relationships on them. See Robert Cohen and David J. Snyder, eds., *Rebellion in Black and White: Southern Student Activism in the 1960s* (Baltimore: Johns Hopkins University Press, 2013), 25–26, 34n36.

23. The concept of intersectionality, pioneered by legal scholar Kimberlé Williams Crenshaw, originated as a way of showing that African American women were marginalized on the basis of gender as well as race. See Kimberlé Williams Crenshaw, "De-Marginalizing the Intersection of Race and Sex: A Black Feminist Critique of Anti-Discrimination, Feminist Theory, and Anti-Racist Politics," *University of Chicago Legal Forum* (1991): 139–67. On recent usage of this concept to analyze other overlapping axes of social inequality, see Tom Bartlett, "The Intersectionality Wars! The Once Obscure Academic Theory Is Now Everywhere. Is That a Good Thing?," *Chronicle Review* (May 26, 2017): b6–7.

24. http://news.wabe.org/post/historical-markers-recognize-role-atlanta-students -civil-rights-movement.

25. Blank, "Birth of Consciousness," 106.

26. Johnnetta Betsch Cole and Beverly Guy-Sheftall, *Gender Talk: The Struggle for Women's Equality in African American Communities* (New York: One World, Ballantine Books, 2003), xi–xxxvi; Guy-Sheftall interview with the author. The scholarly neglect of female student activism in historically black colleges is connected as well to the larger neglect of gender in the historiography of black higher education. See Marybeth Gasman, "Swept under the Rug: A Historiography of Gender and Black Colleges," *American Educational Research Journal* (December 2007): 760–805.

27. Guy-Sheftall interview with the author.

28. Evelyn Terry, letter to the editor, *Spelman College Spotlight*, March 1963.

29. Zinn to Albert E. Manley, January 1958, Zinn papers, Tam, NYU.

30. Guy-Sheftall interview with the author.

31. Staughton Lynd telephone interview with the author, March 11, 2013, transcript in author's possession.

32. Howard Zinn to Ernest and Marilyn Young, n.d.—ca. February 1963, Young papers.

33. "On Liberty at Spelman," student meeting audio recording, March 11, 1963, Zinn papers, Tam, NYU. Excerpts from the tapes/CDs of this meeting have been transcribed and appear in Appendix I of this volume.

34. On President Manley's vision of Spelman, see Albert E. Manley, *A Legacy Continues: The Manley Years at Spelman College, 1953–1976* (Lanham, Md.: University Press of America, 1995). Note, however, that Manley's memoir is not candid about his authoritarian administrative style or his strict enforcement or paternalistic campus regulations. Nor does he mention the student revolt against his authority in 1963 or his clashes with or firing of Howard Zinn. Manley's oral history suggests that his style of governance at Spelman was influenced by sexist assumptions. For example, he said that "in dealing with women [students] one cannot be as blunt with them as one can, or should be with [students who are] men. And that's a distinction that has come out of my experience, that you have to deal with them in a different way. You can come around to the same conclusions, but you don't deal with female students in the same way." "United Negro College Fund Oral History Reminisces of Albert Manley," Oral History Research Office, Columbia University, 1983, Martia Goodson interview with Dr. Albert Manley, August 25, 1981, Washington, D.C., 21–22, Rare Book Room, Butler Library, Columbia University.

35. On Zinn's use of the term "Spelmania," see, for example, his January 14, 1963 diary entry. My interviews with Zinn's colleagues and students at Spelman and reading of the college's student newspaper and yearbook indicate that this term was invented and used by Zinn alone.

36. Dr. Samuel DuBois Cook on Dr. Howard Zinn, October 13, 2015, copy in author's possession, courtesy of Karen Cook.

37. Zinn diary entry, January 20, 1963. Samuel DuBois Cook organized the Town Hall forum so that not only the audience but often the panels of speakers were multiracial. Cook was very fond of Zinn, who was always eager to support him in organizing these forums, and whose activism and defense of student rights Cook admired. So for Cook

the loss of Zinn—after his firing—created a "great void." Cook saw that firing as a violation of academic freedom and signed the faculty letter protesting Zinn's firing. See Dr.
Samuel DuBois Cook on Dr. Howard Zinn, October 13, 2015.

38. For a perceptive discussion of Zinn's *Southern Mystique* and its problematic optimism, as well as a fine summary of the critical reviews of the book by Ralph Ellison,
C. Van Woodward, and Lillian Smith, see Duberman, *Howard Zinn: A Life on the Left*,
63–69.

39. Howard Zinn to Ernest and Marilyn Young, May 13, 1962, Young papers, copy in
author's possession.

40. Howard Zinn to Ernest and Marilyn Young, May 13, 1962, Young papers.

41. Ibid.

42. Howard Zinn to Ernest and Marilyn Young, October 5, 1961, Young papers.

43. Calvin Trillin, *An Education in Georgia: Charlayne Hunter, Hamilton Holmes, and
the Integration of the University of Georgia* (Athens: University of Georgia Press, 1992);
"For Atlanta Too, 1963 Was 'Turbulent, Decisive,'" *Atlanta Journal and Constitution*,
August 23, 2013; Tuck, *Beyond Atlanta*, 115–19; Bayor, *Race and the Shaping of Twentieth-Century Atlanta*, 35–40.

44. See Zinn diary entry, May 10, 1963.

45. "Atlanta's 'Berlin Wall,'" Dec. 18, 1962," *Atlanta Magazine*, December 1, 2011; Tuck,
Beyond Atlanta, 119–27; Justin Nystorn, "Lester Maddox," *New Georgia Encyclopedia*
(Athens: University of Georgia Press, 2004). The situation in Atlanta in 1963 may come
as a surprise to readers who think of Atlanta's white political and business leadership
as moderate and assume that the sit-ins in 1960 won a quick and easy victory in the
struggle to desegregate the lunch counters. But in fact those white leaders cleverly used
delaying tactics and played generational politics—working to divide the city's young
militant student protesters from their more moderate elders who were uncomfortable
with direct action. So despite the Atlanta movement's impressive size and organization,
it took eighteen months to win an agreement to desegregate the city's lunch counters,
much longer than in Nashville. As for the restaurants and hotels, there were desegregation victories at individual sites but no binding citywide agreement, and it took the
Civil Rights Act of 1964 to break the resistance to integration. See Tuck, *Beyond Atlanta*,
110–27.

46. See Zinn diary entry, May 18, 1963.

47. Howard Zinn to Ernest and Marilyn Young, March 2, 1962, Young papers, copy in
author's possession. *Tropic of Cancer* (1934) was Henry Miller's novel that was banned
for its sexual candor. *Strange Fruit* (1944) was Lillian Smith's controversial novel on interracial romance.

48. Howard Zinn, *Albany: A Study in National Responsibility* (Atlanta: Southern Regional Council, 1962). This report came out in November 1962. Zinn had completed an
initial report in January 1962.

49. Howard Zinn, introduction to reprint of his December 1, 1962 *Nation* article,
"Kennedy: Reluctant Emancipator," in Zinn, *Zinn Reader*, 68.

50. Zinn, *You Can't Be Neutral on a Moving* Train, 46–50; "Kennedy: Reluctant Emancipator," in Zinn, *Zinn Reader*, 68–75; "President Chided over Albany, Georgia," *New*

York Times, November 15, 1962; "Dr. King Says FBI in Albany Favors Segregationists," *New York Times,* November 19, 1962; David Garrow, *The FBI and Martin Luther King, Jr.* (New York: Penguin, 1981), 54–55. Note that between his initial and final Albany report Zinn expanded substantially its section criticizing the federal government's failure to protect the rights of African Americans and the freedom movement in Albany. That section, "Where Was the Federal Government?," was three pages in the January 1962 report and eleven pages in the October 1962 draft, which would be published in November. See the January and October Albany report drafts, Zinn papers, Tam, NYU; and Zinn, *Albany: A Study in National Responsibility,* 26–34.

51. Zinn, *Zinn Reader,* 68.

52. The most striking mockery of the Kennedy civil rights record in Zinn's diary came from comedian Dick Gregory lampooning Bobby Kennedy's lethargy on civil rights. See Zinn diary entry, April 12–13, 1963. Zinn was equally critical of JFK's Cold Warrior foreign policies.

53. Taylor Branch, *Parting the Waters: America in the King Years, 1955–1963* (New York: Simon & Schuster, 1989).

54. Zinn to Ernest and Marilyn Young, March 2, 1962, Young papers.

55. For Zinn's opening remarks at the February 11, 1963 debate on abolishing HUAC, see Appendix II to this volume.

56. For Zinn's own discussion of the roots of his engagement with Marxism, see his chapter, "Growing Up Class-Conscious," in Zinn, *You Can't Be Neutral on a Moving Train,* 163–82.

57. Howard Zinn to Ernest and Marilyn Young, n.d., ca. spring 1963, Young papers.

58. Howard Zinn interview with Kathleen Dowdey and Jed Dannenbaum, August 7, 1989, transcript, 3, Ralph McGill papers, Manuscripts, Archives, and Rare Book Library, Emory University. Agnes Scott College was a historically white private college for women in Decatur, Georgia.

59. Zinn referred to himself as a revolutionary in his January 19, 1963, diary entry. But his daughter Myla never heard him refer to himself that way and believes that if he would have labeled himself it would have been as a radical rather than as a revolutionary. Anthony Arnove, Howard Zinn's friend and collaborator, agrees with her, recalling that "the word Howie used most was radical." Myla Kabat Zinn email to the author, September 7, 2017.

60. Zinn diary entry, January 19, 1963.

61. Zinn diary entries, December 24, 1962; January 4 and 13, 1963; April 4 and May 8, 1963.

62. Zinn diary entry, January 13, 1963.

63. Howard Zinn to Ernest and Marilyn Young, December 10, 1961, Young papers. On Zinn's leadership role, dating back to the late 1950s, in the movement to get the Southern Historical Association to stop holding its meetings in racially discriminatory hotels, see August Meier, *A White Scholar and the Black Community: Essays and Reflections* (Amherst: University of Massachusetts Press, 1994), 20–22.

64. In the Zinn papers at NYU there is a letter to Zinn sent in 1994 from an Old Left veteran, "Phil" (whose last name is illegible), who had been a Young Communist League

(YCL) member in Williamsburg, Brooklyn in the 1930s. In this letter Phil seemed to assume that because he had seen Zinn at a YCL meeting "somewhat more than fifty years ago" that Zinn had been a YCL member—though Phil never comes out and asserts such membership. Phil was tentative about Zinn's subsequent participation in Communist demonstrations, writing that "We probably both participated in Times Square demonstrations—with mounted cops charging us; also probably both hung effigies of Hitler (after June 22 [1941, when Nazi Germany invaded the USSR]). Phil to Howard Zinn, May 6, 1994, Zinn papers, Tam, NYU. It is entirely possible, as Phil indicates, that back then Zinn did attend some YCL meetings, as he was close to young Communists and to the Communist worldview on antifascism and class issues in his youth. And in Zinn's memoir he did term these years, when he was close to the Communists and went to Communist-led demonstrations, as "my Communist years." But on the other hand, Zinn never seems to have joined the YCL or Communist Party (CP), and in fact recalled that he "argued with the Communist guys. Especially about the Russian invasion of Finland." Zinn, *You Can't Be Neutral on a Moving Train*, 170–73.

As to whether Zinn was in or close to the CP in his Spelman years, there are grounds for deep skepticism. The best reading of this comes from SNCC activist Dorothy Zellner, who worked with Zinn in SNCC during his Spelman years, and knew many people who were in or close to the CP, and found that none of them interacted with Zinn as if he was in or close to the CP. She viewed Zinn as an independent radical. Dorothy Zellner email to the author, September 16, 2015.

The FBI, on the other hand, claimed that in the mid-1940s and early 1950s Zinn was an active CP member, a claim that Zinn biographer Martin Duberman finds inaccurate. Duberman, *Howard Zinn: A Life on the Left*, 23–25.

65. Though there is no convincing evidence that Zinn was ever a CP member, the 1954 FBI interview of Zinn did indicate in the early Cold War years (the late 1940s) a degree of closeness to Communists and his openness to working with them and supporting them, at least on causes he found admirable. Thus Zinn told the FBI that he may have signed a petition for a Communist city council candidate, that he attended the Paul Robeson concert in Peekskill, New York, that he filed a suit against the state of New York as a result of the anti-Communist riot that disrupted the concert, and that he supported a number of organizations that the Justice Department had labeled Communist fronts. In that interview Zinn denied being a Communist and cited his commitment to nonviolence as distinguishing him from Communists. FBI Report: Howard Zinn, Security Matters, February 24, 1954, Zinn papers, Tam, NYU.

66. For perceptive analyses of Zinn's eclectic, independent radicalism, see Duberman, *Howard Zinn: A Life on the Left*, 198–99; 209–10; Lynd, *Doing History from the Bottom Up*, 21–36; Stephen Bird, Adam Silver, and Joshua S. Yesnowitz, eds., *Agitation with a Smile: Howard Zinn's Legacies and the Future of Activism* (New York: Routledge, 2013).

67. On Zinn's role in founding the non-Western studies program at Spelman, see Albert E. Manley to Marian Wright, October 31, 1961, President Albert E. Manley papers, Spelman College archives (hereafter, Manley papers). Zinn also founded an exchange program where white students spent a year studying at Spelman and Spelman students studied at predominantly white campuses; see Renate W. Wolf to Albert E. Manley, October 17, 1960, Manley papers.

68. Zinn, *You Can't Be Neutral on a Moving Train*, 17.

69. In hosting his African American students at his home, Zinn was crossing another racial boundary. As Spelman alumna Sylvia Cook explains: "I had lived in the South all my life and had never been invited to the home of a white person. Dr. Zinn was one of my professors and would invite our whole class to his home to meet his family and engage in lively intellectual discussions." Cook saw this egalitarianism in his relationship with his students as connected to his intellectual and political iconoclasm, challenging students, as Cook put it, to "hone our critical thinking skills . . . and question the status quo." Karen Cook, email to the author, October 13, 2015.

70. On Zinn's closeness to his Spelman students, see Staughton Lynd et al. to Spelman Board of Trustees, n.d., ca. summer 1964, Zinn papers, Tam, NYU.

71. Zinn, *You Can't Be Neutral on a Moving Train*, 45.

72. Henry West telephone interview with the author, July 18, 2015, tape in author's possession.

73. Ibid.

74. Ibid.

75. Ibid.

76. West was likely correct on the prominence of first-generation college students at Spelman. According to one study, 75 percent of HBCU students in 1964 were first-generation college students (the first in their family to attend college). Working-class and low-income students were far more prominent in HBCUs than in predominantly white colleges and universities. According to one study in 1964, 40 percent of HBCU students but only 8 percent of white students came from families with incomes below $4,000 annually. See McGrath, *Predominantly Negro Colleges*, 38, 48. But on the other hand, the working-class presence in the HBCU student population had a limit, as that population overall was considerably more middle class than black America overall. For example, while only 3.4 percent of employed African American men in 1960 were professional and technical employees, 18.6 percent of the fathers of female HBCU students were in these middle-class work categories (McGrath, *Predominantly Negro Colleges*, 49). Zinn attested to the prominence of both middle- and working-class students at Spelman. See his essay, "Alice [Walker] at Spelman," 4, Zinn papers, Tam, NYU.

77. Henry West telephone interview, tape in author's possession. Spelman campus records attest that West was not exaggerating these restrictions. In fact, punishment, which West did not get into in our interview, was often harsh for students who violated the campus's restrictive social rules. For example, a student in 1957 was barred from leaving campus for a month (the Spelman term for this grounding was "campused") because—after a string of late returns to campus—"she went home after church without permission and returned to the campus at 2:25 pm." Spelman College Social Discipline Committee Minutes, February 21, 1957, Manley papers, Spelman. Two years earlier a couple of students were "suspended without the privilege of returning to Spelman" because "the nightwatchman reported [them] as being [in] a car on Monday night." M. N. Curry, Chairman of the Spelman College Social Discipline Committee, to Albert E. Manley, April 22, 1955, Manley papers. In his memoir, Manley himself—writing in the 1990s—acknowledged that during his presidency Spelman "campus and dormitory rules" were so "strict" that " Spelman students today would find it difficult to believe that

any woman could endure the life lived on the Spelman campus" in the 1950s. Manley, *A Legacy Continues*, 20.

Spelman was not alone in upholding paternalistic social restrictions. Restrictions on female dress, curfews for women students, compulsory chapel, etc. were common on campuses in the era of in loco parentis. What set Spelman apart from other colleges was how resistant its administration was to liberalizing such restrictions and how harshly it repressed students and faculty efforts at such liberalization—through censorship, cutting off scholarship aid, and even firing dissident faculty. Moreover, when compared with the more liberal elite northern women's colleges, Spelman was decades behind in its rigid regulation of student dress. By the 1930s, Wellesley, Vassar, and Smith college students were allowed to wear pants, a privilege Spelman students were still longing to secure in 1963. See Deirdre Clement, *Dress Casual: How College Students Redefined American Style* (Chapel Hill: University of North Carolina Press, 56–60). And while compulsory chapel had been eliminated at Harvard in 1886 and Yale in 1926, such compulsory religious services endured at Spelman into the 1960s—and students who missed those services at Spelman had their grade point average lowered. See Manley, *A Legacy Continues*, 20. Southern women's colleges tended to be conservative socially, with the most enduring restrictions, and Spelman was among the most conservative in such matters. On the origins of such restrictions in the South and on challenges to them, see Amy Thompson McCandless, *The Past in the Present: Women's Higher Education in the Twentieth Century American South* (Tusacaloosa: University of Alabama Press, 1999), 121–58, 213–56.

One can well understand why, in the eyes of radicals West and Zinn, Spelman's social restrictions, dress codes, compulsory chapel, and finishing school ethos seemed outdated and "crazy." But there was a logic to this campus regime, essentially that since black women faced so much discrimination their morality, dress, and deportment needed to be above reproach—and so college in its "finishing school" role groomed them for success in a hostile world. At least this is how the biographer of Willa B. Player, the president of Bennett College (the North Carolina counterpart to Spelman, as a women's HBC) in the 1950s–60s, explains how Player, a courageous progressive in politics, could also support and defend her college's socially conservative finishing school emphasis. See Linda Beatrice Brown, *The Long Walk: The Story of the Presidency of Willa B. Player at Bennett College* (Danville, Va.: McCain Printing, 1998), 107–8.

78. "Cowering Experience," *Spelman Spotlight*, January 1958.

79. Zinn, *You Can't Be Neutral on a Moving Train*, 38.

80. Ibid.

81. West interview with the author.

82. Ibid.

83. Ibid.

84. Ibid.

85. Zinn, *You Can't Be Neutral on a Moving Train*, 30.

86. Howard Zinn to Members of the Board of Trustees of Spelman College, the Spelman faculty, students, alumni, President Manley, and others interested in the future of the college, July 1963.

87. These demands for freedom of movement and "individual dating" were made in response to the ways Spelman student social life had been restricted by rules that required students to be accompanied by fellow students when leaving campus and to have chaperones, as well as by curfews and restrictions on "calling hours."

88. West interview with the author.

89. Ibid.

90. Zinn, *You Can't Be Neutral on a Moving Train*, 41.

91. Ibid.

92. West interview with the author. Although Manley never commented in print on his or the Spelman board of trustees' role in Zinn's firing, he did—in a 1981 oral history interview—discuss the Spelman board's reaction to student protest. Manley indicated that he had great autonomy since the Spelman board did not pressure him to be hard-line because "at Spelman . . . we have a board that understood, I think, what was going on. I'm not saying all the members, but certainly most of them did." And so they "weren't threatening to fire me . . . because the students were protesting." "United Negro College Fund Oral History: Reminisces of Albert Manley," Oral History Research Office, Columbia University, 1983; interview of Manley by Martia Goodson, August 25, 1981, Washington, D.C.), 26, Rare Book Room, Butler Library, Columbia University.

93. Minutes, Spelman College Board of Trustees Meeting, November 15, 1963, 3, Manley papers; Staughton Lynd to Zinn, 2nd letter Thursday [ca. July, 1963], Zinn papers, Tam, NYU; Elbert P. Tuttle to Esta Seaton, July 2, 1963, Zinn papers, Tam, NYU.

94. Zinn himself initially told the press: "The students didn't dismiss me; the faculty did not; the board of trustees did not. . . . It was the president's decision entirely" (*Atlanta Constitution*, July 18, 1963).

95. Minutes, Spelman College Board of Trustees Meeting, November 15, 1963, 3.

96. Lawrence J. MacGregor to Manley, November 28, 1963, Manley papers.

97. West interview with the author.

98. Ibid.

99. Marian Wright Edelman, *Lanterns: A Memoir of Mentors* (New York: Harper, 2000), 31–32.

100. Ibid., 31.

101. Ibid., 30.

102. Ibid., 30, 32.

103. Ibid., 30–32.

104. Ibid., 59 (March 4, 1960 diary entry). On the generational rift between the Atlanta student sit-in organizers and their more tactically conservative college presidents, see Howell Raines, *My Soul Is Rested: The Story of the Civil Rights Movement in the Deep South* (New York: Penguin, 1977), 85; Tuck, *Beyond Atlanta*, 120–24. Spelman sit-in leader Roslyn Pope, who was present in 1960 at the initial meeting between her fellow movement leaders and the presidents of the AU Center colleges, recalled that of the six college presidents at that meeting Manley was among the least supportive of the sit-in movement, seeming "quite distressed about the actions" being discussed by the student protesters. See Roslyn Pope interview with the author. Atlanta movement leader Lonnie King recalled that at the first meeting between sit-in organizers and their college presi-

dents, Manley and three of the other AU Center presidents "discouraged students from participating in the movement," arguing that "students should focus on their class work and let the NAACP fight the racial battle." Lonnie King Jr., "Atlanta Student Movement Timeline, Committee on Appeal for Human Rights (COAHR) 1960–1964," Atlanta Student Movement Commission, 2013, www.crmvet.org/info/60asmtim.htm.

105. Wright Edelman, *Lanterns*, 57. Neither this incident nor any other in which Manley opposed the actions of Spelman's student wing of the civil rights movement in the early 1960s is discussed in his memoir. In fact, Manley's memoir so praises the student movement's battles against segregation that it leaves the impression that he was a supporter of that movement. See Manley, *A Legacy Continues*, 172–76. Manley also presented himself as supportive of the sit-in movement in the only oral history interview he did where he discussed the movement. Unfortunately, the interviewer did not know Spelman's history and so could not press Manley to explain his opposition to Wright Edelman's advocacy of the march on the capitol or his other episodes of opposition to the movement. Nor did she ask him about the student rights struggle at Spelman. See "United Negro College Fund Oral History: Reminisces of Albert Manley," 24–26. Marybeth Gasman offers an illuminating comparison of Manley with other black college presidents in his handling of student civil rights protest. See Gasman, "Perceptions of Black College Presidents: Sorting through Stereotypes and Reality to Gain a Complex Picture," *American Educational Research Journal* (August 2011): 855–64. Note, however, that Gasman's claim that Manley "shifted definitively towards the right" with respect to student protest is not convincing (Gasman, "Perceptions of Black College Presidents," 861). In fact, Manley's political trajectory (such as it was) would seem to shift at least slightly leftward in the late 1960s through and beyond the end of his presidency in the 1970s—when he became more conciliatory toward protests for student rights, signed an open letter with other AU Center presidents protesting police invasions of historically black campuses (in the wake of the Orangeburg Massacre), and expressed support for the student movement pushing for the naming of a black female president as his successor at Spelman. See *Spelman Spotlight*, March and November 1968; Manley, *A Legacy Continues*, 96–101; Guy-Sheftall interview.

106. Wright Edelman, *Lanterns*, 58.

107. Gwendolyn Zoharah Simmons, "From Little Memphis Girl to Mississippi Amazon," in *Hands on the Freedom Plow: Personal Accounts of Women in SNCC*, ed. Faith S. Holsaert, Martha Prescod Norman Noonan, Judy Richardson, Jean Smith King, and Dorothy M. Zellner (Urbana: University of Illinois Press, 2010), 9–32.

108. Ibid., 14–15.

109. Ibid., 14, 16.

110. Ibid., 17–20, 19.

111. Ibid., 21.

112. Ibid., 23–24.

113. Betty Stevens Walker telephone interview with the author, March 29, 2013, transcript in author's possession.

114. Ibid. Audio CD of "On Liberty at Spelman" meeting, March 11, 1963, Zinn papers, Tam, NYU. Also see highlights of this meeting in Appendix I, this volume.

115. Zinn diary entries, January 5, 8, 14; February 4 and 7; March 4 and 28; April 8, 9, 20; and June 8, 1963; *Spelman Spotlight*, May 15 and October 17, 1963.

116. Stevens Walker interview with the author.

117. Mercile L. Johnson to Martha Stevens, February 16, 1961, Betty Stevens Walker papers, copy in author's possession (courtesy of Betty Stevens Walker).

118. Ibid.

119. Stevens Walker interview with the author.

120. Albert E. Manley to parents, October 17, 1960, Manley papers. For an abbreviated published version of his letter, see Lefever, *Undaunted by the Fight*, 61.

121. For King's speech at Spelman in 1960, see Martin Luther King Jr., "'Keep Moving from This Mountain,' Address at Spelman College on 10 April 1960," in Clayborne Carson, ed., *The Papers of Martin Luther King, Jr., Volume V, Threshold of a New Decade, January 1959–December 1960* (Berkeley: University of California Press, 2005), 409–19.

122. Lefever, *Undaunted by the Fight*, 48–49, 50–51; *Spelman College Messenger*, August 1960, 12.

123. *Spelman Spotlight*, February 28, 1962; Lefever, *Undaunted by the Fight*, 132. This pattern of state historically black colleges and their presidents tending to be more repressive of student activism and faculty dissent than their private school counterparts (being intensely pressured to be so repressive by the white supremacist legislatures and state boards of education that hired them and funded their colleges) is documented convincingly by Joy Ann Williamson in *Radicalizing the Ebony Tower: Black Colleges and the Black Freedom Struggle in Mississippi* (New York: Teachers College Press, 2008), 76–80, 114–30; and in Joy Ann Williamson-Lott, "Student Free Speech on Both Sides of the Color Line in Mississippi and the Carolinas," in Robert Cohen and David J. Snyder, eds., *Rebellion in Black and White: Southern Student Activism in the 1960s* (Baltimore: Johns Hopkins University Press, 2013), 62, 68–69. Also see Marybeth Gasman, "Perceptions of Black College Presidents," 853. Among the memoirs of the 1960s, HBCU student activist D'Army Bailey's is the most detailed on the immense pressure that segregationist government officials placed on a state HBCU president to suppress the sit-in movement. See his account of how such pressure led President Felton G. Clark of Southern University in Louisiana to expel the leaders of the student movement sitting in against segregation in D'Army Bailey with Roger Easson, *The Education of a Black Radical: A Southern Civil Rights Activist's Journey, 1959–1964* (Baton Rouge: Louisiana State University Press, 2009), 35–36, 41, 47–49, 90–99, 102, 106, 110–18.

124. Zinn diary entry, February 4, 1963. Manley also pressured the editors of Spelman's yearbook not to dedicate the book to Irene Asbury, a former Spelman dean who resigned her deanship at Albany State College in protest against the refusal of that college's president William Dennis to stand up to local racists, and who would herself become a leader in the Albany civil rights movement. See Zinn diary entry, February 14, 1963. There is some confusion as to the details concerning Asbury's resignation from Albany State. A digital library summary claims that she resigned protesting Dennis's expulsion of forty Albany State student civil rights activists. See https://dp.la/item/f6b3a5cc64af12a3a0a5cf0c9086e022. But Asbury resigned in the summer of 1961 and Dennis did not send his letters of suspension to the thirty-nine Albany State student

civil rights activists until December 1961, so obviously it could not have been the ex-
pulsions that precipitated her resignation. In her memoir, Annette Jones White, one
of the expelled Albany State civil rights activists, writes that Asbury resigned because
Dennis had disbanded the Albany State student government for its antiracist activism
and had forced student civil rights activists to student-teach out of town. But another
of the expelled Albany State students, Bernice Johnson Reagon, writes that Asbury resigned because the Albany State administration insisted on dropping charges against a
racist motorist who had driven onto campus and injured a female student. See Annette
Jones White, "Finding Form for the Expression of My Discontent," and Bernice Johnson Reagon, "Uncovered and Without Shelter I Joined This Movement for Freedom,"
both in *Hands on the Freedom Plow: Personal Accounts of Women in SNCC*, ed. Faith
S. Holsaert, Martha Prescod Norman Noonan, Judy Richardson, Jean Smith King, and
Dorothy M. Zellner (Urbana: University of Illinois Press, 2010), 105, 119–20.

125. Zinn, "Finishing School for Pickets," 45.

126. Howard Zinn to Members of the Board of Trustees of Spelman College, the Spelman faculty, students, alumni, President Manley, and others interested in the future of
the college, July 1963, Zinn papers, Tam, NYU.

127. Blank, "Birth of Consciousness," 78.

128. Ibid., 78–79.

129. Dick Schaap, "Behind the Lines: The Ladies Went over the Wall," *New York Herald Tribune Book Week*, November 8, 1964. On the historical roots of Ellison's fictionalized black college president, see Barbara Foley, *Wrestling with the Left: The Making of
Ralph Ellison's Invisible Man* (Durham: Duke University Press, 2010), 160–64.

130. Howard Zinn to the editor of *Book Week*, November 9, 1964, Zinn papers, Tam,
NYU.

131. Dick Schapp to Howard Zinn, November 17, 1964, Zinn papers, Tam, NYU.

132. Howard Zinn to Members of the Board of Trustees of Spelman College, the Spelman faculty, students, alumni, President Manley, and others interested in the future of
the college, July 1963, Zinn papers, Tam, NYU.

133. Betty Stevens Walker interview with the author.

134. Ibid.

135. Ibid.

136. On the rise of this campus-directed protest and militancy at HBCUs in the late
1960s, see Martha Biondi, *The Black Revolution on Campus* (Berkeley: University of California Press, 2012), 29–40. At Spelman such tactical militancy on campus would not
erupt until 1976 when students demanding the appointment of Spelman's first female
African American president held a two-day lock-in of the college's board of trustees.
See Norman M. Rates, *May Thy Dear Walls Remain: Memoirs of a College Minister at the
Sisters Chapel Spelman College* (Atlanta: Publishing Associates, 2010), 151–52. Also see
epilogue, this volume. Four Spelman students, were, however, involved in the lock-in
of Morehouse College's board of trustees by black power militants in 1969. See Benjamin Mays, *Born to Rebel: An Autobiography* (Athens: University of Georgia Press, 1987),
311–12.

137. Stevens Walker interview with the author. While it is true that as the president of

a historically black women's college, Manley was not free from special pressures to be protective of his college's students (and to shy away from supporting political protests that put their safety at risk), the same could be said of Willa B. Player, the president of Bennett College. Yet she, unlike Manley, was one of the most vocal and consistent supporters of her women's college's student involvement in the sit-in movement. See William Chafe, *Civilities and Civil Rights: Greensboro, North Carolina and the Black Struggle for Freedom* (New York: Oxford University Press, 1980), 80, 96–98, 129; Brown, *Long Walk*, 165–180; Gasman, "Perceptions of Black College Presidents," 852–55.

138. Betty Stevens Walker interview with the author.

139. Ibid.

140. Ibid.

141. Staughton Lynd telephone interview with the author, March 11, 2013.

142. Ibid.

143. Ibid. Zinn made a similar point, but linked it to a larger pattern in the Manley administration's "manner and timing" of reprisals against its critics. Zinn saw his firing as bearing "the same imprint of evasion" as the punishments imposed on student critics: "Students would get letters during the summer when they were already far away, telling them not to return in the fall. A letter denying a scholarship to an honors student who had criticized the administration . . . was also sent during the summer. Actions like these leave no room for due process, for protest. They have the finality of a middle-of-the-night execution." (Zinn to Members of the Board of Trustees of Spelman College, the Spelman faculty, students, alumni, President Manley, and others interested in the future of the college, July 1963, Zinn papers, Tam, NYU).

144. Staughton Lynd interview with the author.

145. Zinn to Members of the Board of Trustees of Spelman College, the Spelman faculty, students, alumni, President Manley, and others interested in the future of the college, July 1963, Zinn papers, Tam, NYU. Perhaps because he wrote this statement at a stressful moment, after being fired, when he wanted to avoid seeing any racial element in his firing, it was one of the few times one finds Zinn writing superficially about race. His statement was particularly one-dimensional in discussing black faculty support of Manley, which he attributes to a "cultural" factor—namely that unlike their white counterparts they had not experienced the more liberal academic culture of northern colleges and universities and thus were not so offended by his repressive acts. What Zinn is missing here is that African American academics, because of racially discriminatory hiring practices at many colleges and universities in 1963, had far fewer job options than white faculty. This alone would make black faculty especially reluctant to challenge their college president as Zinn had. Additionally, at a small president-centered college such as Spelman, Manley would have hired many of the black faculty personally, so there would likely have been an element of personal loyalty that left them disinclined to challenge Manley (compounded by the fact that Manley's black faculty supporters had been at Spelman for years since this was for them the pinnacle of their careers). Finally, there is evidence that some black faculty did feel a sense of racial solidarity with Manley and disliked seeing his authority challenged by a white colleague. So while Zinn is not wrong about cultural conservatism mattering, and surely many black faculty who

worked at Spelman for decades were affected by its conservatism, the deference among those faculty to Manley is far too complex to be attributed to cultural factors alone.

146. Staughton Lynd interview with the author.

147. W. L. James et al. to Albert E. Manley, July 26, 1963, Willis Laurence James papers, Spelman College archives (hereafter Willis Laurence James papers). A similar perspective was voiced by a Spelman faculty member (whose name was deleted by FBI censors) in a private interview with an FBI agent in July 1963, who "advised SA [special agent] . . . that Zinn was relieved of his duties because Spelman 'could not operate with two Presidents.'" July 31, 1963, FBI Field Office File 100-5643, Bureau File 100-360217, "Howard Zinn: Security Matters," Howard Zinn FBI files, Zinn papers, Tam, NYU.

148. W. L. James et al. to Albert E. Manley, July 18, 1963, Willis Laurence James papers.

149. Grady-Willis, *Challenging U.S. Apartheid*, 149.

150. Lerone Bennett Jr., preface in Vincent Harding, *Hope and History: Why We Must Share the Story of the Movement* (Maryknoll, N.Y.: Orbis Books, 2010), ix.

151. Vincent Harding telephone interview with the author, March 26, 2013, transcript in author's possession.

152. Ibid.

153. Ibid.

154. Grady-Willis, *Challenging U.S. Apartheid*, 149.

155. Vincent Harding to Howard Zinn, January 2, 1966 [1967], Zinn papers, Tam, NYU. Note that this letter was missing its final page, which had its author's signature on it. So the identify of its author was unclear until Vincent Harding in our interview confirmed that he had written this letter to Zinn.

156. Vincent Harding, typescript, "When Stokely Met the Presidents: Black Power and Negro Education," 1, in author's possession (courtesy of Vincent Harding). This article by Harding "When Stokely Met the Presidents: Black Power and Negro Education," was published in *Motive* (January 1967): 4–9.

157. Harding, typescript, "When Stokely Met the Presidents," 1–2.

158. Harding, typescript, "When Stokely Met the Presidents," 6.

159. Vincent Harding interview with the author.

160. Gloria [Bishop] and Jim to Howard Zinn, April 8, 1964, Zinn papers, Tam, NYU.

161. Ibid.

162. Marie Thomas telephone interview with the author, September 25, 2013, tape in author's possession. For a summary of Thomas's career as an actress, see Manley, *A Legacy Continues*, 123.

163. Marie Thomas interview with the author.

164. Zinn diary entry, just before Xmas 1962.

165. Marie Thomas interview with the author.

166. Ibid.

167. Ibid.

168. The full text of the Marie Thomas letter can be heard on the CD of the "On Liberty at Spelman" meeting, Zinn papers, Tam, NYU. There is also an extensive excerpt of the letter in Zinn to Members of the Board of Trustees of Spelman College, the Spelman

faculty, students, alumni, President Manley, and others interested in the future of the college, July 1963, Zinn papers, Tam, NYU.

169. Marie Thomas interview with the author.

170. Ibid.

171. Alice Walker email to the author, April 28, 2014; Zinn diary entries, March 7, May 14, May 31, 1963; Alice Walker, *Meridian* (New York: Harcourt, 1976), which is dedicated to Staughton Lynd.

172. Zinn to Members of the Board of Trustees of Spelman College, the Spelman faculty, students, alumni, President Manley, and others interested in the future of the college, July 1963, Zinn papers, Tam, NYU.

173. Ibid.

174. Ibid.

175. Alice Walker telephone interview with the author, July 1, 2015, transcript in author's possession.

176. Ibid.; Alice Walker letter in *Spelman Spotlight*, October 17, 1963.

177. Alice Walker letter in *Spelman Spotlight*, October 17, 1963.

178. Ibid.

179. Staughton Lynd to Howard Zinn, n.d. [ca. October 1963], Zinn papers, Tam, NYU.

180. Alice Walker to Howard and Roslyn Zinn, September 20, 1963, Zinn papers, Tam, NYU. Sisters Chapel was the Spelman campus chapel where in 1963 all students were required to attend morning religious services.

181. Alice Walker, "Saying Goodbye to My Friend Howard Zinn," *Boston Globe*, January 31, 2010.

182. Alice Walker interview with the author.

183. Ibid.

184. Ibid.

185. Ibid. For an informative oral history on how "class colorism" worked at one HBCU, Howard University, see Audrey Elisa Kerr, *The Paper Bag Principle: Class, Colorism, and Rumor and the Case of Black Washington, D.C.* (Knoxville: University of Tennessee Press, 2006), 88–102; see also Kimberly Jade Norwood, ed., *Color Matters: Skin Tone Bias and the Myth of a Post-Racial America* (New York: Routledge, 2014), 1–29. On class colorism at Spelman in the early 1960s, see Gwendolyn Zoharah Simmons's recollections in Blank, "Birth of Consciousness," 99.

186. Alice Walker interview with the author. The opening lines of Paul Laurence Dunbar's poem, "We Wear the Mask," does indeed, as Walker suggests, evoke the way that the oppressive power of whites left blacks masking their true feelings. The poem's opening lines read:

"We wear the mask that grins and lies,
It hides our cheeks and shades our eyes,
This debt we pay to human guile;
With torn and bleeding hearts we smile."

187. Alice Walker interview with the author.

188. Ibid.

189. Zinn, "Finishing School for Pickets," 42.

190. Alice Walker interview with the author. Walker was correct in connecting paternalistic regulations and administration response to student protest at Spelman to fears of rape. Manley in a 1981 oral history interview explained that with regard to student protest in the Atlanta University Center, "all the presidents were concerned about the safety of their students. But I guess, in my situation, I perhaps had additional problems, because here were girls from different parts of the country who had been sheltered and protected at home. All of a sudden [with the sit-ins] they were in jail. And some of those jails were ill kept and poorly supervised. You didn't know whether they were going to get raped or what was going to happen. So I had a different situation from other presidents dealing with women only." "United Negro College Fund Oral History: Reminisces of Albert Manley," Rare Book and Manuscript Library, Columbia University, 24.

191. Alice Walker interview with the author.

192. Ibid.

193. Ibid.

194. Ibid.

195. Ibid.

196. Ibid.

197. Alice Walker to Howard Zinn, n.d. [ca. fall 1963], Zinn papers, Tam, NYU.

198. Alice Walker interview with the author.

199. Ibid.

200. Alice Walker, *The World Has Changed: Conversations with Alice Walker* (New York: New Press, 2011), 147.

201. Alice Walker, "Saying Goodbye to My Friend Howard Zinn," *Boston Globe*, January 31, 2010.

202. Walker, "Saying Goodbye to My Friend Howard Zinn."

203. Alice Walker interview with the author.

204. Herschelle Sullivan to Albert E. Manley, October 26, 1963, Committee A Zinn files, American Association of University Professors (AAUP) Archives, George Washington University.

205. Ibid.

206. Ibid.

207. Ibid.

208. Ibid.

209. Ibid.

210. Ibid. Sullivan's ability to be candidly critical with Manley and yet reaching out to him and not demonizing him seems linked to the relationship she developed with him in her final years as student body president and leader of the student sit-ins downtown. In contrast to his intolerant attitude toward those who challenged his own authority on campus, she found Manley flexible and even sympathetic about the sit-ins. So she would tell him more about the students' antiracist protest plans than her counterparts on some other AU Center campuses would tell their presidents. Thus Manley was often better informed than other presidents, something she thought he appreciated. Though again we are shifting back into oral history—and an interview she gave long after the 1960s—

Sullivan did credit him for giving her "a little rope" in her civil rights activism. So that while Manley, in her words, "certainly did not publicly champion the [sit-in] movement, he was a fighter, we reached a modus operandi that worked, and I think that he was very proud that we were doing what we were doing." Herschelle Sullivan Challenor interview, January 1994, Emory University Library.

211. Albert E. Manley to Robert Van Waes, July 29 and September 26, 1963; Manley to Zinn, June 1, 1963, Committee A Zinn files, American Association of University Professors (AAUP) Archives, George Washington University.

212. Samuel DuBois Cook to Howard Zinn, July 9, 1963, Howard Zinn papers, Tam, NYU.

213. Samuel DuBois Cook et al. to Spelman College Board of Trustees, n.d. [ca. July 1963], Zinn papers, Tam, NYU.

214. R. B. Pearsall to Robert Van Waes, December 2, 1963, Zinn files. AAUP Archives.

215. Ibid.

216. Ibid.

217. Zinn, *You Can't Be Neutral on a Moving Train*, 43.

218. Albert E. Manley to Howard Zinn, January 25, 1964, Zinn files, AAUP Archives. It is also true that though Manley did not raise the morals charge until months after the AAUP took up Zinn's case, the Zinn diary mentions that as early as July 10, 1963 the wife of Morehouse president Benjamin Mays was telling people that "moral questions" were involved in Zinn's firing—though when pressed by Zinn's friend Staughton Lynd she backed away from that statement (Zinn diary entry, July 10, 1963).

219. Albert E. Manley to Winston E. Ehrman, August 15, 1964, Zinn files, AAUP Archives.

220. Zinn, *Southern Mystique*, 136.

221. Howard Zinn to Albert E. Manley, March 5, 1964, Zinn files, AAUP Archives. Here Zinn expressed his outrage that Manley never dared to make such charges in an open hearing before his dismissal, and that Spelman's president would "seize upon an incident where a student and I were arrested by two racist policemen, as the basis for building a web of suspicion and gossip about me."

222. Albert E. Manley to Winston E. Ehrman, August 15, 1964; Albert E. Manley to Robert Van Waes, March 19, 1964, Zinn files, AAUP Archives. Subsequently, Manley's attorney James Groton told the AAUP that affidavits from the arresting officers in the 1960 incident had been obtained by Manley because in 1963 Manley "had received information (from a person Gorton did not identify) to the effect that there had been an improper relationship between Zinn and the coed in question." And it was also noted that Zinn had lied about both the location and other circumstances of the arrest. HIO [Herman I. Orentlicher] to Files, October 16, 1964, Zinn files, AAUP Archives. But Groton did not show the AAUP the affidavits or any other evidence supporting Manley's accusations. Nor did he explain who had told Manley in 1963 that such an affair had occurred or why this information had only surfaced three years after the incident. It is true, however, that on one detail regarding the arrest—its location—Zinn had not been candid with college authorities. Zinn told the AAUP that "he did not state the location of the arrest . . . to protect the girl, who would have been punished for violating her

[dormitory] sign out statement concerning her original destination." Robert Van Waes to Committee A, "Spelman College: Zinn Case, Interview with Professor Zinn," February 12, 1964, Zinn files, AAUP Archives.

223. Manley to Van Waes, March 19, 1964, Zinn files, AAUP Archives.

224. Howard Zinn to Robert Van Waes, August 2, 1963, Zinn files, AAUP Archives.

225. Ibid.

226. Zinn to Members of the Board of Trustees of Spelman College, the Spelman faculty, students, alumni, President Manley, and others interested in the future of the college, July 1963, Zinn papers, Tam, NYU; see also abridged version, Zinn to Whom It May Concern, August 31, 1963, Zinn papers, Tam, NYU.

227. For an excellent summary of the Manley-Zinn battle as reflected in the AAUP's papers, see Duberman, *Howard Zinn: A Life on the Left*, 86–93. Zinn's correspondence to the AAUP regarding the morals charge indicates that he viewed the charge as not merely false but a crude intimidation tactic designed to thwart his AAUP academic freedom case. The charge did not intimidate Zinn, who pursued the appeal well into 1964. For months after Manley's accusation, Zinn held firm, telling the AAUP that the appeal had to go on, that the battle for educational democracy and academic freedom should not be "stopped cold" on account of bogus charges by "an unscrupulous administrator." Howard Zinn to Winston Ehrmann, July 13, 1964, Zinn files, AAUP Archives.

The reason Zinn gave the AAUP as to why he finally abandoned the appeal in November 1964 was that the *Herald Tribune* book review story on his dismissal had misquoted Zinn in ways that were insulting to Manley, and so made it almost impossible for an AAUP investigation "to have a constructive effect on academic freedom at Spelman." Howard Zinn to Louis Jouhlin, November 14, 1964, Zinn files, AAUP Archives. But this argument seems weak, especially considering how strongly and openly critical he had been of Manley in the past. So it seems more likely that the causes were exhaustion, a desire to move on in his life with his new job, and a sense that "with so much time passed" since his firing Zinn was dubious about "how much good an investigation would do at this point." Howard Zinn to Louis Jouhlin, November 14, 1964, Zinn files, AAUP Archives.

228. This confidential statement by Manley is mentioned in the Minutes of the Spelman College Board of Trustees, November 15, 1963, 3, Manley papers.

229. Albert E. Manley to John Alexander, September 16, 1963, Manley papers.

230. Manley to Van Waes, March 19, 1964, Zinn files, AAUP Archives.

231. Manley to Winston E. Ehrman, May 8, 1964, Zinn files, AAUP Archives.

232. Minutes of the Spelman College Board of Trustees, November 15, 1963, 3.

233. Howard Zinn to Bertram Davis, June 21, 1963, Zinn files, AAUP Archives.

234. Manley, *A Legacy Continues*.

235. Beverly Guy-Sheftall telephone interview with the author, March 26, 2016.

236. Lynd interview with the author.

237. Roslyn Pope telephone interview with the author, April 16, 2016, transcript in author's possession.

238. Roslyn Pope email to the author, April 18, 2016.

239. Ibid.; Pope telephone interview with the author.

240. Pope telephone interview with the author.

241. Ibid.

242. Pope email to the author, April 18, 2016.

243. Lynd interview with the author.

244. Alice Walker interview with the author. Beverly Guy-Sheftall heard rumors of Zinn having an affair at Spelman but with a staff member, not a student (Guy-Sheftall interview with the author).

245. Alice Walker interview with the author. When I read her this quote by Walker, Roslyn Pope remarked: "That's a very nice statement. I was just thinking that well, I was not one of the swooners (*laughs*). It was a great friendship. And I miss him and I had looked forward to seeing him in 2010 when we were going to be celebrating the 50th anniversary of the civil rights movements [i.e., the sit-in movement of 1960]. We get together every ten years. And he died just before we were planning to have him come back" (Pope interview with the author).

246. On these infidelities, see Duberman, *Howard Zinn: A Life on the Left*, 187–91.

247. Zinn diary entry, March 18, 1963. Also see Albert E. Manley to Staughton Lynd, September 13, 1962, Manley papers.

248. Zinn interview with Dowdey and Dannenbaum.

Epilogue

1. Spelman College Commencement script, May 15, 2005, Dr. Beverly Daniel Tatum presiding, copy in author's possession, courtesy Beverly Tatum.

2. Ibid.

3. See Duberman, *Howard Zinn: A Life on the Left* (New York: New Press, 2012), 95–318.

4. "Howard Zinn: 'To Be Neutral, To Be Passive in a Situation Is to Collaborate with Whatever Is Going On,'" transcript of National Public Radio Interview of Howard Zinn by Amy Goodman, *Democracy Now*, National Public Radio, April 27, 2005.

5. Ibid.

6. Harry G. Lefever, *Undaunted by the Fight: Spelman College and the Civil Rights Movement, 1957–1967* (Macon, Ga.: Mercer University Press, 2005). DVD of Spelman College convocation, featuring Howard Zinn, October 23, 2003, in author's possession, courtesy of Sarah Thompson—available now at the Howard Zinn papers, Tamiment Library, NYU (hereafter Zinn papers, Tam, NYU).

7. DVD of Spelman College convocation, featuring Howard Zinn, October 23, 2003.

8. Ibid.

9. Ibid.

10. Ibid.

11. Ibid.

12. Ibid.

13. Beverly Daniel Tatum telephone interview with the author, March 17, 2016, transcript in author's possession (hereafter Tatum interview). Actually Zinn in the 1960s had been back to Spelman at least twice after his firing: in the fall of 1963 to pick up his belongings; and in 1966 to do some interviews for his *Harper's* article on the future of historically black campuses. He had also given an antiwar speech at Atlanta University

after the Vietnam War escalated, and had been back to Spelman later to autograph his books. But Zinn had never been formally invited to speak at Spelman since his firing in 1963 until the 2003 convocation that Tatum described and attended.

14. Beverly Daniel Tatum interview.

15. Sarah Thompson telephone interview with the author, July 5, 2016, notes in author's possession.

16. "Howard Zinn: 'To Be Neutral, To Be Passive,'" National Public Radio Interview of Howard Zinn by Amy Goodman, *Democracy Now.*

17. This is not meant to imply that Spelman student activism ceased after Zinn's firing in 1963. Spelman continued to be a source of students active in the black freedom movement, especially in SNCC, such as Gwendolyn (Robinson) Zoharah Simmons (Gwendolyn Robinson in her Spelman years), who played a leadership role in the Mississippi Freedom Summer voting rights crusade in 1964. And in fact when President Manley sought to expel her and another Spelman activist after their arrest in a tumultuous desegregation protest at a restaurant in downtown Atlanta, a demonstration on campus by more than a hundred students and SNCC activists in January 1964—complete with the burning in effigy of Manley—pressured him to reinstate them (on probation). But this campus protest was defensive and not aimed at challenging the whole paternalistic regime at Spelman and its many social and political restrictions, as had been the case back in 1963. On the 1964 demonstration, see Zoharah Simmons, "From Little Memphis Girl to Mississippi Amazon," in *Hands on the Freedom Plow: Personal Accounts of Women in SNCC*, ed. Faith S. Holsaert, Martha Prescod Norman Noonan, Judy Richardson, Jean Smith King, and Dorothy M. Zellner (Urbana: University of Illinois Press, 2010), 20–22; Staughton Lynd to Howard Zinn, January 14, 1964, Zinn papers, Tam, NYU.

18. F. J. Ingersoll Jr. to Mrs. B. Laconyea Butler, August 15, 1966, Zinn papers, Tam, NYU.

19. Ibid.

20. Ibid.

21. Howard Zinn, "New Directions for Negro Colleges," *Harper's Magazine*, May 1, 1966, 75–81.

22. Ibid., 75,

23. Ibid., 76–78.

24. Ibid., 75, 80–81.

25. Ibid., 81.

26. Ibid., 80.

27. Ibid., 80–81.

28. See Martha Biondi, *The Black Revolution on Campus* (Berkeley: University of California Press, 2012).

29. *Spelman Spotlight*, November 1967.

30. Biondi, *Black Revolution on Campus*, 1–42.

31. "Proposal of the Ad-Hoc Committee for a Black University," *Spelman Spotlight*, November 1968.

32. Sisters in Blackness, "Clarification of a Black University," *Spelman Spotlight*, November 1968.

33. "Proposal of the Ad-Hoc Committee for a Black University," *Spelman Spotlight*, November 1968.

34. Ibid.

35. "Dialogue or Monologue? A Statement by President Albert E. Manley," *Spelman Spotlight*, November 1968.

36. Ibid.; "Senior Gripes Voiced," *Spelman Spotlight*, October 31, 1968.

37. This too was similar to the way the deans responded to Zinn's reading of the student government constitution at the "On Liberty at Spelman" protest meeting in 1963, when the dean objected vigorously to Zinn's claim that the constitution gave students control over campus social regulations—she insisted that all decision-making power rested with President Manley.

38. "Dialogue of Monologue? A Statement by President Albert E. Manley," *Spelman Spotlight*, November 1968.

39. "Students Reject Speak Out Agenda," *Spelman Spotlight*, November 1968.

40. Ibid.

41. Ibid.

42. "All Minds on Victory," *Spelman Spotlight*, November 1968.

43. Ibid.

44. "Student Revolution: The Whole Story," *Spelman Spotlight*, November 1968. Note, however, that this "revolution" at Spelman in 1968 did not end all the traditional in loco parentis regulations at the college: compulsory chapel would not be eliminated at Spelman until 1973. See Frances D. Graham and Susan L. Poulson, "Spelman College: A Place All Their Own," in *Challenged by Coeducation: Women's Colleges since the 1960s*, ed. Leslie Miller-Bernall and Susan L. Poulson (Nashville: Vanderbilt University Press, 2006), 240.

45. "Spelman SSGA," *Spelman Spotlight*, November 1968.

46. It may seem odd to find at Spelman a black power campus movement battling for female students' rights, given the sexist tendencies of the black power movement nationally. Certainly on many coeducational campuses the black power movement was male-dominated organizationally and patriarchal ideologically. But since Spelman was a black women's college, its black power movement was shaped primarily by women students who had their own organization, their own campus priorities, and, as we have seen, would effectively use black power discourse and militancy to win rights that women students had long desired at Spelman. On sexism in the black power movement nationally, see Johnnetta Betsch Cole and Beverly Guy-Sheftall, *Gender Talk: The Struggle for Women's Equality in African American Communities* (New York: One World, Ballantine Books, 2003), 79–84; on sexism in the black power movement on coeducational campuses, see Biondi, *Black Revolution on Campus*, 27–28, 58–59.

47. "Proposals of the SSGA Toward a Black University" and "Spelman Student Government Association to the Parents and Guardians of Spelman Students," both in *Spelman Spotlight*, November 1968.

48. Albert E. Manley, *A Legacy Continues: The Manley Years at Spelman College, 1953–1976* (Lanham, Md.: University Press of America, 1995), 93–96.

49. "Students Free 14 Trustees Held at a Black College for Women," *New York Times*,

April 24, 1976; Norman M. Rates, *May Thy Dear Walls Remain: Memoirs of a College Minister at the Sisters Chapel, Spelman College* (Atlanta: PA Inc., 2011), 151–52; Manley, *A Legacy Continues*, 96–101. Manley's account of this protest in his memoir is not only the most thorough yet published, but it is surprisingly sympathetic to the protesters and their demand for a black woman president to succeed him at Spelman. Such sympathy is connected to his own disaffection with Spelman's board of trustees, which had nudged him to retire. Beverly Guy-Sheftall email to the author, July 4, 2016.

50. Ibid. The "lock-in" term and the idea for such a militant mode of protest originated within the AU Center in April 1969 when ten black power student protesters locked in the trustees at Morehouse College—as well as the AU and Spelman trustees in attendance at its meeting. Four Spelman students had participated in this earlier lock-in, demanding black control of the AU Center, renaming it the Martin Luther King Jr. Center, and merging all six of the center's higher educational institutions. See Benjamin E. Mays, *Born to Rebel: An Autobiography* (Athens: Brown Thrasher Books, University of Georgia Press, 1987), 311–13.

51. *New York Times*, April 24, 1976.

52. Beverly Guy-Sheftall telephone interview with the author, March 16, 2016, tape in author's possession (hereafter Guy-Sheftall interview).

53. Tatum interview.

54. Mary Schmidt Campbell email to the author, March 16, 2016.

55. Tatum interview.

56. Ibid.

57. Denise McFall, "Beverly Guy-Sheftall: Rebel With A Cause . . . or Two," *Spelman Messenger* (Spring 2006): 16–19.

58. Guy-Sheftall interview.

59. Ibid.

60. Tatum interview.

61. Guy-Sheftall interview.

62. Tatum interview.

63. Betty Stevens Walker to Howard Zinn, May 12, 2005, Stevens Walker papers, copy in author's possession, courtesy of Betty Stevens Walker.

64. Samuel DuBois Cook to Howard Zinn, June 14, 2005, Zinn papers, Tam, NYU.

65. Tatum interview; Spelman College Commencement script, May 15, 2005, Dr. Beverly Daniel Tatum presiding, copy in author's possession.

66. Howard Zinn to Betty Stevens Walker, August 6, 2005, Stevens Walker papers, copy in author's possession, courtesy of Betty Stevens Walker.

67. Text of Howard Zinn's Spelman College Commencement Speech, "Against Discouragement," May 15, 2005, Howard Zinn, *The Zinn Reader: Writings on Disobedience and Democracy* (New York: Seven Stories Press, 2009), 734.

68. Ibid., 734–35.

69. "Howard Zinn: 'To Be Neutral, To Be Passive,'" National Public Radio Interview of Howard Zinn by Amy Goodman, *Democracy Now*.

Appendix I. "On Liberty at Spelman," March 11, 1963

1. Howard Zinn to Members of the Board of Trustees of Spelman College, the Spelman faculty, students, alumni, President Manley, and others interested in the future of the college, July 1963, Howard Zinn papers, Tamiment Library, New York University (hereafter Zinn papers, Tam, NYU).

2. Samuel DuBois Cook to Howard Zinn, July, 9, 1963, Zinn papers, Tam, NYU.

3. Note that it was not possible to identify all those who spoke at the meeting since some speakers did not introduce themselves and were not introduced. Students or administrators who could not be identified by name are referred to as generic "students" or "administrators" in the transcribed excerpts below.

4. Of Dorcas Boit, who chaired the meeting, Zinn wrote that she was "a student leader who comes from Kenya and who might, in terms of maturity and scholarship, be termed the dean of the African students at Spelman." Zinn to Members of the Board of Trustees of Spelman College, the Spelman faculty, students, alumni, President Manley, and others interested in the future of the college, July 1963, Zinn papers, Tam, NYU.

5. Zinn to Members of the Board of Trustees of Spelman College, the Spelman faculty, students, alumni, President Manley, and others interested in the future of the college, July 1963, Zinn papers, Tam, NYU.

Appendix II. Debate on Abolishing the House Committee on Un-American Activities: Howard Zinn's Opening Statement in Support of Abolition, Emory University, February 11, 1963

1. Howard Zinn to Members of the Board of Trustees of Spelman College, the Spelman faculty, students, alumni, President Manley, and others interested in the future of the college, July 1963, Howard Zinn papers, Tamiment Library, New York University (hereafter Zinn papers, Tam, NYU).

INDEX

Abernathy, Ralph, 30, 110
Agnes Scott College, 15, 123, 148
Albany report, 3, 13–14, 100, 111, 138, 242–43n50
Albany State, 35, 100, 111, 112, 127, 249–50n124
Aleichem, Sholem, 88
Alexander, John, 176
Alien and Sedition Acts (1798), 115
Allen, Chris, 101
Allen, Damaris, 94, 115, 120, 125, 132, 136, 137, 164
Allen, Ivan, Jr., 96, 97, 120, 129, 155, 162
Allen, Robert, 125, 156, 160
Allen, Sadie Sims, 126, 210
Alston, Wallace, 148
American Association of University Professors (AAUP), 86, 124, 136, 139; faculty salaries, 101, 159; Albert Manley and, 65, 67–69, 70–72, 255n218, 255–56n222; Zinn dismissal appeal and, 25, 65, 66, 69–72, 175, 178, 255n218, 255–56n222, 256n227
American exceptionalism, 16
American Federation of Labor, 88
American Friends Service Committee, 99
American Jewish Committee (AJC), 103
American Socialist Party, 88, 155
Amritsar Massacre, 128
antiauthoritarianism, 36
Anti-Defamation League (ADL), 100, 103, 148
anti-Semitism, 81, 86, 168–69
Appeal for Human Rights, 1, 3, 239n9. *See also* Committee on Appeal for Human Rights

Arnett, Trevor, 149
Asbury, Irene, 100, 111, 115–16, 134, 249–50n124
Atlanta Chamber of Commerce, 5, 169
Atlanta University, 1, 7, 23, 29, 58, 79–80, 84, 90, 109, 127, 167, 195
Atlanta University-Morehouse-Spelman (AMS) Players, 82, 118, 131–32

Bacote, Clarence, 93, 94, 102, 152
Baez, Joan, 153, 163, 165
Bailey, Jackson, 117
Baker, Dave, 149
Baker, Ella, 164
Baldwin, James, 101, 146
Banks, Arthur, 120, 125, 127, 135, 161, 169
Bardinelli, Harold, 84, 105, 110, 175
Barenblatt, Lloyd, 135
Barenblatt v. U.S. (1959), 135
Barnett, Ross, 170
Bazelon, David, 163
Beard, Charles, 148
Beasley, Sadye Maria, 132, 169
Belafonte, Harry, 144
Bellamy, Edward, 94
Bennett, Lerone, Jr., 45, 162
Berger, Monroe, 97–99, 101, 104
Bernhardt, Berl, 162
Berrien, Jean, 94
Berrien, Willie Paul, 154
Bezhura, Esta, 85, 138
Bikel, Theodore, 157
Birmingham, Ala., 12, 153, 155, 156
Bishop, Gloria Wade, 48, 49
Black, Charles, 153